THE CAMBRIDGE COMPANION TO
LATINA/O AMERICAN LITERATURE

The Cambridge Companion to Latina/o American Literature provides a thorough yet accessible overview of a literary phenomenon that has been rapidly globalizing over the past two decades. It takes an innovative approach that underscores the importance of understanding Latina/o literature not merely as an ethnic phenomenon in the United States, but more broadly as a crucial element of a trans-American literary imagination. Leading scholars in the field present critical analyses of key texts, authors, themes, and contexts, from the early nineteenth century to the present. They engage with the dynamics of migration, linguistic and cultural translation, and the uneven distribution of resources across the Americas that characterize the imaginative spaces of Latina/o literature. This *Companion* is an invaluable resource for understanding the complexities of the field.

John Morán González is Associate Professor of English at the University of Texas at Austin, where he holds courtesy appointments with the Department of Mexican American and Latino Studies and the Department of American Studies. He is also a Faculty Affiliate of the Center for Mexican American Studies. His publications include *The Troubled Union: Expansionist Imperatives in Post-Reconstruction American Novels* and *Border Renaissance: The Texas Centennial and the Emergence of Mexican American Literature*.

A complete list of books in the series is at the back of this book.

THE CAMBRIDGE
COMPANION TO
LATINA/O AMERICAN LITERATURE

THE CAMBRIDGE COMPANION TO LATINA/O AMERICAN LITERATURE

EDITED BY

JOHN MORÁN GONZÁLEZ
University of Texas, Austin

CAMBRIDGE
UNIVERSITY PRESS

University Printing House, Cambridge CB2 8BS, United Kingdom

One Liberty Plaza, 20th Floor, New York, NY 10006, USA

477 Williamstown Road, Port Melbourne, VIC 3207, Australia

4843/24, 2nd Floor, Ansari Road, Daryaganj, Delhi - 110002, India

79 Anson Road, #06-04/06, Singapore 079906

Cambridge University Press is part of the University of Cambridge.

It furthers the University's mission by disseminating knowledge in the pursuit of education, learning and research at the highest international levels of excellence.

www.cambridge.org
Information on this title: www.cambridge.org/9781107622920

© Cambridge University Press 2016

This publication is in copyright. Subject to statutory exception and to the provisions of relevant collective licensing agreements, no reproduction of any part may take place without the written permission of Cambridge University Press.

First published 2016

A catalogue record for this publication is available from the British Library

Library of Congress Cataloging in Publication data
Names: González, John Morán, editor.
Title: The Cambridge companion to Latina/o American literature / [edited by] John Morán González.
Description: New York, NY : Cambridge University Press, 2016. | Series: Cambridge companions to literature | Includes bibliographical references.
Identifiers: LCCN 2015040744 | ISBN 9781107044920 (hardback) | ISBN 9781107622920 (paperback)
Subjects: LCSH: Latin American literature – 20th century – History and criticism. | Latin American literature – 21st century – History and criticism.
Classification: LCC PQ7081.A1 C347 2016 | DDC 860.9/868073–dc23
LC record available at http://lccn.loc.gov/2015040744

ISBN 978-1-107-04492-0 Hardback
ISBN 978-1-107-62292-0 Paperback

Cambridge University Press has no responsibility for the persistence or accuracy of URLs for external or third-party internet websites referred to in this publication, and does not guarantee that any content on such websites is, or will remain, accurate or appropriate.

For m'ijo Santiago, and all who dwell in latinid@des

CONTENTS

Notes on Contributors	page xi
Acknowledgments	xv
Chronology	xvii
Introduction	xxiii
JOHN MORÁN GONZÁLEZ	

PART I EARLY TRANS-AMERICAN CONTACTS AND CONFLICTS

1 The Trans-American Literature of Conquest and Exile, 1823–1885   3
   RODRIGO LAZO

2 The Trans-American Literature of Empire and Revolution, 1880–1938   17
   LAURA LOMAS

3 Between Ethnic Americans and Racial Subjects: Latina/o Literature, 1936–1959   36
   JOHN MORÁN GONZÁLEZ

PART II LATINA/O LITERATURE SINCE 1960

4 The Aesthetics of Politics: Cultural Nationalist Movements and Latina/o Literature   57
   RICHARD T. RODRÍGUEZ

5 The Cold War in the Americas and Latina/o Literature   72
   RICARDO L. ORTÍZ

6 The 1980s: Latina/o Literature during the "Decade of the Hispanic"   91
   TIFFANY ANA LÓPEZ

7 Trans-American Latina/o Literature of the 1990s:
   Resisting Neoliberalism   111
   LUCÍA M. SUÁREZ

8 From "Latinidad" to "Latinid@des": Imagining the
   Twenty-First Century   128
   PAUL ALLATSON

PART III CRITICAL METHODOLOGIES AND THEMES

9 Latin@ Poetics: Voices   147
   NORMA ELIA CANTÚ

10 Latina/o Life Writing: Autobiography, Memoir, *Testimonio*   161
   ISABEL DÚRAN

11 Queering Latina/o Literature   178
   LAWRENCE LA FOUNTAIN-STOKES

12 Latinos and the Like: Reading Mixture and Deracination   195
   CLAUDIA MILIAN

13 *Mestizaje* and Cyborgism on Either Side of the Line   213
   THEA PITMAN

14 *Historias Transfronterizas*: Contemporary Latina/o
   Literature of Migration   231
   MARTA CAMINERO-SANTANGELO

   Index   247

NOTES ON CONTRIBUTORS

PAUL ALLATSON is an associate professor in the Faculty of Arts and Social Sciences, University of Technology Sydney. He has published widely in the areas of Latino and trans-American cultural studies, and cultural, postcolonial, and sexuality studies more broadly. His publications include *Key Terms in Latino/a Cultural and Literary Studies* (Blackwell, 2007), *Latino Dreams: Transcultural Traffic and the U.S. National Imaginary* (Rodopi, 2002), and the coedited volumes *Exile Cultures, Misplaced Identities* (Rodopi, 2008) and *Celebrity Philanthropy* (Intellect, 2015).

MARTA CAMINERO-SANTANGELO is a professor in the English Department at the University of Kansas. Her books include *The Madwoman Can't Speak, Or Why Insanity Is Not Subversive* (Cornell University Press, 1998) and *On Latinidad: US Latino Literature and the Construction of Ethnicity* (University Press of Florida, 2007). Her book *Documenting the Undocumented: Narrative, Nation, and Social Justice in the Gatekeeper Era* is forthcoming from the University Press of Florida.

NORMA ELIA CANTÚ currently serves as professor of U.S. Latin@ Studies at the University of Missouri, Kansas City. Through publications in the areas of folklore, literary studies, women's studies, and border studies, she engages in critical scholarship on Latinas and Latinos, especially on the border. Her numerous publications include the 1995 *Canícula: Snapshots of a Girlhood en la Frontera*, which chronicles her coming of age in Laredo, Texas. Most recently she edited *Ofrenda: Liliana Wilson's Art of Dissidence and Dreams*. She is a cofounder of CantoMundo, a space for Latin@ poets and a member of the Macondo Writers Workshop.

ISABEL DÚRAN is Professor of American Literature at the Universidad Complutense. Her publications on gender studies, literature, autobiography, and ethnicity includes *Autobiografía: versiones femeninas en la literatura norteamericana del siglo XX* (Universidad Compultense, 1992). She also edited *Miradas Transatlánticas/Transatlantic Vistas* (Fundamentos, 2011). She is currently President of the Spanish Association for American Studies; she was a member of the General Council of the American Studies Association from 2008 to 2011, and served on its International Committee from 2005 to 2011. She has been a Fulbright Fellow twice.

JOHN MORÁN GONZÁLEZ is Associate Professor of English at the University of Texas at Austin, where he holds courtesy appointments with the Department of Mexican American and Latino Studies and the Department of American Studies. He is also a Faculty Affiliate of the Center for Mexican American Studies. He is author of *Border Renaissance: The Texas Centennial and the Emergence of Mexican American Literature* (University of Texas Press, 2009) and *The Troubled Union: Expansionist Imperatives in Post-Reconstruction American Novels* (Ohio State University Press, 2010). His articles and reviews have appeared in *American Literature*, *American Literary History*, *Aztlán*, *Nineteenth-Century Contexts*, *Symbolism*, and *Western American Literature*. In addition to editing *The Cambridge Companion to Latina/o American Literature*, he is coediting (with Laura Lomas) *The Cambridge History of Latina/o Literature*.

LAWRENCE LA FOUNTAIN-STOKES is Director of the Latina/o Studies Program and Associate Professor of American Culture, Romance Languages and Literatures, and Women's Studies at the University of Michigan, Ann Arbor. Born and raised in Puerto Rico, he received his A.B. from Harvard (1991) and M.A. and Ph.D. from Columbia (1999). He is the author of *Queer Ricans: Cultures and Sexualities in the Diaspora* (University of Minnesota Press, 2009), *Uñas pintadas de azul/Blue Fingernails* (Bilingual Press, 2009), and *Abolición del pato* (Terranova, 2013). He coedited an issue of *CENTRO Journal* on Puerto Rican Queer Sexualities (Spring 2007) and is currently working on "Translocas: Trans Diasporic Puerto Rican Drag."

RODRIGO LAZO is an associate professor of English and an affiliate in the Chicano/Latino Studies Department at the University of California, Irvine. He is the author of *Writing to Cuba: Filibustering and Cuban Exiles in the United States* (University of North Carolina Press, 2005). He is the coeditor of the forthcoming collection of essays, *The Latino Nineteenth Century*, and is working on a book-length study of Spanish-language writing in Philadelphia in the early nineteenth century. His articles have appeared in numerous collections and journals.

LAURA LOMAS teaches Latina/o and U.S. Literature at Rutgers University-Newark. Her first book, *Translating Empire: José Martí, Migrant Latino Subjects and American Modernities* (Duke University Press, 2008), won the Modern Languages Association Prize for Latina/o and Chicana/o literature and an honorable mention from Latin American Studies Association Latina/o Section; it analyses Cuban José Martí's role as critical interpreter of American literature, politics, and culture from the perspective of a Latino migrant during the Gilded Age. Coeditor of the forthcoming *The Cambridge History of Latina/o Literature*, Lomas has published numerous essays and book chapters, most recently in *Review: Literature and Arts in the Americas*.

NOTES ON CONTRIBUTORS

TIFFANY ANA LÓPEZ is Professor of Theatre, Film and Digital Production and Tomás Rivera Endowed Chair in the College of Humanities, Arts & Social Sciences at University of California, Riverside. Her writing has appeared in numerous journals and books, including *Theatre Journal, Theatre Topics, A Companion to Twentieth-Century American Drama, Performing the U.S. Latina and Latino Borderlands*, and *Captive Audience–Prison and Captivity in Contemporary Theater*. From 2005 to 2012, she served as editor of *Chicana/Latina Studies: The Journal of Mujers Activas en Letras y Cambio Social*. She is currently completing a book about U.S. Latina/o drama, community engagement, and the processing of trauma.

CLAUDIA MILIAN is Associate Professor of Romance Studies at Duke University and the author of *Latining America: Black-Brown Passages and the Coloring of Latino/a Studies* (University of Georgia Press, 2013).

RICARDO L. ORTÍZ is Chair of the Department of English at Georgetown University, where he is also Associate Professor of U.S. Latin@ Literature. Professor Ortiz's first book, *Cultural Erotics in Cuban America*, was published in 2007 by the University of Minnesota Press; his second book project, which is well under way, is entitled *Testimonial Fictions: Atrocity, Sexuality and History in Post-Cold War US Latin@ Literature*.

THEA PITMAN is Senior Lecturer in Latin American Studies at the University of Leeds. Her research career started with work on travel writing produced by Mexican authors, published in book form as *Mexican Travel Writing* (Lang, 2007). It has since evolved to focus on the subject of Latin American online, and more broadly digital, cultural production. This work is published in article form as well as in the coedited anthology, *Latin American Cyberculture and Cyberliterature* (with Claire Taylor, Liverpool University Press, 2007) and the coauthored monograph, *Latin American Identity in Online Cultural Production* (also with Claire Taylor, Routledge, 2013).

RICHARD T. RODRÍGUEZ is Associate Professor of English and Latina/Latino Studies at the University of Illinois, Urbana-Champaign, where he is also affiliated with the Department of Gender and Women's Studies and the Unit for Criticism and Interpretive Theory. His research, teaching, and writing are grounded in Latina/o cultural studies, literary and film studies, critical theory, and queer studies. The author of *Next of Kin: The Family in Chicano/a Cultural Politics* (Duke University Press, 2009) and many articles and reviews, he is currently writing a book on Latino male sexualities in film and literature.

LUCÍA M. SUÁREZ is Associate Professor of Spanish at Amherst College, where she teaches Latino/a Studies and Caribbean Cultures and Literatures. Her publications include *The Tears of Hispaniola: Haitian and Dominican Diaspora Memory* (University Press of Florida, 2006) and *The Portable Island: Cubans at Home in the World* (coedited with Ruth Behar, Palgrave Macmillan, 2008). Her interdisciplinary work has received generous support from the Ford Foundation, the Rockefeller Foundation, and the Mellon Foundation. She was a Visiting Scholar at The David Rockefeller Center for Latin American Studies (DRCLAS), Harvard University. She is working on a new book, *Framing Cuba: Literary and Film Castings of a Nation and Its Diasporas.*

ACKNOWLEDGMENTS

I would like to thank Ray Ryan, my editor at Cambridge University Press, for his sage advice to a novice volume editor. Thanks also to the editorial and production staff at CUP for their professionalism in making this volume a reality. In particular, Fred Goykhman, Kani Ramamurthy, and Alex Poreda helped bring this volume to fruition in the most professional way. I also extend my appreciation to Sandra Spicher for compiling the index.

As this critical anthology would be nothing without the essays that comprise it, I would like to thank the contributors for their wonderful efforts in creating this collaborative overview of Latina/o literary studies and making it accessible to a wide audience.

CHRONOLOGY

1791–1804	Slave revolt in Saint-Domingue creates the Republic of Haiti
1810–29	Wars of Independence across Latin America
1823	Proclamation of the Monroe Doctrine by the United States
1826	The Spanish-language historical novel *Jicoténcal* is published anonymously in Philadelphia
1836	Texas Revolt and formation of the Republic of Texas
1845	United States annexes the Republic of Texas as the 28th state
1846–48	U.S.-Mexican War begins as a border dispute; the United States claims the Rio Grande is the border while Mexico claims the Nueces River is
1848	Treaty of Guadalupe Hidalgo ends U.S.-Mexican War, resulting in the transfer of Mexico's northern provinces to the United States
1854	Ostend Manifesto calls for the United States to annex Cuba either by purchase or force
1855–57	Filibuster by William Walker in Nicaragua
1858	Exiled Cuban poets in the United States publish *El laúd del desterrado* in New York City
1861–64	U.S. Civil War
1861–67	French military occupies Mexico until driven out by Republican forces under Benito Juárez
1872	María Amparo Ruiz de Burton, *Who Would Have Thought It?*
1885	María Amparo Ruiz de Burton, *The Squatter and the Don*
1891	José Martí, "Nuestra América"
1894	Manuel Zeno Gandía, *La charca*

1898	U.S.-Spanish War results in the transfer of Cuba, Puerto Rico, Guam, and the Philippines to U.S. control
1901	The Platt Amendment reserves the right of the United States to intervene in the affairs of a nominally independent Cuba
1910–20	The Mexican Revolution forces up to a million Mexicans to migrate to the United States
1910s	María Cristina Mena's short stories are published in U.S. magazines.
1912–33	U.S. military occupies Nicaragua
1914	Alirio Díaz Guerra, *Lucas Guevara*
1914–18	World War I
1915-1919	Armed uprising of *los sediciosos* in South Texas, followed by violent reprisals by the Texas Rangers and vigilante groups
1915–34	U.S. military occupies Haiti
1916–22	U.S. military occupies the Dominican Republic
1917	U.S. citizenship is imposed upon Puerto Ricans by the Jones-Shafroth Act
1918	Salomón de la Selva, *Tropical Town*
1925	William Carlos Williams, *In the American Grain*
1926–29	Cristero Rebellion in Mexico sends a new wave of migrants to the United States
1928	Daniel Venegas, *Las adventuras de Don Chipote*
1929–39	The Great Depression; tens of thousands of Mexican nationals and Mexican American citizens alike are deported by the U.S. government
1933	U.S. President Franklin Roosevelt announces the "Good Neighbor Policy"
1933–43	Most active decade of Julia de Burgos's poetic production
1936	Texas Centennial of Independence from Mexico
1936–40	Américo Paredes writes *George Washington Gómez*
1937	Massacre of nationalists by state authorities in Ponce, Puerto Rico
1937	The "Parsley Massacre" of some 10,000 Haitians in the Dominican Republic at the order of dictator Rafael Leonides Trujillo
1937–41	Jovita González and Margaret Eimer coauthor *Caballero*
1938–45	World War II
1942–64	The bracero program admits tens of thousands of Mexican agricultural workers into the United States

1948	Operation Bootstrap initiated in Puerto Rico
1950–53	War on the Korean Peninsula
1952	Puerto Rico becomes a U.S. Commonwealth
1954	Puerto Rican nationalists open fire in the U.S. House of Representatives; Operation Wetback implemented to deport undocumented Mexican migrants in the United States; René Marqués, *La carreta*
1956	Pedro Juan Soto, *Spiks*
1959	The Cuban Revolution overthrows U.S.-backed dictator Fulgencio Batista, initiating the Cuban diaspora to the United States; José Antonio Villarreal, *Pocho*
1960	The United States imposes trade and travel embargos on Cuba
1962	Cuban Missile Crisis
1963	John Rechy, *City of Night*
1965	U.S. military occupies the Dominican Republic after a period of civil unrest following Trujillo's assassination in 1961; Immigration and Nationality Reform Act shifts future immigration to the United States away from Europe and to Asia and Latin America
1965–75	U.S.-Vietnam War
1966–78	Repression during Joaquín Balaguer's "Twelve Years" initiates mass migration from the Dominican Republic to the United States
1967	Rodolfo "Corky" Gonzales, *I Am Joaquin*; Piri Thomas, *Down These Mean Streets;* Luis Valdez, *Los Vendidos*
1969	Pedro Pietri, "Puerto Rican Obituary"
1970	José Montoya, *El Louie*
1971	Tomás Rivera, *… y no se lo tragó la tierra*
1972	Oscar Zeta Acosta, *Autobiography of a Brown Buffalo;* Rodolfo Anaya, *Bless Me, Ultima*
1972–87	ASCO art performance collective active
1973	Oscar Zeta Acosta, *Revolt of the Cockroach People;* Rolando Hinojosa, *Estampas del Valle y otras obras;* Nicholasa Mohr, *Nilda*
1974	Miguel Piñero, *Short Eyes*
1977	María Irene Fornés, *Fefu and Her Friends;* Gary Soto, *The Elements of San Joaquin*
1978	Luis Valdez, *Zoot Suit*
1980s	Endemic poverty, a socialist revolution in Nicaragua, civil wars in Guatemala and El Salvador, and death squads in

	Honduras initiate the great Central American diaspora to the United States
1980	Mariel boatlift brings 125,000 Cubans to U.S. soil; raúlsalinas, *Un trip through the mind jail*
1981	Landmark anthology of women of color feminism, *This Bridge Called My Back*, published; Alurista, *Spik in Glyph?*; Lorna Dee Cervantes, *Emplumada*; Richard Rodriguez, *Hunger of Memory*
1982	Edward Rivera, *Family Installments*
1983	Cherríe Moraga, *Loving in the War Years/ lo que nunca pasó por sus labios*
1984	Sandra Cisneros, *The House on Mango Street*; Arturo Islas, *The Rain God*; Tato Laviera, *La Carreta Made a U-Turn*
1985	Miguel Algarín, *Time's Now*; Helena María Viramontes, *The Moths and Other Stories*
1986	Immigration and Control Reform Act provides path to citizenship for 2.7 million undocumented workers in the United States while enacting more stringent border controls; Ana Castillo, *The Mixquiahuala Letters*; Denise Chávez, *The Last of the Menu Girls*; Cherríe Moraga, *Giving Up the Ghost*
1987	Gloria Anzaldúa, *Borderlands/ La Frontera*; Sandra Cisneros, *My Wicked, Wicked Ways*; Martín Espada, *Trumpets from the Islands of Their Eviction*; Luz María Umpierre, *The Margarita Poems*
1988	Ana Castillo, *My Father Was a Toltec*
1989	U.S. military invades Panama; Lucha Corpi, *Delia's Song*; Virgil Suárez, *Latin Jazz*
1990	Oscar Hijuelos's *The Mambo Kings Play Songs of Love* awarded the Pulitzer Prize for Fiction; Judith Ortiz Cofer, *Silent Dancing*
1990–91	First U.S.-Iraq War
1991	Julia Alvarez, *How the García Girls Lost Their Accents*; Sandra Cisneros, *Woman Hollering Creek and Other Stories*
1992	Los Angeles Uprisings; Cristina García, *Dreaming in Cuban*; Alejandro Morales, *The Rag Doll Plagues*
1992–94	Coco Fusco and Guillermo Gómez-Peña perform *The Year of the White Bear and Two Undiscovered Amerindians Visit the West*

1993	Reinaldo Arenas, *Before Night Falls;* Dagoberto Gilb, *The Magic of Blood;* Graciela Limón, *In Search of Bernabé;* Luis Rodríguez, *Always Running;* Tino Villanueva, *Scenes from the Movie GIANT*
1994	North American Free Trade Agreement (NAFTA) Treaty in force, causing Zapatista rebellion in Mexico; Rafael Campo, *The Other Man Was Me;* Edwidge Danticat, *Breath, Eyes, Memory;* Demetria Martínez, *Mother Tongue;* Esmeralda Santiago, *When I Was Puerto Rican*
1995	Norma E. Cantú, *Canícula: Snapshots of a Girlhood en la Frontera;* Helena María Viramontes, *Under the Feet of Jesus*
1996	Junot Díaz, *Drown:* Achy Obejas, *Memory Mambo*
1997	Francisco Goldman, *The Ordinary Seaman;* Esmeralda Santiago, *América's Dream*
1998	Mario Bencastro, *Odyssey to the North;* Giannina Braschi, *Yo-yo Boing!;* Héctor Tobar, *The Tattooed Soldier*
1998–2000	Guillermo Gómez-Peña and La Pocha Nostra, "Ethno-Techno: A Virtual Museum of Radical Latino Imagery and Fetishized Identities," active on the Internet.
1999	Loida Maritza Pérez, *Geographies of Home*
2000	Ernesto Quiñonez, *Bodega Dreams;* Alina Troyano, *I, Carmelita Tropicana*
2001	9/11 attacks; U.S. military operations commence in Afghanistan; Ana Menendez, *In Cuba I Was a German Shepherd*
2001–07	Los Cybrids active on the Internet
2002	Sandra Cisneros, *Caramelo*
2003	Nilo Cruz's *Anna in the Tropics* is awarded the Pulitzer Prize for Drama; Oscar Casares, *Brownsville;* Manuel Muñoz, *Zigzagger;* Alisa Valdes-Rodríguez, *The Dirty Girls Social Club*
2004	Nina Marie Martínez, *¡Caramba!*
2005	Sesshu Foster, *Atomik Aztex;* Salvador Plascencia, *The People of Paper*
2006	Millions protest proposed anti-immigrant federal legislation; Angie Cruz, *Let It Rain Coffee;* Reyna Grande, *Across a Hundred Mountains*
2008	Junot Díaz's *The Brief Wondrous Life of Oscar Wao* awarded the Pulitzer Prize for Fiction

2009	Oscar Casares, *Amigoland*
2010	Josefina López, *Detained in the Desert*; Luis Negrón, *Mundo Cruel*
2012	Justin Torres, *We the Animals*
2013	Richard Blanco, *One Today;* Raquel Cepeda, *Bird of Paradise: How I Became Latina*
2015	Thawing of U.S.-Cuban relations

INTRODUCTION

JOHN MORÁN GONZÁLEZ

During the past two decades, Latina/o literature has become increasingly recognized as part of world literature, taught not only in the United States and throughout the Americas but also in classrooms from Europe to Asia. This remarkable worlding of Latina/o literature is a testament to its imaginative capacity to artfully depict and theorize the experiences of people of Latin American descent whose migratory journeys have led to the formation of Latina/o communities physically situated within the United States but cognitively situated as a transnational multiplicity of cultural and linguistic practices. Latina/o literature renders in aesthetically powerful ways the dynamics of life-in-diaspora that has become characteristic of the contemporary world, in which migrant flows continuously disturb the boundaries of the nationalisms they exceed, whether that of the sending nation or that of the receiving one. Simultaneously, Latina/o literature indexes the historical development of life-in-diaspora through the specific stages of its unfolding in the Americas over more than two centuries.

Beginning in the early nineteenth century, the first iteration of this process developed in the encounter of British American and Spanish American intellectuals attempting to envision the social, political, and imaginative dimensions of everyday life after the end of European colonialism. Yet over the course of the nineteenth and twentieth centuries, this initial sense of republican unity among American nations gave way to U.S. imperial ambitions and Latin American fears of those ambitions, fears that were realized as the United States continually sought to establish a cultural and political hegemony over Latin America and the Caribbean through its economic and military might. Some of these U.S. interventions in Latin America directly or indirectly created the deterritorialized communities within the United States and the diasporic migrations to the United States that are the basis of contemporary *latinidades*, or the multiple ways Latinas/os enact their trans-American existences.

Thus tracing the complex relationships between the peoples of the United States and Latin America since at least the early nineteenth century, Latina/o literature provides an invaluable account of the changing nature of trans-American interactions between North and South as the Americas unevenly emerged from European colonialism. Given this history, Latina/o literature is neither a recent development stemming from the large migrant flows from Latin America and the Caribbean over the last three decades nor solely the product of the Latina/o social movements of the 1960s and 1970s, although clearly both have heavily influenced the contemporary literature's thematic content as well as greatly accelerated its sheer production. Reflecting its trans-American situation, Latina/o literature is fundamentally a bilingual tradition, whose relative output in Spanish, English, Spanglish, and sometimes indigenous languages reflects the specific social conditions and aesthetic choices available at any given historical moment and context.

The Cambridge Companion to Latina/o American Literature is designed to reach a wide audience that would come to it from general literary anthologies of Latina/o literature such as *The Norton Anthology of Latino Literature*. The first principle to acknowledge, in conceptualizing the contours of *The Companion*, is the fundamental recasting of what *latinidades* means within the field of Latina/o literary studies. Like Latina/o literature, Latina/o literary studies is on the cusp of becoming similarly globalized as transnational methodologies make for new conceptual possibilities. While the field has grown substantially over the past two decades as an institutional presence and in methodological sophistication, the direction and force of the change has yet to be fully charted. Most obviously, the demographic changes in the nature and intensity of migrant flows to the United States from Latin America and the Hispanophone Caribbean during the Cold War and its aftermath have enlarged the number of communities from which Latina/o writing emerges, thereby altering the field's imagined subjects of inquiry. Initially starting as disparate community-supported literary history fields during the 1960s (i.e., as Chicano studies and Puerto Rican studies), Latina/o literary studies has expanded since the 1990s to include the literature of other Latino groups such as Cuban Americans, Dominican Americans, and U.S. Central Americans. While Cuban American literature often benefited institutionally for its perceived anticommunism, Dominican American and especially U.S. Central American literature have had to fight against an invisibility propagated by normative field definitions of *latinidades*.

In addition, Latina/o studies has changed via its encounters with other academic fields, emerging from its original focus as the university arm of community empowerment into a semiautonomous scholarly field. At least since the great mobilizations of indigenous communities against the

1992 Columbian Quincentenary, Latina/o literary studies has entered into critical conversations with American Studies, Latin American Studies, and other literary fields. The scholarly conversations across these fields over the past quarter-century have been mutually transformative. In large measure, the "transnational turn" in American Studies can be attributed to the focus upon trans-migrant, cross-border analyses central to Latina/o studies. Likewise, Latin American Studies has increasingly turned to Latina/o studies to understand the flow of people, capital, and culture across national borders, with particular attention to how migrants negotiate competing nationalist, economic, political, and cultural transitions in a post–Cold War environment. In turn, interaction with American Studies and Latin American Studies has worlded Latina/o literary studies, bringing the study of Latina/o literature into closer comparative contact with oral traditions and literature of the Americas, whether in English, Spanish, or indigenous languages. Much the same can be said for the proliferation of theoretical and methodological approaches that have lead Latina/o studies away from concerns about cultural authenticity and identity to those of coloniality, sexuality, and racialization as operations of power, drawn not only from Continental theory but also from indigenous, black, feminist, queer, and other subaltern knowledges.

Complimenting the new spatial dimensions of Latina/o literary studies has been the deepening of its temporal dimensions. When the field was first founded, scholars of Chicano and Puerto Rican literature were hard-pressed to identify many literary texts written or published prior to the 1950s. Thanks to the archival research and methodological insights about the archive made possible by the Recovering the U.S. Hispanic Literary Heritage Project (itself an outgrowth of the movement against the Eurocentric triumphalism of the Columbian Quincentenary), scholars have convincingly demonstrated how Spanish colonial-era texts dating to the sixteenth century should be considered as key antecedents to Latina/o literature with regards to its origins in hemispheric coloniality. In addition, recent research into the nineteenth century has greatly expanded the number and scope of Latina/o literary texts, and, furthermore, the Recovery Project has made many of these texts widely available for classroom use either through literary anthologies or reprints, providing widespread accessibility for adoption in university courses.

Periodization has historically been a key manner by which literature has been contextualized, with the original Romantic sense that the finest literature of a given moment somehow best captured the *Zeitgeist* or "Spirit of the Age." At later moments, periodization offered the comfort of a quasi-scientific categorization of literature into qualitatively identifiable moments or movements. What periodization tenders is basically a large-scale way of understanding groups of literary works in relation to each other across a specific "era," but in a way that necessarily excludes texts that fit neither the temporal markers assigned to a particular grouping, nor the formal qualities supposedly characteristic of that grouping, nor the cultural values subsequently assigned to it by the field. In some sense, the periodization of literary history says less about the "era" that produced certain texts than about the schema by which literary historians study said texts. Nonetheless, periodization remains a useful organizational tool for literary and critical anthologies as long as the developmental teleology implied by periodization is checked by an acknowledgment that discontinuity and multiple pathways are as important, and sometimes more so, for a field with such heterogeneous origins and trajectories. For the *Companion*, I indicated the presence of related but not continuous or teleological developments for Latina/o literature in two ways. First, only two of the three major divisions are "historical"; the third is methodological. Second, individual chapters within the historical divisions, when limned by exact years, have overlapping beginning and end dates to indicate the messiness of their contextual existences. The year 1960 remains a significant transitional date for the *Companion*, in large measure following the periodization set forth by the Recovery Project.[1]

However considered, the spatial and temporal elaboration of Latina/o literature and its study have transformed what had been previously been taken by the dominant academy as a minor, late twentieth-century phenomenon into a multilingual, poly-temporal expression of trans-American contestation and cooperation. It is precisely these dimensions of Latina/o literature that have lead to its increasingly globalized study, as the movements of migrants, capital, commodities, and cultures from the global South to the global North and sometimes back again necessitates not only transnational frameworks of interpretation but comparative ones as well. This principle guided both the historical sections and the methodological ones, such that the emphasis is on underscoring the transnational dimensions of Latina/o literature. While this is by now a familiar move with deep and convincing justifications, the task of the *Companion* is to make this aspect central to the way the field is presented from the start. Hence, in the historical sections, the trans-American connections, especially as wonderfully elaborated by Recovery Project scholars for the nineteenth century, are stressed in the colonial and early republican phases. Contemporary Latina/o literary studies has rightly rejected national borders as the limits of knowledge, following the increasing insistence of Latina/o communities on maintaining and celebrating transnational ties. To that end, and to highlight the historical arc of reciprocity put into motion by U.S. colonial and neocolonial policies

INTRODUCTION

in Latin America, the refugee, exile, and migrant streams associated with such U.S. interventions take center stage. But rather than focus specifically on 1848 or 1898, the idea is to imagine the consequences of conquest for Latina/o literature over the course of decades; in the same way, the global Cold War serves as a key framework for the post-1960 chapters, especially as not only Cuban migration but also Dominican and Central American migrations can be traced in large measure to U.S. Cold War policies and interventions in those regions. The chapters on more recent Latina/o literature extends this focus on the transnational by taking neoliberalism and the rise of the Internet as points of departure.

Besides disrupting any notion of historical periodization being able to tell the "complete" story of Latina/o literature, the *Companion's* closing section on critical methodologies foregrounds just how these shape not only which questions get asked about Latina/o literature but also how they influence the status of particular authors, texts, and genres. For instance, the critical focus on normative systems of gender and sexuality by Latina feminism and queer studies has brought genres that focus on the social negotiations of gendered and queer subjects within hostile social environments, such as poetry and life writing, into the forefront of Latina/o critical inquiry. Likewise, the centrality of migrants to the present articulation of *latinidades* has brought narratives of migration to the fore, not only as a present reality but as a long-standing phenomenon.

Organization of the *Companion*

Part I examines these developments within Latina/o literature from the early, heady days of trans-American exchanges to the grim reality of Latina/o abjection during the first half of the twentieth century. As Rodrigo Lazo demonstrates, the trans-American literary encounters of the early nineteenth century, as portrayed within poetry and travel narratives, map out the hopeful possibilities of a Western hemisphere of sister republics united against the tyranny and corruption of European colonization. This alliance of hope was not to last, as the United States would, by the 1820s, begin to imagine itself as an "Empire for Liberty," and the rest of the Americas as its protectorate under the Monroe Doctrine. By the 1840s, Manifest Destiny, or the self-granted providential right of the United States to spread across the North American continent, made possible the taking of Mexico's northern half in a war of conquest (the U.S.-Mexican War of 1846–48).[2]

As a result, the early nineteenth-century dream of sister republics gave way by mid-century to an increasing fear and wariness of the United States throughout Latin America. The invasion and conquest of a sister republic, followed by the increasingly harsh racialization of those Mexicans in the annexed territories who chose to become U.S. citizens, fostered a deep and abiding distrust of the imperial ambitions of the United States to dominate the Americas. As Laura Lomas shows, Cuban expatriate José Martí articulated in the 1880s and 1890s what we may now recognize as a working-class migrant Latina/o subjectivity, critical not only of local inequalities of race and class within the Gilded Age United States but also of major differences in power between American nation-states as well. Even while he organized fellow exiles against the Spanish colonialism still ruling Cuba, Martí criticized the retention of colonial epistemologies and institutions in Latin American republics, warning that social hierarchies of race would invariably weaken the ability of Latin America to fend off the incursions of the United States, "the giant with seven-league boots." Martí died fighting for Cuban independence in 1895, four years before his worst fears would be realized by the U.S. seizure of Cuba, Puerto Rico, Guam, and the Philippines as a result of the U.S.-Spanish War of 1898. Cuba would gain nominal independence in 1902, albeit under U.S.-imposed conditions, while the Philippines would remain under direct U.S. rule until 1946. The colonial status of Puerto Rico and Guam has only nominally changed since 1898.[3]

During the first half of the twentieth century, the terms of U.S. national inclusion for Latinas/os, whether citizens or not, became the central subject of the first substantial body of Latina/o literature to be written in English, as I discuss in my contribution. Coming from the first generation of *Mexico-tejanos* [people of Mexican descent in Texas] to have fully encountered the English-only public educational system, writers such as Jovita González and Américo Paredes engaged the novelistic tradition in English in their examinations of race, class, gender, and power in the South Texas borderlands during the 1930s. Spurred into writing by the Anglo-Texan discourses of racial triumphalism during the Texas Centennial of 1936, these authors provided socially symbolic responses to the pressures of modernity upon Mexican descent communities. As I discuss in my essay, José Antonio Villarreal's 1959 novel *Pocho*, once considered the "first" Chicano novel, highlights what appeared to be the key ideological impasse for "the Mexican American generation": how to imagine social agency in something other than the individualist terms allowed by U.S. nationalist discourses.[4]

In contrast, the Puerto Rican literature of the 1950s directly engages the impact of U.S. administrative colonialism of the Island and the resulting diaspora of Puerto Ricans, particularly to New York City. René Marqués's play *La carreta* [*The Oxcart*] traces the forced migration of a poor *jíbaro* [peasant] family from the hardscrabble but dignified life on the Island's central mountains, to the crowded and vice-ridden slums of San Juan, and finally to the cold mean streets of New York. In modernist, fragmented fashion, Pedro Juan Soto's *Spiks* picks up where *The Oxcart* leaves off, tracing the deprived and dehumanized experiences of Nuyoricans as they attempt to navigate an economic and racial system that exploits them economically while stripping them of dignity and culture. Significantly, these bilingual authors chose to write their works in Spanish rather than English, reflecting the highly charged politics of language associated with the Island's colonial status; while English was the linguistic medium of hopeful incorporation into the United States for many Mexican American writers of this period, Spanish was the preferred language of national independence for Puerto Rican authors.[5]

Part II of the *Companion* examines the contemporary production of Latina/o literature, starting with the Chicano and Boricua social movements of the late 1960s and early 1970s until the dawn of the present millennium. In this period, the sheer quantity of Latina/o literature increases dramatically, as changes in U.S. immigration policy after 1965, the impact of the Cold War on Latin America, the global decolonization movement, and the intensification of neoliberal economic policies created not only new transnational migrant communities but also the critical political consciousness among those communities to oppose their further exploitation and marginalization. As Richard T. Rodríguez demonstrates, the cultural and political nationalisms of the Chicano and Boricua movements formed a key moment in mass mobilization and the proliferation of poetry, novels, and drama, even if the cultural nationalist imaginaries expressed within these works were limited by sexist and heteronormative assumptions.[6]

The trans-American nature of Latina/o literature in the twentieth century becomes immediately clear when the huge impact of the Cold War (1945–91) is taken into consideration. As Ricardo Ortíz shows, the twin pillars of U.S. foreign policy for Latin America in this period – the protection of U.S. economic interests and the containment of Soviet-influenced communism – lead to interventionist policies throughout the region. These included CIA-sponsored coups (Guatemala, 1954; Cuba, 1961; Chile, 1973), covert proxy wars (Nicaragua, 1980s), military invasion and occupation (Dominican Republic, 1965–66; Panama, 1989), and support for numerous repressive dictatorships, including those of Rafael Trujillo in the Dominican Republic (1930–61), Fulgencio Batista in Cuba (1933–44, 1952–59), the Duvaliers in Haiti (1957–86), and the Somozas in Nicaragua (1936–79). U.S. support for repressive governments in Guatemala and El Salvador, especially during the civil wars in those nations during the 1980s, lead to near-genocidal campaigns against indigenous communities. All told, these interventions created the political and economic circumstances that led to mass migrations from Latin America to the United States, thereby shifting the nature of *latinidades* as imagined within the United States from a Chicano-Puertoriqueño axis to a multivalent nexus that predominantly featured diasporic communities from Cuba, Central America (especially Guatemala, El Salvador, and Honduras), and Hispaniola (Haiti and the Dominican Republic) as well as Mexico and Puerto Rico.[7]

Widely proclaimed at its onset to be "The Decade of the Hispanic," the 1980s proved to be less about the dawn of widespread Latina/o influence in the United States and more about the uneven incorporation of Latinas/os into national institutions. As Tiffany Ana López illustrates, Latina feminist writers and theorists such Gloria Anzaldúa, often in conversation with African American women and other feminists of color, created increasingly complex writings not only about economic exploitation and racist marginalization but also about the sexism and homophobia of the previous decade's cultural nationalist movements. Simultaneously, the relative opening of U.S. institutions of higher education and the arts to Latinas/os during the late 1960s and early 1970s allowed for the increasing professionalization of Latina/o literary production by the early 1980s. Authors such as Sandra Cisneros and Oscar Hijuelos received advanced degrees in creative writing, while the Hispanic Playwright Laboratory at INTAR, cofounded by dramatist María Irene Fornes, directly or indirectly trained a number of important Latina/o dramatists such as Cherríe Moraga and Nilo Cruz. Other Latina/o poets and playwrights, notably Nuyoricans Miguel Piñero and Tato Laviera and Chicanas/os Lorna Dee Cervantes and Luis Valdez, continued the critical legacies of the *movimientos*. Even as relative access to U.S. institutions opened new avenues of expression, Latina/o writers still confronted the numerous crises facing the Latina/o community, including the AIDS epidemic, the demonization of poor communities by Reaganomics, and the influx of Central American and Dominican refugees caused by U.S. Cold War policies in Latin America.

Two trends during the 1990s defined the trans-American dimensions of that decade for Latina/o literature. As Lucía Suárez outlines, the first of these is best exemplified by the implementation of the North American Free Trade Agreement (NAFTA) in 1994, which further integrated the economies of the United States, Mexico, and Canada into a common market. Neoliberalism, or the set of economic theories behind NAFTA and other so-called free-trade agreements, favored the privatization of corporate gain while socializing corporate risk. This arrangement placed Mexico's weaker economic sectors at a major disadvantage relative to the stronger economic sectors of the United States, and while certain sectors of the Mexican economy prospered under NAFTA, the vast majority of small-scale agricultural production faltered, causing hundreds of thousands to move across the border *al norte*. Neoliberal economic policies spread throughout the Americas during the 1990s, often resulting in profound internal turmoil as austerity measures jeopardized the ability of nations to care for the well-being of the citizenry. The second galvanizing event of this decade was the Columbian Quincentenary of 1992, in which the colonial discourses of European discovery and exploration were challenged by indigenous nations of the Americas, characterizing the celebrations as the legitimation of the five centuries of genocide, exploitation, and land theft that followed Columbus's arrival in the Americas. The 1994 Zapatista uprising in the Lacondon rainforest of the southern Mexican state of Chiapas brought these two key aspects of the 1990s together, as the largely indigenous rebels launched their attack on January 1, 1994, the first day that the NAFTA treaty was implemented.

Even as the effects of neoliberal trade policies set large-scale migrations into motion, Latina/o literature deployed new expressive practices that participated within the cultural manifestations of neoliberalist individualism while coalescing a new, critical Latina/o perspective. After the awarding of the 1990 Pulitzer Prize for Literature to Oscar Hijuelos's *The Mambo Kings Play Songs of Love*, a new generation of Latina/o writers gained access to major New York publishing venues hoping to capitalize on the growing and formally legitimated Latina/o book market. Successful authors from the 1980s such as Sandra Cisneros, Ana Castillo, and Helena Maria Viramontes, along with newer arrivals such as Julia Alvarez, Cristina García, Esmeralda Santiago, Junot Díaz, and Héctor Tobar, published or reprinted their works through New York publishers, thus gaining far wider distribution and recognition for their works in the global literary scene. Taken together, the literature of the 1990s articulated the new complexities of *latinidades*, exploring the trans-American articulations of specific Latina/o communities as formed across borders while building a shared sense of culture and history within the United States.[8]

Latina/o literature in the twenty-first century engages the complexities of the contemporary moment, including the impact of global data networks that not only provide new venues for artistic expression and social networking but also represent the possibilities of refiguring the concerns and very nature of *latinidades* in the material complexity of present-day migrations worldwide. As Paul Allatson argues in his essay, contemporary Latin@ narratives signal a significant turn from the identarian representational imperatives of the previous three decades to more loosely authenticated forms of identification and disidentification, a shift indicated in large measure by the widespread adoption of postmodernist narrative techniques or at least a marked disinterest in the forms of realism primarily associated with cultural nationalist movements. A new generation of Latin@ writers such as Gianni Braschi, Oscar Casares, Susana Chávez-Silverman, Maya Chinchilla, Nina Marie Martínez, Salvador Plascencia, José Rivera, Roberto José Tejada, Edwin Torres, Justin Torres, and Rodrigo Toscano engage in what Allatson terms post-racial representational practices distanced from the concerns of ethno-nationalisms. As such, contemporary Latin@ literature creates the possibilities of new trans-American, transnational, or transcultural forms of community, solidarity, and artistic practice not previously imaginable, thereby creating a dynamic and fluid redefinition of *latinidades*.

Part III of the *Companion* is dedicated to highlighting topical and methodological approaches to Latina/o literature. While not meant to be all-inclusive of these approaches, the selections in this section nonetheless represent major currents in the scholarship. Poetics, the focus of Norma Elia Cantú's essay, is arguably the historical core of Latina/o literature, with deep roots in the oral traditions of pre-Columbian and colonial-era communities. Poetry was also a mainstay of Spanish-language newspapers and periodicals since the mid-nineteenth century and the preferred aesthetic language of the Boricua and Chicano movements of the late 1960s, but, as Cantú relates, poetry retains an important role in the articulation of *latinidades* today.

Isabel Dúran charts the rise of Latina/o life writing as a central discursive site for the development of Latina/o writing. Going beyond making the personal political, Latina/o life writing – as expressed through the genres of autobiography, memoir, and *testimonio* – differs from the normative dimensions of the first two genres by translating an essential feature of the third: explicitly situating the life experiences of the individual within the life of the community and its social imbrications with other communities or social formations. This articulation of the individual and the communal allows for Latina/o life writing to critically interrogate two interrelated dynamics: the impact of the social in the formation of the individual, and the individual's capacity to effect social change.[9]

Latina/o literature has always been queer, as Lawrence La Fountain-Stokes reminds us. While the experiences of LGBTI (lesbian, gay, bisexual, transgender, intersex) Latinas/os have been narrated in literature since at least the late nineteenth century, one need not limit the question of "queering Latina/o literature" to the representation of LGBTI identities or experiences; as La Fountain-Stokes points out, all of Latina/o literature is queer if one takes queering as a methodological imperative to examine any processes of power/knowledge that creates social hierarchies of difference, including those of racialization, gendering, and class structuration. In a related sense, to queer Latina/o literature would be to take it out of its United Statesian frame of reference and to resituate it within a trans-American framework, all the while attendant upon the key ways the construction of social difference, and particularly those surrounding sexuality, structure regimes of power/knowledge.[10]

In her contribution, Claudia Milian takes up the question of what it means to be Latin@, not as an identity but rather as a constantly changing intersection of diasporic discourses, migrations, and material histories. "Latin@" highlights precisely the contingency, rather than rootedness, of "Latinness," so that to find where "Latin@" begins and ends is to find not origins and genealogies, but rather the epistemological flux of the term as it negotiates the changing conditions of the coloniality of power in the Americas. Tracing the concept of "the Latin 'diaspora' diaspora," Milian suggests how "dominiyorkian" Raquel Cepeda's memoir *Bird of Paradise: How I Became Latina* (2013) reveals the ever-mobile rearrangement of *latinidades* as configured through, against, and by the processes of migration.[11]

Latinas/os were quick to adopt the Internet as potential space for innovative aesthetic production in the 1990s, as Thea Pitman documents. Given the transnational configuration of the Internet, its virtual spaces seemed ideal for Latin@ expressive practices in its questioning of national boundaries; at the same time, the digital divide in access to this space reinforced the same social hierarchies that created invidious social difference in the first place. Pitman compares the approaches of two performance groups that staked a critical virtual presence during the first decade of the Internet: La Pocha Nostra, featuring the globally recognized performance artist Guillermo Gómez-Penā, and Los Cybrids, a more recent group composed of "digital natives." Reflecting this generational difference, La Pocha Nostra generally used the Internet to extend performances into the virtual realm, while Los Cybrids focused on the virtual space itself as the site of performance. In both cases, these two collectives challenged the racial, gendered, class, and heteronormative discourses underlying the use of, and discussions about, the Internet as a potentially liberatory space.[12]

As the question of migration from the global South to the global North, documented or otherwise, looms ever larger as a defining aspect of the current world economic, political, and cultural system, Latina/o literature has provided the aesthetic grounds of socially symbolic acts that reimagine the meaning of said migration beyond U.S. nationalist concerns about border security, domestic job losses, and inassimilable aliens. As Marta Caminero-Santangelo writes, Latina/o literature traces the cultural and material histories of communities formed and reformed through migration, such that even older Chicana/o communities in the U.S. Southwest change under the influence of more recent Mexican and Central American migrations; similarly, the Puerto Rican communities of New York City have changed through interactions not only with Dominican migrations but also with African American and other communities. In both cases, the interactions between more established Latina/o communities with continued migration from Latin America renovates the sense of *latinidades* within the United States while reinforcing trans-American linguistic, cultural, and economic ties. This dynamic in turn brings about cultural transformations in Latin America nations as remittances, goods, and people circulate between the Americas, South and North.[13]

Taken together, the chapters of *The Cambridge Companion to Latina/o Literature* highlight not only the deep historicity of this literature within the cultural imaginary of the Americas but also its increasing relevance for world literature at a time of unprecedented globalization of migratory experiences. Taken in its own right, Latina/o literature underscores how the circulation of people, commodities, and ideas has shaped the history of the Americas through the creation of migrant imaginaries.[14] Studied alongside other migratory imaginaries created in the flow of people, commodities, and ideas between Europe and Africa, between the Middle East and Asia, or between wherever difference forces or inspires mass migrations, Latina/o literature can help illuminate the creative transcultural responses developed for community survival wherever they may be needed.

Notes

1 However, the Recovery Project itself is currently reconsidering the significance of 1960 as a meaningful periodization of its work.
2 For further instances of early trans-American interactions, see Rodrigo Lazo, *Writing to Cuba: Filibustering and Cuban Exiles in the United States* (Chapel Hill: University of North Carolina Press, 2005); Kirsten Silva-Gruesz, *Ambassadors of Culture: The Transamerican Origins of Latino Writing* (Princeton, NJ: Princeton University Press, 2001); Anna Brickhouse, *Transamerican Literary Relations and the Nineteenth-Century Public Sphere* (Cambridge: Cambridge University Press, 2005); Marissa K. López, *Chicano Nations: The Hemispheric Origins of Mexican American Literature* (New York: New York University Press, 2011); Raúl Coronado, *The World Not to Come: A History of Latino Writing and Print Culture* (Cambridge, MA: Harvard University Press, 2013).
3 For a full treatment, see Laura Lomas, *Translating Empire: José Martí, Migrant Latino Subjects and American Modernities* (Durham, NC: Duke University Press, 2008).
4 See John Morán González, *Border Renaissance: The Texas Centennial and the Emergence of Mexican American Literature* (Austin: University of Texas Press, 2009) for an in-depth treatment.

INTRODUCTION

5   To learn of these dynamics in the life of the foremost Puerto Rican poet of the era, see Vanessa Pérez Rosario, *Becoming Julia de Burgos: The Making of a Puerto Rican Icon* (Urbana: University of Illinois Press, 2014).
6   For more on the dynamics of Chicano cultural nationalism, see Richard T. Rodríguez, *Next of Kin: The Family in Chicano/a Cultural Politics* (Durham, NC: Duke University Press, 2009).
7   For more on the Cuban American literary context, see Ricardo L. Ortíz, *Cultural Erotics in Cuban America* (Minneapolis: University of Minnesota Press, 2007).
8   Lucía Suárez specifically examines this dynamic for Haitian American and Dominican American fiction in *Tears of Hispaniola: Haitian and Dominican Diaspora Memory* (Gainesville: University Press of Florida, 2006).
9   For a trans-Atlantic, rather than trans-American, reading of Chicana/o life writing, see Isabel Dúran, "A Transatlantic Approach to Chicano Lifewriting" in *Interculturalism in North America: Canada, United States, Mexico, and Beyond*, eds. Joseph Raab and Alexander Greiffenstern (Hamburg/Tempe, AZ: Wissenschaftlicher Verlag Trier/Bilingual Press, 2013): 133–148.
10 Lawrence La Fountain-Stokes explores the articulations of queerness in the Puerto Rican diaspora in *Queer Ricans: Cultures and Sexualities in the Diaspora* (Minneapolis: University of Minnesota Press, 2009).
11 Claudia Milian's *Latining America: Black-Brown Passages and the Coloring of Latina/o Studies* (Athens: University of Georgia Press, 2013) explores the complexity, if not incoherence, of the term *latinidad* when used as a totalizing theoretical singularity.
12 Thea Pitman has examined the question of cyber-identities in Latin America in two critical anthologies, both coedited with Claire Taylor: *Latin American Cyberculture and Cyberliterature* (Liverpool: Liverpool University Press, 2008) and *Latin American Identity in Online Cultural Production* (London: Routledge, 2012).
13 See Marta Caminero-Santangelo's *On Latinidad: U.S. Latino Literature and the Construction of Ethnicity* (Gainesville: University Press of Florida, 2009) for the role of migration in forming Latina/o identities in the United States.
14 For a fuller discussion of the concept of migrant imaginaries in the Latina/o context, see Alicia Schmidt Camacho, *Migrant Imaginaries: Latino Cultural Politics in the U.S.-Mexico Borderlands* (New York: New York University Press, 2008).

PART I

Early Trans-American Contacts and Conflicts

I

RODRIGO LAZO

The Trans-American Literature of Conquest and Exile, 1823–1885

When José María Heredia arrived off the coast of Cape Cod in 1823, his first impression was desolation. "I did not see one man, not one animal, not one insect," he wrote in a letter to his beloved Emilia, who had remained behind in Cuba as Heredia escaped from authorities pursuing him for plotting to overthrow the Spanish colonial government.[1] Off the coast of Massachusetts, a ferocious December wind tormented the thin Heredia as he made his way to a lighthouse. The scene reminded him of Miltonic verses: the "immense solitude" leading to Satan's throne. "They passed, and many a region dolorous, / O'er many a frozen, many a fiery Alp, / Rocks, caves, lakes, fens, bogs, dens, and shades of death, A universe of death," Milton writes in *Paradise Lost*, as if he also knew about having to escape from a tropical island in fear for his life.[2] Heredia had probably read Milton in French from the 1805 translation by Jacques (L'Abbé) Delille. At the lighthouse, Heredia encountered a veteran of the War of 1812 who took pity on the shivering poet. As Heredia told it, the veteran, who was missing a leg, took the exile's cold hand and whispered something that sounded like consolation. But the English language was incomprehensible to Heredia. And thus Heredia's initial impression of the United States was one of "total isolation."

Movement and migration are defining characteristics of this figure whose life and work exemplify the trans-American dimensions of nineteenth-century Latina/o literature. As Heredia traveled throughout the northeastern United States and other parts of the Americas, he developed a body of work that spoke to hemispheric perspectives, politics in his home country, and the pain of exile. As such, his poems and other writings were marked by dislocation even as they spoke about specific contexts. Heredia's trajectory differs in important ways with the situated lives of many contemporary Latina/o subjects, who are either born in the United States or immigrated to U.S. sites. Heredia, who went to Mexico in 1825, did not remain long in the United States and cannot be tied to one location. Although he published and wrote important work in the United States, including some of his best-known poems, Heredia has been most commonly situated in Cuban literary history for expressing the exilic spirit of many important intellectuals from that country. As Kirsten Silva Gruesz has noted, many of the U.S. writers involved in nineteenth-century trans-American encounters defy easy categorization. "Many were exiles, expatriates, im-/emigrants, or determined cosmopolites," she writes. "Others seem, in a way, hypernational: iconic figures rendered representative of a country, celebrated in patriotic engravings and statues now superannuated, both aesthetically and ideologically."[3] The national histories of Latin American countries have offered a conceptual home for some of these writers, although at times in their lives they moved in and out of various nations and even across the Americas. That movement complicates national classification.

Heredia's feeling of "total isolation" on the shores of Massachusetts is the product of social, geographic, and even linguistic dislocation. Rather than view his trans-American journey as creating a new geographic space of the Americas, I want to emphasize the force of dislocation. "Trans-American" movement calls for crossings and changes that create the discomfort of feeling out of place; it is at once across America and beyond the United States, so that even as Heredia stops in U.S. sites, he is never integrated or integrates himself into the United States. Rather than invoke a hemispheric geographic space that stands in as a map for a field of writing from North to South, "trans-American" emphasizes disruption, which is in part created by sociopolitical conditions.

For those nineteenth-century figures that we claim retroactively as part of Latina/o literature, writing became a nexus for the consideration of political upheaval, governmental reorganization, economic transformations, and personal separation. Their writing, which included literary genres but just as often pamphlets and newspapers, encode disruption and tumult both at the subjective level of the speaker and in the subject matter. Most of the intellectuals who made their way to the United States from Spain and Latin America in the 1810s and early 1820s published political tracts primarily. For example, the texts published in Philadelphia by Vicente Rocafuerte, José Alvarez de Toledo, and Manuel Torres show how intellectuals deployed essays and translations to further their cause.[4] As the nineteenth century continued, the sites of publication became more varied, and so did the socio-political upheavals affecting their communities. Some writers continued to emphasize political writing and journalistic work, and periodicals became one of the most important venues for publication. Another trajectory also emerged: the politically minded writer who turned to literary forms in the United States without extricating him or herself from the trans-American revolutionary changes of the time. In some cases, literary forms were imbedded in the political content of newspapers and other forms of publication.

Nineteenth-century trans-American writing is intricately bound with (and sometimes the result of) political and military conflicts, including the Latin American wars of independence, the U.S.-Mexico War, and U.S. expansionist designs in the Caribbean. From the novels of María Amparo Ruiz de Burton to the essays of José Martí, texts engage with and sometimes explicate trans-American connections and dislocations. Early in the century, some writers expressed admiration for U.S. republican forms of government and saw the potential for alliance. A notion of a hemispheric Americanism that would stand in anticolonial opposition to Europe influenced some writers; this perspective was intertwined with constitutional readings of social organization and often de-emphasized class and racial hierarchies affecting Latin American societies. As the century went on, it became clear that the United States, despite the proclamations of equality in its founding documents, would not prove an easy ally to the nation-states of Latin America. After the U.S.-Mexico War, writers increasingly saw that U.S. expansionist ideology was intertwined with depictions of populations south of the border as undemocratic and racially inferior. Filibustering expeditions to take over Cuba and Central America in the 1850s were supported not only by economic interests but also by ideological arguments.[5] After the U.S. Civil War, projects for territorial acquisition were driven by industrial capitalism's hunger for new commodities and markets. By the time Martí was publishing his essays in the 1880s, it was clear that the aspirations for hemispheric American republican solidarity had given way to realpolitik driven by the ascendancy of the U.S. empire. Trans-American writers recognized that U.S. nationalist agendas inspired by white supremacy were at odds with notions of equality beyond U.S. borders.

These historical conditions remind us that approaching nineteenth-century writing demands putting contemporary notions of Latina/o subjectivity in dialogue with conditions encountered by writers at the level of print culture and in the sociopolitical arena. Contemporary debates about *latinidades* bring forward difference rather than point to a monolithic subjectivity, and those differences cut across national affiliations (Cuban American versus Chicana/o), racial formations, immigration and citizenship status, gender, and sexuality. Given the complex proliferation of identities in Latino America today, the hermeneutic challenge is not how to reconcile a bounded notion of identity with a historical condition in which such a notion did not circulate. Rather, the challenge is how to bring forward the textual remains of the past in a way that recognizes its contexts and considers the ways those texts generate a multiplicity of meanings. Difference emerges both in the past and the present. This involves working across languages, genres, print culture formations, and literary histories.

At times the desire of writers and publishers to reach readers beyond the United States meant that much of the literature appeared in periodicals. Because of their size and thinness, newspapers and other serial publications were easier to transport on ships and circulate, if necessary, clandestinely. Newspapers and other periodicals appeared from East to West in very different contexts, and they provide a view into the heterogeneity of concerns among writers and their communities. While publications put out by Cubans and Puerto Ricans provided news of importance to the Caribbean, periodicals in the West grappled with the effects of U.S. expansion on populations that had previously been part of Mexico. The periodical press supported local communities and kept an eye on events in the homeland of origin. This dual vision crossing the Americas spreads not only from the content of the articles in periodicals but also onto the language of literary texts. Newspaper pages often included poems, stories, and serialized novels, often as supplementary material to the main news and concerns. Newspapers such as *El Mensagero Semanal* (Philadelphia and New York, 1828–29), *La Verdad* (New York, 1848–60), *La Patria* (New Orleans, 1846–50), *La Voz de la América* (New York, 1865–67), and *La República* (San Francisco, 1885) were established to connect U.S. readers with Mexico, Cuba, Puerto Rico, and other places.[6] The conditions of periodical print culture may be the most important consideration in the analysis of trans-American nineteenth-century writing.

The archival conditions of such material lead to a state of fragmentation. To work in the nineteenth-century Spanish press is to confront an incomplete archive. In some cases, repositories of those documents do not have a complete run of a newspaper and researchers may even have to settle for a single issue. A researcher may come across a reference to a writer's participation in a particular periodical only to find that the periodical is available only in a fragmentary form. The result is that nineteenth-century Latina/o writing is as much about discrete pieces and incomplete information – indeed, about epistemological stopping points – as it is about the recovery and reconstitution of print culture conditions. Given these conditions, reading may involve focus on an isolated text that raises more questions than answers.

An effect of the periodical press for readers today is that it creates sites of analysis rather than a body of literature that we can connect to particular writers. While books and collections of writing emphasize an individual author, newspapers and journals are at times difficult to place. Because many articles and poems went unsigned in the nineteenth-century periodical press, it is not always possible to connect the published material with a specific writer. The result for literary historical work is a tension between the production of a writing subject (the emergence of a notable writer) and the more collective production of a periodical press that sometimes speaks not only to but also for a community. The periodical press emphasizes the "collective" value of minor textual production, which in extreme case shows that "there are no possibilities for an individuated enunciation that would belong to this or that 'master' and that could be separated from a collective enunciation."[7]

A handful of the writers in nineteenth-century United States, including Ruiz de Burton and Martí, have been elevated to the status of prominent literary figures. But to think of them in relation to literary distinction emphasizes the individual attainment of mastery and thus elides the lack of mastery (and the discomfort) that was created by exile and conquest at the level of entire populations. The tension between an individual writer and larger social context was a concern for Edward Said, writing about the twentieth century: "It is apparent that, to concentrate on exile as a contemporary political punishment, you must therefore map territories of experience beyond those mapped by the literature of exile itself. You must first set aside Joyce and Nabokov and think instead of the uncountable masses for whom UN agencies have been created."[8] This tension between, on one hand, a humanistic emphasis on individuation and, on the other hand, conditions that sought to deny identity to populations have an analogy in the historical reading of Latina/o literature in that we must simultaneously recover and contextualize the writers themselves even as the historical record shows a more collective scene of dispersal and textual fragmentation.

Part of that recovery and contextualization calls for working in at least two languages. With the exception of María Amparo Ruiz de Burton's novels and a few sporadic publications, the majority of the poems, novels, and stories that appeared were published in Spanish and sometimes aimed at readers outside of the United States. These include the anonymous novel *Jicoténcal* (1826) as well as the collection of poems *El laúd del desterrado* (1858). The importance of Spanish means that scholars working on this nineteenth-century material must translate as a practice of reading. That is to say, translation itself becomes a form of interpretation. Because most of the materials, sometimes in bits and pieces, are not available in English, a critic must provide snapshots of the original. The choice of which texts, passages, or even sentences to bring forward in an article is a result of critical emphasis but also a reminder that the original materials are not easily accessible.

The Spanish language positions this literature and print culture between the expansion of one empire (Spain) and that of another (United States). As a language, Spanish is colonial in that it was used by the Spanish empire to dominate vast territories (one of the initial colonial languages of the Americas and in use in Florida, New Mexico, and California prior to the founding of the United States). But Spanish is also marginalized in that it becomes a minority language in the nineteenth-century United States. As a language of exiles, migrants, and conquered people, Spanish takes on the characteristics of what Gilles Deleuze and Félix Guattari have associated with the "minor," at once deterritorialized and displaced (even excluded) but also full of revolutionary potential because of its alterity. "We might as well say that minor no longer designates specific literatures but the revolutionary conditions for every literature within the heart of what is called great (or established) literature."[9] As such, the Spanish-language periodical press in nineteenth-century America can be considered a minor remain of a period that is often read in U.S. literary studies as belonging to the writers of the so-called American Renaissance (Whitman, Emerson) and their late-century counterparts (Twain, James). Spanish challenges English-only conceptions of U.S. literary history. The revolutionary conditions, to pick up on Deleuze and Guattari's words, are not so much in the content of the language itself but in the materiality of the Hispanophone press, the fragmentation of its remains.

One periodical, which remains today only in partial run, provides insight into the role of literature in the periodical press. On October 3, 1829, *El Mensagero Semanal* out of Philadelphia published a front-page letter focusing on a polemic debate about the literary merits of Heredia as poet. The writer of the letter attacked the editors of *El Mensagero* for being "extremely cautious, considering that as Spanish journalists and compatriots and colleagues of the poet, it was your duty to tell us something of his merit."[10] The editorial team at *El Mensagero* included Cubans, and thus the references to Heredia's compatriots. In response to the call to evaluate Heredia's poetry, the editors *El Mensagero* noted that their paper did not focus primarily on literature. They continued:

> *El Mensagero* no es otra cosa que una gaceta destinada á dar noticia de los acaecimientos politicos, y á hacer mas variada su lectura, si las circunstancias lo permiten, con los progresos mas notables de algunas artes y ciencias, ó con algunos articulos de util aplicacion á la isla de Cuba, ó finalmente con los chistes y agudezas del ingenio."[11]

> ["The Messenger" is nothing more than a gazette intended to give accounts of political events, and we aim to reach a broader readership, if possible, by relaying the most notable accomplishments in arts and sciences, or with articles of relevance to the island of Cuba, or in the last instance with a few jokes and sharpness of wit.]

Although it promoted Heredia's poetry, the newspaper did not position itself as a site for literary criticism, in part because of limited print space. Here the use of the Spanish *gaceta* (gazette) is important because it implied a periodical that covered commercial and governmental topics. And yet *El Mensagero*'s support of the poet displayed an implicit understanding of Heredia as a writer of the Americas in contra-distinction to the European and particularly Spanish domains of literature.

The newspaper's reluctance to get involved in that type of a dispute (despite publishing Heredia's poems) shows its commitment to a cosmopolitan tenor in which political events and commercial news took precedence over artistic concerns and proto-nationalist considerations. To the assumption that they should evaluate Heredia's poetry because they share a homeland (Cuba) with the poet, the editors wrote that *El Mensagero* did not have the space to provide a thorough and informed critique of literature. Without negating a Cuban affiliation, they also resented the belief that they would praise Heredia simply because of their common island home. "Who has said that because we are Spanish journalists and compatriots and companions of the poet, we are obliged to critique his poems?"[12] The use of the term "Spanish journalists" shows the broader Hispanicism informing the way writers referred to one another. The nineteenth century had no common ethnic label such as Latino or Hispanic; regular usage in English-language publications was "Spanish" or "Spanish American."

The appearance of *El Mensagero* as part of a Hispanophone print culture context, and the fight for Latin America's future raging behind it, cannot be divorced from the publication of Heredia's collection of poems, *Poesías*, published in New York in 1825, which featured some of his best-known verses. In some selections, we see a desire for a repetition of U.S. events in other countries. In his poem "A Washington," written during a visit to Mount Vernon, Heredia connects his Romantic longing for immortality with the U.S. president:

> Viva imagen de Dios sobre la tierra,
> libertador, legislador y justo,
> Washington inmortal, oye benigno
> el débil canto de tu gloria indigno,
> con que voy a ensalzar tu nombre augusto.
>
> [Vivid image of God on earth,
> liberator, legislator just,
> immortal Washington, listen benevolently
> to the faint, indignant song that exalts
> your glory and your majestic name.]

These lines from the opening stanza to this paean are driven by Heredia's desire for the repetition of the verses in the future. The invocation of a god-like Washington positions the president-general as a figure that carries Heredia's poetry into the future while also connecting the poetic voice to the president's "indignant" position against tyranny. Ultimately, Washington is deployed as inspiration for the countries of the southern Americas struggling to form governments after colonial rule. That type of exchange – Spanish-language poet at Mount Vernon sending verses about a U.S. president in a southern direction – showed the intricate dialogues that emerged in nineteenth-century trans-American writing.

My discussion of the important role of Hispanophone print culture to literary productions, which creates a panorama of the minor, shows the unusual place of the novels by Ruiz de Burton within Latina/o literature. The publication of *Who Would Have Thought It?* (1872) and *The Squatter and the Don* (1885) in English is an anomaly among U.S.-based nineteenth-century writers of Latin American descent. Although she was fluent in her native Spanish, Ruiz de Burton's decision to publish novels in English and her engagement with U.S. culture and politics help us situate her in several other critical frameworks, among them sentimental novels, historical romance, and fictions of Reconstruction. One effect of this commitment to the English language is that she has become almost canonical in Anglophone U.S. literary study, if by canonical we mean a frequency of inclusion in syllabi and the number of articles published about an author. Scholars who might not otherwise be inclined (or be able) to read Spanish trans-American literature can turn their attention to Ruiz de Burton.

Like Hispanophone writers from Mexico and Cuba, Ruiz de Burton contended with the role of empire in the Americas, particularly the conquest of the southwestern United States. In response to the U.S.-Mexico War, *The Squatter and the Don* offers a portrait of the challenges faced by an elite California family at risk of losing their land and calls attention to the illegal U.S. appropriation of territory previously owned by Mexicans. Together with the satirical *Who Would Have Thought It?*, the two novels raise questions about race and ethnicity in the United States and Mexico. Scholars have noted the contradictory positions of Ruiz de Burton, whose fiction and life at times reflect her upper-class status.[13] Ruiz de Burton also adopts certain racial hierarchies and is consumed with drawing a distinction between elite white Mexicans and the indigenous populations at the periphery of societies in California and Mexico, even if she is not always successful.[14]

While Ruiz de Burton's fiction differs in important ways from other trans-American nineteenth-century writing, she herself does share a social position with many of the figures. Like certain light-skinned Latin American

Creoles who move through an elite trans-American circuit, Ruiz de Burton criticizes certain aspects of empire-building (on the part of Spain and the United States), but she is unwilling to overturn certain racial and social hierarchies.[15] The political positions of Ruiz de Burton and Cuban Creole exiles, for example, are not commensurate. Ruiz de Burton would have bristled at the support of expansionism expressed by Cuban exiles that allied themselves with the likes of John L. O'Sullivan, whose writings named the ideology and practice of "Manifest Destiny." And yet despite her skepticism about the role of the United States in relation to its southern neighbors, Ruiz de Burton does share with many others a transnational vision that continuously places the United States in dialogue with another country. This is apparent, for example, at the end of *Who Would Have Thought It?* when Julian and Lola end up together in Mexico. The marriage plot eventually brings together a Mexican woman and a U.S. man, but it is in Mexico that they decide to make their home. In turn, a novel concerned about corruption in the U.S. political system ends with a scenario in which the two protagonists decide to depart. That is not to say that Mexico becomes a panacea. At one point that country is criticizes for "being an independent government" that "lets its Indians live as they please, and its more civilized citizens take care of themselves as best they may."[16] Rather, my point is that even after decades in the United States, Ruiz de Burton's gaze remains fixed at least in part on the country of her birth. That is also apparent in the letters she writes, particularly those to Mariano Vallejo, in which she discusses the future of Mexico and its need to remain united rather than hang itself with the rope knitted by its "sister Republic," a rope by the name of Manifest Destiny.[17]

In her letters, available in a collection edited by Rosaura Sánchez and Beatrice Pita, we see Ruiz de Burton's fragmented and dislocated self at work. Born in 1832 in Baja California, Ruiz de Burton was a teenage girl when U.S. troops invaded her hometown of La Paz. It was as a result of this conflict that she met her future husband, U.S. Army Captain Henry S. Burton. After the war, Capt. Burton helped Ruiz and her family move to Monterey, California, where they became U.S. citizens. For almost twenty years of marriage, the couple traveled around the United States as Capt. Burton was posted to different cities. After his death in 1869, Ruiz de Burton returned to the family's ranch near San Diego, where she spent the rest of her life fighting for a rightful title to the land. While Ruiz de Burton is an example of someone crossed by the U.S. border rather than crossing the border herself, she does share with Heredia and many other trans-American writers a penchant for movement.[18] The letters show her moving around U.S. cities, even as she kept her eyes on Mexico. Like some of the impoverished Cuban exiles, Ruiz de Burton in later life was constantly fighting debt and looking for sources of money. And yet, as Sánchez and Pita note, at various points in her life "[s]he moved in the social circles of the politically and economically powerful, both in the United States and Mexico, on the basis of her personal charisma, her attractive demeanor, her status as the wife of a West Point officer, and her capacity to construct herself as a landowner in both California and Baja California" (550).[19]

One letter that captures Ruiz de Burton's relentless engagement with trans-American political conditions – including the future of Mexico, U.S. expansionism, and transatlantic influences – was composed in Staten Island, New York, in 1869 and sent to Mariano G. Vallejo. In it, Ruiz de Burton jokes with Vallejo about various matters and then releases a stream of invective against Benito Juárez, the United States, and French Revolutionary leaders (Robespierre, Marat, and Danton), only to confess that she still hurts from the execution of Maximilian, the French-installed emperor of Mexico, calling that event "the assassination of our nationality" [el asesinato de nuestra nacionalidad]. The letter is a tour de force of convoluted politics, at once critical of the U.S. empire and embracing of the French invasion, all of it finally supported by her defense of "la raza Latina," with France as the ultimate example of the race's accomplishment. She writes, "History does not lie and history tells us how glorious has been the course of the Latin race" [La historia no miente y la historia nos dice cuan gloriosa ha sido la Carrera de la raza Latina].[20] Here Ruiz de Burton provides an entry into an intellectual shift toward a notion of *Latin* America in the nineteenth century, driven in part by efforts to turn away from a Spanish genealogy by drawing together France and "Latin" countries.[21] Ruiz de Burton buys a French imperialist position that valorizes that country not only above Anglo-Saxon and Germanic countries but also Spain itself. In the end, however, she finds that the deposing of Maximilian will turn Mexico into one of the "miserable Hispano American Republics of this continent" [las miserable Repúblicas Hispano Americanas de este continente].

The conditions created by imperial powers and the attempts to establish new governments in the Americas often pushed writers to place political concerns alongside forays into literary form. Responding to colonialism and conquest, whether on the part of Spain or the United States, was one of the important elements in *El laúd del desterrado*. This 1858 poetry collection, culled from U.S.-based newspapers that had published many of the poems, was produced by exiled Cuban writers caught in that island's colonial predicament: Cuba was simultaneously a territory of Spain and an island desired for annexation by expansionists in the United States. *El laúd del desterrado* featured selections by seven Cuban poets, including Heredia, who had been exiled or migrated to the United States. At least half the poems had been previously published in Spanish-language periodicals in New York and New Orleans. As a product of U.S.-Cuba print culture connections, the book wove a transnational versification that responded to the colonial scene in Cuba even as it grappled with U.S. conditions.[22]

The collection is filled with exilic longing for the home country and vituperative lines against Spain's administration of its colony. The opening lines to Miguel Teurbe Tolón's Petrarchan sonnet "Resolución" capture both:

> Yo sin patria ni hogar, en tierra extraña,
> Errante marcharé por senda oscura:
> Yo apuraré mi cáliz de amargura,
> Brindis letal de la opresora España.[23]
> [Lacking country and home, in a strange land,
> I will wander through a dark path,
> Exhausting my bitter chalice,
> A lethal salute to Spain.]

Without claiming the United States as a new home, the speaker prefers the chill and strangeness of the exile land to the challenge of returning to Cuba to witness the island as a "slave" to Spain. The double implication of slavery, both colonial and economic, would seem to point to that as an important dimension of his work. But for Tolón and most of his comrades in exile, slavery in the 1850s took a back seat to their insistence that Cuba be dislodged from Spanish control. For writers in Tolón's circle, slavery was a convenient metaphor as well as an actual condition, despite its presence in Cuba until the 1880s. Cuban exiles are in large part curiously silent on slavery in the United States, in part because of their attempt to avoid abolitionist debates and draw support in the United States for their cause. Because Tolón and others supported the annexation of Cuba to the United States in the 1840s and 1850s, they were willing to forego the discussion of abolition. These types of negotiations and even some of the alliances made point to the contradictory positions that writers often adopted.

One of the writers who integrated himself into this trans-American circuit was Juan Clemente Zenea, whose life and work are connected to periodical print culture in the United States and various revolutionary movements in Cuba. Until recently, literary history had regarded him largely as one of Cuba's foremost romantic poets.[24] But the separation inherent in exile, what Said calls the "unhealable rift forced between a human being and a native place," manifested itself in the tortured relationship of Zenea's publications to the island home. His essays and poems appeared in the New York-based papers *El Filibustero* and *El Mulato* in the 1850s, and Zenea went on to become heavily involved in U.S.-based exile politics. While on a mission to communicate with rebels during Cuba's Ten Years' War (1868–78), Zenea was captured and executed by Spanish authorities. His "Diary of a Martyr," a cycle of sixteen poems written on scraps with a pencil while imprisoned prior to his execution, was published first in the New York newspaper *El Mundo Nuevo* in 1871. A chronicle of impending death, the martyr cycle offers verses without references to specific Cuban landmarks or to locations in New York. The following stanza captures the contradictory effects of exilic literature, at once invoking terminal loss and the enriching effects of composition: "Yo canto como los pájaros, / yo entonces lanzo a los aires / en la voz de la alegria / la expression de hondos pesares" [I sing like the birds / and thus hurl into the clouds / in the voice of happiness / an expression of deep grief].[25] Unlike his poems in *El laúd del desterrado*, the martyr verses do not refer to the political context that has led Zenea to a military execution. But how does imprisonment affect what Zenea chooses to include in his final verses? Are the turns toward abstraction precisely one of the effects of the real political conditions under which he composes his poems? These questions, not easily answered, point us to the immediate context of literary production.

Zenea's situation points us toward a set of conditions important to this nineteenth-century literature of exile and conquest. Zenea's poems and essays are tied to a periodical print culture. His work is in dialogue with a transnational community. And his language, both the Spanish language but also his working in various politically inflected registers, provides a context for which an Anglophone literary history cannot account. The minor in Zenea's poetry is itself part of the U.S. context of Latina/o literary history. As Zenea's work shows, the periodical press was deployed to address issues not only in the United States but also in other countries. The result is a body of work that cannot be contained within a nation. I have considered texts here that point to a trans-American spatial configuration for the field of Latina/o literary and cultural history. Exile and conquest are dominant conditions – and thus dominant themes – in this literature. Writers attempted to respond to the colonial predicaments created by competing empires in the Americas, and the result was a fragmented literary production that indicates a historical alterity rather than continuity in Latina/o literary history.

Notes

1 Emilia was the name Heredia used in his writing for Pepilla Arango Manzano. "Carta Sobre los Estados Unidos," in *Niagara y Otros Textos*, ed. Angel Augier (Caracas, Venezuela: Biblioteca Ayacucho, 1990), 249.
2 *The Complete Poetical Works of John Milton*, ed. Douglas Bush (Boston: Houghton Mifflin, 1965), 246.

3 Kirsten Silva Gruesz, *Ambassadors of Culture: The Transamerican Origins of Latino Writing* (Princeton, New Jersey: Princeton University Press, 2001):14.
4 For an excellent article on Toledo, see Nicolás Kanellos, "José Alvarez de Toledo y Dubois and the Origins of Hispanic Publishing in the Early American Republic," *Early American Literature* 43.1 (2008), 83–100. See also Lazo, "La Famosa Filadelfia: The Hemispheric American City and Constitutional Debates," in *Hemispheric American Studies*, ed. Caroline F. Levander and Robert S. Levine. Recent work by Raúl Coronado and Emily Garcia continue to recover the publications and contexts for intellectuals in the early nineteenth-century United States. See Coronado's *A World Not to Come: A History of Latino Writing and Print Culture* (Cambridge, MA: Harvard University Press, 2013) and Emily García, "On the Borders of Independence: Manuel Torres and Spanish American Independence in Filadelphia" (forthcoming).
5 Ideological notions of Anglo/Spanish hierarchy appeared in various Anglophone texts, such as Richard Henry Dana Jr. in *To Cuba and Back: A Vacation Voyage* arguing that "Creoles" could not govern themselves.
6 For a bibliography of periodicals, see Nicolás Kanellos with Helvetia Martell, *Hispanic Periodicals in the United States, Origins to 1960* (Houston, TX: Arte Público, 2000), 137–277. Studies of the nineteenth-century U.S. Hispanophone press include A. Gabriel Meléndez, *Spanish-Language Newspapers in New Mexico, 1834–1958* (Tucson: University of Arizona Press, 2005) and Doris Meyer, *Speaking for Themselves: Neomexicano Cultural Identity and the Spanish Language Press (1880–1920)* (Albuquerque: University of New Mexico Press, 1996).
7 Gilles Deleuze and Félix Guattari, *Kafka: Toward a Minor Literature*, trans. Dana Polan (Minneapolis: University of Minnesota Press, 1986), 17.
8 Edward Said, *Reflections on Exile and Other Essays* (Cambridge, MA: Harvard University Press, 2000), 175.
9 Deleuze and Guattari, 18.
10 The original Spanish: "estremadamente cautos, pues aun cuando les tocaba como á periodistas españoles y compatriotas y *camaradas* del poeta, decirnos algo de su mérito." Unless otherwise noted, all translations from Spanish-language texts are mine. "De los anales de ciencias, etc." *El Mensagero Semanal*, October 3, 1829.
11 "De los Anales de Ciencias, Etc.," *El Mensagero Semanal*, October 3, 1829, 50.
12 "¿Quie le ha dicho que por que séamos poeriodistas españoles, y compatriotas y *camaradas* del poeta, ya estamos en la obligacion de criticar sus poesias?" "De los Anales de Ciencias, Etc.," *El Mensagero Semanal*, October 3, 1829, 50.
13 The bibliography on Ruiz de Burton has grown considerably in the last two decades. An exemplary set of essays can be found Amelia María de la Luz Montes and Anne E. Goldman, *María Amparo Ruiz de Burton: Critical and Pedagogical Perspectives* (Lincoln: University of Nebraska Press, 2004).
14 John Morán González has characterized *The Squatter and the Don*'s failure to transfer white upper-class privilege from the Californio family to the U.S. nation in relation to "new cultural logistics of nationalism modeled not by the family but by the corporation." See "The Whiteness of the Blush: The Cultural Politics of Racial Formation in *The Squatter and the Don*," in Montes and Goldman, *Ruiz de Burton*, 155.
15 *The Squatter and the Don*, for example, is brutal in its attack on monopoly capitalism and corruption in the U.S. court system as well as its depiction of

squatters who attempted to take lands previously belonging to Californios. But it is also concerned with distinguishing white land-owning Californios from lower-class Anglo Americans and indigenous populations.
16 María Amparo Ruiz de Burton, *Who Would Have Thought It?* (Houston, TX: Arte Público Press, 1995), 194.
17 Ruiz de Burton to Mariano Vallejo, September 14, 1869, in *Conflicts of Interest: The Letters of María Amparo Ruiz de Burton*, ed. Rosaura Sánchez and Beatrice Pita (Houston, TX: Arte Público Press, 2001), 301.
18 In one of her letters, Ruiz de Burton invokes the phrase *"alma atravesada"* to speak about herself. *Conflicts of Interest*, 301.
19 Sánchez and Pita, *Conflicts*, 550.
20 Ruiz de Burton to Mariano Vallejo, September 14, 1869.
21 For an insightful discussion of France and the invention of "Latin America," see Mónica Quijada, "Sobre el Origen y Difusión del Nombre América Latina," *Revista de Indias* No. 214 (1998).
22 For a longer discussion of *El laúd del desterrado*, see my book, *Writing to Cuba: Filibustering and Cuban Exiles in the United States* (Chapel Hill: University of North Carolina Press, 2005), 53–56.
23 *El laúd del desterrado*, ed. Matías Montes-Huidobro (Houston, TX: Arte Público, 1995), 41.
24 Cintio Vitier, *Lo cubano en la poesía*, (La Habana: Instituto del Libro, 1970, 2nd ed.): 177.
25 Quoted in Angel Aparicio Laurencio, *Diario de un mártir y otros poemas* (Miami, FL: Ediciones Universal, 1972), 13.

2

LAURA LOMAS

The Trans-American Literature of Empire and Revolution, 1880–1938

During the period of 1880–1938, Latina/o writers such as José Martí, Manuel Zeno Gandía, Julia de Burgos, Salomón de la Selva, María Cristina Mena, Daniel Venegas, and William Carlos Williams addressed readers in English or Spanish and in print venues at various sites throughout the Americas, thereby constructing literary exchanges within what we have come to think of as a trans-American field. Following Kirsten Silva Gruesz, Anna Brickhouse, and José David Saldívar, we may define the field that contains these disparate writers of Latin American origin as "trans-American," as the scope and anti-imperialist angle of their texts demand a term more partial and limited than "pan-American," "transnational," or "hemispheric" labels that have gained currency in U.S. American Studies. Moreover, the term "trans-American" requires attention to the process of *cultural translation* involved in writing about the United States in Spanish or about Mexico or Nicaragua in English, or in more conventionally moving across languages, or interpreting North America from a perspective informed by Latin American and Latina/o cultural formations. Transamerican Latina/o literature of this period thus provides a story of migratory routes rather than the root of a single nation and pushes Latina/o literary studies toward comparative methodologies that attend to language difference and multiple national cultures within the United States.

During the turn from the nineteenth century to the twentieth, the moving borders of empire and people migrating from Latin America to the United States set *latinidad* in motion, not only along the border that delineated the United States from Mexico after 1848 but also in the context of migration from the Hispanic Caribbean, Mexico, and Central America as a result of U.S. imperial intervention in the first decades of the twentieth century. While migratory sojourners have long figured as contributors to the formation and innovation of national literatures and especially to the emergence of *modernismo* in Spanish and of modernism in English, the recovery of late nineteenth- and early twentieth-century Latina/o writing through the

Recovering the U.S. Hispanic Literary Heritage Project has made it possible to read foundational texts of multiple national traditions simultaneously as defining the parameters and preoccupations of Latina/o literature. The readership and print community for this literature may have deep roots in the early nineteenth century, as Kirsten Silva Gruesz has argued, but the trans-American scope gains new salience with the formal emergence of U.S. imperial annexations, occupations, and interventions.

In the period of exile and migration during the protracted struggle for national independence in the Hispanic Caribbean, and as Revolutionary armies of Francisco I. Madero, the anarchist Magón brothers, Emiliano Zapata, and Pancho Villa toppled the dictatorship of Porfirio Díaz in Mexico, the dueling forces of empire and revolution became key themes and defining forces of Latina/o literature. During the late nineteenth and early twentieth centuries, the Spanish and Portuguese empires lost their last vestiges of formal governance in the Americas, and the United States became an unquestionably imperial force. Only in the latter half of the twentieth century does the United States acknowledge its role as an empire, despite its earlier annexations of Mexico's northern half, Puerto Rico, and the Philippines and its earlier military occupations of Cuba, Nicaragua, the Dominican Republic, and Haiti. Only in response to decolonization and civil rights movements – struggles that continue into the twenty-first century – does the United States begin to address the second-class racialized status of Caribbean, Mexican, and other Latin American migrants resident in the United States. In other words, the decolonial critique demanded by the social movements and cultural expression of the late twentieth century forces a recognition of the earlier writers as not simply national figures of Latin American literary history, but directly relevant to Latina/o literary history as well.

Writers such as María Cristina Mena, Salomón de la Selva, José Martí, Manuel Zeno Gandía, and William Carlos Williams, whose homeland directly experienced or would undergo occupation or annexation, underscored the way North American aesthetics, economics, and objects of consumption represented modernization as both bedazzling and bamboozling for the lands south of the U.S.-Mexico border. Martí attributed common cultural forms and interests to these homelands of the Latin American diaspora in the United States. If this period begins with a call to collective resistance to imperialism and self-affirmation in Martí's Spanish-language manifesto "Our America" (1891), Salomón de la Selva, in his 1918 English-language collection of poetry *Tropical Town*, condemns North American readers' "dirty" dollar and directly rejects U.S. influence by likening its economic interests as a "greenish leprosy" in "A Song for Wall Street" (75).

In contrast to leading anti-imperialists, such as philosopher William James who opposed U.S. imperialism because it would incorporate large numbers of undigestable or unmeltable brown bodies into the (fictively white) nation, these writers draw on a critique of European and Yankee privilege, of the miserable conditions of workers, of the vulnerability of women, and of the role of government in facilitating corrupt imperial economics, which each had observed firsthand from their vantage point as migrants "in the monster" or from the perspective of the colonized territory (Martí *Selected Writings* 347).

Trans-American texts informed by the prism of *latinidad* and steeped in the knowledge of Spanish and North American invasion and expansion speak out about the economic stratification and corruption fostered in many American nations during what Mark Twain called the Gilded Age. These texts offer a trenchant critique of the interconnected logic of extracting raw materials from Latin America, of exporting manufactured U.S. goods to Latin American markets, and of disciplining the bodies of Latina/o workers in the United States during border crossings. As these practices tended to render working-class Latina/o migrants more vulnerable to exploitation and more cautious about organizing to resist abuse, Latina/o literature introduces a critical consciousness by documenting the experiences of peasants in Puerto Rico or of Latina/o migrant workers to the United States as a way of warning readers about the dangers of adopting the United States as a model for political, aesthetic, or economic imitation.

Revolution and Empire in Cuba, Puerto Rico and Beyond: A Critique of "Imported Ideas" and the "Bad Copy"

Latina/o writers' critique of the Spanish colonial regime and of the looming U.S. imperial presence suggests that an emergent nationalist and Latin Americanist imaginary often overlaps with heterogeneous Latina/o perspectives during this period. With the twinned shouts of Lares and Yara of 1868, struggles for national independence erupted in Puerto Rico and Cuba in the wake of Spain's Glorious Revolution, threatening to remove these last and most valuable pearls from the crown of the Spanish empire in the Americas. What became the protracted and bloody Ten Years War in Cuba, along with the abolition of slavery in 1873 in Puerto Rico and in 1886 in Cuba, propelled waves of migrants, including many recently liberated from slavery, from the two remaining Spanish island colonies to U.S. cities along the Eastern seaboard, in particular South Florida and the New York City metropolitan area. At a time when immigrants poured out of ships at the feet of New York's Statue of Liberty from an impoverished Europe, when Edison's electric lights began to flood city streets, and the White City of Chicago's Columbian Exposition of 1893 projected the United States as a pinnacle of civilization and modernity for fledgling Spanish American republics and for the world, Latina/o writing assumed the difficult task of critically translating the remarkable and sometimes terrifying experiences in *el norte* to readers in Latin America and the Caribbean, and eventually for readers in the United States.

Major Latina/o writers from the 1880–1938 period engage in the work of cultural translation and transculturation, terms that derives from postcolonial theory, anthropology, cultural studies, and translation studies, and refers to the work of interpretation – in two directions – across cultural and colonial difference, including languages, national borders, and other categorical differences, on terrain marked by the asymmetries of power that derive from empire and the displacement it provokes. Mary Louise Pratt, drawing on a tradition defined by Fernando Ortiz that revises a diffusionist model of unidirectional, European colonial influence, calls the spaces in which cultural translation takes place a "contact zone." Although Pratt, and Angel Rama before her, used Ortiz's concept of transculturation to discuss Latin American literature and culture, the notion of movements of influence in two directions across borders illuminates thinking about the trans-American Latina/o literature of empire and revolution, when writers begin to translate the cultural implications of coloniality, slavery, and empire for readers on the both sides of the border. This translation of empire, I have suggested, contributes to the founding of what Deleuze and Guattari describe as a minor literature, or a subordinate literary and cultural tradition within and in the process of subverting and remaking the dominant – in this case, U.S. – literature. By infiltrating and then rendering in literary form the imperialist norms they encountered in the north, Martí, de la Selva, Williams, Mena, Venegas, and others translate the cultures and critical perspectives of the occupied, the annexed, and the migrant for readers in Latin America or the United States, with an eye to change the policies and trajectory of an imperial United States. In this move, Latina/o writing establishes a connection between the racializing of multiethnic Latina/o subjects inside the United States and the discourses of race that undergird and apologize for U.S. imperial expansion.

Let us consider the response to these intersecting axes of racialization and imperialism, for example, in José Martí's March 25, 1889 Letter to the Editor of the *Evening Post* in New York, known as "Vindication of Cuba," which he simultaneously published in Spanish as a pamphlet titled *Cuba y los Estados Unidos* along with translations of the articles to which his Letter to the Editor responds. This intervention in the debates about Cuba's future makes plain the experiences of racism of Cubans resident in the United States, "where [the Cuban's] ability is denied, his morality insulted, and his character despised" ("A Vindication of Cuba" 263). Martí's letter suggests these acts of racial disdain do not merely reflect a U.S. attitude toward Cuban residents who, as Martí notes, "do not want to return" (267). This letter and pamphlet also expose how the discourse about Cubans in the United States, draws on stereotypes about the entire group as a "people of destitute vagrants or immoral pigmies ... an 'effeminate' people" to fuel and justify annexation of a neighboring island (264).

The trans-American literature of empire and revolution asserts Latino/a difference as present within the not yet fully recognized heterogeneity of North America, without losing sight of the trans-American implications of such racial discourses. In a key early example of this inscription of Latina/o difference, José Martí's 1880 essay "Coney Island," published initially in Bogotá, Colombia, defines his disillusionment with the promise of democratic political and economic opportunity that led many immigrants to the United States in the first place: "[H]owever much the first impressions may have gratified their senses, enamored their eyes and dazzled and befuddled their minds, the anguish of solitude possesses them in the end" (*Selected Writings* 92). The frustrated expectations of the "men [sic] of our Hispanoamerican peoples who live here" differentiate a group of migrants with distinct aesthetic and social criteria for defining cultural value or common sense (92). These subjects who perceive the spectacle of Coney Island with suspicion echo the ironic excess that the writer of the English-language "Impressions of America (By a Very Fresh Spaniard)" (1880) comments upon in the United States, where everyone merely "*looks* like his own master" (32, my emphasis). The North America of the 1880s pretended self-government in a society marked by extreme class differences, racial terror, and European-style imperial ambitions, and Latina/o writing comments on these contradictions.

The North American culture seems to these Latina/o writers to be preoccupied with material consumption and an unconvincing performance of unfailing happiness: the correspondent reporting on "Coney Island" (1880) ironically notes the "absolute absence of any visible sadness or poverty" (92–93). In the viciously Anglocentric environment in which Theodore Roosevelt associates "True Americanism" with speaking only English, a milieu that Martí describes in his diary as living "as if under a hail of blows" (287), the chronicler's aestheticizing appeal to superior Latin American–influenced taste develops into a more radical position of public dissent in his chronicles about the massacre of Chinese miners in Wyoming in 1885, the state-sponsored killings of the Chicago anarchists in 1887, the mob violence in "The Lynching of the Italians" (1891), and the spectacular savagery of white citizens lynching a black man in "A Town Sets a Black Man on Fire" (1892). Martí ends his career as a journalist reporting on U.S. culture with an unequivocal declaration on "The Truth about the United States" (1894), in which he asserts the "crude, unequal and decadent character of the United States, and the continual existence within it of all the violence, discords, immoralities and disorders of which the Hispanoamerican peoples are accused" (333). He proposes translation of U.S. journalism into Spanish as a means of unmasking this "crude" inequality in the United States for readers across the Americas.

This keen consciousness of the United States' imperial or economic ambitions, not only for the Caribbean and South America but also with respect to Mexico, tempers self-critique with a call to action. In the opening lines of "Our America" published in New York and in Mexico, when Martí addresses the "prideful villager," he alludes to the Latin American leaders in their respective countries, who assembled at the invitation of the U.S. Secretary of State James G. Blaine for the first Pan-American conference in 1889–90. Martí observes the persistence of coloniality in the tendency among his elite interlocutors to attune themselves more to the fashions and ideas of Paris, Madrid, or New York than to ideas emerging from the indigenous, African-descended, and *mestizo* majorities of their nations: "America … endures the weary task of reconciling the discordant and hostile elements it inherited from its perverse, despotic colonizer with the imported forms and ideas that have in their lack of local reality, delayed the advent of a logical form of government" (292). The Mexican American writer María Cristina Mena repeats this exhortation to draw on the cultural forms and knowledge of the people who make up the nation's majority in her "My Protocol for our Sister Americas" (1943): "[O]ne can't very well ignore the PEOPLE – the masses – who are the Nation" ("Protocol" 358). Martí, de la Selva, Williams, and Zeno Gandía similarly affirm the creative self-definition of the majorities of the American nations, an idea that will have radical implications in a few decades when non-Hispanic whites are projected to become a minority in the United States. These Latina/o writers demand ideas and forms that embrace and articulate the interests of the working people of color majority, for only this perspective will offer a viable program for decolonization.

This call to creative self-affirmation and decolonization interestingly repeats itself in the language of the Filipino Revolutionary José Rizal, who published his philosophical Spanish-language text *El Filibusterismo* in 1891, the same year Martí published "Our America." Rizal's romantic nationalist turned cut-throat saboteur of the colonial system, Simoun, challenges Basilio to see the limitations of liberal appeals for Hispanization or reform within the Spanish system: "That's just the road to becoming a bad copy" (55). Simoun's radical and militant vision, like that of Martí after the founding of the Cuban Revolutionary Party in 1892, aims to strike at the roots of all vestiges of coloniality. Filipino revolutionaries, with whom Martí had contact during his last years, found inspiration in the Cuban and Puerto Rican revolutionary imaginaries. Reading Rizal together with Martí reveals the pernicious and trenchant legacy of the Spanish system, in which any expression of independent thinking was condemned by the Spanish authorities as *filibusterismo*, or subversion.

The Question of Antiracism in Hispanic Caribbean Writing

This climate of race-based exclusion fostered by the 1882 Chinese Exclusion Act, the U.S. Supreme Court case *Plessy vs. Ferguson* in 1896, and the rise of lynching in this period enforced the stark racial and class hierarchies that characterize post-slavery societies such as the United States. In this context, Martí's controversial antiracist declaration that "there is no race hatred, because there are no races," diverges radically from the prevailing nineteenth-century tradition of scientific racism. In Martí's essays addressed to the revolutionary movement and the migrant community or to Latin American leaders, such as "With all and for the Good of All," "My Race," or "Our America," the emergence of the nation must redress centuries of racism, for racism and colonialism are intertwined. The notion that, by ending slavery and the colonial regime, it would be possible and necessary to put an end to centuries of racialization, coupled with the crucial role of black leadership by Antonio Maceo and others in positions of authority in the revolutionary forces, convinced many Cubans and Puerto Ricans of African descent to risk their lives fighting against Spanish colonialism. But this view also suggests a naïve misconception of how easy it would be to disentangle institutions and psyches from the entrenched legacies of racial hierarchy and enslavement. As Lourdes Martínez-Echazábal has pointed out, the nationalist program did not eliminate racism in the new Cuban republic, and Martí's premature death does not permit us to learn whether he would have endorsed the struggle of the Partido Independiente de Color, the suppression of which in 1912 resulted in the Cuban army's massacre of 3,000–4,000 who took up arms to oppose a law that prohibited the creation of political organizations based on racial differences. More generally, the resistance fighters of 1912 sought to challenge the marginalization of black Cubans in a country that many black Cubans and Puerto Ricans had sacrificed their lives to create.

Among those Puerto Ricans who initially joined the independence movement was Arturo Alfonso Schomburg, who supported anticolonialism to the extent that he was among the signatories of the documents that led to the creation of the Partido Revolucionario Cubano. However, after the annexation of Puerto Rico and the dismantlement of racially mixed associations such as the Union Maceo-Martí, and in light of the racism that continued more virulent than ever in Cuba and the United States, Schomburg turned fully to the project of building the largest archive of books by and about people of African descent in the Americas. This shift in his attention, his adoption of an English spelling of his name for certain periods of his life, and his composition of his major essays in English – including "The Negro Digs up his Past," which appeared in Alain Locke's *The New Negro* (1925) – perhaps suggests his disillusionment with the abiding racism in the anticolonial project despite Martí's exhortations, or perhaps, due to the insufficiently acknowledged racism persistent in Cuban nationalism just as it was created, with an official silence about race, as Ada Ferrer has suggested. Lisa Sánchez González, Frances Negrón Muntaner, and Antonio López argue that Schomburg's affiliation with blackness should be read as a redefinition of *latinidad* as always-already black.

Popular Collective Action as a Way out of Coloniality in Zeno Gandía's *The Pond*

Much as "Our America" asks the *criollo* elite to recognize their dependency on, rather than authority over, the peasants or working people of African and indigenous descent whom they claimed to represent, Manuel Zeno Gandía's novel *The Pond* (*La Charca*) brings into focus what Juan Flores has called the "interlocking worlds" of the 1894 novel's two main protagonists, the coffee plantation owner Juan del Salto and the poor peasant girl Silvina (Flores, "Introduction" 13). The axis of asymmetry here does not address the hierarchical structures of race or imperialism that we might expect, as Zeno Gandía witnessed emancipation firsthand, which his own slave-owning father vehemently opposed. Zeno Gandía, a medical doctor by training, sidesteps the question of race during the 1887 *compontes*, when Afro–Puerto Ricans bore the brunt of the state's suppression of an emergent liberal autonomist movement for reform, as Jesse Hoffnung-Garskof has shown. This repression of artisans of color – coincident with the massive mobilizations for an eight-hour day in the United States, led by the Spanish-speaking mixed-race anarchist Lucy Parsons – in turn transformed Sotero Figueroa and his adopted son Francisco Gonzálo Marín, and perhaps also Martí, into revolutionaries, for all joined and led militant organizations in New York in the wake of the *compontes* and the Haymarket anarchist hangings. The unresolved antagonism that defines the dramatic buildup of *The Pond* builds on the tensions between landowners and workers, or between the privileged male landowners and sexually abused peasant women who lived and worked on del Salto's coffee plantation.

Zeno Gandía's text critically assesses the way the culture of colonialism prevented the oppressed coffee plantation workers and the women who depended on them from denouncing abuses they suffered or claiming their rights as citizens and human beings. The emergent social force of "el negocio" – that is, the unscrupulous business dealings, usury, and murder associated with the unsympathetic characters Andújar, Galante, Gaspar, and Deblás, two of whom launch an import-export business by the end of the novel – leads the reader to suspect that U.S. capitalist modernity on the island's horizon would merely amplify these abusive practices.

The more radical stance of later Puerto Ricans writers who emigrated to New York after the Jones-Shafroth act imposed U.S. citizenship in 1917, including Jesus Colón, Bernardo Vega, and Julia de Burgos, locates the hope to end the gridlock of these interlocking forces with the creativity of working people. The poetic persona of "To Julia de Burgos" rebels against the gendered, consumerist, elite-identified "lady" that her colonized society expected her to be, and instead situates herself among the masses who do break into protest with torches in hand. De Burgos's poetry, journalism, and memoirs explicitly endorse socialism and anti-imperialism, all while documenting the life of the Puerto Rican diaspora in relation to the broader formation of *Pueblos Hispanos*, which is also the title of Juan Antonio Correbtjer's newspaper where Julia de Burgos and many others published short essays in Spanish that affirm an ongoing connection between the Puerto Rican diaspora and peoples throughout the Caribbean and Latin America. Julia de Burgos launched her career as the most important Puerto Rican poet with her collection, *Poema en Veinte Surcos/Poems in Twenty Furrows*, in 1938, just prior to her movement away from Puerto Rico to New York via Cuba.[1] Juan Flores asks us to consider Zeno Gandía and Julia de Burgos as major writers of an American literary tradition, and Julia de Burgos's remarkable experiments with a divided poetic persona and the use of the authorial name as a third person in her poems make major contributions to poetics of the early twentieth century.

Zeno Gandía's *The Pond* – like Daniel Venegas's novel *Don Chipote* and Maria Cristina Mena's stories to which we will shortly turn – makes a vital contribution to this phase of Latina/o writing by depicting the popular culture of the peasants as offering the most effective and creative response to coloniality on the island. Two scenes in the novel depict the solidarity and collective action of the peasants as a source of inspiration for the paralyzed Juan del Salto and his overseer, Montesa. First, having been whipped the previous day, Inés Marcante, a worker on the plantation, heroically rescues a fourteen-year-old boy from drowning when the river in their village floods. Second, after Gaspar steals the savings of the elderly and impoverished Marta, the workers on the plantation draw on the popular cultural riches of island to express their anxious desire for an alternative to the capitalist prescriptions of hoarding and hard work. Both scenes demonstrate the view that the way out of the stench and stagnancy of the miasma, or *charca*, of coloniality will derive from popular, collective practice and working-class celebrations of life:

> The couples revolved around the hall like the links of a chain pump.... The billowing wave of humanity stirred incessantly, knee striking knee, each couple sharing the same breath, feeling at every instant collisions of tender delicacy and the friction of short hair tingling against foreheads, creating currents of restless love – of desires mortified by the nearness of the unattainable object that tantalized them – the warm soft desire of a life filled with anxiety for pleasure and happiness (107).

With the force of a pump, the dancers' bodies work together to extract from the difficult conditions of their lives a now globally influential cultural form of music and dance. Indeed, rhythms of Puerto Rican and Cuban music that continue to tropicalize the urban landscape of the United States, to reference Guillermo Cotto-Thorner's metaphor, derive from traditions on the islands of making music influenced by African drums and indigenous percussion instruments such as the *güiro* (which Zeno Gandía specifically refers in this section). Unlike the solitary or elite academic reflections of Juan del Salto, the peasants who work for him collaborate to give original form to their collective future. Already the narrator evokes the power of this cultural practice to engender pride and affirmation of Puerto Rican-ness in the face of colonialism upon leaving the island: "away from home, it [the music] was touching ... swelling one with pride for having been born there" (108).

Latina/o Perspectives on the American Dream Myth

Literature by writers born in Latin America who migrated to the United States and did not affiliate culturally and politically presents a serious exception to a long-standing and celebrated tradition of ethnic immigrant writing that portrays the United States as the land of opportunity and an exemplary nation where it is possible to experience freedom and progress unavailable in the migrants' places of origin. Daniel Venegas's novel of Mexican migration to the United States offers an exemplary definition of the genre of "Hispanic immigrant literature," which according to Nicolás Kanellos deconstructs the American Dream myth by documenting the lack of upward mobility for Latina/o workers.

Like Zeno Gandía's *The Pond*, Venegas's *Las Aventuras de Don Chipote, o Cuando los pericos mamen* (*Don Chipote, Or When Parrots Breast-Feed*) affirms the creative power of popular working-class culture, in a kind of writing that formally calls attention to its intended working-class audience of "Chicana/os" in Los Angeles (a term that makes an early appearance in this text). With vernacular language and broad dialect, Venegas's 1928 novel uses humor to empower working-class migrants to criticize, survive, and overcome the myriad injustices that they faced in the United States. Whereas Zeno Gandía's or Martí's Spanish-language texts, although opposed to a certain kind of European-identified elite intellectual, speak from a position distinct and separate from the peasants, working classes, and people of color whom they charged the self-critical intellectuals – like themselves – to represent or govern with more justice, Venegas's narrator affects the position of an organic intellectual, who uses the working-class dialect as an artistic resource to approach the unrepresentable predicament of Chicana/o migrants. Despite his abandonment of Doña Chipota and their children, Don Chipote gains the reader's sympathy by hard work, unlike the despicable Pitacio, who after sojourning in the United States returned to the Chipote's village to induce Don Chipote to migrate *al Norte* by misrepresenting it as a fabulous land of opportunity: thus the title and narrator of Venegas's novel suggests that Mexican migrants to the United States will achieve the wealth and equal status associated with the American dream, "when parrots breastfeed," which is to say, never.

In this text originally written in Spanish, the narrator of *Don Chipote* criticizes the tendency of Mexicans who elect upon arrival in the United States to assimilate and forget their cultural origins and their first language.[2] Among the horrors that Mexicans face upon migrating, Venegas's narrator mentions specifically the system of debt peonage by which bosses and suppliers so indebted migrants that, even after working incredibly long hours, they found themselves with more debt than earnings at the end of the season. The narrator comments with shock on U.S. citizens' lack of concern about the violation of Chicana/o labor rights, and reprimands established Chicana/os for their lack of solidarity with – or worse, their artful preying upon – the vulnerability of those "greenhorns" or "cholos" who have recently arrived (51). The narrator complains about reductive stereotypes of Mexicans as "drunken tramps" and *charros*, in the popular theater productions frequented by Don Chipote in Los Angeles, and where working migrants like Don Chipote and Venegas participated actively in the audience, or, as in Venegas's case, as a playwright (117).[3]

Venegas's novel portrays the routes and rituals of migration upon traveling between the United States and Mexico, and thus suggests the communication and ongoing connections among people in Mexico and migrants of Mexican origin resident in the North. Moreover, the novel assumes a trans-American readership of potential migrants or of current or past migrants now resident in the United States. The novel portrays the dehumanization that migrant subjects experienced in crossing the border, laboring in the fields, dealing with the judicial system or other public institutions, and even in negotiating social interactions, such as the interactions Don Chipote has with a flapper upon whom he lavishes all of his attention and funds, at least until Doña Chipota finds her errant husband in Los Angeles.

This novel's account of the forced derobing and application of pesticides in the shower scene suggests the text's canniness about the disciplining and vulnerability of the bodies of migrants from Mexico during and after border crossing, a humiliating ritual which renders migrants less able to respond to unjust working conditions or to the abuses of the suppliers and bosses. In chapter four, the narrator details the physical process of crossing the border from Ciudad Juarez to El Paso, which begins with the border officer failing to understand anything Don Chipote says, and Don Chipote unable to understand the officer. At this impasse in verbal communication, the *gringo* guard forces Don Chipote "into a room where his fellow countrymen were taking off their clothes to enter the shower" (35). The humor of this scene plays simultaneously on the audience's own recollections and survival of this collective delousing, and in the heterosexual normativity that the reader is invited to perform by laughing at Don Chipote who "actually takes pleasure in the first humiliation that the *gringo* forces on Mexican immigrants!" (35)[4] The novel invites a trans-American readership of Greater Mexico to develop a critical consciousness about these abuses and calls for solidarity with both Don Chipote and Doña Chipota, who eventually return to their homestead in Mexico and begin their lives again, having gained nothing except the consciousness of the impossibility of return.

In its recursive screening of the same scenes of "peace and calm" back in the Chipotes's Mexican village, where Don Chipote continues to "poke at his oxens' asses" just as he did in the opening scenes, the book's epilogue characterizes the transformation the migrant's consciousness. Now Don Chipote dreams his life as if he were the protagonist of a film, with a modernist self-reflexivity: "And in his dreams he saw bitter adventures, in which he had played the protagonist, unwind like a movie reel, sweetened by the remembrance of his flapper's love" (160). This screen-memory simultaneously springs from his unconscious as an object of obsessive desire. At the same time it triggers an awareness of the real – that is, the long history of harsh difficulties of Latina/o migrants – and of the imaginary narratives and representations of that history. Because it unwinds like a movie reel, the memory both captivates the audience and distorts the audience's memory of the bitter adventures in the North.[5]

Latina/o Modernism of María Cristina Mena, Salomón de la Selva, and William Carlos Williams

Writers such as the relocated Mexican María Cristina Mena and the Nicaraguan Salomón de la Selva – who immigrated to the United States as a child and began to compose stories or poetry in English – articulate a critical distance from the ideology of the American dream, and thus present a challenge to Kanellos's division of Latina/o literature into immigrant Spanish and "native" English categories. Whereas Kanellos limits the interrogation of the American Dream to immigrant texts in Spanish, and posits that the children of immigrants who write in English usually reinforce and celebrate the promise associated with life in the United States (3), these texts invite us to consider other factors besides language, generation, or migratory status – such as class, relationship of the homeland to the empire, political critique, and gender – in shaping English-language subjectivities that dismantle the American dream and the United States as model.

As migrants or children of migrants, Salomón de la Selva, María Cristina Mena and William Carlos Williams, all of whom published in English, go beyond affirmation or rejection of the dominant culture to demand and engage in a redefinition of the literary tradition and culture of the United States. These early twentieth-century pioneers of Latina/o modernism in English write against the American grain (as Kutzinski suggests with respect to Williams) in order to affirm the sovereignty and dignity of their homelands that the United States must learn to respect and to invent in English-language literary texts "a new art form itself – rooted in the locality which should give it fruit" (Williams *Autobiography* 176). Thus drawing on a simultaneously local, multilingual, and trans-American cultural archive, these Latina/o writers define a mode of modernist poetry or prose that articulates a Latina/o difference rather than imitating European, Yankee, or other Old World traditions. This orientation seems to directly echo Martí's affirmation of "our wine," and "our Greeks," or the mestizo American culture over reheated leftovers of coloniality.

The task of translation between Mexico or Nicaragua and the United States provided María Cristina Mena and Salomón de la Selva with the materials that they transformed into prose and poetry in their twenties, after arriving in the United States in the first decade of the twentieth century at age fourteen and eleven, respectively. While Mena had already developed fluency in Spanish, English, French, and Italian thanks to her elite upbringing in Mexico, and de la Selva had earned a scholarship from the Nicaraguan congress to study English, both spent formative years in the United States and began to convey a Latina/o critical distance from the dominant culture of their country of residence. Their bodies of work (Mena's entirely in English and de la Selva's mostly in Spanish, after his English-language debut) bear the marks of the revolutionary upheaval in their countries where the working class and peasant masses sought to transform the extreme class and racial hierarchies of Central America and Mexico. Mena's upper-class parents sent her to the United States to escape the unrest leading up to the 1910 revolution, and she takes the revolution as a theme in her stories, "The Sorcerer and General Bisco" and "A Son of the Tropics," in which Carmelita and Tula elect to become *soldaderas* in the revolution. De la Selva witnesses firsthand as a solider in the British military the massive carnage of World War I, but moreover he directly engages in intellectual and activist resistance to U.S. occupations of Nicaragua. The so-called "Banana Wars" began in 1910 while de la Selva was still in the United States, but they cumulated with Agusto César Sandino's armed revolution from 1927 to 1933, and de la Selva became one of Sandino's most outspoken supporters during his residence in Mexico after returning from England, and while writing for working-class newspapers in Panama and Nicaragua. Much of de la Selva's prose has appeared in a three-volume anthology; current translation and scholarship activity suggest that de la Selva's stature as a Nicaraguan, a Latin American, and a Latino writer will continue to grow.

Mena, de la Selva, and William Carlos Williams circulated in cosmopolitan literary worlds, to which they contributed by experimenting not primarily with form, but with a dissenting sensibility and a new mode of poetic language. De la Selva knew and translated Rubén Darío – the leading spokesperson of the movement that came to be known as *modernism* – into English; he became closely acquainted with Edna St. Vincent Millay when he was teaching at Williams College, and his English-language poetry reveals their shared adherence to classic lyrical forms while introducing a startlingly intimate poetic persona. De la Selva knew Williams's college interlocutor Ezra Pound and Anglophone modernism through contact in London after World War I, which helps explain the more radical formal experiments of his Spanish-language text *El Soldado Desconocido* (The Unknown Soldier) of 1922, which featured Diego Rivera's artwork on the cover and which has not yet appeared in English, like most of de la Selva's later work. Similarly, Mena was married to Australian playwright and journalist Henry Kellett Chambers, and exchanged correspondence and visits with D. H. Lawrence and Aldous Huxley. T. S. Eliot selected Mena's story, "John of God, the Water-Carrier," for reprinting in *The Monthly Criterion*, after which it was chosen for *The Best Short Stories of 1928*.

Both Mena and de la Selva assumed the role of cultural translators with vehemence and dissented from the dominant conceptions of their home countries. De la Selva openly interrogated U.S. views of Nicaragua as a banana republic that existed for North American bankers and capitalists to exploit. Mena's stories in mainstream magazines such as *The Century, Cosmopolitan, American Magazine and Household*, educate Anglophone readers by teaching them not only to pronounce the names of the Aztec God of War, Huitzilopochtli and his mother, Cuatlicue – "Weet-zee-lo-potchtlee," by explaining pronunciation, "Kwaht-lee-quay, with the accent on the 'lee'," in her "Birth of the God of War" – but also to consider as the narrator does, that Cuatlicue, mother of the Aztecs' "protector-genius" who was destined to fame in key works of twentieth-century Chicana feminism, led a more "charming" life than that lived by Virgin Mary, who "remained on this sad earth as the wife of a carpenter" (69).

Mena asks her Anglo readers to compare cosmologies and recognize Aztec equality if not superiority, much as she critically assesses the implications of "a spirit named 'modern improvement,'" from the angle of the indigenous working-class Mexican. "John of God the Water Carrier" invites a critique of the introduction of automated U.S. pumps from insofar as they would displace – and offer no real benefit – to the titular character Juan de Dios, who delivered water to people's homes. In "The Gold Vanity Set," her readers encounter a familiar white tourist snapping photographs of "Indians" as part of a frenzy of exotic consumption, but as told through the eyes of the tall, slender, strong, rebellious, and beautiful Petra, whose picture the white tourist has just taken. Mena counteracted stereotypical portrait of Mexicans as exotic, backward, and in need of U.S.-styled modernization that littered the pages of *The Century Magazine* and the minds of its readers.

Living in the interstices of cultures, and translating back and forth between the imperial center and peripheral Central America and the Caribbean, Latina/o writers of the late nineteenth and early twentieth century innovated the national literatures of the United States, Nicaragua, Cuba, Puerto Rico, and beyond, simultaneously creating landmarks of a Latina/o literary tradition that challenges the scope and significance of the singular national, monolingual traditions. Lisa Sánchez González's recontextualization of William Carlos Williams as part of the Puerto Rican diaspora in light of his anticolonial activism and the influence of his Puerto Rican mother, Elena Hoheb, invites us to consider this canonical writer in relation to other Latina/o writers who engaged modernism. In *Yes Mrs. Williams*,

Williams affirms that the home in which he grew was a Spanish-speaking household. He copies into this text his mother's most hermetic and humorous comments and her constant movement back and forth between Spanish and French. Here the reader encounters Elena's spellbinding version of Corneille's *Horace*, ending in the famous curse of the empire: "Rome enfin que je hais!" According to Williams, "All her contempt and even hatred that we had earned in this benighted country [i.e., the United States] through the years was contained in that anathema" (*Yes* 18). This Latina/o critique of U.S. imperialism informs his lack of interest in the turn to Europe for poetic inspiration, in contrast to his friend Ezra Pound and many others modernists who moved to Europe to become expatriates. Like Martí in his last and most widely read poetry collection, *Versos sencillos*, Williams privileges the common voice, and specifically the local working-class idiom of Paterson, New Jersey. Williams's critique of empire becomes undeniable as his archival excavation of early American history – *In the American Grain* – confronts his readers with the "orgy of blood" brought about by European colonists to the Americas. The "we" of those who arrived (in which he includes himself) is ironically excoriated as "'heavenly m[e]n' bent on murder" (*In the American Grain* 41).

While turning away from "imported" Yankee and European ideas, these Latina/o writers participated in the definition of futurity and a redefinition of the modern forms of poetry and of the social, there and here, in light of the periphery's transculturation of the center. David Colón, in his evocation of Salomón de la Selva's "Deep Translation and Subversive Formalism," notes the poet's aspiration to stage the reversal whereby the peripheral or provincial speaks to and defines a "co-experience" of distinct Americas (27) nonetheless reveals that "my people and your people are the same" (*Tropical Town* 84). De la Selva articulates this desire by inviting his readers to view "his" Nicaragua, so that the reader in the North must see that her humanity and indeed her future is caught up with his Nicaragua's struggle, survival, and difference. De la Selva, in his philosophical meditation on the historical production of our common trans-American present in the closing poem of *Tropical Town and Other Poems*, affirms Martí's declaration of the universal sources and interlocutors for his *Versos sencillos*: "Yo vengo de todas partes, y hacia todas partes voy" [No boundaries bind my heart/ I belong to every land] (20–21). Emblematic of the trans-American literature of empire and revolution we have examined here, de la Selva's poem "Of Time and Song" invites the reader to think across the linguistic and other borders that render our perceptions at once untranslatable, and yet necessarily in communication: "Thus, on and on/ all days are somehow linked, all songs are one" (*Tropical Town* 161).

Notes

1 See Vanessa Pérez Rosario, *Becoming Julia de Burgos: The Making of a Puerto Rican Icon.*
2 See my translation of Martí's critique of Latin American immigrants who quickly adopted U.S. citizenship, spoke in the language of power and cultural capital, English, and attempted to hide the "last drops of his mother's milk" that lingered as a telltale sign of their foreign origin and their mother tongue in "Thinking Across, Infiltration and Transculturation," 18.
3 Kanellos's research has revealed that Venegas created many musical comedies for blue-collar audiences, but also works of drama in which renowned Mexican actress Virginia Fábregas acted.
4 I am grateful to my students and to Andrew Lester in particular, whose work on this text illuminated the forbidden homoerotics of this shower scene and of other homosocial spaces in the novel.
5 I am indebted to John Morán González for calling my attention to this film metaphor and its implications.

Works Cited

Burgos, Julia de. *Song of the Simple Truth: Obra poética completa/the Complete Poems of Julia de Burgos.* Comp. and Trans. Jack Agüeros. Willimantic, CT: Curbstone Press, 1997.
Colón, David. "Deep Translation and Subversive Formalism." *Journal of Philosophy: A Cross-Disciplinary Inquiry* 7.17 (2012): 11–27.
Colón, Jesus. *A Puerto Rican in New York and Other Essays.* New York: Monthly Review Press, 1982.
De Burgos, Julia. *Song of the Simple Truth: Complete Poems of Julia de Burgos.* Ed. and Trans. Jack Agüeros. Boston: Beacon Press, 1997.
De la Selva, Salomón. *Antología Mayor. 3 volumenes.* Sel. Julio Valle-Castillo. Ed. Francisdo Arrellano Oviedo. Managua: Colección Cultural Centro America, and Fundación Uno 2007.
   El soldado desconocido. México: Cultura, 1922.
   Tropical Town and Other Poems. Ed. with an Introduction by Silvio Sirias. Houston, TX: Arte Público Press, 1999.
Deleuze, Gilles and Félix Guattari. *Kafka: Towards a Minor Literature.* Trans. Dana Polan. Minneapolis: University of Minnesota Press, 1986.
Ferrer, Ada. "The Silence of Patriots: Race and Nationalism in Martí's Cuba." In Belnap, Jeffrey, and Raul Fernández, eds. *José Martí's "Our America": From National to Hemispheric Cultural Studies.* Durham, NC: Duke University Press, 1998, 228–49.
Flores, Juan. "Introduction" to Zeno Gandía, Manuel, *The Pond (La Charca): Puerto Rico's Nineteenth-Century Masterpiece.* Princeton, NJ: Markus Wiener Publishers, 1999, 13–32.
   Divided Borders: Essays on Puerto Rican Identity. Houston, TX: Arte Público Press, 1993.
Gruesz, Kirsten Silva. *Ambassadors of Culture: The Transamerican Origins of Latino Writing.* Princeton, NJ: Princeton University Press, 2002.

Hoffnung-Garskof, Jesse. "To abolish the law of caste": merit, manhood and the problem of colour in the Puerto Rican liberal movement, 1873–92," *Social History* 35.3 (2011): 312–42.

James, William. "Address at the Annual Meeting of the New England Anti-Imperialist League," in *Report of the Fifth Annual Meeting of the New England Anti-Imperialist League*. Boston: New England Anti-Imperialist League, 1903.

Kanellos, Nicolás. *Hispanic Immigrant Literature: El Sueño del Retorno*. Austin: University of Texas Press, 2011.

History of Hispanic Theater in the United States: Origins to 1940. Austin: University of Texas Press, 1990.

Kutzinski, Vera. *Against the American Grain: Myth and History in William Carlos Williams, Jay Wright and Nicolás Guillén*. Baltimore: Johns Hopkins University Press, 1984.

Lomas, Laura. "Thinking-Across, Infiltration and Transculturation: José Martí's Theory and Practice of Post-Colonial Translation in New York" *Translation Review* (Fall 2011) 81: 13–35.

Translating Empire: José Martí, Migrant Latino Subjects and American Modernities Durham, NC: Duke University Press, 2008.

López, Antonio. *Unbecoming Blackness: The Diaspora Cultures of Afro-Cuban America*. New York: New York University Press, 2012.

Martí, José. *Selected Writings*. Trans. and Ed. Esther Allen. New York: Penguin, 2002.

Versos sencillos: A Dual Language Edition. Trans. Anne Fountain. Foreword Pete Seeger. Jefferson, NC: McFarland & Company, Inc. Publishers, 2005.

Martínez-Echazábal, Lourdes. "Martí y las Razas [Martí and Race]: A Re-Evaluation." *Re-Reading José Martí One Hundred Years Later*. Binghamton: State University of New York Press, 1999.

Mena Chambers, María Cristina. *The Collected Stories of María Cristina Mena*. Ed. with an Introduction by Amy Doherty. Houston, TX: Arte Público Press, 1997.

"My Protocol for our Sister Americas," reprinted by Margaret A. Toth, *Legacy: A Journal of American Women Writers* 30.2 (2013): 355–60.

Ortiz, Fernando. *Cuban Counterpoint: Tobacco and Sugar*. Trans. Harriet de Onís. Durham, NC: Duke University Press, 1995.

Pérez Rosario, Vanessa. *Becoming Julia de Burgos: The Making of a Puerto Rican Icon*. Champaign: University of Illinois Press, 2014.

Pratt, Mary Louise. *Imperial Eyes: Travel Writing and Transculturation*. London: Routledge, 1992.

"Modernity and Periphery: Toward a Global and Relational Analysis." In *Beyond Dichotomies: Histories, Identities and the Challenge of Globalization*, ed. Elisabeth Mudimbe-Boyi. Albany: State University of New York Press, 2002.

Rama, Angel. *Writing across Cultures: Narrative Transculturation in Latin America*. Ed and trans. David Frye. Durham, NC: Duke University Press, 2012.

Rizal, José. *El Filibusterismo*. Trans. Harold Augenbraum. New York: Penguin, 2011.

Roosevelt, Theodore. "True Americanism." *The Forum* (April 1894).

Saldívar, José David. *Trans-Americanity: Subaltern Modernities, Global Coloniality and the Cultures of Greater Mexico*. Durham, NC: Duke University Press, 2012.

Sánchez González, Lisa. "Modernism and Boricua Literature: A Reconsideration of Arturo Schomburg and William Carlos Williams." *American Literary History* (2001): 242–64.

Schomburg, Arthur A. "The Negro Digs up His Past." In Alain Locke, ed. *The New Negro, an Interpretation*. 1925; New York: Atheneum, 1992, 231–37.

Venegas, Daniel. *The Adventures of Don Chipote, or, When Parrots Breast-Feed*. Ed. Nicolás Kanellos. Trans. Ethraim Cash Brammer. Houston, TX: Arte Público Press, 2000.

Williams, William Carlos. *The Autobiography of William Carlos Williams;* 1951. New York: New Directions, 1967.

   In the American Grain: Essays by William Carlos Williams. Introduction by Horace Gregory. New York: James Laughlin, 1956.

   Yes, Mrs. Williams: A Personal Record of My Mother. New York: McDowell Obolensky, 1959.

Zeno Gandía, Manuel. *The Pond (La Charca): Puerto Rico's Nineteenth-Century Masterpiece*. Trans. Kal Waggenheim with Introduction by Juan Flores. Princeton, NJ: Markus Weiner Publishers, 1999.

3

JOHN MORÁN GONZÁLEZ

Between Ethnic Americans and Racial Subjects: Latina/o Literature, 1936–1959

During the period from the Great Depression through the early Cold War, Latina/o literature highlighted the various social contradictions that the presence of Mexican Americans, Puerto Ricans, and other transnationally situated Latina/o populations posed for U.S. nationalism. Authors such as Américo Paredes, Jovita González, José Antonio Villarreal, René Marqués, and Pedro Juan Soto interrogated the ongoing operations of the coloniality of U.S. power as expressed through the racially limned incorporation of the Mexican-descent populations of the U.S. Southwest and the further consolidation of U.S. colonial rule over Puerto Rico. These writers used the imaginative forums of the novella, novel, and drama to interrogate U.S. racialist narratives that considered Latinas/os as inassimilable "foreigners" unfit for citizenship even as they could be exploited as a cheap, docile workforce. As these narratives relied on the nationalist mapping of the United States as racially white in opposition to the imagined non-whiteness of Latin America, Latina/o literary responses engaged the question of how Latina/o individuals and communities asserted claims to inclusion within the U.S. national imaginary while simultaneously insisting on the fundamentally trans-American dimensions of their experiences. If U.S. nationalism insisted on the relinquishing of linguistic and cultural practices perceived as "foreign" while maintaining race as its indelible marker, then Latina/o literature of this period would both critically interrogate the terms of nationalist inclusion and trace the epistemological operations of power in the making of race, colonial subjection, and national incorporation.

Two key moments frame the production of Latina/o literature during this period. The first of these occurred at the height of the Great Depression in 1936, when Mexican American intellectuals and writers forcefully critiqued the anti-Mexican discourses of the Texas Centennial and began to imagine the "Mexican American" as the harbinger of a new relationship between U.S. nationalism and people of Mexican descent. The second of these occurred during the mid-1950s, when Puerto Rican authors initiated a sustained critical examination not only of the U.S. colonial domination of Puerto Rico but also of the specific economic policies put into effect in the late 1940s. Operation Bootstrap, the major U.S. initiative to "modernize" the Puerto Rican economy, resulted in a mass exodus from the Island to the United States mainland, principally New York City, thus creating the diasporic conditions that forged Nuyorican expressive culture as a new kind of modernism.

The Texas Centennial and the Emergence of Mexican American Literature

The Texas Centennial of 1936 proved to be a key catalyst for the consolidation of a new social and literary movement for and among people of Mexican descent. While anti-Mexican sentiment had always informed the racial contours of Anglo-Texan identity, the centennial celebration of Texas's independence from Mexico in 1836 cast that event, and the subsequent greatness of Texas in U.S. history afterwards, to the racial superiority of white Texans over those that they considered their inferiors: African Americans, Native Americans, and Mexican Americans. Domination of the latter group in particular defined Texan greatness, as Texas Centennial discourses propagated a reductive narrative about the Texas Revolution that cast honest, hardworking, freedom-loving Anglo-Texans against despicable, lazy, tyrannical Mexicans. Ignoring the complicated political alliances in 1836 that joined federalist-minded Anglo-Texans and *tejanos* (Texans of Mexican descent) against the depredations of Mexican President Santa Ana's centralist government, Texas Centennial discourses celebrated the absolute subordination of all considered "Mexicans" – whether U.S. citizens or not – as a cheap, docile labor force for a modernizing Texas. While people of Mexican descent, as legally "white," were not subject to racial segregation by law as were African Americans, nonetheless other legal practices and informal customs regarding their treatment resulted in largely the same condition, violently reinforced by police brutality and persistent expressions of anti-Mexican sentiment in the dominant media and by the general public. Mobilizing the past to justify the continued racial domination of people of Mexican descent in the present, Texas Centennial discourses saturated the print and radio media in Texas during the mid-1930s, emphasizing how categorically antithetical all "Mexicans" were to U.S. ideals of individual freedom, social modernization, and participatory democracy.

Mexican American literature as it emerged during the 1930s has its origins in the response of Texas Mexican intellectuals to a crisis for Mexican-descent communities in the United States some two decades earlier. Inspired by the military success of revolutionaries during the Mexican Revolution, the 1915 uprising of *tejano* ranchers against the economic and social displacements occurring in the Lower Rio Grande Valley was not only the last organized armed uprising against U.S. rule in South Texas but also a crushing reminder of how the Mexican population was at the mercy of local and state authorities; terrible reprisals and collective punishment were meted out by the Texas Rangers and Anglo-Texan vigilantes, resulting in hundreds, if not thousands, of Texas Mexican deaths. The brutal state suppression of *los sediciosos* [the seditious ones] convinced Texas Mexican intellectuals of the necessity of adhering to a nation-state that could afford communal protection from such depredations; many felt that the mobilization of the U.S. Army into the Texas-Mexican borderlands during the 1915 Borderlands War prevented even worse treatment by local and state authorities.

During the 1920s, some people of Mexican descent began to emphasize U.S. citizenship as the answer to state violence and racial discrimination. In 1929, three like-minded organizations merged to create the League of United Latin American Citizens (LULAC), expressly dedicated to asserting the rights of U.S. citizens of Mexican descent in all matter of governance and public law. Although often narrowly categorized as a civil rights organization, the LULAC of the 1930s had an ambitious goal for which its members developed a cultural strategy that involved aesthetics, linguistics, and manners as much as it did a political strategy that involved civic education, government lobbying, and antidiscrimination lawsuits. As a full-fledged social movement, LULAC desired no less than the complete reorientation of citizens of Mexican descent away from Mexico and toward the United States in matters of public importance for the well-being of their communities. While this goal has sometimes been characterized by later historians as that of the wholesale abandonment of Mexican culture and the Spanish language in a doomed attempt to gain an impossible "whiteness," it is more instructive to note that LULAC's desire for Mexican Americans to learn the English language, engage in electoral politics, and generally participate in U.S. civic life points to a pragmatic interaction with the nation-state that did not extend to matters of private life. For the private sphere, LULAC advocated for the retention of the Spanish language, the preservation of Mexican moral standards and gender roles, and the teaching of a proud Mexican history and tradition. The term "Mexican American" arises at this historical moment to describe the subject imagined by LULAC as the result of this reorientation of people of Mexican descent to the United States.

Jovita González and Eve Raleigh's coauthored historical romance, *Caballero: A Historical Novel*, brilliantly captures this LULAC aesthetic strategy, albeit with a biting criticism of the organization's invidious gender politics that would keep women subordinate to men and a regressive sexual politics that advocated a strict heteronormativity. Written between 1937 and 1939 but not published until 1996, *Caballero* tells of romantic encounters between enemy lovers during the U.S.-Mexican War of 1846–48, when the United States annexed Mexico's northern half through conquest. Set in the contested Lower Rio Grande Valley of South Texas, the narrative allegorizes the wholesale – out of necessity – reorientation of the region's Mexican population to all things United Statesian through four distinct kinds of courtships between Anglos and Mexicans. The first of these is the high romance between Lt. Robert Warrener of the occupying U.S. Army, scion of a wealthy Virginia plantation family who fled an arranged marriage, and Susanita, daughter of the aristocratic ranchero Santiago Mendoza y Soría. Susanita's sister Angela finds herself in a much more pragmatic marriage with Alfred "Red" McLane, an aspiring political boss who realizes the importance of the Mexican vote to the area's future elections. Luis Gonzaga, the "effeminate" younger son of Don Santiago who prefers painting to soldiering, joins his fortunes to those of U.S. Army Captain Devlin in order to realize his goal of formal training in Europe. While all of these romantic relationships model what González and Raleigh hoped would be the mutually beneficial, and mutually respectful, relationship between Anglos and Mexican Americans, this last relationship in particular points to the homoerotics of collaboration implicit in its allegorization. Besides the relationships between people, the seducing of Mexican labor into the relative freedom of contract labor over the informal economic and social slavery of debt peonage completes the narrative's imagining of the equitable integration of people of Mexican descent into the U.S. political and social imaginary.

However, these fundamental changes in the political, economic, and social relationships in South Texas create significant conflicts, with tradition-minded Mexicans portrayed as stubbornly adhering to an outmoded model of patriarchal privilege. Don Santiago's older son Alvaro, depicted as having all the vices of a baronial seigneur without any of the noblesse oblige that his father demonstrates on occasion, dies not in battle against the hated "Yanquis" but as a result of his own moral failings, having provoked a duel against a Texas Ranger whom he found wearing the ring he had given to his favorite prostitute. The regal Don Santiago, who vows never to acknowledge U.S. sovereignty and forbids his daughters from even looking at *Americanos*, finds himself defied at all turns by those he considers his inferiors as his tyrannical reign crumbles before a new system that values individual freedom over filial piety and companionate romance over patriarchal domination. Unwilling to adapt to the new political and social circumstances that promote consent over coercion, Don Santiago finds his world crumbling around him, dying as the land itself, the bulwark of his patriarchal domain, gives way in a landslide that kills him. Ironically, his body is found by Warrener, the son-in-law for whom Susanita defied him. Not only is the new owner of the patriarchal inheritance of Rancho La Palma de Cristo but also father of the next generation of *tejanos*, as Susanita is pregnant with his child.

Writing at nearly the same moment as González and Raleigh in the same Texas-Mexico borderlands, Américo Paredes likewise aimed to counter Texas Centennial discourses with his novel, *George Washington Gómez: A Mexicotexan Novel*, but in such a manner that also critiqued what he considered the shortcomings of a LULAC-style approach. Like *Caballero*, Paredes's novel was published well after it was written between 1936 and 1940, only seeing publication in 1990. But rather than imagine the possibility of a multicultural U.S. citizenry as it coalesces across cultural differences as does *Caballero*, *George Washington Gómez* interrogates the ways that U.S. nationalism leaves no space for the "Mexicotexan" within its racialized imaginary. The novel's titular protagonist is born in 1915, into the violence of Anglo reprisals against *los sediciosos* that claims the life of his blameless father. Although named by his father after the first U.S. president, the boy answers to the indigenous Mexican-inspired name of "Guálinto," a moniker given to him by his maternal uncle Feliciano, who helps his sister, Guálinto's mother, rear the child. Guálinto experiences life in the border town of Jonesville-on-the-Grande as middle-class Texas Mexican youth whose subjectivity is formed by institutional U.S. discourses of nationalist pride and upward mobility as well as regional Mexican discourses of resistance to the white supremacy of Anglo-Texans. The U.S. public school system instructs Guálinto in the former even as it functions to expel most Texas Mexican children into the unskilled labor force, while the Mexican folk ballads of border conflict known as *corridos* educate him in the latter, especially since his uncle Feliciano is the virtual embodiment of those values as a former *sedicioso*.

The two competing discourses manage to coexist until adulthood, when questions of interracial sexuality, the blatant racialization of political and economic power, and the revelation of the circumstances surrounding his father's death cause Guálinto to doubt his familial expectations to become "leader of his people" in their collective struggle against racial domination. Attending the University of Texas in Austin at a time only a handful of Mexican-descent students could enroll, Guáltino returns to Jonesville-on-the-Grande some seven years later as "George G. Gómez," a high-powered real estate attorney whom the town's LULAC-like group, comprised of his high school friends, approaches for aid in organizing for local political power. But rather than assume the community leadership role as envisioned by LULAC's emphasis on a U.S. education, George harbors a secret that is all but laid bare by his brusque rejection of their request and his concomitant contempt for all things Mexican. The powerful final scene between George and his uncle Feliciano reveals not only the secret but also the degree to which the LULAC strategy of Mexican American engagement with U.S. institutions backfires on the very community it was supposed to help. Ultimately, Paredes argues, LULAC failed to understand the power of racialist epistemologies enacted within U.S. educational institutions and their power to change the very subjectivities of those (very few) individuals of Mexican descent allowed access to them. LULAC's approach to structural change through the education of individuals not only had no chance of succeeding but also imperiled future community progress as those co-opted by the educational system would be redeployed to further police racial, linguistic, and national boundaries instead of challenging them.

As evidenced by *Caballero* and *George Washington Gómez*, Mexican American writers of the 1930s not only strove to counter the racially invidious portrayal of their community within Texas Centennial discourses but also engaged in a heated debate within their community about how to address the ongoing coloniality of power as structured by hierarchical relations of race. This debate was particularly salient during the 1930s as communities of Mexican-descent people were themselves divided by citizenship status, given the mass migrations from Mexico during and after the Mexican Revolution. In this sense, LULAC's turn to U.S. citizenship as the ideological grounds on which to make their demands for Latina/o civil rights was an attempt to disarticulate race from nationality from within white supremacist discourses, which cast all Mexicans, regardless of legal citizenship status, as forever foreigners to the United States; in other words, "Mexicans" were considered foreign precisely because they were transnationally linked by language, culture, and race to Mexico. LULAC attempted to disarticulate those aspects from nationality, claiming that the term "Mexican American" was not an oxymoron but rather an ethnic Americanism that had not received its proper due. Critics of LULAC such as Paredes asserted that, to the contrary, U.S. nationalism would reject such claims for the Mexican-descent masses and extract a fierce loyalty from the Mexican American elites at a terrible cost. The question of how to imagine an alternative communal strategy that acknowledged the transnational situation of Mexican-descent people outside Mexico would lead Paredes, who would become a prominent Chicano Studies scholar during the second half of the twentieth century, to formulate the still-influential concept of "Greater Mexico," or the imagined Mexican trans-nation in diaspora.

If *Caballero* and *George Washington Gómez* depicted the Great Depression–era plight of the long-established *tejano* community as it responded to the encroachment of Anglo-Texan modernity, the relation of the first- and second-generation Mexican migrants to U.S. nationalism would be the subject of José Antonio Villarreal's influential novel *Pocho*. While published in 1959, well after the Texas Centennial of 1936, this *bildungsroman* nonetheless plays out the conceptual implications of the "Mexican American" as a subject position through protagonist Richard Rubio's dual encounters with traditional Mexican masculinity and U.S. modernity. As the transnational extension of what has traditionally been considered the quintessentially Mexican genre of the novel of the Mexican Revolution, the narrative traces the origins of the first great wave of Mexican migration to the United States as a result of the violent displacements of the Mexican Revolution of 1910–20. Richard's father, Juan Manuel Rubio, is a loyal soldier of Francisco "Pancho" Villa's army, who abandons the country and the Revolution after Villa's assassination in 1923. Forced into exile *al norte*, Juan Rubio becomes a laborer and family man, raising numerous daughters but focusing on his only son Richard, whose subject formation as a Mexican American is the novel's primary concern. Even as Richard's formative experiences differentiate his subjectivity from that of his Mexican father's, the latter always reminds the former of the limits of social agency granted to Mexican-descent people in the United States: "'You are an American with that black face? Just because your name is Rubio does not mean that you are really blond'" (133).

Set in the agricultural towns and fields of California's Santa Clara Valley during the Great Depression, *Pocho* depicts the process of Richard's becoming Mexican American between his family's Mexican cultural values regarding the Spanish language and traditionally patriarchal gender roles and his quest to define his own existence against the social demands placed on him from all quarters, whether United Statesian or Mexican. From an early age, Richard frames the question of subjective agency as one of either being convinced or coerced to fill particular social roles by institutions such as the family, school, or religion. Resolved not to let any institution determine his individual being, Richard decides to become a writer, a subject position that he believes will allow him to create his own fate. Literacy, Richard finds, opens up new imaginative alternatives to the world he lives in, although the fact that his schooling is solely in English means that his newfound sense of literary freedom is bound to that language; excluded from his formal education, Spanish becomes a utilitarian language of newspapers that seemingly offers no alternative imaginaries for him. Yet, even with this caveat, literature allows Richard to imagine himself outside the institutional strictures of a racialized school system that considers Mexican American children as future menial workers, of an increasingly unstable family life marked by conflict between his father and mother over the gendered division of labor, and of his friends' peer pressure to participate in homosocial bonding through adolescent male sexual rituals. Richard's ambivalence toward what he believes to be the dominance of group identities over individual ones means that he disidentifies with all the social groupings he encounters – ranging from his own family and childhood friends to later acquaintances such as *pachucos* or even other would-be writers – even as he befriends them in an effort to go beyond his otherwise preset social circles.

Try as he might, Richard cannot escape his historical situation, which results in him inhabiting not only his own conceptual framework of the individual against the collective but also the cultural space of the *pocho*, or the person of Mexican descent in the United States whose very being exhibits the contradictory stresses placed on it by the racialized, conflictual relationship between Mexican and U.S. ideologies of the self and the respective obligations, or lack thereof, to the collective.

Richard's multicultural circle of friends includes Spanish, Portuguese, Italian, Japanese, and Anglo youth whose varied experiences as racialized subjects inform Richard's sense of his own racialized place within the contemporary United States. The police harassment and beating of Richard and his friends introduces him to the racialized policing of those boundaries, but perhaps the most extreme example of the disruptive potential of being between worlds is the disintegration of Richard's family over the course of the novel. While Juan Rubio insists on maintaining the patriarchal prerogatives of traditional Mexican masculinity, his wife Consuelo refuses her gendered role as submissive housekeeper "as a symbol of her emancipation" in the United States; after a fight during which Richard is injured trying to separate the couple, his father moves out, only to move in with another woman. While conceding that his mother and sisters face an even more rigid interpellation into predetermined gender roles than he does, Richard nonetheless advocates the deferral of individuality for women even as he insists on his own: "What was done was beyond repair. To be just, no one could be blamed, for the transition from the culture of the old world to that of the new should never have been attempted in one generation" (135). For Richard, the "transition" from a patriarchal Mexican family structure anchored by the complete surrender of women to the roles of daughter, wife, and mother to a United Statesian model of the relatively consensual association of individuals results in ruin if Mexican women act to realize their individuality rather than submit to their prescribed social roles.

With his father's departure, Richard finds himself in the unwanted role of "man of the house," complete with financial responsibilities to maintain his mother and sisters. Fearing his complete incorporation into precisely the normative social role of familial breadwinner that he considers the greatest threat to his individual agency, Richard decides to enlist in the U.S. Navy a few months after the U.S. entry into World War II. The novel ends on this decidedly ambiguous note of Richard joining a war effort that he considers "wrong" and an institution seemingly antithetical to any notion of individuality; nevertheless, the war is also "his only alternative" to what he believes to be the death of his individuality at home (184). While resisting the closure of a definitive answer about the *pocho*'s subjectivity in entering (or exiting) U.S. modernity, the novel does foreground the question of what the ultimate cultural, linguistic, and familial cost of doing so might be.

Operation Bootstrap, the Island Colony, and the Nuyorican Diaspora

Although Puerto Ricans had been living and writing in the United States at least since the late nineteenth century, the U.S. seizure of Puerto Rico after the U.S.-Spanish War of 1898 utterly transformed the migratory possibilities for Puerto Ricans even as it continued the Island's colonial status under a new flag. The granting of U.S. citizenship to Puerto Ricans by the 1917 Jones-Shafroth Act did little to quell popular agitation for independence by the Puerto Rican Nationalist Party, led by famed anticolonialist orator Pedro Albizu Campos. By the late 1930s, popular protests against U.S. colonial policies broke out throughout the Island, which were met with severe repression by the U.S. authorities. The bloodiest of these was the Ponce massacre on Palm Sunday of 1937, in which nineteen unarmed civilians in a peaceful march were gunned down by police on the orders of the U.S. military governor of the Island. Although Albizu Campos was subsequently imprisoned for agitating for Puerto Rican independence, other nationalists continued advocating for the cause, using both popular protest and armed resistance. Among the most notable instances of the latter include an assassination attempt on U.S. President Harry S. Truman in 1950 and an armed attack, lead by Lolita Lebrón, on the U.S. House of Representatives in 1954. The political status of the Island had formally been defined by the U.S. Congress as that of a "Commonwealth" in 1952, but this small measure of local autonomy scarcely satisfied those who believed that the Commonwealth designation (Estado Libre Asociado) continued the Island's colonial status under a more palatable name during the era of post–World

War II decolonization movements. Early twentieth-century U.S. economic policy had favored transformation of the Island's diverse agricultural production into monocultural sugarcane plantations controlled by U.S. corporations, thereby immiserating a high percentage of the population and creating the economic conditions that led to the mass migrations of the 1940s and 1950s.

Seeking to "modernize" Puerto Rico's economy, Governor Luis Muñoz Marín initiated Operation Bootstrap (Operación Manos a la Obra) in 1948, which encouraged the start-up of U.S.-owned industrial enterprises on the Island through generous tax exemptions and rental reductions for industrial production. Operation Bootstrap was, in essence, a colonial policy that attempted to rapidly transform a small-scale agrarian peasantry into an industrial working class. The consequent economic displacements forced *jíbaros* [peasants] to seek gainful employment first in the Island capital of San Juan and then, together with urban Puertorriqueños, in New York City. By the late 1950s, more than 500,000 Puerto Ricans had migrated to New York City, gaining national recognition through mainstream depictions such as *West Side Story* (theater, 1957; film, 1961). However, even while attempting a sympathetic portrayal of working-class Puerto Rican characters, such representations relied on racialized stereotypes of Puerto Ricans as hot-tempered, knife-wielding malcontents who largely refused to melt into the U.S. ethnic immigrant narrative. Such narratives largely exonerated the white mainstream for the blatant and sometimes violent racism that greeted the Puerto Rican arrivals.

During the mid-1950s, Puerto Rican writers began documenting the Puerto Rican diaspora, initiated by U.S. colonial policies on the Island, as the subject of drama and fiction. The iconic portrayal of this era remains René Marqués's *La carreta* (1954). Translated into English as *The Oxcart*, the three-act play traces the various displacements of a *jíbaro* family from their ancestral home in the lush yet unrenumerative Puerto Rican mountains, to the slums of San Juan, and finally to the crowded *barrios* of the Bronx. The promise of greater economic opportunity remains elusive in every stage of this journey, through which Luis Muñoz Marin's boosterism on behalf of Puerto Rico's modernization offers the family only bitter disillusionment. Poor yet close-knit with a proud dignity in their mountain home, the family gradually loses its cohesion as poverty, racial discrimination, and an illusory belief in the American Dream hammer the lives of family patriarch Don Chago, his daughter Doña Gabriela, and her children Juanita, Luis, and Chaguito.

Act One directly addresses the question of land usage policy under U.S. colonial rule, demonstrating how the concentration of agricultural lands into corporate sugarcane plantations, along with predatory lending practices, forced *jíbaro* landowners off their small holdings. Losing their thirty-acre property due to a mortgage default, the family of *La carreta* is torn between the rural romanticism of Don Chago, who wishes to remain in the mountains regardless of poverty and hardships, and the machine-minded modernism of Luis, who imagines that a better life is to be had in the industrialized cities of San Juan and New York. This conflict is in part fueled by Luis's guilt over being his father's son but not his mother's, a secret that Doña Gabriela has kept from him but that he knows nonetheless. The familial drama is augmented by the nascent delinquent tendencies of Chaguito but even more so by Juanita's budding sexuality; one of Doña Gabriela's rationales for supporting the family's uprooting is to nip Juanita's young romance with a neighboring farmer in the bud. With both Luis and Doña Gabriela viewing the move to San Juan as the solution to their immediate problems, the family leaves their home behind, all save the elderly Don Chago, who chooses to live and eventually die in a cave within his beloved mountains.

In Act Two, the family's situation a year later has gone from bad to worse; they live in the heavily polluted, crowded slum ironically named *La Perla* in San Juan that offers no jobs, no privacy, and many illegal activities. The promised schooling for Changuito never materializes, and he is eventually arrested for absconding with a tourist's change. Luis, who vowed not to work the land but only in a factory upon his arrival in the capitol, is forced to labor as a gardener, a job he despises. Doña Gabriela watches with increasing concern as Juanita, encountering the illicit world of the urban sex trade, grows worldly beyond the circumscribed rural situation of the mountainside. Ever seeking what he considers to be modernity, Luis insists that a move to New York City, with better job and schooling possibilities, would remedy their problems, so the family packs up once again.

Act Three is set one year later in Morrisana, the Puerto Rican *barrio* of the Bronx. Luis has obtained his longed-for factory job, but by now the family has truly separated, as only Luis and Doña Gabriela live together in a cramped apartment while Chaguito and Juanita have gone their separate ways, the former incarcerated for criminal activity and the latter employed as a sex worker. If the living and economic conditions aren't quite as bad as in *La Perla*, nonetheless they now have to contend with rampant discrimination from white New Yorkers as well as pervasive police brutality; even as Luis, Juanita, and Doña Gabriela debate the merits of returning to the Island to farm the mountainside, a young Puerto Rican man is gunned down in their apartment building's stairwell for stealing a pocketbook. The play ends with Luis's death in an industrial accident, killed by the very machinery he idolized as the symbol of modernity and success. Devastated but determined, Juanita and Doña Gabriela vow to return to the Island mountainside, not simply to live as before, but to bring change to Puerto Rico. Their clarion call is for a national identity and morally uncorrupted family, rooted in the land as a bulwark against the U.S. colonial policies that alienate Puerto Ricans from their beloved homeland and send them into a dehumanized exile on a cold urban island.

Pedro Juan Soto's *Spiks* (1956) amplifies the sense that Puerto Rican life in diasporic exile on the U.S. mainland is a modernist nightmare, not only from a political or economic angle but more crucially from an existential one. Set entirely in the Nuyorican landscape, this novella consists of seven loosely related short stories interspersed by six paragraph-length sketches, or *miniaturas*; the title, a common racial epithet of the era used by whites to insult people of Latin American descent, indicates the emotionally difficult nature of the narrative. Each of these thirteen segments offers a glimpse into the daily struggles of working-class Nuyoricans to not only to find economic subsistence but also to gain a modicum of dignity in an environment that precludes its existence. Puerto Rican men battle substance abuse, chronic unemployment, mental health issues, police harassment, and their own fragile sense of masculinity that often expresses itself in habitual belligerence or violence toward each other and especially toward Puerto Rican women. These women, in turn, face issues of abandonment, poverty, unwanted pregnancies, abusive relationships, mental health issues, and a general lack of access to resources that might alleviate or improve their lives.

Unlike the predominantly realist aesthetic of Marqués's *La carreta*, *Spiks* more deeply engages the cosmopolitan aesthetic of modernism in its narrative construction. The sketches and *miniaturas* are told in an oblique, fragmented manner, often with little or no narratorial contextualization to determine the speaking character; readers are subsequently thrust into stream-of-consciousness narration that portrays the subjective experiences of the characters, who face alienation, marginalization, and outright violence at the hands of other Puerto Ricans as well as the police. But while a listing of the formal modernist characteristics would align the narrative squarely within a canonically modernist narrative, the specificity of their articulation points to an alternative formulation of literary modernism, one that eschews the universalist modernist experience of alienated humanity. Rather, *Spiks* suggests that the mid-1950s Nuyorican existence resides within an imposed, rather than autochthonous, modernity, whose colonial matrix intensifies the experience of community fragmentation, the subsequent alienation between individuals, and the resulting violence that erupts from such conditions.

The *miniaturas* function as near-instantaneous flashes of these moments in consciousness, providing fleeting glimpses into the subjective experience itself or its immediate aftermath. *Miniaturas* 1–3 show the bloody aftermath of embattled masculinities; in *Miniatura 3*, the disemboweling of Chano by the barber he insulted is depicted only by "whishwhash, whishwhash" of the barber's razor as it slices an "x across Chano's chest and belly" (48). *Miniaturas* 4–6 are given over to the social traps and swindles, some made by the dominant society but others made by Nuyoricans themselves, that typify the Puerto Rican immigrant's experience of New York. Most telling in the latter respect is *Miniatura 5*, in which the utter inadequacies of the public school system in educating the newcomers is ultimately not due to the lack of classroom discipline confronting the teacher's "porcelain face," but rather the subtractive schooling offered to the new arrivals. Emphasizing to her Puerto Rican students that their native Spanish is considered a learning deficit by the school system, the class instructor seeks to replace it with English-only language instruction. Seeking to teach "the sounds of English," the white teacher calls upon "Gorzia," prompting the derisive reply, "Y que Gorzia […] his name is García, teach!" Said-named student responds to his teacher's request in bilingual fashion: "García stood up, waited for the laughter to subside, and, hiding his impudence behind the pimples and blackheads on a face tanned by the sun, said: 'The soun [sic] of English is …' and in Spanish, 'the asshole of English!'" (62) García schools the teacher in the power of the powerless's laughter, scatologically associating English with fatuous school policy and thereby turning, if only momentarily, the power dynamic enacted by that policy on its head. The narrative powerfully suggests that the white privilege enacted by a racially inflected monolingualism within the U.S. public school system, and not the students' mother tongue, is what the teacher's "porcelain face" attempts, and fails, to enforce.

If the *miniaturas* offer glimpses into Nuyorican life, then the seven short stories of *Spiks* elaborate particular aspects of that life as they shape the subjective experiences of class, gender, and race under colonial modernity. As with *Miniatura 5*, "Bayaminiña" offers the most direct portrayal of how Puerto Rican immigrants are semi-incorporated into the lowest levels of New York's economic activity, a structural position that often leads to conflict with the police. Vacillating between unemployment and underemployment, Nuyoricans such as the cart vendor survive on the edges of the urban economic order selling "cod fritters, blood sausage, and banana fritters" without the costly Department of Health permit (59). Given a ticket and a court summons by a beat cop, the desperate vendor throws himself on the fragile, makeshift glass cart of glass, wood and tin, destroying his meager livelihood in an act of protest against the system that excludes him from the

American Dream. His plea of "Gimme a job, saramabich, gimme a job!" registers the fundamental contradiction of the Puerto Rican diaspora: migrating from an impoverished Island to the U.S. mainland for better economic opportunities only to find those opportunities even more circumscribed linguistically and racially in the midst of great wealth.

The other stories focus on the material and psychological tolls that life in New York City takes on Puerto Rican migrants of the 1950s. "The Innocents" tells the heartbreaking decision of one family to place a mentally disabled boy named Pipe in a mental institution after his mother and sister find themselves unable to watch and care for him due to the unfamiliar urban environment and long working hours. The breaking of familial ties in this manner would have been considered anathema on the Island, where an intimate village life would allow for the communal care of Pipe. In essence, the story illustrates some of the unintended consequences of migration for families and the psychological trauma that ensues from bowing to the pressures of urban life. Pipe's stream-of-consciousness ramblings sum up the dismay of "the innocent" (i.e., naïve) Puerto Rican migrants upon reaching New York: *"and there's no roosters and there's no dogs and there's no bells and there's no river wind and there's no movie buzzer and the sun doesn't come in here and I don't like [...] and the cold sleeps sits walks here inside and I don't like it"* (45) (italics in original). Pipe's mother sums up their experience in New York as the negation of life in Puerto Rico, saying wearily, "'In Puerto Rico this woudn' of happened'" (43).

Defined as a series of negations compared to Puerto Rico, the migrant experience of New York takes its toll on Puerto Rican masculinity in its never-ending frustration of male hopes, ambitions, and dreams. In "Champs," a sixteen-year-old outcast named Puruco hopes to make a big name for himself in the barrio by defeating the local gang's big shot, the pool shark Gavilán. While skilled, Puruco is naïve enough to believe that the contest isn't rigged in his opponent's favor, instead misconstruing Gavilán's nonchalance at losing a couple of games almost as badly as his own chances of winning within the gang's favorite hangout. Rather than recognize how the entire scenario is geared to guarantee his defeat, Puruco insists on viewing the match as an individualistic, meritocratic contest with the corresponding rewards that such street cred would bring, namely the reputation of being "the neighborhood macho, the man with a hand in everything – numbers, dope, the chick from Riverside Drive slumming in the barrio, the rumble between this gang and that to settle men's affairs" (65). The degree of his gullibility is underscored by his attribution of Gavilán sudden resurgence of skill to *bilongo*, or witchcraft. Contemptuously kicked out of the pool hall by his opponent, Puruco is left to regain his wounded masculinity through violence on those even less powerful than himself; slapping a young boy to the sidewalk for no reason, Puruco's snarled comment to his victim hints at the kind of masculinity he not only aspires to but has already performed: "'Wachout, man. I'll split yer eye'" (69).

Besides depicting the deformation of Nuyorican masculinity as the logical outcome of the collective misapprehension of a rigged system, other stories such as "Captive," "Absence," and "God in Harlem" focus on the resulting implications for relationships between men and women. Primarily told through female protagonists, all three narrate the dissolution of the Puerto Rican family as it lies at the intersection of the Island's colonial situation and the migrant's colonial citizenship in New York. The opening story of *Spiks*, "Captive" is the only one set in Puerto Rico, albeit in the diasporic space of San Juan's airport. Seventeen-year-old Fernanda is New York–bound, but not to search for a job; she is being sent by her mother for an extended visit with her brother in order to defuse the explosive familial conflict caused by her brief affair with her sister's husband. Even as Fernanda searches in vain for her unnamed lover in the crowded airport terminal, she holds onto the illusion that she can lure him away from her sister Inés. Only once the plane takes off does she realize, in an epiphany, not only the absurdity of her dream but also the profundity of her separation from the family and the Island to which she can never return, nor see in the same way again. Depicting this experience as a collective loss, the narrative includes overheard fragments of other migrant voices as they travel to New York in search of employment, to rejoin loved ones, or to report on the condition of Puertoriqueños there.

"Absence" and "God in Harlem" deal with the gritty and tragic experiences of Nuyorican women in their relationships with absent or abusive men. In the former story, Altagracia is haunted by the memory of her long-absent husband Mario, who abandoned her more than three years earlier after moving to New York. Driven to alcoholic despair, Altagracia neither holds a job nor leaves her apartment building; her despondent mother thinks that she *"looks more and more like a mummy every day"* (53) (italics in original). Altagracia speaks of the unseen spirit of her husband, who refuses to allow her to move on with her life after his abandonment because "'[h]e don' want no one to love me'" (51). The narrative hints that Mario's experiences as a conscripted soldier in the U.S. military during the Korean War has resulted in trauma that has rendered him incapable of performing the socially normative duties of a husband. Mario's wartime trauma manifests itself through a belligerent, jealous masculinity; Altagracia's drunken retelling of parties past to an empty room significantly includes episodes where Mario's own excessive drinking has lead to fits of rage over the attention his wife received from other men. In this sense, Altagracia's own alcoholism and mental illness, brought about by his abandonment of her, makes her another casualty of that conflict and the U.S. colonial policies that forced Puertoriqueño men onto the Cold War battlefield.

The closing story of *Spiks*, "God in Harlem," recounts a sex worker's attempts to find social redemption and acceptance through an unplanned, and initially unwanted, pregnancy. While in a drunken state, twenty-two-year-old Nena is impregnated by the slick but vicious Microbio [Microbe], whose very name suggests his malevolent existence on the streets as a con man and petty criminal. While Nena recognizes Microbio's insufficient maturity to assume the role of a father, she nonetheless demands financial assistance from him after she rules out an abortion out of fear of the then-illegal, and therefore highly risky, procedure. After religious flyers start mysteriously appearing all over town, including one announcing the arrival of the Apocalypse on "NEXT SUNDAY, 11 A.M. 114 ST. & MADISON AVE," Nena grows increasingly obsessed with envisioning the destruction of the current world and its rebirth, a vision that parallels her own hopes that parenthood will set her, and perhaps even Microbio, into a new, more respectable life (86).

Microbio himself professes to be a changed man, but this turns out to be a ruse to dupe Nena out of her cash savings. When Nena confronts a drunken Microbio about this latest con, the latter beats the expectant mother so hard that the fetus dies as a result. Despondent about the death of her unborn child and her dreams of transformation, Nena attends the advertised coming of God, only to find a street preacher vying against the jeers of the unbelieving crowd that has come to mock him. Still carrying the now-dead fetus in her womb, Nena insists to them that "'God-is-here God-is-here God-is-here,'" knowing "neither pain, nor hate, nor bitterness" as "[s]he is being born" (92). These last lines of the story are not as much a repudiation of either the hapless street preacher's hope of religious salvation or the hostile crowd's sarcastic skepticism as they are a firsthand account of the birth of Nuyorican modernity. Drawing parallels to the Irish modernity that, as William Butler Yeats envisioned in "The Second Coming," roughly "slouche[d] towards Bethlehem to be born," Soto casts Nuyorican modernity's harsh, irony-laced birth in Harlem as portending an intensification of colonial trauma for Puerto Ricans in the diaspora, defined by the exploitation of migrant labor, the destruction of traditional cultural values and rural family life, and the escalation of violence in everyday life. This profoundly pessimistic view of the Puerto Rican diasporic experience typifies the view of the nationalist literary writers of la Generacíon del '40 [the Generation of 1940] such as Soto and Marqués. Nuyorican writers of memoirs of the same era, such as Luisa Capetillo, Jesús Colón, and Bernardo Vega, affirm the lasting contributions of Puerto Ricans despite their colonial citizenship, a stance taken up by the literary authors of the Boricua Movement and beyond. In a move that signaled this subsequent generation's intent not only to reverse the effects of U.S. colonialism on Puertoriqueños but also to highlight the resiliency and creativity of the diaspora, Tato Laviera gave his landmark 1979 collection of poetry the title of *La Carreta Made a U-Turn*.

Conclusion

The Latina/o literature in the period from the Great Depression through the early Cold War era critically interrogates the conditions of colonial modernity foisted on the Mexican Americans and Puerto Ricans, albeit with crucial differences in the ways each community experienced the cultural displacements and deterritorialization generated by settler colonialism in the U.S. Southwest and administrative colonialism's economic policies in Puerto Rico. In both instances, Mexican American and Puerto Rican writers not only chronicled the disintegrative and uneven effects of modernity but also called for communal responses to such conflicts, including the formation of social movements such as the League of United Latin American Citizens (LULAC), which fought for Mexican American civil rights on the specific basis of U.S. citizenship. If such antiracist strategies failed to address the peculiarly colonial nature of that racialization, or the transnational configuration of the communities involved, nonetheless such movements demonstrated that Latinas/os did not let the ravages of modernity go unchallenged.

Likewise, the Mexican American and Puerto Rican literature of this period would, in criticizing the colonial present, lay the imaginative groundwork for engaging colonial modernity in ways in dialog with, but distinct from, the cosmopolitan literary modernism of the same period. If the latter focused on the generalized experience of the fragmentation and alienation of the individual as modernity affected the white urban elites of Europe and the United States, the former highlighted the fragmentation and social marginalization of racialized working-class communities as colonial modernity fundamentally altered the terms of their existence. Simultaneously, if works of canonical literary modernism introduced a new aesthetic vocabulary through which to describe the cosmopolitan experience of modernity, then the Latino/a literary works of this period likewise developed innovative forms and bilingual/bicultural narration to aesthetically engage the partial, incomplete, or alternative modernities created by coloniality and the collective response of Latinas/os to it. While less known than the literature produced by the Chicano and Boricua movements of the late 1960s and the early 1970s, not to mention the Latina/o literature produced after that, the

Mexican American and Puerto Rican literature of the 1930s through the 1950s reveals critical engagements with social and aesthetic questions that have yet to be fully explored.

Works Cited

González, Jovita, and Eve Raleigh (Margaret Eimer). *Caballero: A Historical Novel.* College Station: Texas A&M University Press, 1996.

Marqués, René. *The Oxcart (La Carreta).* Translated by Charles Pilditch. New York: Charles Scribner's Sons, 1969.

Paredes, Américo. *George Washington Gómez: A Mexicotexan Novel.* 2nd ed. Houston, TX: Arte Público Press, 1993.

Soto, Pedro Juan. *Spiks.* Translated by Victoria Ortiz. New York: Monthly Review Press, 1973.

Villarreal, José Antonio. *Pocho.* New York: Anchor, 1989.

PART II
Latina/o Literature Since 1960

4

RICHARD T. RODRÍGUEZ

The Aesthetics of Politics: Cultural Nationalist Movements and Latina/o Literature

In her contribution to a guidebook for black writers published in 1975, titled *A Capsule Course in Black Poetry Writing*, renowned African American poet Gwendolyn Brooks reflects on the heady years that gave rise to a discernable and decidedly black literary culture:

> 1966. 1967. 1968. Years of explosion. In those years a young black with pen in hand responded not to pretty sunsets and the lapping lake water but to the speech of physical riot and spiritual rebellion. Young blacks went to see *The Battle of Algiers* rather than the latest Rock Hudson movie. Young blacks stopped saluting Shakespeare, A.E. Housman, T.S. Eliot. They began to shake hands with Frantz Fanon, Malcolm X – gulping down the now "classic" *The Wretched of the Earth*, the *Autobiography* and *Message to the Grass Roots*. And after such seeing, after such gulping, there *had* to be a Difference. There had to be hard reckonings. There had to be an understanding that NOW the address must be to blacks; that shrieking into the steady and organized deafness of the white ear was frivolous – perilously innocent; was "no 'count." There were things to be said to black brothers and sisters and these things – annunciatory, curative, inspiring – were to be said forthwith, without frill, and without fear of the white presence.[1]

With her insistence that "black life is different from white life," Brooks spotlights an anti-assimilationist discourse that can also be detected in a body of Latina/o literature emerging during and around the same historical moment.[2] Indeed, young Chicana/o and Puerto Rican writers forcefully took the task the normalizing tenets of white American culture and promoted a counter-hegemonic politics that was simultaneously about affirmation and resistance. Speaking of the activists who belonged to these movements as a whole, political theorist Cristina Beltrán notes that "[b]ringing together a paradoxical mix of cultural nationalism, liberal reformism, radical critique, and romantic idealism, the Chicano and Puerto Rican movements created a new political vocabulary, one emphasizing resistance, recognition, cultural pride, authenticity, and fraternity (*hermanidad*). The movements – organizations, issues, and events – left a profound legacy."[3] With a focus on the cultural workers both directly and indirectly involved in these movements, I argue that novelists, playwrights, and poets in particular contributed to this "new political vocabulary." Moreover, rather than reflect on the various aesthetic principles based on form and stylistic technique adopted by a range of Latina/o authors, this essay maintains that Chicana/o (or Mexican American) and Puerto Rican (or Boricua) writers during the 1960s and 1970s engaged with an aesthetics of politics – or, in other words, how political action decisively contours the terms of expressive content – seeking to represent and mobilize their respective communities.[4]

For French theorist Jacques Rancière, "'aesthetic practices'," or "forms of visibility that disclose 'artistic practices'," "'do' or 'make' from the standpoint of what is common to the community." Such artistic practices for Rancière are additionally significant for "the relationships they maintain to modes of being and forms of visibility" (8).[5] Indeed, "modes of being and forms of visibility" for Chicana/o and Puerto Rican writers during the civil rights and cultural empowerment era dovetailed with the cultural nationalist sentiment informing social movements aiming to appraise and confirm collective history and struggle. While there are many thematic currents comprising the politicized aesthetics informing Latina/o literary production at this given moment, here I elaborate on the rejection of assimilation into mainstream U.S. society, the contestation of racism through racial-ethnic self-consciousness, and the claims to space and place for formulating collective experience. These particular themes are informed by and convey the emergent cultural nationalisms predicated on the struggle for social justice.

Staging Affirmation

To fully understand the discourses of affirmation and resistance in 1960s and 1970s Latina/o literature, one must acknowledge the intellectual and literary precursors who paved the way for later generations of activist-writers. In a speech delivered to the Associated Press in 1936, political figure, writer, and attorney Pedro Albizu Campos waxed poetic about the independence of Puerto Rico from the United States and the attendant necessity of Puerto Rican nationalism. According to Albizu Campos (whose consciousness was ignited after subjection to racism as a soldier in the U.S. Army during World War I and as a law student at Harvard University), "It stands to reason – it stands to common sense – that we must be a free nation in order to survive as a people. The future of those not yet born depends on respecting the independence of Puerto Rico. That respect alone – the respecting of Puerto Rico's independence – is what Puerto Rican nationalism is all about."[6] Crucial for defining the terms of debate regarding the Island's need for independent status or, alternatively, its dependence on the United States as a territory, state, or commonwealth, Albizu Campos's words also served as a source of influence for Puerto Ricans on the mainland. To be sure, the naming of Puerto Rican nationalism and its collectively felt affective energies would prove essential to foment a growing cultural and political awareness during the 1960s and 1970s in places like New York City and Chicago.

For Chicana/o writers, the Mexican Revolution of 1910 – with its heroic male figures like Emiliano Zapata and Francisco "Pancho" Villa – would serve as a source of cultural nationalist inspiration. Likewise, the Partido Liberal Mexicano (PLM), an anarchist group cofounded by Ricardo Flores Magón and an indelibly motivating force for the Revolution, was adopted by Chicana/o activists and served as, according to historian Emma Pérez, "a foundation for contemporary Chicano nationalist discourse."[7] Exemplary of this point is how the PLM's symbol – featuring a muscular shirtless man holding a flag that reads "Tierra y Libertad" – appeared on the back cover of the early issues of the Chicano studies journal *Aztlán*, whose first issue appeared in 1970.

While she does not connect Albizu Campos to the writers she identifies as charting a "'New School' of cultural intellectual politics" or a "Nuyorican Renaissance," literary critic Lisa Sánchez González understands the later generation of essayists, poets, novelists, playwrights, and journalists as "characteristically concerned with social justice" and "discourses of anticolonial resistance and civil rights." Rightly observing how "these writers represent a vast range of lifestyles and varied perspectives, the primary underlying concern among them as a group is the construction, through literature, of Boricua cultural citizenship as an organic – and organically resistant – North American formation."[8] Indeed, as a result of decades of social and economic disparagement after their migration from the Island, Puerto Rican writers assisted in flipping the script on their portrayal by the dominant culture by foregrounding quotidian struggles that were either maligned or ignored. Furthermore, despite their supposed ability to lay claim to rights as citizens, Puerto Ricans, like Chicanas/os born in the United States, were more often than not granted second-class status due to racial and ethnic difference.

Sánchez González singles out two texts exemplifying the "new Boricua literary sensibility": Piri Thomas's autobiographical novel *Down These Mean Streets* (1967) and Nicholasa Mohr's novel *Nilda* (1973). "As civil rights-era fictions," she argues, "both novels explore how the Boricua community responded to the tremendous historical shifts that occurred during the postwar period in the continental United States."[9] While both

Down These Mean Streets and *Nilda* richly detail the histories of Puerto Ricans in New York City since the first half of the twentieth century, the publication of these books during the late 1960s and early 1970s provided their then-contemporary readers with a deep sense of knowledge pertaining to racial, class, and gender inequality. This in turn would ignite a Boricua consciousness shaped by historical awareness and therefore inspiring attention paid to the enduring discrepancies within the Puerto Rican diaspora.[10]

Self-identified Chicano writers Rudolfo Anaya and Tomás Rivera, like Nicholasa Mohr and Piri Thomas, keyed in to the pressing community issues that helped scaffold a literary tradition charged by a political aesthetic fashioned by struggle. Rivera's ... *y no se lo tragó la tierra/And the Earth Did Not Part* (1971), a series of fourteen vignettes about lives of migrant workers who bear the harsh realties of toiling in the fields of Texas and in the Midwest, illustrates the physical and psychological traumas associated with backbreaking fieldwork while gesturing to the potential for collective uplift in the face of labor oppression. Rivera's narrator, most likely a reflection of Rivera's own life as a young migrant worker, provides the text's focalization by which an anti-assimilative and communally empowering literary chronicle surfaces. Anaya's *Bless Me, Ultima* (1972), with its young protagonist Antonio functioning in a similar fashion to Rivera's narrator, incorporates various indigenous and spiritual elements (such as *curanderismo*) prominently featured in the work of many Latina/o novelists, poets, and playwrights.

Other Chicano writers – Oscar "Zeta" Acosta, Miguel Mendez, and Rolando Hinojosa-Smith, among many more – would similarly publish works that forcefully made the case for a literary politic that defied the dominant social order. Whether foregrounding the experiences of the assimilated-cum-politicized Mexican American (Acosta's *The Autobiography of a Brown Buffalo* [1972] and *Revolt of the Cockroach People* [1973]), undocumented workers on the U.S.-Mexico border (Mendez's *Peregrinos de Aztlán/Pilgrims of Aztlán*, 1974), or racial violence in the lower Rio Grande Valley of Texas (Hinojosa-Smith's *Estampas del Valle y otras obras/ Sketches of the Valley and Other Works*, 1973), early Chicano literature (that is, literary texts that were identified as part of a Chicano agenda) signaled an aesthetic that was unapologetically intent on upholding a politically attentive cultural discourse.

As the era witnessed an increasing demand for narratives of collective consciousness, Latina/o writers and activists sought earlier published texts that matched their goals and ambitions. For example, Piri Thomas credits Pedro Juan Soto's 1956 collection of stories *Spiks* (written in Spanish but translated and published in English in 1973) as a necessary early book that spoke to the lives of Puerto Ricans in "Nueva Yawk." (In an interview, Thomas questions why Soto isn't given his due credit: "Why don't they mention his name as one of the fine pioneers?")[11] In the Chicana/o context, José Antonio Villarreal's 1959 novel *Pocho* was embraced by some as a literary antecedent despite the author's resistance to this categorization. After the book's initial publication, a trade paperback edition of *Pocho* was published in 1970 by Doubleday/Anchor, most likely to meet the demand for Chicana/o literature generated by the sweeping momentum of the Movement at the time. In an introduction to the 1970 edition (which Villarreal would soon denounce and thus understandably cut from the subsequent 1989 edition), historian Ramón E. Ruiz writes: "In the literature of the American Southwest, *Pocho* merits special distinction. Its author is the first man of Mexican parents to produce a novel about the millions of Mexicans who left their fatherland to settle in the United States. Not until 1970 did another Mexican-American duplicate this feat."[12] Observant to the fact that Villarreal is quite like his novel's protagonist and writes from the "motherland" of the United States about those who, unlike himself, hail from the "fatherland" of Mexico, Ruiz, however, accuses Villarreal of failing to highlight in the novel the racism experienced by Mexican Americans. Running counter to how the book would supposedly link up to the goals and revolutionary spirit of the movement, Ruiz questions the novel's ability to appropriately feed into the cultural nationalist principles of the Chicana/o community.[13]

A Poetics of Resistance

Aside from the prose work penned by then-contemporary Latina/o writers and the various literary forerunners writers and scholars wished to embrace as part of an aesthetic-political project, the poetry surfacing during the 1960s and 1970s would not only overlap with the various Latina/o movements but would often develop within them. Indeed, a poetics of resistance would lead to the proliferation of verse with cultural nationalist leanings.[14] Impoverished neighborhoods, racism in education, overrepresentation in prison, the disproportionate numbers of Latinos drafted in the Vietnam War, and job discrimination were some of the many reasons why Puerto Rican and Chicana/o activists – from New York to Los Angeles, Denver to Chicago – put pen to paper.

A range of Latina/o social movements jump-started across the country reflecting the concerns of their respective local constituencies.[15] For Chicanas/os, the movement was symbolized by organizations like the United

Farm Workers (UFW), United Mexican American Students (UMAS), the Crusade for Justice, and the paramilitary group known as the Brown Berets. For Puerto Ricans, the Young Lords (or the Young Lords Organization or the Young Lords Party) represented the nationalist goal of communal liberation. The Young Lords originated in Chicago as a street gang before developing into an organization, committed to fighting for Puerto Rican self-determination and collective sustenance, which soon migrated east to New York City. According to its Minister of Defense David Pérez, the group's "cry is a very simple and logical one. Puerto Ricans came to this country hoping to get a decent job and to provide for their families, but it didn't take long to find out that the amerikkkan dream that was publicized so nicely on our island, turned out to be the amerikkkan nightmare."[16] Understandably, the 1971 organization-penned book *Palante: The Young Lords Party* was dedicated to "Don Pedro Albizu Campos, the President of the Nationalist Party, who from the 1920s to his death in 1965, carried the message of freedom throughout the nation."[17]

In his riveting memoir, Young Lord Miguel "Mickey" Melendez recounts the organization's 1969 occupation of the First Spanish Methodist Church of East Harlem, renamed "the First People's Church," to demand space in the building to provide programs and services for the local community. The church would take on a "new role as the social, cultural, and political center of El Barrio" not only because of events such as a screening of Gino Pontecorvo's influential film *The Battle of Algiers* (presented by none other than Budd Schulberg and Elia Kazan) but also because it was where "for the first time many of us heard our generation's poet laureate Pedro Pietri's 'Puerto Rican Obituary'."[18] It was here, in 1969, that Pietri first read his moving poem, and it would thereafter continue to operate as a clarion call for mobilizing Puerto Rican activists.

"Puerto Rican Obituary" is a poignant reflection on the trials and tribulations faced by Puerto Ricans migrants in the face of racism and economic disenfranchisement in the United States. It pivots on the experiences of five individuals – Juan, Miguel, Milagros, Olga, and Manuel – forced to live and die day after day and thus cast as the undead in a country that has consigned them to a perpetual dead-end existence. Yet the poem aspires to turn the tables on U.S. colonialism by asserting the life-sustaining worth of Puerto Rico, the indigenous, African roots of Puerto Ricans, and life-saving potential of one's cultural heritage required for escaping the dilemmas faced by the poem's five destitute subjects. Insisting on "The geography of their complexion/PUERTO RICO IS A BEAUTIFUL PLACE/PUERTORRIQUENOS ARE A BEAUTIFUL RACE," the poem props up Juan, Miguel, Milagros, Olga, and Manuel as victims of colonialism who might have lived "If only they/Had used the white/supremacy bibles/For toilet paper purpose/And made their Latin Souls/The only religion of their race."[19]

Puerto Rican writer Miguel Piñero's poem, "Declaration 1968," also makes clear how poverty, social marginalization, and racial oppression served as catalysts for fueling consciousness and mobilization. Beginning from childhood, the narrator recounts the various reasons that lead to the keen awareness of personal and communal subjugation.

> This child ...
> this child felt the cold storms of winter
> on those hot summer days ...
> this child went hungry on the banquet table
> of the church ...
> this child played with roaches and rats for pets
> and found her sister lying dead
> beneath a bottle cap ...
> YES, MOTHERFUCKERS, I AM MILITANT

The poem further details the immediate loss of innocence and its attendant childhood psychological damage ("this child was innocent/of the big money plays/was ignorant of the teachers'/racist ways") while interrupting this recounting with two additional boldfaced declarations ("YES, I AM A RADICAL" and "YES, YOU DEGENERATE MOTHERFUCKERS, I AM A REVOLUTIONARY") to provide the necessary evidence for illustrating how an activist is formed and fashioned.

Similar to Pietri's and Piñero's poems, Rodolfo "Corky" Gonzales's "I am Joaquín" is indebted to the nationalist, revolutionary discourses espoused by the movement to which it is aligned.[20] Indeed, Gonzales – a former boxer and Democratic Party advocate turned radical activist – was a key organizer of the Denver-based Crusade for Justice. According to Chicano movement scholar Carlos Muñoz, Jr., "In 1967 [Gonzales] wrote an epic poem entitled *I Am Joaquín*, which was distributed to the UMAS, MASC and MAYO student leadership throughout the Southwest by La Causa Publications in Oakland, California. This poem was published in book form in 1972. *I Am Joaquín* did not offer its readers a well-defined radical ideology, but it did provide a critical framework for the developing student movement through its portrayal of the quest for identity and its critique of racism."[21]

Whereas Gonzales's instructive essay "Chicano Nationalism: The Key to Unity for La Raza" might be said to offer the "well-defined radical ideology" Muñoz renders absent in the poem, Gonzales's epic poem indeed subscribed to the belief in cultural nationalism's utmost importance for collective liberation. This is evident in final lines of the poem, as the nominal subject of the poem, "Joaquín," ultimately functions as the vehicle through which the community must mobilize:

> I am the masses of my people and
> I refuse to be absorbed.
>   I am Joaquín.
> The odds are great
> but my spirit is strong,
>   my faith unbreakable,
>   my blood is pure.
> I am Aztec prince and Christian Christ.
>   I SHALL ENDURE!
>   I WILL ENDURE![22]

Furthermore, one can also point to the document *El Plan Espiritual de Aztlan*, often referred to as "The Chicano Movement Manifesto," which was penned by three poets – Gonzales, Alurista, and Juan Gómez-Quiñones – for evidence of the literary impulse of cultural nationalism, or what I've identified as the aesthetics of politics.

Cultural nationalism has plausibly undergone critique for the ways it often assumes male-centered, patriarchal, and heteronormative prerogatives. Yet that did not deter Chicanas from also penning poems akin to Gonzales's. Take as a case in point Margarita Virginia Sánchez's 1973 poem, "Escape."

> Last week,
> I had been white
> … we were friends.
>
> Yesterday,
> I was Spanish
> … we talked …
> once in a while.
>
> Today
> I am a Chicano
> … you do not know me.
>
> Tomorrow,
> I rise to fight
> … and we are enemies.[23]

Written when Sánchez was only thirteen years old, "Escape" indexes how the Chicano movement infused youth with a political sensibility that countered the expectation of racial self-hatred to instead embraced a new racialized political project. Rejecting the labels "white" and "Spanish" – the former an accommodation to the dominant Anglo culture and the latter a more suitable identification that refuses a historically shamed identity like

"Mexican" – reveals the narrator's desire to embrace the re-signified and intentionally confrontational, anti-assimilationist, and counter-establishment term "Chicano." And yet one suspects, given the presumption of masculinist identification required by a large segment of movement leadership (the precedence of "o" over the feminine "a"), that Sánchez is unable to explicitly identify as a "Chicana."

Indeed, the spirit of cultural nationalism left little room for contradiction and often depended on binary oppositions ("us" versus "them") to frame what was deemed the discourse of revolution. Luis Valdez's 1967 one-act play, *Los Vendidos* and Sacramento-based Chicano poet José Montoya's 1969 poem, "El Vendido," thus cast the "sell-out" or "traitor" as soulless and absorbed by a culture of individuality and nothingness. Montoya fittingly begins his poem about el vendido by classifying him as a "Blunt, dull pain." Yet it is this pain that the narrator deeply feels for it represents the betrayal of his people and a rich, revolutionary history:

> Bequeathing penitence
> Upon my sanguine hopes
> Sorry remnants of
> Once regal Dons
> Yet earlier Yaquis
>
> Vestiges fading fast
>
> From the pain
> That hurts my Raza
> Concerned now
> With boats in the
> Driveway, the Boy Scouts
>
> And the World Series

The threat of assimilation looms large in Montoya's poem, as the seductive lure of a whitewashing popular culture has eclipsed the memory of one's royal historical genealogy.[24] For Chicanas, the refusal to subscribe to this genealogy by assuming a back-seat role to men is grounds for classification as a *malinchista*, a traitor to "La Raza" whose betrayal is likened to the betrayal of Malintzin Tenepal (or La Malinche) for purportedly selling out her people as the mistress and translator of Spanish colonizer Hernán Cortes.[25]

Despite the precarious roles women played on the stage of movement militancy, they also turned supposedly revolutionary discourses on their head by addressing the men in the movement who were ostensibly entitled to women's sexuality. This is clear in Lorna Dee Cervantes's poem, "You Cramp My Style, Baby."

> You cramp my style, baby
> when you roll on top of me
> shouting, "Viva La Raza"
> at the top of your prick.
>
> You want me como un taco,
> dripping grease,
> or squeezing masa through my legs,
> making tamales for you
> out of my daughters.
>
> You "míja"
> "míja" "míja" me
> until I can scream
>
> and then you tell me,
> "Esa, I LOVE
> this revolution!
> Come on Malinche
> gimme some more!"[26]

Scholars like Dionne Espinoza, Maylei Blackwell, and María Cotera have recently observed in their work on feminism and the Chicana/o movement that women not only fought to carve out spaces within male-dominant organizations during the 1960s and 1970s; they also parted ways with these groups to create alternative movements for which gender egalitarianism was not at odds with the desire for Chicana/o empowerment and liberation.

A Place for Us

While cultural nationalism need not always find itself tethered to an actual physical location, Chicanas/os and Puerto Ricans did in fact pinpoint both "homelands" to which one may harken back as well as institutions where creative self-expression was realized. Given how a common bond between Chicanas/os and Puerto Ricans is spatial displacement due to political and economic tyranny (within the United States and their respective lands of origin – Mexico and Puerto Rico), Latina/o writers took to embracing the mythical native soils of their people – Aztlán and Borinquen, respectively – while attempting to determine by their own accord the institutions for demarcating their contemporary experiences. Aztlán, the legendary homeland of the Aztecs thought to coincide with the current U.S. Southwest, is the symbolic location mapped by spiritual and topographical coordinates in which Chicana/o identity is often anchored. The adjective "'Boricua,'" according to Lisa Sánchez González, "references the indigenous (Taíno) name of Puerto Rico's main island, Borinquén."[27] Similar to Aztlán,

Borinquén was the location par excellence for affixing indigenous (in this case Taíno) histories.

Although literary texts that conveyed a cultural nationalist disposition may have originated as orally transmitted or published in mimeograph form, major New York publishing houses like Bantam Books and Vintage Books (subsidiaries of Random House) took note of the demand for literary texts to furnish the historical and cultural frameworks in which to situate new Chicana/o and Puerto Rican social movements. Fittingly, two anthologies published by Vintage Books – *Aztlán: An Anthology of Mexican American Literature*, edited by Luis Valdez and Stan Steiner and published in 1972; and *Borinquen: An Anthology of Puerto Rican Literature*, edited by María Teresa Babín and Stan Steiner and published in 1974 – met the demands for cultural nationalist principles by publishing both precolonial contact documents alongside explicitly literary pieces focused on contemporary cultural and political phenomena.

Because institution building was essential for carving out spaces for Latinas/os, Chicanas/os and Puerto Ricans also realized the need to create their own publishing houses and public settings for the reception of their work. Indeed, part and parcel of the militant ethos of cultural nationalism was the importance of creating counter-institutions for the publication and circulation of Latina/o literature. Initiated in 1967 by Octavio I. Romano-V., a professor at the University of California at Berkeley, Quinto Sol Publications was an independent publishing house that ushered forth foundational texts in Chicana/o literature, including none other than Anaya's *Bless Me, Ultima* and Tomás Rivera's *... y no se lo trago la tierra/... and the Earth Did Not Part*. As an institution, Quinto Sol not only published important literary texts but, as part of its wider project, fostered important social science–grounded scholarship (namely with the journal *El Grito: A Journal of Contemporary Mexican American Thought*) that challenged stereotypes and "historical distortions" about Mexican American and Latina/o populations in predominantly Anglo-penned scholarship. With *... y no se lo tragó la tierra/... and the Earth Did Not Part* and *Bless Me, Ultima* as the first two winners of the Premio Quito Sol, the press also published Hinojosa-Smith's aforementioned *Estampas del Valle y otras obras/Sketches of the Valley and Other Works* and Estela Portillo Trambley's *Rain of Scorpions and Other Writings* (1975).[28]

Established in the Lower East Side neighborhood of Manhattan, the Nuyorican Poets' Café functioned as a performance space for the recitation and dissemination of creative work generated by the local Latina/o community.[29] Founded and maintained by Pedro Pietri, Miguel Algarín, and Miguel Piñero, the café functioned as a democratic institution in which people of various walks of life could publicly share their work. But it was also the space in which a distinct Puerto Rican – or Nuyorican – aesthetic developed and gave rise to the notable talents of its founders and their associates.[30]

While this essay has been concerned with two distinct literary and cultural nationalist traditions, these traditions in no way existed in isolation from one another. In fact, Chicana/o and Puerto Rican writers were well aware of each other's work, drawing influence from the way their fellow Latina/o scribes sought to create spaces and places for the liberation of their constituencies. Furthermore, Chicana/o and Puerto Rican writers often recognized the geopolitical points of connection that bridged their work across physical expanses. For example, in his introduction to Miguel Algarín's book of poems *Time's Now/Ya es Tiempo*, Rudolfo Anaya writes: "[Algarín's] poems moved me, immediately. I write these notes as my response, because Miguel understood that the poem goes out to connect, to share, and if I as a Chicano from the Rio Grande could make the connection to his world, then he had built one more bridge, and now the isla of Manhattan was connected to the isla of Aztlán."[31] Like the Puerto Rican activists who attended the historic Denver Youth Conference organized by the Crusade for Justice and Chicana/o activists who visited Chicago to acquire strategies from Puerto Ricans involved with the Young Lords, Latina/o writers across the continent were attentive to and in productive dialog with each other.[32]

La Lucha Continua: The Lasting Impact of Narrating the Nation

It has almost become conventional in Latina/o literary and cultural studies to denounce the cultural nationalisms permeating the literary production of the 1960s and 1970s. As I have written elsewhere, the careless conflation of "nationalism" and "essentialism" has led to a dismissal of the advantageous features of narratives about communal empowerment.[33] Well aware of the way cultural nationalism can assume anti-feminist and anti-queer standpoints through an uncritical embrace of normative comprehensions of *la familia*, Chicana lesbian writer Cherríe Moraga argues, "What was right about Chicano nationalism was its commitment to preserving the integrity of the Chicano people."[34]

Additionally, cultural nationalism did not always lead to self-containment and result in the refusal to consider international or transnational matters. On the contrary, cultural Latina/o nationalist discourses were often in dialog with Third World thinkers (Puerto Rican poet Jesús Papoleto Meléndez writes of a "revolutionary sister" who's read "Mao & Marx, Che & Lenin") as well as writers of color from the United States.[35] In her 2011 study *Chicano Nations: The Hemispheric Origins of Mexican American Literature*, Marissa López argues that Chicana/o cultural nationalism is hardly a myopic construction given how it remarkably signals the dynamic interplay of national and spatial factors crucial for ascertaining the transnational and global underpinnings of Latina/o literary histories.

Hardly exempt from co-optation from multicultural marketing and adoption by mainstream presses for the sake of profit, the Chicana/o and Puerto Rican literature stemming from the 1960s and 1970s nonetheless represents an essential moment in the genealogy of Latina/o letters. For without its compelling calls to action through its unflinching claims to cultural nationalist beliefs, future generations of writers could not have found their voices given the tenacious hegemonic forces that are quick to disassociate politics from aesthetics and adamantly deny their inextricable affiliation.

Notes

1 Gwendolyn Brooks, Keorapetse Kgositsile, Haki R. Madhubuti, and Dudley Randall, *A Capsule Course in Black Poetry Writing* (Detroit, MI: Broadside Press, 1975), 3–4.
2 In *Next of Kin: The Family in Chicano/a Cultural Politics* (Durham, NC: Duke University Press, 2009), I maintain that the politicized sentiment emerging from a particular era cannot be contained by a rigid demarcation of time given the way that sentiment's energies not only develop from earlier moments but continue to seep into and inform the cultural sensibilities of future generations. For example, "the 60s" do not simply end with the start of the 1970s but persist in the form of an enduring cultural politics. While the years Brooks mentions are also pivotal for U.S. Latinas/os, this essay examines literary texts stemming from the late 1960s and proliferating into the late 1970s.
3 Cristina Beltrán, *The Trouble with Unity: Latino Politics and the Creation of Identity* (New York: Oxford University Press, 2010), 21.
4 A brief clarification on my use of terms is in order. While "Chicana/o" is often used interchangeably with "Mexican American," the former identity category represents a defiant stance toward assimilation (and usually understood as an adopted practice by the previous generation of people of Mexican descent born and/or raised in the United States) in favor of upholding the historical realities of *mestizaje* and indigeneity. Like "Chicana/o," "Boricua" might be understood as shorthand for Puerto Rican, but it also signals the reclamation of an indigenous past for Puerto Ricans in light of colonial amnesia.
5 Jacques Rancière, *The Politics of Aesthetics*, translated and edited by Gabriel Rockhill (London: Bloomsbury, 2013), 8.
6 Pedro Albizu Campos, "Puerto Rican Nationalism" (translated by Roberto Santiago), in *Boricuas: Influential Puerto Rican Writings – An Anthology* (New York: Ballantine Books, 1995), 29.
7 Emma Pérez, *The Decolonial Imaginary: Writing Chicanas into History* (Bloomington: Indiana University Press, 1999), 57.

8 Lisa Sánchez González, *Boricua Literature: A Literary History of the Puerto Rican Diaspora*, 103.
9 Ibid., 103.
10 See Humberto Cintrón, "Poet, Writer, a Voice for Unity: An Interview with Piri Thomas" in Andrés Torres and José E. Velázquez, ed., *The Puerto Rican Movement: Voices from the Diaspora* (Philadelphia: Temple University Press, 1998), 263–79, and "Pa'lante: An Interview with Nicholasa Mohr" in Bridget Kevane and Juanita Heredia, *Latina Self-Portraits: Interviews with Contemporary Women Writers* (Albuquerque: University of New Mexico Press, 2000), 83–96, for confirmation of how family and community histories in New York City would inspire and influence Thomas's and Mohr's foundational texts.
11 Humberto Cintrón, "Poet, Writer, a Voice for Unity: An Interview with Piri Thomas," 269.
12 José Antonio Villarreal, *Pocho* (Anchor/Doubleday, 1970), vii.
13 While beyond the purview of this essay, one might further consider the difficulty behind unearthing earlier literary texts to conceive of a genealogy of Latina/o letters that aims for an uncomplicated, seamless understanding of community coherence and shared cultural politics. Many scholars have addressed this very issue in relation to the Recovering the U.S. Hispanic Literary Heritage Project housed at the University of Houston.
14 For more on the Chicano and Puerto Rican movements, see, respectively, Carlos Muñoz, Jr., *Youth, Identity, Power: The Chicano Movement* (New York: Verso, 1989) and Andrés Torres and José E. Velázquez, ed., *The Puerto Rican Movement: Voices from the Diaspora* (Philadelphia: Temple University Press, 1998).
15 Though the demographics of distinct locations reflected the particular histories of migration (the East Coast with its predominantly Puerto Rican presence and the Southwest with a largely Mexican-origin populace), Chicago and various towns and cities in the Midwest boasted uniquely pan-Latina/o communities given how labor demands influenced overlapping migration patterns from Latin American and the Caribbean. Take, for example, Chicago-based Chicana writer Ana Castillo who writes of "the Latino movement that burned throughout the Midwest" during the 1970s. See Castillo's introduction to *My Father Was a Toltec* (New York: Anchor Books, 2004), xxii.
16 David Pérez, "Free Clothes for the People" (1970), in *The Young Lords Reader*, ed. Darrel Enck-Wanzer (New York: New York University Press, 2010), 219.
17 I cite here from the recent edition of *Palante*, published as *Palante: Voices and Photographs of the Young Lords, 1969–1971* (Chicago: Haymarket Books, 2011).
18 Miguel "Mickey" Melendez, *We Took the Streets: Fighting for Latino Rights with the Young Lords* (New York: St. Martin's Press, 2003), 126.
19 Pedro Pietri, "Puerto Rican Obituary," in *The Young Lords Reader*, 79.
20 I am referring to "I am Joaquín" here as a poem rather than a book (which it was published as in 1972 by Bantam Books). Similarly, "Puerto Rican Obituary" was published as an eponymously titled book in 1973 by Monthly Review Press, yet, unlike *I am Joaquín*, it also included additional poems.
21 Muñoz, Jr., *Youth, Identity, Power*, 60–61.
22 Rodolfo "Corky" Gonzales, *I am Joaquin/Yo Soy Joaquín* (New York: Bantam Books, 1972), 100.

23 Margarita Virginia Sánchez, "Escape," in *We Are Chicanos*, ed. Phillip Ortego (New York: Washington Square Press, 1973), 208.
24 José Montoya, "El Vendido," *In Formation: 20 Years of Joda* (San José, CA: Chusma House Publications, 1992), 2.
25 See Norma Alarcón, "Chicana's Feminist Literature: A Re-vision Through Malintzin/or Malintzin: Putting Flesh Back on the Object," in Cherríe Moraga and Gloria Anzaldúa, ed., *This Bridge Called My Back: Writings by Radical Women of Color* (New York: Kitchen Table Press, 1983), 182–90.
26 Lorna Dee Cervantes, "You Cramp My Style, Baby," *El Fuego de Aztlán*, 1:4 (Summer 1977): 39.
27 Lisa Sánchez González, *Boricua Literature*, 1.
28 Quinto Sol Publications would eventually become Tonatiuhl-Quinto Sol International Inc. (TQS Publications), which Romano oversaw until his death in 2005 at the age of eighty-two. For an excellent account of Quinto Sol, see John Alba Cutler's "Quinto Sol, Chicano/a Literature, and the Long March Through Institutions," *American Literary History*, 26:2 (Summer 2014): 262–94.
29 I use Latina/o here rather than Puerto Rican given the insights of the forthcoming work of Professor Karen Jaime from Cornell University who argues that the Nuyorican Poets' Café was since its inception a space that fostered pan-Latino, multiracial expressions.
30 For a sampling of representative writings, see *Nuyorican Poetry: An Anthology of Puerto Rican Words and Feelings*, ed. Miguel Algarín and Miguel Piñero (New York: William Morrow & Company, Inc., 1975).
31 Rudolfo Anaya, "On Time's Now," introduction to Miguel Algarín, *Time's Now/Ya es Tiempo* (Houston, TX: Arte Público Press, 1985).
32 For further evidence of these points, see Mirelsie Velazquez's groundbreaking essay "Solidarity and Empowerment in Chicago's Puerto Rican Print Culture," *Latino Studies*, 12:1 (Spring 2014): 88–110.
33 *Next of Kin: The Family in Chicano/a Cultural Politics* (Durham, NC: Duke University Press, 2009).
34 Cherríe Moraga, "Queer Aztlán: The Re-formation of Chicano Tribe," *The Last Generation* (Boston: South End Press, 1993), 148–49.
35 Jesús Papoleto Meléndez, "sister, para nuestras hermanas," in *Nuyorican Poetry*, 113.

5

RICARDO L. ORTÍZ

The Cold War in the Americas and Latina/o Literature

As early as 1950, the influential American political scientist and diplomat George F. Kennan wrote the following in an infamous "Memorandum" to then-U.S. Secretary of State Dean Acheson about U.S. policy toward Latin America in a still-emerging Cold War context: "The military significance to us of Latin American countries lies today ... importantly in the extent to which the attitudes of Latin American peoples may influence the general political trend in the international community," a trend which, in Kennan's eyes, could dangerously shift toward a greater sympathy for the Soviet and communist pole in the dialectical struggle for global supremacy between West and East. Kennan continued: "If ... the general pattern of allegiance of the Latin American countries to ourselves were to be seriously disturbed and a considerable portion of Latin American society were to throw its weight morally into the opposite camp, this, together with the initial military successes which the Russians would presumably have in Europe, might well turn the market of international confidence against us and leave us fighting not only communist military power, but a wave of defeatism among our friends and spiteful detraction among our enemies elsewhere in the world" (599–600). Kennan wrote his "Memorandum" after a brief trip to various parts of South America to assess both the political and cultural climate of the continent's wide variety of societies and peoples with respect to looming geopolitical conditions. It matters that Kennan's analysis focuses as explicitly as it does on questions of mass sentiment and psychology: his concerns are with the direction in which peoples of the continent might throw their "moral weight," and what that might in turn do to a "market of international confidence" susceptible to "waves" of "defeatism" or "spiteful detraction," and on the part of other global actors in the moment lined up either for or against U.S. interests, interests that were cultural and social, perhaps even moral and spiritual, as well as economic, political, and military.

While Kennan's initial argument suggests some genuine respect for the sovereign will and legitimacy of claims to self-determination among the

United States' sibling republics in the New World, much of his commentary in the rest of his "Memorandum" reveals more candidly the by turns patronizing and cynical nature of U.S. foreign policy toward the region in the decades to follow. "It seems to me unlikely," he confessed to Acheson, "that there could be any other region of the earth in which nature and human behavior could have combined to produce a more unhappy and hopeless background for the conduct of human life than in Latin America" (600). Based on the litany of similarly egregious and unflattering generalizations that follow this opening, Kennan concludes that while sincere, nonviolent attempts to win over minds and hearts of its Latin American neighbors' citizens should be the United States' priority, "where the concepts and traditions of popular government are too weak to absorb the intensity of communist attack, then we must concede that harsh governmental measures of repression may be the only answer; that these measures may have to proceed from regimes whose origins and methods would not stand the test of American concepts of democratic procedure; and that such regimes and such methods may be preferable alternatives, and indeed the only alternatives, to further communist successes" (607); and given, finally, that for Latin America "the danger of a failure to exhaust the possibilities of our mutual relationship is always greater to them than it is to us," Kennan concludes that "we can afford to wait, patiently and good-naturedly," for geopolitical rapprochement because "we are more concerned to be respected than to be liked or understood" (622).

Kennan's "Memorandum" thus stands as a cornerstone, blueprint, and rationale for much of the history of the geopolitical drama that would unfold in the Western Hemisphere largely but not exclusively as a function of the United States' Cold War–inflected foreign policy in the region. In quick succession in the course of the following decades, Kennan's thinking resonates through the events typically invoked as defining of U.S.–Latin American relations in the mid- and late twentieth century. This list includes the 1954 ouster via CIA-backed coup-d'état of Jacobo Arbenz, the democratically elected president of Guatemala; the extensive series of attempts (including, among other strategies, embargo, invasion, and assassination) since 1959 to limit the influence, stability, and longevity of Fidel Castro's communist revolution in Cuba; the 1972 ouster in another CIA-sponsored coup of socialist President Salvador Allende in Chile; the installation of brutally, murderously repressive military dictatorships, such as Augusto Pinochet's in Chile and neighboring countries of the Southern Cone; the aggressive reaction in Central America to the ascendance of Nicaragua's Sandinista party after the 1979 overthrow of the U.S.-friendly dictator Anastasio Somoza (a reaction that led to the installation of violent and repressive military juntas in such countries as El Salvador and Guatemala to quell similar popular and indigenous insurgencies there in the 1980s, and to the financing, equipping, and training of anti-Sandinista "contra" forces in the countries neighboring Nicaragua); and the decades-long willingness to tolerate additional bloody, repressive, kleptocratic dictatorships like those of Rafael Trujillo in the Dominican Republic from the 1930s to the 1950s and the Duvaliers, father and son, in Haiti from the 1950s to the 1980s. As this inventory of the proxy "wars" (international and civil) fought in the New World under the geopolitical aegis of the Cold War suggests, most of these conflicts played out as a series of competitions mostly among differently authoritarian regimes, some siding with the United States, others with the Soviet Union, and usually with the better interests of the popular masses of their countries only indirectly or remotely in mind.

This decades-long dictatorial dialectic found a crystalizing articulation in the work of the political scientist Jeane Kirkpatrick, in many ways the intellectual heir of George Kennan, and an architect of the Reagan administration's foreign policy in the last decade of the Cold War. In her famous 1979 essay, "Dictatorships and Double Standards," Kirkpatrick distinguishes between "traditional" autocracies friendly to the United States and "revolutionary" autocracies friendly to the other side, offering a series of rationales and alibis favoring U.S. tolerance of the former, regardless of the degree to which such autocracies repressed their own people. "From time to time," Kirkpatrick observes at one point, "a truly bestial ruler can come to power in either type of autocracy – Idi Amin, Papa Doc Duvalier, Joseph Stalin, Pol Pot are examples – but neither type regularly produces such moral monsters ... There are, however, *systemic* differences between traditional and revolutionary autocracies that have a predictable effect on their degree of repressiveness. Generally speaking, traditional autocrats tolerate social inequities, brutality and poverty, whereas revolutionary autocracies create them" (49). In the thirty years separating Kirkpatrick's statement from Kennan's, one might detect a significant refinement in the rhetoric that rationalizes the more palatable tendency among "traditional autocrats" to "tolerate" rather than to "create ... social inequities, brutality and poverty," but such a formula significantly fails to describe the known historical legacies of a Trujillo or a Pinochet, or of the pro-U.S. juntas in Argentina, Guatemala, or El Salvador. Kirkpatrick's account of the political situation in Latin America nevertheless directly influenced U.S. foreign policy through the end of the Reagan administration's years in power, and through the end of the Cold War.

One hears, for example, in President Ronald Reagan's speech to the nation in May 1984 a more publicly accessible version of Kirkpatrick's refinement of Kennan. Early in the speech Reagan sounds an almost dove-ish tone, declaring: "The defense policy of the United States is based on a simple premise: We do not start wars. We will never be the aggressor. We maintain our strength in order to deter and defend against aggression, to preserve freedom and peace. We help our friends defend themselves." In many ways the speech also reaffirms a benign vision of Pan-American unity in the ideals of national independence and republican democracy running through twentieth-century U.S. presidential speeches about Latin America, from Roosevelt's "Good Neighbor Policy" to Kennedy's "Alliance for Progress." "Central America," Reagan argues in 1984, "is a region of great importance to the United States. And it is so close: San Salvador is closer to Houston, Texas, than Houston is to Washington, DC. Central America is America. It's at our doorstep, and it's become the stage for a bold attempt by the Soviet Union, Cuba, and Nicaragua to install communism by force throughout the hemisphere." But by its conclusion, the speech comes back around to the central case it needs to make to finance the arming of the Salvadoran military to handle a native insurgency putatively backed by the governments of Cuba and Nicaragua: "As I talk to you tonight, there are young Salvadoran soldiers in the field facing the terrorists and guerrillas in El Salvador with the clips in their rifles the only ammunition they have. The lack of evacuation helicopters for the wounded and the lack of medical supplies if they're evacuated has resulted in one out of three of the wounded dying. This is no way to support friends, particularly when supporting them is supporting ourselves." The discursive elisions here are telling: a conflict pitting "soldiers" fighting heroically for a government named only as the U.S.'s "friends" against nameless "terrorists and guerrillas" whose only possible motives are "terror" and "war," does little to clarify the conditions under which the friendly government those soldiers are defending was installed, or to underscore the extreme "social inequities, brutality and poverty" that might have initially provoked a domestic insurgency on the part of populations who in Reagan's narrative only figure as violent agents of anarchy and crime.

Latino America and Latino American Literature of the Cold War

The politically complex and violently fluid set of conditions that characterize the "Cold War in the Americas" necessarily elude easy summary, and have been the subjects of endless and ongoing scholarly study and analysis. These conditions, among other consequences, resulted in dramatic forms of demographic displacement across the new world from the 1950s onward. Starting with the exile of individuals and families fleeing threats to their safety and their lives based on their opposition to various national regimes and opposition movements, and continuing through larger and more sustained forms of exodus of significant or even entire sectors of a society in response to political and economic changes, from revolution and programmatic repression to forms of currency and labor market collapse, in a variety of countries in the region, one powerful consequence of these conditions has been the increasing, intensifying, and diversifying of the process of "Latinizing" U.S. society and culture in the last half of the twentieth century. If in 1960 the Latin American–descended population of the United States was dramatically majority Mexican American and concentrated in the Southwest and West Coast, with a smaller percentage of mainland Puerto Ricans and others from the "hispanic" Caribbean living in the New York City area, by 2000 the Latino population very directly reflected the impact of the Cold War, especially in the Caribbean and Central American regions. During the 1960s, almost one million Cubans fled the Castro revolution, most of them settling in South Florida, followed in later decades by tens of thousands of their compatriots; Dominicans and Haitians initially left in smaller numbers to escape the Trujillo and Duvalier regimes, respectively, then migrated in much greater numbers, and mostly to New York and Florida, climbing in both cases into the hundreds of thousands, when those regimes collapsed, fleeing the societies and economies they had each so successfully ravaged; similar numbers fled extreme political violence and economic hardship in Guatemala and El Salvador, especially after 1980, thus diversifying the Latino population of the West Coast, especially in Los Angeles, and bringing an unprecedentedly large diasporic Latino presence to the Washington, DC, area. There were also smaller but still important emigrations out of a number of additional countries from the southern American hemisphere, including (in no particular order) Colombia, Venezuela, Nicaragua, and Brazil.

In the first decade of the twenty-first century, therefore, Latino America had been transformed (thanks in great part to some decidedly unintended consequences of U.S. Cold War policy) into a poly-cultural, poly-ethnic, poly-national amalgamation of distinct but melding and coalescing subgroups, all of them exercising transformative effects on most regions of the country, from the South to the Midwest to the Northwest, and from numerous rural and exurban areas to almost every major American metropolitan center: from Los Angeles, Miami, and New York to Chicago, San Francisco, Boston, Orlando, and Washington. Latino American reality therefore felt like an entirely different experience by the end of the twentieth century than it did in the years when modern Latino American critical and political consciousness first came into being; in the early to mid-1960s, as Chicano and Nuyorican civil rights movements first began to mobilize politically and to develop ideologically, the focus was understandably on immediate demands for social, political, and economic justice for the historically marginalized communities these movements represented, in time extending to more ambitious goals tied to Third World nationalist independence movements, and eventually to forging more consolidated forms of pan-Latino unity in the U.S. context. These dynamics also influenced the institutional establishment and rise of Chicano and Nuyorican studies programs in the 1960s and 1970s, which began their lives as interdisciplinary formations combining methodologies from the social sciences, history, the humanities, and the arts in order to fashion what became, in the following decades, influential disciplinary formations like critical race studies, ethnic studies, and certain forms of cultural studies. Simultaneously, emergent forms of both Latina/o literary practice and Latina/o literary studies began to, on the one hand, render and explore more fully the Latino experience in all the imaginative, expressive, and aesthetic registers available in literature, and, on the other, to organize critical and scholarly projects to shape the various histories of those practices into reliably and institutionally knowable and teachable formations.

Ironically, however, while the work of Latina/o writers of the Cold War years primarily reflected Cold War concerns through a common interest in liberation movements within the United States (including forms of both Chicano and Puerto Rican nationalism) and solidarity with such movements in the rest of the world, it was only in the decade following the end of the Cold War that Latina/o writers and their work both began to reflect more directly the practical consequences of those forty years of foreign policy on such high-impact zones as Central America and the Caribbean, and on their diasporic extensions in the United States itself. Two *testimonios* of the 1980s and early 1990s that best laid the groundwork for the literary explosion to follow were, again ironically, both composed originally in Spanish, and by figures who spent minimal to minor portions of their lives in the United States, and both putatively works of nonfiction that suffered in light of their considerable notoriety from attacks to their claims to veracity: *I, Rigoberta Menchú*, by the indigenous Guatemalan activist (recorded in 1982 and soon transcribed and translated into several languages), received international acclaim during the 1980s before some of its own claims were brought into question at the end of the decade); and the literary memoir *Before Night Falls* by the exiled, queer Cuban novelist and poet Reinaldo Arenas (published in English in 1993, just three years after the writer's suicide in the final stages of his long battle with HIV/AIDS). Menchú's life story, despite its arguably negligible errors, informed a vast readership in no uncertain terms of the murderous brutality of the Guatemalan military's repression of the country's peasant and indigenous insurgency, especially in the 1970s and early 1980s. Arenas's memoir, despite its gossipy informality and tendency toward emotional exaggeration, likewise described in compelling detail the systematic, pervasive, and brutal forms of personal surveillance, control, and detention that the Castro regime exercised daily on its most vulnerable and marginalized citizens. Both born into abject rural poverty and enduring childhood illiteracy in their countries during periods of severe political and social turmoil, both embodying some of the most precarious forms of "bio-political" existence in Cold War Latin America (the indigenous Guatemalan woman from a community targeted by death squads, the Castro-era queer dissident turned Reagan-era gay man fighting AIDS) and both following distinct but in many ways complementary tracks into literacy, literary and cultural notoriety, and political activism, Menchú and Arenas together make a striking case for the complexity of the Cold War's legacy on Latin and Latino America, and their texts made an equally compelling case for the interest of various reading publics to encounter that history and its legacy in literary and quasi-literary form. While Menchú has mostly lived in exile in Mexico or back in Guatemala working on the causes of indigenous and women's rights in her country, her *testimonio* continued to circulate widely in the United States and even worldwide, often serving as a foundational text for explorations of not only Guatemalan history but also Guatemalan American history since the 1980s. While Arenas died by his own hand in 1990 before he ever saw the success of his memoir and, through republication, the rest of his literary works, *Before Night Falls* continues to stand as a foundational work of Cuban American literature of the Cold War thanks to its firsthand accounts of both queer life in Castro's Cuba in the two decades following the revolution and queer life in a Cuban-exile, Reagan-era America where the writer found himself just as distressingly marginalized and cast out.

Five Representative Novelists

While Cold War themes and concerns appear in work representing all major literary genres, this discussion focuses on five writers of literary fiction whose major works together provide a comprehensive account of Latina/o literature's defining engagements with the historical formations that arguably determined their writers' very existence as members of their various Latin American diasporic settlements on U.S. soil. All five of these writers have been producing their major work, and in each case quite prolifically, in the decades following the Cold War; they are two men and three women, representing four distinct diasporic subcultures but in their work exploring many others, and among them they have won or been nominated for the National Book Award, the MacArthur Fellowship, the National Book Critics Circle Award, and the Pulitzer Prize; as recently as 2014, all remain active producers of important literary work.

Julia Alvarez

While she is also a poet, essayist, and writer of young adult fiction, Julia Alvarez is mostly known for her works of literary fiction, starting with 1991's *How the García Girls Lost Their Accents* and including *In the Time of the Butterflies* (1994), ¡Yo! (1997), *In the Name of Salomé* (2000) and *Saving the World* (2006). Cold War themes pervade Alvarez's work. Her family fled the Dominican Republic in the early 1960s because they feared the Trujillo regime would target them if Alvarez's father's opposition to it was discovered; novels based on her family's more private, domestic immigrant experience in the United States, such *García Girls* and ¡Yo!, necessarily rely on the United States' support of Trujillo's dictatorship as at least the backdrop for their narratives of immigrant Dominican American struggle and settlement in the following decades. Her more frankly historical novels, like *Butterflies* and *Salomé*, explore in much greater detail the conditions of Dominican life under Trujillo in the 1940s and 1950s (*Butterflies*) and conditions of transnational Latina/o life in the hemisphere over the decades spanning both the Trujillo and Castro regimes (*Salomé*).

Of all her works, *In the Time of the Butterflies* most centrally focuses on the Cold War context in which U.S. support of a "friendly" dictator as vicious as Rafael Trujillo resulted in extremely degrading conditions of political and personal life for all Dominicans not in the dictator's inner circle, and especially for Dominican women. *Butterflies* famously reimagines the lives of the four Mirabal sisters, all of whom participated in the resistance against Trujillo in the 1950s and three of whom were murdered by his henchmen in 1960. The surviving sister, Bélgica (nicknamed Dedé), reflects in the novel's epilogue on the challenges before the Dominican Republic in the years following her sisters' murders, and Trujillo's own assassination the following year. She remembers a visit to her sisters' memorial from then-Dominican President Joaquín Balaguer just after he took office. "He sat right there," Dedé recalls, "telling me his story. He was going to do all sorts of things … He was going to get rid of the old generals with their hands still dirty with Mirabal blood. All those properties they had stolen he was going to distribute among the poor. He was going to make us a nation proud of ourselves, not run by Yanqui imperialists" (310). Quickly, however, the reader learns that Balaguer's presidency collapses, and that Trujillo's profoundly destructive impact on Dominican life would take much longer, and more considerable forms of practical and psychological struggle, to overcome. "When it all came down a second time," Dedé tells us, "I shut the door ... Anyone had a story ... about the coup, the president thrown out before the year was over, the rebels up in the mountains, the civil war, the landing of the marines. I overheard [on] one of the talk shows on the radio ... someone analyzing the situation ... 'Dictatorships,' he was saying, 'are pantheistic. The dictator manages to plant a little piece of himself in every one of us.' Ah, I thought ... So this is what is happening to us" (311). Alvarez thus manages to weave through what might otherwise strike the reader as a minor scene, a brief anecdote in the larger historical narrative that is *Butterflies*' to tell, all of the salient elements required to account for not only Trujillo in the U.S.-created Cold War context, as well as the challenges facing the Dominican people on the island in the years post-Trujillo (including an occupation by U.S. marines), but also the political and economic conditions leading to the dramatic emigration of so many Dominicans from the island and to the U.S. mainland. In many ways *Butterflies* is a text that swallows its own tale: as an American novel written in English and published in 1994, its largest and most enveloping, informing context is that of the American foreign policy that in the course of the Cold War established conditions in a neighboring country that would eventually propel the ongoing, diasporic Dominicanization of American life, and American literature, thanks to texts like *In the Time of the Butterflies*.

Héctor Tobar

This logic of radical historical self-reference can describe all the additional examples of literary fiction covered here, but these texts will all approach that logic from very different angles or for very different purposes. The Guatemalan American journalist and novelist Héctor Tobar, for example, in a novel published just four years after Alvarez's *Butterflies*, alternates his narrative almost equally between a past setting in war-torn Guatemala in the 1980s and a "present" one in Guatemalan-diasporic Los Angeles in the weeks leading up to the Rodney King riots of 1992. Originally a reporter for the *Los Angeles Times* who won a Pulitzer Prize for team coverage of the riots, Tobar then earned a Master of Fine Arts degree from the University of California, Irvine on the strength of his first novel, 1998's *The Tattooed Soldier*. In addition to its chronological and geographical alternations between Guatemala and Los Angeles, *Soldier* also uses a free indirect style of third-person narration to alternate between the perspectives of its two main characters; both are young Guatemalan immigrant men who flee their homeland to escape the ravages of the civil war there, but one, Antonio Bernal, does so in fear of his life after a death squad murders his wife and their child in retribution for the wife's perceived anti-government activism, and the other, Guillermo Longoria, is the leader of the death squad responsible for those murders. The Guatemalan narratives trace the two protagonists' lives to their inevitable collision at the moment of the murders, and the Angeleno narrative mostly traces Antonio's efforts to track and eventually take revenge upon Guillermo once he recognizes him playing chess in MacArthur Park, thanks to the distinct jaguar tattoo on one of the ex-soldier's forearms.

Like Alvarez, Tobar weaves references to the Cold War pervasively through his text, both implicitly and explicitly. In one striking passage that recalls Menchú's descriptions in the *testimonio* of atrocities inflicted on indigenous Guatemalans by the junta's death squads, Tobar imagines just such a scene of mass murder, but from the perspective of the perpetrator, not the victim. In rendering such a scene from Longoria's point of view, Tobar presents to the reader a detailed account of the force of ideological indoctrination on the kind of young men the Guatemalan army regularly abducted, as they do Guillermo, into violent service. In a sustained flashback scene set in Los Angeles, Tobar has his soldier remember:

> He was called Guillermo when he was a child. In the army he became "Longoria." Longoria knew things Guillermo never dreamed of. The army was a cruel place ... But the army made you a man. The army made you do terrible, violent things, but they were things that had to be done ... This thing they were fighting was a cancer, and sometimes the children were contaminated with it too ... The parents passed the virus along to their children. It made you want to kill the parents again and again, even after they were dead, because if it wasn't for the fucking parents you wouldn't have to kill the children ... The noisy children [in Los Angeles] who lived in the Westlake Arms could not be contaminated with the virus because they were not in Guatemala, because they would not grow up to take up arms against the government. These children were rowdy and insolent, but they did not carry red flags, they did not threaten Guatemala's sovereignty. They only rode bicycles and bounced balls. (63–64)

Tobar trains a meticulous journalist's eye on the chilling details of Longoria's experience, and on the stupefying ideological rationalizations that both compel and excuse the behavior at the heart of that experience. The jump here from the recent past of the last bloody decade in Cold War– and civil war–era Guatemala to the novel's narrative "present" in a multicultural United States just emerging from that Cold War and into its own uncertain future is shortened by the symbolic comparison of two populations of

Guatemalan children, one living in a Guatemala where their parents' association with the "cancer" of a left-wing politics that might bring their country more fully into the orbit of an already declining communist Soviet empire marks them for murder, the other living a precarious diasporic urban life in the post–Cold War, multicultural, neoliberal, metropolitan city (one about to experience its own form of destabilizing state failure with the impending riots), but a life, at least for these displaced immigrant children, meaningfully bereft of all potential to pose a direct threat to the still-triumphant imperial-national state: "They only rode bicycles and bounced balls."

Edwidge Danticat and Junot Díaz

Almost perfect contemporaries of one another, the Haitian American writer Edwidge Danticat and her Dominican American counterpart Junot Díaz have together and since the mid-1990s been complementing and complicating Julia Alvarez's literary project of historical retrieval both by expanding the scope of their literary accounts of Cold War dictatorships' ongoing re-traumatizations of subject populations by bringing the legacies of the Duvalier regimes' impact on Haiti to bear on a larger history of the island of Hispaniola as a whole, and by focusing more explicitly than Alvarez on the roles that race, gender, sexuality, class, and culture have played in reshaping the ongoing protean formations of Afro-Latino-Caribbean-diasporic identity. Junot Díaz's career is perhaps the most spectacularly successful at the levels of both commercial success and critical acclaim of all the writers discussed here; *Drown*, his 1996 collection of short stories, débuted to considerable praise, and his first novel, *The Brief, Wondrous Life of Oscar Wao* (2007), was awarded the Pulitzer Prize for fiction; including his 2012 short story collection *This Is How You Lose Her*, all of Díaz's literary fiction has been devoted to explorations of Dominican and Dominican American life in all the ways that it bears the scars of the murderous brutality of the Trujillo era. Given his remarkable notoriety, this section will not focus on Díaz but instead on his Hispaniolan compatriot Edwidge Danticat; together, however, they represent the generational extension of Julia Alvarez's efforts to make sense of the historical legacies of Cold War dictatorship for Hispaniolans both on and off the island, and through a much more prolific portfolio of work in the first decades of the twenty-first century.

Like Díaz, Danticat's first publication, the 1994 novel *Breath, Eyes, Memory*, débuted to considerable acclaim, and she has remained a prolifically active writer and editor over the following twenty years: her major works include the story collection *Krik? Krak!* (1996), novels like *The Farming of Bones* (1997) and *The Dew Breaker* (2004), and the essay collection *Create Dangerously: the Immigrant Artist at Work* (2010). Also like Díaz, Danticat is the recipient of a MacArthur "Genius" Award (2009) and her 2007 memoir, *Brother, I'm Dying*, won a National Book Critics Circle Award. *The Dew Breaker* (2004) was published, auspiciously or not, the year of bicentennial of Haiti's independence from France; the text reads simultaneously as a novel and a collection of disparate but related stories, connected primarily through most characters' interaction with a "dew breaker," a member of first Francois, then Jean-Claude Duvalier's personal armies of henchmen, the Tontons Macoutes. The central "dew breaker" character finds uneasy redemption when he escapes Haiti with a woman who becomes his wife, and together they settle into nondescript lives as a couple with a young daughter in Haiti's diasporic settlement in Brooklyn, New York. This central family does not appear in every story; instead, many of the stories involve characters whose only relation to them is their having been brutally victimized, directly or indirectly, by the father while he served the Duvaliers as a Macoute.

Such a victim/survivor is Beatrice Saint Fort, the title character of the story "The Bridal Seamstress." Beatrice too has escaped Haiti for Haitian New York, and there she has led a successful career as a maker of bridal gowns for young Haitian American women. Planning to retire, Beatrice receives a visit from another young Haitian American woman hoping to write a story about the seamstress' career for a local Haitian American newspaper. The young reporter, Aline Cajuste, instead uncovers not only the tragic causes of Beatrice's flight from Haiti to America but also the persistence of the horrors of Beatrice's torture in Haiti via the re-traumatizing work of memory: "What are you going to do after you retire?" Aline asks quite innocently in the course of her interview; "Move, again," Beatrice responds, and when Aline counters with "Why?", Danticat has the older woman tell us the following:

> "We called them *choukèt lawoze*," Beatrice said, the couch's plastic cover squeaking beneath her. "They'd break into your house. Mostly it was at night. But often they'd also come before dawn, as the dew was settling on the leaves, and they'd take you away. He was one of them, the guard." Beatrice removed her open-toed sandals and raised her feet so Aline could see the soles of her feet. They were thin and sheer like an albino baby's skin. "He asked me to go dancing with him one night," Beatrice said, putting her feet back in her sandals. "I had a boyfriend, so I said no. That's why he arrested me. He tied me to some type of rack in the prison and whipped the bottom of my feet until they bled. Then he made me walk home, barefoot. On tar roads. In the hot sun. At high noon. This man, wherever I rent or buy a house in this city, I find him, living on my street." (131–32)

Beatrice's testimony to Aline in this scene traces the emotional and psychological consequences of traumatic violence, as borne in body, heart, and mind by those who suffer that violence most directly, to their necessary manifestation in discourse, first in the older woman's confession, then in Aline's decision following the interview that the story she's ethically obligated to tell as a reporter is of Beatrice's survival (and of the suffering and survival of others like her), not her retirement, and in turn in Danticat's own commitment to render in imaginative form lives like those of both these characters, and at such a pivotal moment in their own lives and in the lives of the people(s) they represent. The matrilineal "line" thus connecting Beatrice to the "A-line" who finds her true vocation in retelling Beatrice's real story both deviates and reinforces the never-married, childless Beatrice's already maternal force in the lives of the younger women she presumably dresses for marriage and motherhood; Aline, who the reader knows to be in love with another woman, can in turn nurture and sustain her community through her words, and her work, in powerful ways that mirror but not exactly duplicate the work of the bridal seamstress, and of the writer who created them both. For this reason, Danticat gives Aline the closing, reflective lines in the story: "Growing up poor but sheltered in Somerville, Massachusetts, Aline had never imagined that people like Beatrice existed, men and women whose tremendous agonies filled every blank space in their lives. Maybe there were hundreds, even thousands, of people like this, men and women chasing fragments of themselves long lost to others. Maybe Aline was one of them. These were the people Aline wanted to write about now ..." (137–38).

Cristina García

Like all the other writers under discussion here, the Cuban American novelist Cristina García has enjoyed an active, prolific literary career in the twenty-five years following the end of the Cold War. In addition to a verse collection and various edited volumes, García published six novels from the early 1990s to the mid-2010s, beginning with the National Book Award–nominated *Dreaming in Cuban* (1992) and including *The Agüero Sisters* (1997), *Monkey Hunting* (2003), *A Handbook to Luck* (2007), *The Lady Matador's Hotel* (2010), and *King of Cuba* (2013). Born in Cuba and raised in Brooklyn, García worked as a journalist for *Time* magazine's Miami bureau before launching her literary career in the early 1990s and moving to Los Angeles, where she lived for many years. García's early novels focused quite centrally on the histories of the Cuban revolution and the consequent exile of so many Cubans to the United States, paying special attention not only to the impacts of these historical events on Cuban and Cuban American women but also to the active roles her women characters played in making the historical world that in turn made them. García's years in Los Angeles, however, exposed her to the larger impact of the Cold War on the Latino and Latin American world beyond the scope of its specifically Cuban spaces, and in particular both her fourth and fifth novels (*Handbook* and *Lady Matador*, respectively) in part take on the task of exploring the Cold War's impact on both a regional-hemispheric and even global scale.

A Handbook to Luck, primarily set in Tobar's multicultural Los Angeles from the late 1960s to the late 1980s, follows a trio of main characters whose paths cross in southern California as a result of their home countries' various experiences as vital fronts in the global Cold War. They include a Cuban father and son, an Iranian woman who meets and falls in love with the Cuban son when he becomes a young man, and a young Salvadoran woman who flees her country in the 1970s and by the end of the novel is a U.S. citizen, working for the same Cuban American son, and married to a Korean immigrant entrepreneur who was once her boss. *The Lady Matador's Hotel* both expands the global scope of *Handbook*'s narrative world by including characters from additional countries central to Cold War history, and contracts its narrative world both spatially by having all of her major characters converge on an unnamed Central American capital city most likely fashioned after Guatemala City, and temporally by having all the events in the primary narrative occur in the course of an intensive week as the city prepares for the first-ever Battle of the Lady Matadors in the Americas, in which the novel's Japanese-Mexican-American title character is training to compete. That character, Suki Palacios, shares García's imagined transnational stage with a wide variety of fellow protagonists, including a female German attorney specializing in the adoptions of Central American children by First World couples, a male Korean factory owner desperately in love with his pregnant teenaged indigenous employee, and a Cuban-exile poet in town with his American wife hoping to adopt a child to save their failing marriage. Unlike *Handbook*, *Lady Matador* refuses to specify explicitly its setting in time or place, allowing García some freedom to ruminate more inventively about the general conditions of life in a twenty-first-century Americas still reeling from Cold War–era pathologies producing wounds that even two decades later refuse to heal.

The narrative from *Lady Matador* that most explicitly traces the edges of such a wound involves two characters who in important ways collect the Guatemalan thread at work in this discussion, from the ouster of Arbenz in 1954, to Menchú's testimonial accounts of military atrocity in the 1970s, to Tobar's imagined accounts of precarious life in Guatemalan America as the

Cold War ended. In a place and time of unsteady post–Cold War peace, a female ex-guerrilla named Aura Estrada finds herself working at the hotel in her country's capital where dignitaries and others are converging for the Battle of the Lady Matadors; as the novel and the week of anticipation open, Aura discovers that staying at her hotel is a colonel in the country's army who had previously participated in atrocities, including the burning alive of Aura's brother. But before even identifying him exactly, encountering the colonel and his cronies as she serves them lunch provokes the following reflection from Aura:

> Dozens of military men from around the Americas, old fraternities of criminals, are making the ex-guerrilla nervous. Today they are her customers, gathered in groups of seven and eight, fussing over their fried pork chops and eggs. It astounds her that these men can sit around like princes without fear or restraints ... Aura rarely prays but when she does it's to her beloved dead: to Papi, who passed away when she was ten of a blood disease the curanderas couldn't heal; to her brother Julio, set aflame by a sadistic army patrol while defending the family's cornfield; to Mamá, who, after helplessly witnessing her only son's death, stopped eating and sleeping until her soul joined his; to Aura's lover, Juan Carlos, blown apart by a land mine ... If she begins to tally the savagery, she wouldn't stop ... Yes, there were coffins, pine-wood coffins stacked up to the sky. The civil war might've ended years ago, but the grief, the grief is flourishing still ... Aura is convinced that the entire country has succumbed to a collective amnesia. This is what happens in a society where no one is permitted to grow old slowly. Nobody talks of the past, for fear their wounds might reopen. Privately, though, their wounds never heal. (7–9)

García's narrative in part follows Aura in her attempt to avenge her brother's life in ways that roughly parallel the revenge narrative propelling Tobar's *Tattooed Soldier*. Beyond that, however, García's literary project combines elements of both Menchú's *testimonio* in its insistence on "tally[ing] the savagery" that continues to haunt so many hundreds of thousands of survivors, and the descendants of survivors, of so much violence and so much death (and in all places in our post–Cold War world that Latinas/os might call home), and Tobar's project in his own historically committed literary fiction to counter proactively a collective, national, and diasporic "amnesia" that paradoxically, and tragically, ensures that "grief [will] flourish" still and that too many "wounds never heal." Joining Alvarez's Dedé, Tobar's Antonio, and Danticat's Beatrice, García's Aura provides an additional imagined embodiment of survival's possibility, memory's vitality, and imagination's necessity, in the common struggle to live on, and live better, in a world where political calculation's basic wager is never fully in the interest, or on the side, of life, human or otherwise. García's "pine-wood coffins," we know twenty-five years after the Cold war, continue "stack[ing] up to the sky."

Two Poets and a Conclusion

García's colonel also recalls another famous "Colonel" emerging from the literary fallout of the Cold War era in the Americas. In "The Colonel," a poem composed in 1978 about her experiences in an already war-torn El Salvador, the American poet Carolyn Forché famously testifies to an experience she had visiting an army officer's home for dinner:

> The colonel returned with a sack used to bring groceries home. He spilled many human ears on the table. They were like dried peach halves. There is no other way to say this. He took one of them in his hands, shook it in our faces, dropped it into a water glass. It came alive there. I am tired of fooling around he said. As for the rights of anyone, tell your people they can go fuck themselves. He swept the ears to the floor with his arm and held the last of his wine in the air. Something for your poetry, no? he said. (16)

In 1978, the war in El Salvador was already forcing many Salvadorans to flee north to safety, but the United States had yet to feel the full demographic impact of the exodus to follow. For a poet like Forché, the concern at the time was to give voice to all the dead whom the severed ears represented, and to have that voice resonate wherever her poetry could give it sound. In "San Onofre, California" (1977), another poem in the same collection (*The Country Between Us*, 1981), the poet finds herself in the relative if deceptive safety of her coastal California setting confessing that, while "we feel/it is enough to listen/to the wind jostling lemons,/to dogs ticking across terraces," this collective "we" must also concede "knowing that while birds and warmer weather/are forever moving north,/the cries of those who vanish/might take years to get here" (9). One hears, already in 1978, "the cries of those who vanish" echoing in Forché's self-admonishing lines. All of the literary material covered here, from Menchú to Arenas, from Alvarez and Tobar to Danticat and García, reflects the historical fact of the dramatic "movement(s) north" of so many individuals and so many communities carrying with them, if nothing else, memories of their own of hearing similar "cries of those [many] who vanish[ed]" in a world of bloody conflict that persisted for decades, from Kennan's 1950s to Kirkpatrick's 1970s to Reagan's 1980s.

Over the "years" that it has taken for so many additional "cries" to "get here," an insistent and coherent post–Cold War Latina/o literary project has emerged in and as a compellingly historical formation. As recently as

2009, the Salvadoran American poet William Archila (born in El Salvador in 1968, emigrating to the United States in 1980) published *The Art of Exile*, a verse collection that directly gives voice to the "vanish[ed]" whose "cries" Forché feared would "take years to get here." Archila devotes the poem "This Earth," for example, to remembering a friend, Memo, murdered in "the war": "a fisherman brought him home in an orange/plastic bag: a leg, an arm, one brown shoe still on./ He was found by the side of a lake … I thought of him barefoot, darkening the ground,/the wings of black birds covering his body" (21–22). Archila vacillates here between frank descriptions of his friend's mutilated and dismembered body, its reduction to parts ("a leg, an arm, one brown shoe still on"), and the more ambiguous image of a body either protected and kept whole or picked apart by scavengers, "cover[ed]," as he sees it, by "the wings of black birds." Time passes, and Archila's speaker reflects on the prospect that, while the earth might swallow the buried dead, the dead in turn claim the earth, perhaps in part by mingling substantially with it:

> So many months have gone by, so many buried
> under stones, their once stiffened bodies now dust.
> Somewhere in the mist, I know the earth,
> cold and damp with rain, belongs to them.

And if the earth belongs to the dead, if the dead become in turn the ground, the life-giving earth beneath the feet of the living, then Archila's speaker can find "Memo under my feet," can "love the smell of wet dirt," and can carry Memo's living memo(ry) with him: "I will cup my hands, carry this earth in my pockets" (22). This "earth" in the poet's "cup[ped] … hands," then "pocket[ted]" in his memo(ry) and transported, made transportable through migration and by the vehicle of his poetic and literary imagination, thus years later brings back to renewed life, and gives renewed voice, to the "cries" of all those who, like Memo, "vanish." This "earth" is earth beyond geography, and beyond geopolitics; instead, as Archila imagines it protecting and even reviving his murdered friend, it offers itself up as a geo-poetics, where territories belong to no one in belonging to everyone, where human communities and populations survive and even thrive not merely in memory or in the imagination but also in fact, and where political designations naming both territories or populations, like America(n), Central America(n), Latin(o) America(n), and so forth finally stop serving as alibis for practical policy predicated on the proposition that consideration, to take back Forché's Colonel's words, for "the rights of anyone" can ever completely trump consideration for the rights of everyone.

Bibliography

Alvarez, Julia. *In the Time of the Butterflies*. Chapel Hill, NC: Algonquin Books, 1994.
Archila, William. *The Art of Exile*. Tempe, AZ: Bilingual Press, 2009.
Arenas, Reinaldo. *Before Night Falls: a Memoir*. Trans. Dolores M. Koch. New York: Viking, 1993.
Arias, Arturo, ed. *The Rigoberta Menchú Controversy*. Minneapolis: University of Minnesota Press, 2001.
Avelar, Idelber. *The Letter of Violence: Essays on Narrative, Ethics, and Politics*, New York: Palgrave, 2004.
Baker-Cristales, Beth. *Salvadoran Migration to Southern California: Redefining El Hermano Lejano*. Gainesville: University Press of Florida, 2004.
Beasley-Murray, Jon. *Posthegemony: Political Theory and Latin America*. Minneapolis: University of Minnesota Press, 2010.
Beverley, John. *Testimonio: On the Politics of Truth*. Minneapolis: University of Minnesota Press, 2004.
Danticat, Edwidge. *Create Dangerously: the Immigrant Artist at Work*. Princeton, NJ: Princeton University Press, 2010.
The Dew Breaker. New York: Knopf, 2004.
Díaz, Junot. *The Brief, Wondrous Life of Oscar Wao*. New York: Riverhead Books, 2007.
Forché, Carolyn. *The Country Between Us*. New York: Perennial Library, 1981.
Franco, Jean. *The Decline and Fall of the Lettered City: Latin America and the Cold War*. Cambridge, MA: Harvard University Press, 2002.
García, Cristina. *The Lady Matador's Hotel*. New York: Scribner, 2010.
Hamilton, Nora and Norma Stoltz Chinchilla. *Seeking Community in a Global City: Guatemalans and Salvadorans in Los Angeles*. Philadelphia: Temple University Press, 2001.
Holden, Robert H. and Eric Zolov, eds. *Latin American and the United States: A Documentary History*. Oxford: Oxford University Press, 2011.
Kennan, George F. "Memorandum by the Counselor of the Department to the Secretary of State," March 29, 1950. U.S. Department of State. *Foreign Relations of the United States 1950, 2: The United Nations and Latin America*. Washington, DC: GPO, 1976: 598–624.
Kirkpatrick, Jeane. *Dictatorships and Double Standards: Rationalism and Reason in Politics*. New York: Simon and Schuster, 1982.
Laguerre, Michel. *Diasporic Citizenship: Haitian Americans in Transnational America*. New York: St. Martin's Press. 1998.
López-Calvo, Ignacio. *God and Trujillo: Literacy and Cultural Representations of the Dominican Dictator*. Gainesville: University Press of Florida. 2005.
Menchú, Rigoberta. *I, Rigoberta Menchú: an Indian Woman in Guatemala*. Trans. Ann Wright. Verso: London and New York, 1984.
Moreiras, Alberto. *The Exhaustion of Difference: The Politics of Latin American Cultural Studies*. Durham, NC: Duke University Press. 2001.
Ocasio, Rafael. *A Gay Cuban Activist in Exile: Reinaldo Arenas*. Gainesville: University Press of Florida. 2007.
Reagan, Ronald. "President Reagan: U.S. Interests in Central America." U.S. Department of State. *Current Policy* No. 576 (May 9, 1984): 1–5.

Rodríguez, Ana Patricia. *Dividing the Isthmus: Central American Transnational Histories, Literatures and Cultures*. Austin: University of Texas Press, 2009.
Saldaña-Portillo, María Josefina. *The Revolutionary Imagination in the Americas and the Age of Development*. Durham, NC: Duke University Press, 2003.
Suárez, Lucia. *The Tears of Hispaniola: Haitian and Dominican Diaspora Memory*. Gainesville: University Press of Florida, 2006.
Tobar, Héctor. *The Tattooed Soldier*. New York: Delphinium Books, 1998.
Zilberg, Elana. *Space of Detention: The Making of a Transnational Gang Crisis Between Los Angeles and San Salvador*. Durham, NC: Duke University Press, 2011.

6

TIFFANY ANA LÓPEZ

The 1980s: Latina/o Literature during the "Decade of the Hispanic"

The 1980s marks an incredibly significant period in Latina/o literature that signals the advent of contemporary writing in the field. Some critics see the 1980s as a chasm between the vibrant movement-based literary production of the 1970s and the mainstream publication activity of the 1990s. Hinged between these two pivotal decades is the 1980s, a critically vital time when Latina/o writers are publishing in a variety of venues, drawing on past traditions, expanding and breaking boundaries, grappling with definitions of identity and culture, speaking in multiple voices, and writing with a sense of charting new paths. The activity and experimentation of the period presages the Latina/o literary boom in mainstream publishing that emerges at the cusp of the 1990s featuring Rudolfo Anaya, Sandra Cisneros, Ana Castillo, Denise Chávez, and Mary Helen Ponce and the advent of professionalized Latina/o authors represented by book agents and publicists. Notably, while in the 1990s these writers appear new to the mainstream, all were already well-established voices in Latina/o literature with several of their signature works (i.e., *The House on Mango Street*, *Sapogonia*) first published in the mid-1980s by smaller presses, such as Arte Público Press and Editorial Bilingüe / Bilingual Review, founded with the specific mission to shepherd the publication of Latina/o literature.

During the 1980s, Latina/o literature extends conversations launched during the 1970s about such pivotal matters as civil rights, women's liberation, environmentalism, labor, educational access, and affirmative action. Latina/o authors also engage with pressing issues at the cultural forefront of the 1980s, most significantly affirmative action, institutionalized racism, immigration, diasporic identity, the AIDS crisis, the military industrial complex, environmentalism, the war on drugs, economic recession, and the decline of government commitment to programs addressing social inequity. Latina/o literature produced during this moment is characterized by defining itself as a distinct body of writing with its own literary themes and narrative contours, including Spanglish, code-switching, caló, and other hybrid forms of linguistic word play. Genre is a significant area of experimentation, with writers expanding the very framework of the writing by working across genres and inventing hybrid forms. Matters of training, craft, and aesthetics are thus critically important to reading Latina/o literature from this period and to understanding writers as practitioners of a literary art.

The term "decade of the Hispanic" is said to have captured a collective sense of optimism about the perceived evolving prominence of Hispanics in the public sphere. However, some cultural critics viewed the term as principally a marketing ploy and the source of journalistic hype, since the actual numbers of Latinas/os in business, politics, and education were comparatively quite low, with, for example, Hispanics comprising only 1 percent of elected officials in the country. Referencing the multitude of billboard advertising posted throughout California with beer companies targeting Latinas/os, Richard Montoya, Ric Salinas, and Herbert Siguenza, the trio of Chicano satiric authors and performers known as Culture Clash, quipped, "The decade of the Hispanic turned out to be a weekend sponsored by Coors." The term "Hispanic" itself was a source of contestation, inviting cheeky yet pointed criticism from Latina/o voices – "It's not my panic; it's his panic" – to comment on the imposition of wording said to have evolved not from community-based movement but rather the U.S. census. The literature of the period illustrates authors invoking a range of terms to reference identity: Hispanic, Latino, Mexican American, Chicano, Puerto Rican, Nuyorican, Boriqua, Afro Latino, Cuban American, Cubano. Within each of the different cultural subgroups that comprise Latinos as a collective group, there are also shifts taking place in the articulation of identity with public debate about matters of representation. When it was revealed that the novel *Famous All Over Town* (1983) was written by non-Latino author Daniel James (using the Latino pen name Danny Santiago), it generated much conversation about issues of authenticity and a fraught history of the mainstream reading Latino writers through the lens of the stereotype. Another example of the shift under way about identity during this time is Cubans in the U.S. transitioning to thinking about themselves more as immigrants than exiles. Nation, gender, and sexuality become critically central to definitions of a larger Latina/o community, with Gloria Anzaldúa's *Borderlands / La Frontera* (1987) and Cherríe Moraga's *Loving in the War Years* (1983) representing the employment of new literary forms to articulate the complexities of identity and arrive at more nuanced ways of thinking about the intersectional influences of home and language including matters of race and class in the construction of identity. This is further exemplified by the "a/o" split that comes into fruition during the decade as a means to clarify the importance of gender to definitions of community, the "a/o" emphasizing that "Latino" refers an all male group and "Latina/o" refers to a group inclusive of both men and women.

The decade also experiences what is known as the "Culture Wars," an impassioned debate that spilled over from universities into the popular culture over whether or not there was a foundational canon of classic literature that should be mandatory and taught to all students. Many defended the notion of a canon, feeling classic authors represented the very best model of what literature had to offer and should be the foundation for study to facilitate a national development of literacy and civic culture with all students benefiting from shared reading of a single canon of writing. Others felt the notion of a canon served to preclude attention to work by women writers and authors of color and that the argument of excellence avoided bringing necessary attention to matters of diversity and created a destructively false division between diversity and excellence. The Culture Wars were additionally significant in their impact on how Latina/o literature was approached as a field, putting pressure on Latino studies and ethnic studies to justify their existence as disciplines. It is not uncommon to hear stories from scholars trained during the 1980s about having to defend the study of Latina/o literature as a full-fledged field and legitimate area of academic inquiry. This reactionary climate motivated scholars and writers to bring a strong spotlight to the work of documenting and charting the existing history of the literature leading up to contemporary Latina/o literary production.

Latina/o literature as a whole illustrates authors engaged in the craft of writing and displays a range of literary influences from the United States to Latin America and beyond. Notably, the forms and themes of Latina/o literature produced during the 1980s reflect not only the specificity of community but also the larger national sociopolitical climate informing the work. Over the course of this decade, the country experienced eight years of the Reagan administration and the first two years of the George H. W. Bush presidency, with legislation effectively undoing the gains of civil rights and social reforms of previous decades. While Hispanics constituted approximately 9 percent of the population nationally, 22 percent of Hispanics were living in poverty, a rate more than double that for the non-Latino population. In 1986, Congress passed the Immigration and Control Reform Act, which offered amnesty to many immigrants. The nation saw the rise of Republican conservatism, with the religious right emerging on the scene and pressuring for the address of morality as a central political issue. The Reagan administration's refusal to immediately address the AIDS crisis as an urgent national health care issue created outrage among many communities, including Latinas/os, who felt the administration was willfully turning its back on huge numbers of society for being poor, gay, and/or brown. Along with the influx of immigrants from Spanish-speaking countries in the midst of civil war and other forms of economic instability and political unrest, English-only laws were passed in eighteen states. At the same time the phrase "the decade of the Hispanic" heavily circulated in the media, there was also increasingly heated political rhetoric against affirmative action, bilingual education, and immigration.

This cultural climate is important to understanding how Latina/o writers are speaking on not just one but several counts: their writing demonstrates a response to both national issues and culturally specific issues that may or may not always intersect. This is particularly true for writers strongly aligned with multiple communities not yet in conversation with one another. Feminist and queer Latina/o writers from this period explore the movement across different spaces of identity and the work to create a space where Latinas/os can express identity inclusive of contradictions and complexities. Previously, the pressures of racism created a cultural environment that saw the sole claiming of Latino identity as the priority with identification as feminist or gay viewed as affiliating with a white elite power structure. Writers from the 1980s contest this and affirm the importance of conceptualizing Latina/o identity as inclusive and asserting that the incorporation of feminist and queer work not only expands but also strengthens community building.

One of the most important developments during the decade is the formal training of Latina/o writers. Latina/o authors embrace writing as a profession and their presence in writing programs brings attention to the literature being produced by and about Latino writers. A new generation of professionalized authors emerges from the university, in large part a result of the previous decade's hard-won success in creating programming designed to emotionally, intellectually, and financially foster first-generation students through college and empower them to pursue work in the creative arts as well as fields traditionally viewed as meriting the combined effort and expense of a college education, such as business, law, and medicine. This generation includes Julia Alvarez, Gloria Anzaldúa, Olivia Castellano, Denise Chávez, Sandra Cisneros, Judith Ortiz Cofer, Cristina García, Oscar Hijuelos, José Montoya, Cherríe Moraga, Albert Alvaro Ríos, Gary Soto, and Helena María Viramontes. Notably, many of these figures secured faculty positions at universities where they actively attend to the future development of the field as appointed writers and teachers. The 1980s also indicates a time of increased inclusion of Latina/o literature within the college curriculum as many English departments reacted to the Culture Wars by granting more attention to multicultural literature. Additionally during this time, Latino studies further solidifies as an academic field, with literature providing an important body of work through which to explore the evolution of Latinas/os as a people and culture.

During this period, publishing houses and editorial collectives played a key role in the development of Latina/o literature. Arte Público Press is the oldest and most accomplished publisher of contemporary and recovered literature by U.S. Hispanic authors. The press was founded in 1979 by Nicolás Kanellos to address a huge publishing need, since very few Hispanic authors at that time were finding publication with mainstream presses. As a literature scholar, Kanellos was keenly aware that unpublished work remains invisible to the academic archive and, unless the visibility of a work is maintained through oral performance, it will not be available for future generations to engage. During the 1980s, Arte Público Press published across the genres of Latina/o literature, from poetry and plays to short stories, novels, and essays. The list of Arte Público Press authors published during this period is as historically important as it is artistically impressive and includes Sandra Cisneros, Judith Ortiz Cofer, Lucha Corpi, Victor Cruz, Roberto Fernández, Genaro González, Rolando Hinojosa, Tato Laviera, Miguel Piñero, Elias Muñoz, Mary Helen Ponce, Tomás Rivera, Gary Soto, Sabine Ulibarrí, Luis Valdez, Victor Villaseñor, and Helena María Viramontes. Kanellos issued many pivotal volumes spotlighting the work of Latina/o authors, including *A Decade of Hispanic Literature: An Anniversary Anthology* (1982). Kanellos also founded *The Americas Review*, which evolved from an earlier journal (*Revista Chicano-Riqueña*) and served as the springboard for Arte Público Press. Other publishing outlets, including small presses such as Floricanto, Quinto Sol, Mango, and Pajarito as well as university- and research center–affiliated presses, played a major role in the development of the literature during this period. University archive collections, such as those at Stanford University and the University of California at Santa Barbara, are additionally important resources for following work from the period.

During the 1980s, journals played a significant role in the evolution of Latina/o literature because they provided a timely featured space for writers to publish work and authors and readers alike to learn more about the field. An examination of journals from the period evidences the development of stories into novels, poetry into chapbooks, and personal essays into memoirs and autobiographies. Bilingual Review Press is another vitally important publisher that also featured its own journal, *Bilingual Review / La Revista Bilingüe*. Founded by literature scholar Gary Keller, the press was brought to Arizona State University in 1986. *Revista XhismeArte* (also called *ChismeArte*) is another historically important journal from the period, published by the Los Angeles Latino Writers Association, a pioneering group directed by the poet Luis. J. Rodriguez, with novelist Helena

María Viramontes leading as literary editor. Issue number 7, "The Woman's Issue" (1981), is regarded as a landmark publication for its emphasis on the political dimension of work by established and emerging voices, with a cover image by the formative Chicana visual artist Barbara Carrasco.

Another vitally important press from this period is Kitchen Table: Women of Color Press, publisher of the groundbreaking anthology *This Bridge Called My Back* (1981), edited by Cherríe Moraga and Gloria Anzaldúa. Originally published by Persephone, a queer feminist press, *Bridge* went out of print and gained renewed publication with Kitchen Table, founded by Barbara Smith and Audre Lorde with Moraga as cofounder of the organization. The press reissued *Bridge* and launched as a new press focused on publishing work by women of color. The anthology was critically groundbreaking because it reflected an uncompromising feminism and frankly posed its intervention through prose, poetry, personal narrative, and analysis by Afro-American, Asian American, Latina, and Native American women. The titles of its six sections introduced concepts and methodology that continue to direct thinking about Latina/o literature, such as "The Roots of Our Radicalism," "Theory in the Flesh," "Speaking in Tongues," and "El Mundo Zurdo" (a title later given to the annual conference established in tribute to the life and work of Gloria Anzaldúa). The volume articulated the role of the Latina writer as part of larger movements and affirmed Latina identity as complex and inclusive of not only race and culture but also gender, class, and sexuality. *This Bridge Called My Back* sent a shock wave that dramatically shifted the work being produced in Latina/o literary studies by affirming the centrality of feminist consciousness and the voice of the Latina writer as an author whose vision is hugely relevant and stands in conversation with an intersection of writers and readers across the lines of race, class, culture, gender, sexuality, and nation. Moraga played a pivotal role as an anthologist; coterminous with her work with *Bridge*, she also coedited *Cuentos: Stories by Latinas* (1983), with Alma Gómez and Mariana Romo-Carmona. As a writer who positions her work in relationship to social movement, Moraga's publication activities during the early 1980s exemplify her leadership in the field through her fierce commitment to coalition building among various communities inclusive of feminist and queer politics.

Norma Alarcón is a groundbreaking Latina/o literary scholar and contributor to *Bridge* whose work is pivotal to Latina/o literature of the 1980s. She exemplified the academic as public intellectual, using her position and voice as a literature scholar to build from higher education in ways made meaningful to a larger public beyond the boundaries of the university. Her work as a writer and publisher expanded and clarified the field. She promoted and contextualized authors, including the many different communities from which they worked, producing several groundbreaking essays that served to distinguish a Latina feminist theory. Among the most notable of her essays from the 1980s are: "Chicanas' Feminist Literature: A Re-vision Through Malintzin/or Malintzin: Putting Flesh Back on the Object" (1981); "'What Kind of Lover Have you Made Me Mother?': Toward a Theory of Chicanas' Feminism and Cultural Identity Through Poetry" (1985); and "Traddutora, Traditora: A Paradigmatic Figure of Chicana Feminism" (1988). Alarcón's publishing of her work in collections such as *Women of Color: Perspectives on Feminism and Identity* (1985) and *Changing our Power: An Introduction to Women's Studies* (1988) illustrates the practice she modeled in forging Latina literary criticism as critically multidisciplinary and politically intersectional. Among her editorial contributions, Alarcón founded the journal *Third Woman* after attending the Midwest Latina Writers Workshop in 1980 with Sandra Cisneros and Ana Castillo in the audience. She envisioned *Third Woman* to fill the void of journals run by, about, and for Latina writers and to intervene on the "special issue" syndrome in which journals published Latinas as part of a focused issue but seldom within the regular cycle of publication. Her additional goal was to promote coalition building, the journal providing, in Alarcón's words, "a space for Latina self-invention, self-definition and self-representation." *Third Woman* was founded in Bloomington, Indiana, in 1981, under the auspices of the Indiana University's Chicano-Riqueño Studies Program. Of the significance of the journal to Latina/o literary production during the 1980s, Latina/o cultural studies professor Catherine Ramirez writes, it "exposed the limitations of cultural nationalism and forged links between Chicanas, Latinas, and other Third World Women. In doing so *Third Woman* situated Chicana literature during a burgeoning feminist, woman of color literary movement." In 1986, Third Woman Press moved to the University of California at Berkeley where Alarcón, Moraga, and Castillo edited the final volume of the *Third Woman Journal*, titled *The Sexuality of Latinas* (1989). The significance of the volume's focus on sexuality and gender as pivotal to ongoing conversations about Latina/o studies is indicated by Third Woman Press evolving the volume into a 1993 anthology of the same title also edited by Alarcón, Castillo, and Moraga.

In looking at the emergence of Latina/o literary criticism during the 1980s, there are several key scholars who devoted more than a decade of their careers (from the prior decade and in many cases well into the present moment) to articulating and documenting the field. The role of scholars working in the capacity of editors is fundamental because they identify important conversations, trends, and voices in the field and then variously stage conversations in print to extend their expert vision to a broader readership. In this way, those working as editors and anthologists during the 1980s make the field legible and shape how it is further understood, extending the work of such earlier foundational critics as Luis Leal and Antonia Castañeda. During the decade, María Herrera-Sobek and Helena María Viramontes twice served as an editorial team with the anthologies *Beyond Stereotypes: The Critical Analysis of Chicana Literature* (1985) and *Chicana Creativity and Criticism: Charting New Frontiers in American Literature* (1988). Herrera-Sobek also published her poetry in a collection with Alicia Gaspar de Alba and Demetria Martínez, *Three Times a Woman: Chicana Poetry* (1989). These works had significant impact on critical discussion of trends, debates, and advances in the field; they brought attention to major and emerging writers and further illustrated the distinct features of Chicana literature and literary criticism as well as the significant ways work in the field illustrated an engagement with questions and themes being explored within the larger framework of American literature and literary criticism. This work is also historically significant for how it exemplifies the ways Latina/o literature scholars in the 1980s worked in direct collaboration with authors. During the 1980s, partnerships between scholars and creative writers as well as the content of their collaborative work represented a fundamental ideology carried over from the 1970s: that art making is central to critical practice.

Academics and writers together played an active and vital part in building the literary arts scene and working to document the evolution of the literature and make it widely known and available to readers. Launching the decade's strong publication activity through the genre of anthologies, Gary Keller and Francisco Jiménez produced the important edited collection, *Hispanics in the United States: An Anthology of Creative Literature* (1980). Another pivotal team comprised of a scholar and creative author is Francisco Lomelí and Rudolfo Anaya with their anthology *Aztlán: Essays on the Chicano Homeland* (1989), which provides source documents from movement history as well as critical essays. Drawn from Mexican cultural mythological, Aztlán was conceptualized as a homeland rooted in the lands of Mexico (the present-day U.S. states of California, Nevada, Utah, Arizona, New Mexico, Colorado, and Texas) viewed as unjustly brokered to the United States as a result of the U.S.-Mexican War. Aztlán was employed as a central concept during the Chicano Movement to represent the historical vestiges of colonial oppression and the ongoing need for resistance. In the 1980s, Aztlán became central to thinking about issues of nationalism and identity politics. By reminding of the fragile gains made during the 1970s, it served the advocacy of continued attention to patterns in history as well as the affirmation of cultural pride. Lomelí also edited the comprehensive reference work, *The Dictionary of Literary Biography* (1989), with Don Shirley. Lomelí's distinction as a literary historian and editor is rooted in his earlier collection, *Chicano Literature, A Reference Guide* (1985), coedited with Julio Martínez. Rudolfo Anaya played a further vital editorial role by bringing attention to the significance of genre in thinking about Latino literary production with *Cuentos Chicanos: A Short Story Anthology* (1984), coedited with Antonio Márquez. He also focused thinking on the significance of region in reading Latino literature with his edited collections, *Voces: An Anthology of Nuevo Mexicano Writers* (1987) and *Tierra: Contemporary Short Fiction of New Mexico* (1989). Teresa Córdova coedited two important collections, *Chicana Voices: Intersections of Class, Race and Gender* (1986) and *Chicano Struggle, Analysis of Past and Present Efforts* (1984), with John García. A groundbreaking scholar from the period is Juan Bruce-Novoa, with his *Chicano Authors: Inquiry by Interview* (1980) and *Chicano Poetry: A Response to Chaos* (1982). These works were pathbreaking because they identified the field of Latina/o literary study by illustrating methodological approaches to analysis and inquiry. In this way, they opened the doors for future scholars and encouraged continued writing in the field by legitimizing Latina/o literature as a critically significant and historically important branch of American literature.

Anthologies of literature and literary criticism are central to looking at the development of Latino literature generally but most especially during the 1980s, when several anthologies and edited collections facilitated unprecedented access to Latina/o authors that readerships previously had to independently discover or encounter through specialized channels, such as college courses, book festivals, or community readings. These projects were brought to fruition by a range of voices, including scholars, creative artists, librarians, and bibliographers, and covered the spectrum of literary activity. *Cuban American Writers: Los Atrevidos* (1988), edited by Carolina Hospital, was the first anthology of Cuban American literature published in English. Over the course of the decade, there is a consistent flow in the publication of notable anthologies and single-author works that immediately played a role in crystalizing the definition of Latina/o literary studies and signaling the contributions of leading scholars and creative artists in the field: *Flor y Canto IV and V: An Anthology of Chicano Literature from the Festivals Held in Albuquerque, New Mexico, 1977, and Tempe, Arizona, 1978* (1980) edited by Margarita Cota-Cárdenas; *Chicanos: Antología histórica Y literaria*, edited by Tino Villanueva (1980); *Breaking Boundaries: Latina Writing and Critical Readings* (1980), edited by Asución Horno-Delgado et al.; *Chicano Literature* (1982), by Charles Tatum; *Woman of Her*

Word – Hispanic Women Write (1983), edited by Evangelina Vigil; *Literature Chicana – Creative and Critical Writings Through 1984* (1985), edited by Andrés Rodríguez and Roberto Trujillo; *Five Poets of Aztlán* (1985) edited by Santiago Daydí-Tolson; *Contemporary Chicana Poetry: A Critical Approach to an Emerging Literature* (1985), edited by Marta Sánchez; *Chicano Poetry, A Critical Introduction* (1986) by Cordelia Candelaria; *Nosotras: Latina Literature Today*, edited by María Boza, Beverly Silva, and Carmen Valle (1986); *Contemporary Chicano Poetry: An Anthology* (1986), edited by Wolfgang Binder; *Compañeras: Latina Lesbians* (1987), edited by Juanita Ramos; *Las Mujeres Hablan: An Anthology of Nuevo Mexicana Writers* (1988), edited by Tey Diana Rebolledo, Erlinda Gonzales-Berry and Teresa Márquez; *U.S. Hispanic Autobiography* (1988), edited by Julián Olivares et al. A culminating selected and annotated bibliography of work published in the field including throughout the entirety of 1980s can be found in *Criticism in the Borderlands*, edited by Héctor Calderón and José David Saldívar (1991).

Theater is a foundational genre in Latina/o literature because it organically brings together various literary forms grounded in oral, spoken, and gestural traditions. Furthermore, because plays are written to engage an audience, to literally stage a conversation for further exploration and engagement, dramatic literature deeply reflects contemporary issues and the social world. A written play must be understood as only half a text that is fully completed by a creative team that renders the work into performance in front of a live audience in a theater space, be that a public street, town hall, or university theater. Theater is therefore very much about the issue of embodiment, how the body factors into who people are and how they inhabit the world. It is also about expressing the relationship between what people say and what people do. So many of the issues at the cultural forefront of the 1980s, such as the Iran-Contra scandal, were precisely about the dissonance between appearance and actuality, the actors and the directors. Plays written during the decade help readers in the present better understand the issues at the forefront of national and cultural politics. In looking at dramatic literature generally, it is important to acknowledge there is a politics to the publication of dramatic literature, with mainstream publishers typically only publishing plays that have had a nationally regarded successful commercial run.

María Irene Fornés is the most important Latina/o dramatist from the 1980s. A Cuban-born author, her work emerges from the tradition of the avant-garde. She defined playwriting as a form of "painting with words." This is reflected in the stylistic characteristics of her plays, which often include detailed notes about the visual impact of set design and other aspects of staging. Actors have described her dialogue as both challenging and exciting for the ways it seeks to be tersely poetic while representing everyday speech patterns. In interviews from the period, Fornés openly eschewed labels and categories, such as Hispanic or lesbian, because she felt they set up narrow expectations about the work a writer might produce and imposed a fixed frame of reference that deformed how critics, readers, and audiences approached the work. Her plays addressed issues that were central to the 1980s, such as environmentalism, literacy, domestic violence, and political unrest in Latin America. Among her signature plays from the period are: *The Danube* (1982); *Mud* (1983); the Obie award winning *Sarita* (1984); *Conduct of Life* (1985); and *Abingdon Square* (1988), for which she also received an Obie. Her plays are published in the collected volumes *María Irene Fornés: Plays* (1986) and *Promenade and Other Plays* (1987). Notably Fornés was a 1990 finalist for the Pulitzer Prize for Drama for *What of the Night* (1989), making her the first Latina/o playwright to be nominated for this award.

Fornés also had major impact during the 1980s as a writing teacher and mentor. She is cofounder (with Max Ferrá) of the Hispanic Playwrights Lab at International Arts Relations (INTAR) in New York City. Her goal in founding the lab was to create a space for the training of Latina/o playwrights because she was concerned that the many talented Latina/o dramatists she encountered felt there were few Latina/o role models representing a writer's life as a dramatist. Additionally, as someone trained in the avant-garde, Fornés believed that diversity – of thought, art, and artists – is foundational to the vibrancy and excellence of the American theater and was struck by the lack of Latina/o playwrights featured on the American stage. With the Hispanics Playwrights Lab, Fornés provided a foundational space for artistic training that acknowledged cultural specificity and cultivated craft, most especially in the writing of provocative plays intended to move and challenge audiences. She is legendary for admonishing students to be clear about the difference between producing art and participating in politics, a message that empowered a generation of Latina/o writers to expand the frame of their thinking to privilege accountability to art as well as to community building and social change. Fornés's teaching has influenced nearly every Latina/o dramatist writing today, from Cherríe Moraga to Nilo Cruz, either directly as a participant in the Hispanic Playwrights Lab, or indirectly as a student working with a former student of the Lab, such as Migdalia Cruz or Caridad Svich, carrying forward her visionary teaching exercises.

José Cruz González is another significant voice in Latina/o dramatic literature as a project director and a theater artist with a special focus on plays for young audiences. He launched and led South Coast Repertory's Hispanic

Playwrights Project (HPP), inaugurated in 1986. During its tenure, the HPP prompted the submission of more than a thousand manuscripts, of which more than fifty received workshops and more than half went on to full productions at SCR and other resident theaters. Among the works produced at SCR during the 1980s: *Once Removed* by Eduardo Machado (1986); *Birds* by Lisa Loomer (1986); *The Promise* by José Rivera (1987); *Passion* by Ana Maria Simo (1987); *My Visits with MGM (My Grandmother Marta)* by Edit Villarreal; *Young Valiant* by Oliver Mayer; *Shadow of a Man* by Cherríe Moraga; *Trafficking in Broken Hearts* by Edwin Sánchez.

On the scholarly front during the 1980s, Jorge Huerta published several groundbreaking works that effectively established the field of Latino theater studies. These include *Chicano Theater: Themes and Forms* (1982), *Necessary Theater: Six Plays About the Chicano Experience* (1989), and *Nuevos Pasos: Chicano and Puerto Rican Drama* (1989), coedited with Nicolás Kanellos. As a theater historian and arts practitioner, Huerta produced work that offered an informed reading of drama and performance that documented the field while also sharing the perspective of those on the creative front lines. He introduced the phrase "necessary theater" to capture the ways Chicano theater troupes such as El Teatro Campesino and Teatro de la Esperanza were using plays to stage an intervention to end oppression. As the leading professor in Latino theater studies, Huerta also had influence training a generation of theater artists and scholars. Luis Valdez is among the playwrights whose work he critically documented, and his former students include the dramatists Carlos Morton and Josefina López.

Luis Valdez is one of the most important Latina/o playwrights of the decade. As a movement-based theater artist, during the 1980s he extended the continuity of his work from the previous decade as the founding artistic director of El Teatro Campesino. In the 1980s, Valdez's plays affirmed culturally specific and politically grounded storytelling, exemplified by *Bandido* (1981), *Corridos* (1982), and *I Don't Have to Show You No Stinking Badges* (1986), which directly explored the political ironies of the "decade of the Hispanic" in a story that featured Latina/o veteran professional film actors relegated to the roles of extras, perpetually cast as stereotypes who are always visibly present yet in the background or visually controlled as marginalized figures. In the 1980s, Valdez's work in theater extends into film with the cinematic version of his signature work, *Zoot Suit* (Universal Pictures, 1982) and *La Bamba* (Columbia Pictures, 1987), his adaptation of the biography of late 1950s rock singer Ritchie Valens.

Miguel Piñero is another significant playwright of the 1980s. His most noted work, *Short Eyes* (1974), holds the distinction of being the first Latino play on Broadway, next followed by Luis Valdez's *Zoot Suit* (1979), and then in the 1980s by Reinaldo Povod's *Cuba and His Teddy Bear* (1986). Notably, all three plays feature Latina/o characters as criminalized subjects, a pattern that concerns Latino literary critics who wonder why the Latino outlaw continues to be what makes Latina/o subjects legible to Broadway theater and Hollywood film. Within the context of Latina/o literature, these plays make important contributions to the reading of Latinas/os who come from difficult circumstances. Piñero's signature plays from the 1980s include: *La Bodega Sold Dreams* (1980); *The Sun Always Shines for the Cool; a Midnight Moon at the Greasy Spoon; Eulogy for a Small Time Thief* (1984); *Smuggler's Blues* (1984); and *Outrageous: One Act Plays* (1986).

In addition to INTAR, the New World Theater at the University of Massachusetts, Amherst, under the direction of Roberta Uno, is an incredibly important institutional space for the advancement of Latina/o theater, and the university houses a most impressive historical archive of work from the period. In the 1980s, there was also the publication of the anthology *On New Ground: Contemporary Hispanic American Plays* (1987), edited by M. Elizabeth Osborn, which made readily available for study several important Latina/o plays and affirmed the critical significance of Latina/o dramatic literature to American drama. Other notable plays from the 1980s include Carlos Morton's *Rancho Hollywood* (1980) and *The Many Deaths of Danny Rosales and Other Plays* (1983) as well as *Johnny Tenorio* (1983), which together explored themes of Chicano masculinity and interpersonal struggle. Denise Chávez's *How Junior Got Throwed in the Joint* (1981) was performed at the State Penitentiary of New Mexico, Santa Fe, and her *Novena Narrative* (1987), a work with a national tour, had a particularly strong influence on Latina writers' thinking about storytelling in performance. Eduardo Machado is one of the most produced playwrights of the period with *The Modern Ladies of Guanabacoa* (1983), *Broken Eggs* (1984), and *In the Eye of the Hurricane* (1989). José Rivera is a significant playwright known for his lyricism with one of his most critically important works, *The House of Ramón Iglesia: A Drama in Two Acts* (1983), produced during this time. Estela Portillo Trambley is a voice who is foundational to looking at the evolution of Latina playwrights, with her work from this period represented by the collection *Sor Juana and Other Plays* (1983). Dolores Prida is one of the most important feminist voices from the 1980s; she wrote plays in both English and Spanish, and her works *Coser y Cantar* (1981), *Savings* (1985), and *Pantallas* (1986) explore the roles of women in business and commerce as well as family and community. In 1984, Richard Montoya, Ric Salinas, Herbert Sigüenza, Marga Gomez, Monica Palacios, and José Antonio Burciaga formed the socially and politically charged comic performance group Culture Clash; the group later revised itself with Montoya, Salinas, and Sigüenza as its three members, who then wrote and nationally toured *The Mission* (1988). Gomez and Palacios are major figures in Latina feminist performance during the 1980s, working at the junctures of comic performance and solo theater. Cherríe Moraga's *Giving Up the Ghost: Teatro in Two Acts* (1986) is a landmark play from the decade, drawing on the *testimonio* genre to tell a story about two feminist Chicana lesbians grappling with histories of violence and oppression, including sexual assault and heteropatriarchy. Evelina Fernández's *How Else Am I Supposed to Know I'm Still Alive* (1989) is a critically acclaimed work from the period that explores the friendship between two women sharing their dreams as well as their life struggles. Josefina López's *Simply María or The American Dream* (1989) marks the playwright's debut as the youngest produced Latina/o dramatist with a play that endures as an inspiring coming-of-age story. During the late 1980s, the performance artist Guillermo Gómez-Peña was experimenting with hybrid forms in the realm of theater and visual culture to trouble conversations about issues of immigration and identity politics, represented by his "Border Culture: The Multicultural Paradigm" (1989).

Poetry is by far the genre with the most publication activity during the 1980s. Poetry provides a vehicle for experimentation in voice and form, documenting social issues, even sounding an alarm. The poetry of the time also reflects currents in feminism and various movements under way in arts and politics. Poets associated with the Nuyorican Poets Café, for example, illustrate the precursor aesthetics of hip-hop and rap. Among the authors associated with this arts and cultural space are: Tato Laviera, whose published books of poetry published during the 1980s include *Enclave* (1981), *La Carreta Made a U-Turn* (1984), and *Mainstream Ethics: Etica Corriente* (1988); Nuyorican Poets Café founder, Miguel Algarín, *On Call* (1980) and *Time's Now* (1985); Pedro Pietri, *Telephone Booth Number 190* (1980) and *Traffic Violations* (1983); and Sandra Maria Esteves, *Yerba Buena: Dibujos Y Poemas* (1980) and *Tropical Rains: A Bilingual Downpour* (1984).

Chicano poets in the Southwest also experiment with aesthetics and engage with themes of social movement through poetry as a genre that facilitates exploring the contours and possibilities of language as a means to expand consciousness. José Montoya, a master poet of the Chicano Movement renowned for his wordplay and puns, had strong influence on the generation of poets working in the 1980s. Alurista is another major figure that wrote in English and Spanish as well as bilingually, incorporating street slang from both languages, represented in the witty title *Spik in Glyph?* (1981). Jimmy Santiago Baca began writing poetry in prison and published several volumes of poetry during the decade, including *Swords of Darkness*

(1981), *Downtown* (1981), *What's Happening* (1982), *Immigrants in Our Own Land & Selected Early Poems* (1982), *Poems Taken from My Yard* (1986), *Martín: &, Meditations on the South Valley* (1987), and *Black Mesa Poems* (1989). Across the scope of these writers one finds an exploration of many themes, including labor, racism, incarceration, and masculinity.

There is a tremendous surge in the publication of Latina poets during the 1980s that illustrates the turn to poetry as an incredibly potent site to explore issues central to feminist discourse: private versus public parenthood, mother-daughter relationships, culturally proscribed gender roles, spirituality, and sensuality. Carmen Tafolla published with an ear toward future generations with *Patchwork Colcha, A Children's Collection: Poems, Stories & Songs in Spanish and English* (1980), and her book *Curandera* (1983) is regarded as exemplifying literary language and code-switching; she also published the genre-crossing *To Split a Human: Mitos, Machos y la Mujer Chicana* (1985). Lorna Dee Cervantes's *Emplumada* (1981) had a tremendous impact on thinking in the field about Chicana poetics, the collection viewed as landmark work for its deployment of form to grapple with pressing questions about self and community. Sandra Cisneros's poetry boldly takes on the themes of sex and desire in *Bad Boys* (1980) and *My Wicked, Wicked Ways* (1987). Ana Castillo's work offered a fiercely vocal persona concerned with redefining spirituality and sensuality and situating both as political issues, illustrated in *Women Are Not Roses* (1984) and *My Father Was a Toltec* (1988). Other landmark poets from this decade include: Alma Villanueva, *Golden Glass* (1981) and *Life Span* (1984); Pat Mora, *Chants* (1984) and *Borders* (1986); Judith Ortiz Cofer, *Peregrina* (1986) and *Terms of Survival: Poems* (1987). It is significant that during the 1980s many of these authors were writing across genres, a further illustration of how this was a moment in which writers felt free to work in various forms. Additionally significant Latina poets from the period include: Olivia Castellano, *Blue Mandolin, Yellow Field* (1980), *Blue Horse of Madness* (1983), and *Spaces That Time Missed* (1986); Gina Valdés, *There Are No Madmen Here* (1981) and *Comiendo Lumbre: Eating Fire* (1986); Luz Maria Umpierre, *The Margarita Poems* (1987); and Evangelina Vigil-Piñón, author of *Thirty An' Seen a Lot* (1982) and translator of the definitive edition of Tomás Rivera's short story collection/poetic novella, *... y no se lo tragó la tierra* (1987). A signature book of poetry is Rosario Morales and Aurora Levin Morales's *Getting Home Alive* (1986), coauthored by mother and daughter about their grappling with personal and political issues across their generations. A landmark collection distinguishing Latina poetry of the 1980s is *Three Times a Woman: Chicana Poetry* (1989), featuring the work of Demetria Martinez, Alicia Gaspar de Alba, and María Herrera-Sobek.

Gary Soto is one of the most distinguished and prolific poets from the decade. His work celebrates daily life and speaks with humor. Among his published works are *The Elements of San Joaquin* (1977), *Father Is a Pillow Tied to a Broom* (1980), *Where Sparrows Work Hard* (1981), *Black Hair* (1985), *Small Faces* (1986), and *Off and Running* (1986). Alberto Ríos is a pivotal voice from this period renowned for his moving and lyric storytelling, often exploring themes of family and history in the compact space of poetry with the books *Sleeping on Fists* (1981), *Whispering to Fool the Wind: Poems* (1982), and *Five Indiscretions: A Book of Poems* (1985). Juan Felipe Herrera is one of the decade's signature voices know for his vibrant wordplay and fearless experimentation with form and theme. His work includes *Exiles of Desire* (1983) and *Mission Street Manifesto: For All Varrios* (1983). Ray González is renowned for the reflective quality of his work in *From the Restless Roots* (1986) and *Twilights and Chants: Poems* (1987). Other important figures from the decade include: Victor Hernandez Cruz, *By Lingual Wholes* (1982); Tino Villanueva, *Shaking Off the Dark* (1984); Leo Romero, *Celso* (1985); Martín Espada, *Trumpets from the Islands of Their Eviction* (1987); and Luis J. Rodríguez, *Poems Across the Pavement* (1989). These works exemplify the bold construction of persona with these male authors working to simultaneously affirm and interrogate definitions of masculinity.

Short story collections are another important genre for reading Latino literature of the 1980s. These works often carry the force of novels. Two of the most critically significant collections from the period are Tomás Rivera's ... *y no se lo tragó la tierra/ And the Earth Did Not Devour Him* (bilingual edition, 1980) and Sandra Cisneros's *The House on Mango Street* (1983). Both are coming-of-age narratives with characteristics that place them within the genres of the short story as well as the short novel. Rivera's collection tells the story of a young boy and his experiences with trauma and violence as a child migrant farmworker. Cisneros's book centers on a young girl growing up in an urban landscape navigating the hazards of girlhood while yearning for a place to call home. Both works are considered literary classics and have inspired film and theatrical adaptations. Other landmark short story collections from the decade are Nicholasa Mohr's *Rituals of Survival: A Woman's Portfolio* (1985), Helena María Viramontes's *The Moths and Other Stories* (1985), Denise Chávez's *The Last of the Menu Girls* (1986), and Nicholasa Mohr's *El Bronx Remembered: A Novella and Stories* (1986) and *In Nueva York* (1988). These works include stories in the bildungsroman tradition charged by a personal voice so deftly drawn it appears autobiographical. All gained the attention of critics for the ways they documented the experiences of girlhood and womanhood, exploring complicated interpersonal and social dynamics while also pressing central questions about politics, culture, gender, and power. Viramontes is considered one of the most exceptional authors writing in the genre of the short story and widely respected as both an editor and master teacher. All of the aforementioned short story collections remain regarded as foundational works in the field.

There is a notable body of authors working principally in the genre of the short story, among them: José Antonio Burciaga, *Sammy y los Del Tercer Barrio* (1983); Mary Helen Ponce, *Recuerdo: Short Stories of the Barrio* (1983); Dagoberto Gilb, *Winners on the Pass Line* (1985); and Sabine Ulibarrí, *El Cóndor and Other Stories* (1988). As many authors in the 1980s embraced working across genres, established writers in other mediums produced short story collections during the period. These include: Rudolfo Anaya, *The Silence of the Llano: Short Stories* (1982); Alberto Ríos, *The Iguana Killer: Twelve Stories of the Heart* (1984); Luz María Umpierre, *Y Otras Desgracias and Other Misfortunes* (1985); and Nash Candelaria, *The Day the Cisco Kid Shot John Wayne* (1988).

There is an exciting range of novelistic work produced during the 1980s. Marking the commencement of the decade is Luis Sánchez's *Macho Camacho's Beat* (1980), a comic novel about Puerto Rico and the influences of popular culture on thinking about identity. Rudolfo Anaya builds from his foundational early novel *Bless Me, Ultima* (1972) with several works: *The Legend of La Llorona: A Short Novel* (1984); *The Adventures of Juan Chicaspatas* (1985); *Lord of the Dawn: The Legend of Quetzalcóatl* (1987); and *The Farolitos of Christmas* (1987). Nash Candelaria is another major voice whose work focuses on the people of New Mexico; his novels *Not by the Sword* (1982) and *Inheritance of Strangers* (1985) explore the history of the Rafa family. Aside from his many books of poetry, essays, and novels, Rolando Hinojosa is the author of the fifteen-volume Klail City Death Trip novel series, a multigenerational narrative about a fictional county in lower Rio Grande Valley of Texas. His publications during the 1980s include: *Rites and Witnesses* (1982); *The Valley: A Re-Creation in Narrative Prose of a Portfolio of Etchings, Engravings, Sketches, and Silhouettes by Various Artists in Various Styles, Plus a Set of Photographs from a Family Album* (1983); *Partners in Crime* (1985); and *Klail City* (1987), for which he was the first Chicano author to receive the prestigious Premio Casa de las Américas award. Oscar Hijuelos is one of the most important novelists of the decade with *Our House in the Last World: A Novel* (1983) and *The Mambo Kings Play Songs of Love* (1989), which was recognized by a Pulitzer Prize for Fiction in 1990. Other important novelists and works published during the decade include: Richard Vasquez, *Another Land* (1982);

José Antonio Villarreal, *Clemente Chacón: A Novel* (1984) and *The Fifth Horseman* (1984); Roberto Fernández, *Raining Backwards* (1988); Genaro González, *Rainbow's End* (1988); Virgil Suárez, *Latin Jazz* (1989); and José Yglesias, *Tristan and the Hispanics* (1989).

The 1980s is a distinguishing decade in Latina/o literature for the emergence of novels that feature gay and lesbian characters and explore related themes that engage the intersections between Latina/o and queer identity. John Rechy is among the most important novelists, unabashedly writing about sexuality and a range of relationships. His works include: *Rushes* (1981); *Numbers* (1981); *The Sexual Outlaw* (1981); and *Tiger's Wild* (1986). Arturo Islas's *The Rain God* (1984) is highly regarded for its poignant illustration a cultural moment during the AIDS crisis and the process of grappling with cultural trauma. Michael Nava launched his career as a novelist with the first two of his seven-volume Henry Rios mystery series starring an openly gay criminal defense attorney: *The Little Death* (1986) and *Goldenboy* (1988), for which he was among the first recipients of the highly prestigious Lambda Literary Award. Elías Muñoz's *Crazy Love* (1989) is a novella that looks at the underside of the American Dream and is groundbreaking in its exploration of childhood sexual assault as experienced by a young male. Jaime Manrique's *Colombian Gold* (1983) is another significant novel and looks at the life of a young gay immigrant in Manhattan.

Novels produced by Latinas during the 1980s also reflected the incredible sea changes under way as women of color shifted the lens that had been brought to the reading of their work. Among the decade's novels written by Latinas are: Margarita Cota-Cárdenas, *Puppet: A Chicano Novella* (1985); Angela de Hoyos, *Woman, Woman* (1985); Ana Castillo, *The Mixquiahuala Letters* (1986); Mary Helen Ponce, *Taking Control* (1987); Alma Villanueva, *The Ultraviolet Sky* (1988); Judith Ortiz Cofer, *The Line of the Sun* (1989); Lucha Corpi, *Delia's Song* (1989); Mary Helen Ponce, *The Wedding* (1989). Castillo's *The Mixquiahuala Letters* illustrates the ways Latina writers additionally experimented with form, the novel told through a series of numbered letters with the author recommending different sequences for reading.

Memoirs and autobiography are pivotal genres to the reading of Latina/o literature during the 1980s because they are precisely about the articulation of self and model grappling with the tensions between imposed expectations for identity performance and definitions of the self that are by nature complicated and contradictory. Richard Rodriguez's *Hunger of Memory: The Education of Richard Rodriguez* (1981) is one of the decade's most important works in the genre. The memoir recounts the author's experience obtaining a college education under the support of affirmative action programming and the personal losses he perceived as a result of being labeled. The book remains a source of contention for many readers who take issue with the ways the book was embraced and promoted by political conservatives invested in ending programming that specifically targeted historically marginalized students. Edward Rivera's *Family Installments: Memories of Growing Up Hispanic* (1982) tells the story of his family's journey from Puerto Rico to New York, and continues to be regarded as a pivotal immigration story. Cherríe Moraga's *Loving in the War Years / lo que nunca pasó por sus labios* (1983) is understood as a most critically significant memoir of the 1980s. The work is foundational to Latina feminist and queer studies because it offered a theoretical groundwork for understanding the specificity of oppression for Latinas generally and Latina lesbians specifically. Additionally, the memoir's incorporation of multiple genres (poetry, essay, *testimonio*) exemplifies how Latinas engaged with narrative form to arrive at new ways of speaking about life experiences. Gary Soto's *Living Up the Street: Narrative Recollections* (1985) stands in conversation with his short story collection of the same title and illustrates how Latina/o writers often work across genres to process the same story, working from personal experience as a springboard for creative exploration. Rudolfo Anaya's *A Chicano in China* (1986) reflects on his time living in China and the connections he draws between Chinese and Chicano cultures. Gloria Anzaldúa's *Borderlands / La Frontera: The New Mestiza* (1987) is one of the signal works of the 1980s and regarded as a foundational to Latina/o literary studies. It is also a multi-genre work that employs personal experience and *testimonio* as the engine for theorizing the history of the border as fundamentally linked to a history of trauma whose wounds have yet to be fully addressed. The book is groundbreaking in its frank and poetic exploration of how the author feels shaped through the legacy of colonial oppression and the language she discerns to make the personal violence she endured generative to the collective work of cultural healing and social change. The work continues to be celebrated and engaged through an annual conference held by the Society for the Study of Gloria Anzaldúa.

The 1980s, the so-called decade of the Hispanic, marks a vitally important moment in Latina/o literary production. It is a time of great experimentation with an incredible outpouring of work in multiple genres, with many writers defying categorization and working across mediums in a gesture of resistance against the larger culture's narrow lens of reading their work through such labels as Hispanic. By the end of the decade, Latina/o writing strongly clarifies how Latina/o literature reads as its own tradition of writing and additionally belongs to a broader field of American literature. The range and volume of literature produced during the 1980s reflects the cultural climate of the decade, the resonance of work from the past, and a setting of the stage for the works to follow.

Acknowledgments

I would like to publicly acknowledge Esmeralda Arrizón-Palomera for her bibliographic research contributions to this essay. Her assistance facilitated the range of references charted in this essay. I would also like to thank Karen Mary Davalos, Eliza Rodriguez y Gibson, Patricia Herrera, Lisette Lasater, and AnneMarie Perez for their conversations with me about the work.

7

LUCÍA M. SUÁREZ

Trans-American Latina/o Literature of the 1990s: Resisting Neoliberalism

In the 1990 census, the Latina/o population in the United States was 22.3 million; by 2000, this number soared to 35.3 million.[1] The decade in between proved to be pivotal for two major reasons. First, the U.S. focus shifted from the Cold War and communism to a renewed preoccupation with illegal migrations from the global South. Through the manipulation of sensationalistic stereotyping, the news media spotlighted Latin American and Caribbean peoples illegally crossing borders by night to Texas, Arizona, New Mexico, and Southern California and desperately traveling on makeshift rafts to Florida. These migrants were portrayed as desperate masses that contained drug dealers, gang members, and thieves threatening public safety. A conservative chorus responded: this hemorrhage of human unwanteds had to be deterred. The U.S. government consequently began the construction of a projected 2,000-mile border fence with Mexico, of which 62 miles were erected by 1998.[2] Second, just as this campaign against Latin American and Caribbean migrations started to rage, mainstream trade presses, including Penguin, Plume, Simon and Shuster, Harper and Row,[3] Norton, and Random House, enthusiastically published the stories of Latinas/os and small, university, Hispanic and Latina/o presses produced more than thirty anthologies by and about Latinas/os.[4] Adopted as part of a multicultural canon throughout the country, authors such as Sandra Cisneros, Ana Castillo, Esmeralda Santiago, Julia Alvarez, Junot Díaz, and Cristina García began gracing high school and college reading lists. Their writings nuanced issues of migration, class, race, gender, and sexuality in the United States and explored the complex relationships that exist between two homeland identities.

Latinas/os are at once peoples to be despised and kept out and members of plural communities that are an indelible part of the U.S. national picture. The two narratives presented, alien and American, dangerous and assimilated, underscore a discursive duality that continues to afflict the nation's largest minority population. In effect, this parallel situation – aggression against, and mainstream inclusion of Latinas/os – presents two distinctive chronicles that can be traced to ideologies of dispossession based on racializing worldviews produced during the colonial period, and, more recently, further grafted by neoliberal principles. Despite the fact that many Latinas/os are economically stable and even wealthy, the media features the disadvantaged. Latinas/os are affronted by stereotypes that deny their personal experiences and ignore their socioeconomic plurality and the sociopolitical mechanisms that have historically prevented poor populations from attaining the "American dream." On the one hand, without adequate education, sustainable employment, or access to health benefits, the impoverished are hard-pressed to enter the realm of agentic citizenship in any country. On the other hand, the presence of Latina/o literary voices and characters proves that they constitute a fundamental fiber of the American nation. At issue is a binary of dispossession versus personhood, continued exclusion in light of selectively accepted inclusion.

This binary accentuates the dual discursive narratives of Latinas/os as foreign and uninvited (escaping wars, political oppression, and extreme poverty in their native lands) and national (belonging for generations to the terrain of the United States or annexed into its borders). Reminiscent of long-established European strategies of deprivation, individual and communal Latina/o experiences are hierarchically divided along economic lines that define them as either failures or achievers. According to this narrative, the despondently poor and unskilled cannot belong, while those who gain education and visibility, through literature for example, are imagined to be of another ilk. This rationale is based on values of possessive individualism. At issue are the schisms produced by popular conceptualizations of freedom (individual responsibility for economic success) in contrast to lived experiences where agency is negated to those individuals who have no possessions and continue to be victims of sociocultural prejudice and semantic slurring.

In response to limiting binary narratives, Latina/o literatures of the 1990s offer a fertile ground for numerous, inherently varied, historically differentiated trans-American histories to flourish. Resistant of sweeping economic and political generalizations, this literary corpus underscores the universal desire for a good life (sustainable work, health benefits, education, and the possibility for upward social mobility) sought by Latin American and Caribbean people on U.S. soil. Thus, what it is to be human in the public sphere is reframed from a place where the private is valued substantively. Latina/o literatures of the decade underscore the fact that Latina/o communities include newly arrived, established, and migrant peoples responding to a vast array of circumstances. They contextualize the extensive differences that include status identifications such as immigrant, exiled, diaspora, refugee, hyphenated (Cuban-American, Mexican-American), re-territorialized (*Mexicanos, tejanos, californios*), and recuperative (Chicanas/os). Latina/o literatures are complex, casting light onto all of the ways in which peoples from Latin America, the Caribbean, and annexed territories have historically been exploited and kept from assimilating into the American dream. Simultaneously, they prove that Latinas/os are a part of the mainstay of American culture, succeeding in meaningful ways.

A significant question arises: Can a few select literary "stars" truly open the door to inclusion, understanding, and an organic acceptance of the numerous "bodies" of Latin American and Caribbean peoples in the United States? In this chapter, I outline the political premises of possessive individualism and neoliberalism, and their lasting legacy, to explicate the narrative constructs foundational to contemporary portrayals of Latinas/os. I propose that autobiography, fiction, and testimonies function as resources that assist Latinas/os in actively claiming their experiences and valuing their contributions in a trans-American context, within and beyond the United States.

Labeling: Acts of Derision and Dispossession

Since the colonial period, Latin American identity politics have been built on a series of systems meant to extract labor and land for a ruling elite (conquistadors, plantation owners, U.S. transnational corporations). Fundamentally, these systems were based on presumptions that were androcentric, European, and misogynistic. According to Audrey Smedley, the historical tenets of inequality, exclusion, and servitude date back to the Spanish during the Inquisition (1478–1834), when policies of conversion, dispersion, and extermination were brutally implemented, and the English "enclosure movement" in the fifteenth century, when communal lands and meadows were turned into private property.[5] In Spain, the ostracized consisted of the Jews and the Moors, and, in England, the colonized people of Ireland. The Spanish and English labeled Jews, Moors, the Irish, Africans, and (later) indigenous nations of the Americas as barbarous and uncivilized. The colonizers "all shared a common belief that those whom they conquered were in some sense 'savages,' despite the recognized diversity among the indigenous cultures and the different conceptions of savagery among the Europeans."[6] Defining them with repulsive and negative adjectives such as deceitful, lazy, disorderly, dirty, licentious, untamed, wild, and uncontrolled, the colonizers justified the exploitation and genocides that they enacted. By the seventeenth century, a unifying political way of viewing the world was established in English society that juxtaposed the English merchant to the barbaric, unruly savage. Smedley explains that the English systematically disadvantaged the

Irish: English laws prohibited the Irish from owning land, learning skills or crafts, or serving on juries. Merchant wealth was further amassed through religious and national laws that foreclosed education and work for their subjects in Ireland. English capitalist ventures made some men very wealthy and reduced the rest to abject poverty.[7] Accordingly, the "principal identity [of the latter] was that of cheap labor."[8] The Irish resisted the English empire, turning their plantation ventures into failures. The resulting "saga of tension and hostility" between the English and the Irish served to affirm accusations against the latter that the Irish were "rude, beastly, ignorant, cruel and unruly infidels."[9]

The relationship between the end of feudalism, the rise of private property, and the extension of the savage/civilized binary is at the root of the racial worldview in place today.[10] This worldview was driven by the notion of possessive individualism, which was established by Locke with the three words: "Life, Liberty and Estate."[11] These three words, Smedley proposes, demarcated an era whereby "the English concepts of individual personhood, autonomy, and freedom" impacted "economic, religious, social institutions, values, laws and customs."[12] In other words, society was cast between the deserving rich and the undeserving poor. According to C. B. MacPherson, possessive individualism defines "man [as] free and human by virtue of his sole proprietorship of his own person," casting "human society [a]s essentially a series of market relations."[13] Smedley continues:

> These ideas and ideals as well as Locke's general vision of civil rights and human liberties were transported to the American colonies in varying forms and modifications, and ultimately became part of the economic worldview, and rhetoric, of most Americans.[14]

The constructs of possessive individualism are at the core of contemporary neoliberal discourse and economic policies.

According to political scientist Javier Corrales, neoliberalism's rise was propelled by numerous factors, including "theoretical refinement, Nobel prizes, model cases, rising technopols, smart packaging, and plenty of international sticks and carrots."[15] The Nobel Prizes won by its leading proponents, Friedrich von Hayek and Milton Friedman in 1974 and 1976, respectively, brought worldwide attention to neoliberal ideas. Subsequently, the debt crisis of 1982 left Latin American countries desperate and ready to engage in extreme measures. After several years of increased levels of inflation, economies were devastated: the middle class shrank and poverty skyrocketed within months.[16] Countries, hungry for solutions, turned to neoliberalism, which focused on fiscal austerity, reduced state intervention, and massive privatization. Technopols, or U.S.-trained Latin American economists, returned to their native countries in the 1980s, championing pro-market ideas.[17] Corrales continues that "neoliberal ideas and scholars seemed unstoppable" by the end of that decade.[18] In brief, price pressures and creditor incentives offered by the International Monetary Fund (IMF), the World Bank, and the United States motivated many countries to espouse neoliberal reforms enthusiastically, if not drastically. For example, Pinochet welcomed the Chicago Boys, Friedman and his disciples, to consult on the Chilean economy. Mexico opened "free trade" negotiations with the United States through NAFTA, Argentina enforced "strict monetary policies and a convertibility law," Peru sanctioned a "massive privatization program," Venezuela developed "sweeping banking liberalization," and Ecuador implemented "strict dollarization."[19]

While these policies had strong proponents, their opponents noted that neoliberal programs resulted in higher taxes, job losses for many, and discontinued social services.[20] Critics felt that targeted social programs espoused by neoliberals increased inequality because the cutbacks were severe and unevenly implemented.[21] The debates as to which was worse, the previous statism or the imposed neoliberalism, remained strong; under statism, "poverty exploded," yet under neoliberalism, "an uneven distribution of power" was enforced, which was "intrinsically biased against domestic actors relative to external ones."[22] The most consistent critique among sociocultural scholars against neoliberalism throughout Latin America and the Caribbean was that the countries were ignoring their populations in selling their goods to the world market. Rosario Santos's edited collection of short stories, *And We Sold the Rain*, clearly references this general feeling of a nation selling out to global political and business players.[23] Corrales observes that "market reforms ... paid insufficient attention to poverty, inequality and access to social services."[24] Reminiscent of previous strategies of exclusion mastered by the English and the Spanish, the economic reforms ushered by neoliberals disadvantaged the already poor and further stratified the haves and have-nots.

Neoliberal narratives of freedom strongly reference dialectics of possessive individualism, arguing for merit-based social mobility and ignoring inherent structures of cultural and social dispossession. While, in theory, immigration and assimilation are the expected outcome for all who arrive to the United States, in reality, neoliberalism's focus on possessive individualism imposes parameters of equal treatment that, in effect, deepen existing inequality and violence. Asking disadvantaged people to function as equals sets them up to fail. Consequently, the neoliberal rhetoric of incorporation, production, and reproduction has produced a greater economic and narrative disparity between the excluded and the included. Ideologically, a conspicuous schism between concepts of freedom and attainment of agency are at play. Neoliberals would argue that everyone has the freedom to succeed and become an individual with the right to ownership. However, the reality is that growing global poverty necessitates migration by creating a large underclass of disposable bodies, unwelcomed and abused because they are labeled as different and dangerous. Minority groups (i.e., Afro-descendent, indigenous, queer, women, children) who have escaped poverty and violence in their home nations and survive urban poverty and marginalization in their host country are the most acute victims of the resulting hierarchies of dispossession. Their circumstances preclude the possessive individualism they need in order to become active citizens of any nation.

While the media features this disparity in an evident, if not exaggerated, manner, the reality is also deeply nuanced and ambivalent. Rossini and Ybarra note that inclusion is possible and real, as attested by Nilo Cruz, a Latino playwright who won the Pulitzer Prize for drama,[25] and, I would add, Junot Díaz's more recent Pulitzer Prize for fiction. Rossini and Ybarra quote David Román and Brian Herrera's statement that the success of Latino performers and "accurate 'cultural representation' on Broadway may sometimes precede the success of Latino performers in authentic local productions."[26] However, Rossini and Ybarra continue, these success stories "elide the shifting relations of art, capital, and identity."[27] They argue that there is a fundamental ambivalence of "neoliberal governmentality and identity politics, in which the protected freedom of individuals (and corporations as individuals) allows for visibility and voluntarist freedom to articulate individual identity claims as long as one is safely ensconced in a world of production and consumption."[28] In other words, the visibility gained by a select few responds to a culture of consumption that satisfies market trends such as multiculturalism. Often, the trends represent plural communities without truly believing in their inclusion, keeping old hierarchies in place, and homogenizing Latinos/as by featuring only those who fit into the mainstream. Those who make it could be singled out as individuals, not reflecting their communities or the nations they come from, but rather embodying a story of assimilation and success, as safe "others" who both are different and capable of blending in. Rossini and Ybarra suggest that while "the 1990s was a time of diversification, articulated within the rhetoric of affirmative action," the decade did not introduce cultural transformations or sociocultural expansion.[29] There was a disconnection between representation of the successful individual and acceptance of Latina/o communities with distinctive histories within the United States. The logistics of migration and immigration in globalized labor markets complicates the relationships between the individual, production, and consumption. Can the individual create new paradigms that counter the debilitating beliefs of the neoliberal individual and build new communities?

Writing: Creating Community through Literature

Concertedly, the Latina/o literary production of the decade presented narratives of Latina/o lives that valued their individual achievements, recognized the significance of their communities and national origins, and exposed the inherent classism, racism, and sexism to which they were often subjected. Much of the literature references specific historical, political moments that have necessitated migration or continued movement between borders. For example, Nicholasa Mohr's autobiography, *Growing Up Inside the Sanctuary of My Imagination* (1994),[30] depicts her memories of growing up female, poor, and Puerto Rican, and provides an intimate picture of how Operation Bootstrap (begun in 1949 to industrialize the Island) impoverished Puerto Rico. Mass migrations led to further poverty as a disproportionate part of the population that moved offered unskilled labor and suffered from severe discrimination.

In her epilogue she discloses a telling anecdote. She had been invited to write her autobiography by a press agent who later rejected her manuscript because it was not filled with the expected "world of nefarious exploits."[31] Mohr was shocked that, despite her talent and education, her agent still saw her as a Puerto Rican, who by default had to have had that kind of experience.[32] Mohr makes it clear that she had no stories to tell about gang wars, sex, or violence. She had been a good child, an outstanding student, and had never engaged with any kind of drugs. That agent was "dissatisfied" with the text; the author refused to invent a world to affirm all of the negative stereotypes that belittled her community and would misrepresent her life. Instead, she put her vignettes away, until another editor, Ellen Rudin at Harper and Row, recognized the value of her honesty.

Mohr highlights the importance of her Island's *cuentos* and her imagination to continue making up stories in which she was a protagonist, meriting all of the good that was systematically denied her by a conspicuously racist and classist culture. She recalls how special Christmas was as all of the family gathered to sing, cook, eat, and tell stories: "*el cuento puertorriqueño*, storytelling was also used as a way to mollify any number of crises ... Soon we were all enthralled, forgetting our grief, our hunger, or our anguish. When the story was over, our stress had lessened and once more life appeared endurable."[33]

With her text, Mohr presents three critical points. During her childhood in the United States during World War II, she could not find representations of people like her in literature. "On the screen, all the cowboys and war heroes were white Americans. Native Americans and Mexicans were the bad guys," she explains.[34] She achieved an education despite a public school system that ostracized her. She was reprimanded by a teacher ("Why don't you folks try to speak like real Americans"[35]) and recalled how her junior high school counselor would not allow her to apply to Music and Art High School because she would be using up the space of another student who could really go to college. Finally, her mother's life and words served as her anchor and greatest inspiration. Mohr observed how hard her mother worked to sustain her children, and how much she sacrificed to be a good wife. At age fourteen, Mohr heard her mother's final advice before she succumbed to cancer: "Be somebody, *mi hijita*, and have a life that will bring you joy and fulfillment. Let that joy come from within you."[36] She listened to her mother and chose a path for herself where she did not affirm any negative stereotypes, becoming an artist and later an acclaimed writer. Mohr emphasizes, "There are two major components that have helped me survive and thrive. The first was my imagination and the powers of my creative life. The second was my mother's faith in me and her determination that I succeed."[37] Her individual success highlights all that her community has to offer, and all that Latina women and their children can attain, despite rampant stereotyping, blatant ostracism, and structural oppression. Her book makes it clear: poverty is not synonymous with criminality.

Esmeralda Santiago's memoir *When I Was Puerto Rican* (1994) further supports the idea that Puerto Rican lives are multiple, resilient, and not defined exclusively by poverty.[38] The first of eleven children, raised by a single mother, Santiago exposes her childhood memories of extreme poverty on the Island, her mother's determination to go to New York to find a better life, and how education changed her experiences.[39] Her story underscores the particularities of the Puerto Ricans experience, being classified as neither white nor African American while being both American citizens and immigrants.

Cuban American and Cuban immigrant writings, such as Cristina García's novel *Dreaming in Cuban* (1992) and Reinaldo Arenas' memoir *Before Night Falls* (1993), further testify to the many circumstances that shape Latina/o memory and migration throughout ever-evolving historical periods (i.e., Cuban independence, the 1959 revolution, the 1980 Mariel exodus).[40] *Dreaming in Cuban* details family memories, traumas, and sociopolitical tensions through three generations of women (grandmother, mother, daughter) who have different relationships to Spanish colonialism, Fidel Castro's communism in Cuba, and democracy in the United States. The latter text denounces the ostracism experienced by homosexuals in Cuba in the 1970s and repercussions of life with AIDS in the United States. Through fiction and memoir, García and Arenas outline the vast differences in social, racial, and political affiliation and sexual orientation embodied by Cuban American Latinas/os.

Dominican American life stories, which until the 1990s had been mostly invisible in the U.S. literary market, received critical acclaim with books that include Julia Alvarez's *How the García Girls Lost Their Accents* (1991) and *In the Time of the Butterflies* (1994), Junot Díaz's *Drown* (1996), and Loida Maritza Pérez's *Geographies of Home* (1999).[41] Each book unveils a different dimension of Dominican American experiences. Julia Alvarez refocuses international attention on class and immigration with the García Girls whose father is a physician escaping political persecution, and reclaims the lives of the famous Mirabal Sisters, who were murdered opposing the brutal dictatorship of Rafael Leónidas Trujillo.[42] Junot Díaz, at first reading, offers the expected fare of macho violence in the hood and in the marginal spaces of his native country. But a closer reading reveals a crafty critique of the limitations of machismo and violence, as the protagonist Yunior is actually a gentle soul searching for his own safe place and life alternatives.[43]

Loida Maritza Pérez's novel *Geographies of Home* is a bittersweet story that exposes the inherited double consciousness of many postcolonial subjects, struggling to avoid being objects of continued public disdain and internalized self-negation. At home, her parents find safety and authority in religion; her sister scrubs herself with Brillo to cleanse herself and, perhaps, to lighten her skin; and Iliana, the protagonist, goes to college hoping to leave this world behind and discover her own pathway to the "American Dream." In her college far from home, she discovers relentless racism. Pérez submits this stark description:

> For a year and a half she had lived in a town whose pristine appearance had deceived her into believing, because she had wanted desperately to believe, that, having entered into the company of the elite, she would never again suffer hunger or abuse. She had clung to this belief despite hearing the word "NIGGER" erupt from the lips of strangers; seeing swastikas scrawled on the walls of synagogues; and witnessing women, marching to "take back the night," attacked for calling attention to the town's hidden violence. When classmates had presumed to know the inner workings of those of her race and class – inferring their inherent laziness, lack of motivation, welfare dependency and intellectual deficiency – she had stopped up her ears and gradually trained her eyes not to see. Yet rage turned her body against itself, transforming her stomach into an acidic mass that heaved bitterness into her mouth.[44]

These lines confirm how multilayered and tacit mechanisms of dispossession of "different" individuals continue to destroy their attempts to become possessive individuals in the classical sense. Notably, the novel exhibits how these mechanisms exist as much in the public realm of the elite as in the private confines of immigrant households, whose members suffer the traumatic scars of violations imposed in their native lands by dictators and postcolonial structures of power.

In addition, Pérez's story describes the methods employed to maintain dignity against all odds. While the father seeks support through the church, the mother finds strength through the practice of Afro-Caribbean religious rituals. The protagonist, Iliana, herself resorts to education. Her entry into an elite college is challenged, not because of her talent, but (reminiscent of the writings of Frantz Fanon) because of the evident color of her skin. Iliana reaches maturity only when she claims her self-worth in the described miasma of derision; she belongs to both worlds – impoverished and elite, Dominican and American – with a newfound compassion for herself and the family she once sought to escape. *Geographies of Home* is an immigrant bildungsroman whereby the central character gains racial awareness, understands family affiliations, and assumes Dominican national pride. Through writing, the author affirms her own place in the U.S. educational system and proposes a foundational analysis of the place of Dominican Americans in the United States.

The literary output of Chicana writers Sandra Cisneros and Ana Castillo during the 1990s testifies to the violence women and children in precarious situations (i.e., extreme poverty in the borderlands, illegal status in the United States) endure and survive. Their stories reposition the purviews of illegal and legal status and the arbitrariness of neoliberal ideology. Specifically, they challenge the invisibility of their protagonists' historical worth and accent their undeniably heroic actions.

Feminist literary critic Sonia Saldívar-Hull suggests that Cisneros does not gloss over the "contradictions embodied and experienced by Mexican immigrant women of color who live in poverty in the wealthiest country in the world and never experience themselves as fully constituted citizen subjects in a Mexican or US context."[45] Saldivar-Hull explains that the political action facilitated by transnational, transfronteriza practice of *feminismo popular* is a "type of border feminism [that] articulates a feminist materialist aesthetics that enables us to reexamine an emergent formation of feminism on the border, a formation characterized by specific types of movements of Mexican women across geopolitical boundaries and borders."[46] She maintains that Cisneros "skillfully rewrites la novella," and presents a new Chicana feminism that moves past convoluted abstraction and seeks to address the real-life difficulties faced by Chicana women."[47]

Ana Castillo also deftly employs fiction to describe the lives of women who are not in the annals of history, but whose accounts deserve credit on numerous levels. For example, the character Doña Felicia in *So Far From God*[48] details the struggles of the dispossessed and the dignity required to stay alive, working in alternative yet worthy ways. Orphaned at a very young age, Doña Felicia had been a young and illiterate mother; an autodidact, she learned to read and write in Spanish and English. She escaped deportation by joining the army during World War II, trained as a nurse, and went to France where she learned to speak French. An undocumented woman who witnessed the murder of her own children in anti-Mexican border country, she devoted herself to her community. In her role as a healer (trained nurse and spiritual guru), she became useful from the margins of the nation to her undocumented and marginalized community. Her story shows how an individual in the globalized labor market is both alone and connected. While she does not count officially as a citizen of any country, her work is critical to the spaces she occupies. Her status is invisible only in the census report; in reality, her labor is productive, creating new circles of community that counter negative labels pummeled against illegal and poor peoples.

The *testimonios* in *Telling to Live: Latina Feminist Testimonios* (2001) offer a daring counterpoint to these fictions. For this text, the Latina Feminist Group, composed of professional women who understand the extensive variation they embody, collaborated throughout the decade in conferences, workshops, and summer institutes. Through their teamwork they question the interstices between the personal and the professional and forge testimony as a site of affirmation, resistance, and recuperation for themselves and their various communities (professional, national, Latina).[49] They shed light on the centrality of family and education in their lives and examine how their work has been undermined, limited, and even challenged because of continued stereotyping of their Latina identities. Their stories show the mechanisms at play between structural narratives of denigration that condone continued exploitation and individual strategies of resistance to these historically embedded hierarchies of power. In the process, they signal the frustrations Latinas have felt as a result of the "marginalization of difference" within macho hierarchies of power and feminist stratifications. They offer "a politicized understanding of identity and community"[50] and witness "incredible journeys of achievement despite expectations of failure."[51] "Sharing," they argue, "can begin a process of empowerment."[52] They also acknowledge the risk of developing new hierarchies even within Latina feminist projects and recognize their need to "constantly negotiate difference" among themselves.[53] Conscientiously they give valence to the intimate, which is often rejected in academia, precisely to make it central to academic and other professional, esteemed worldviews, thereby proving that theory can be made from experience.

The Latina Feminist Group premises *Telling to Live* on the concept of *papelitos guardados*:

> [*Papelitos guardados* have] hybrid meanings for us: protected documents, guarded roles, stored papers, conserved roles, safe papers, secret roles, hidden papers, safe roles, preserved documents, protected roles ... [the phrase] evokes the process by which we contemplate thoughts and feelings, often in isolation and through difficult times.[54]

While the collection gives voice to and names many women in this process, it is telling that a number of the chapters are published anonymously. "Latina Anónima" freckles the content pages. Author anonymity evidences the challenge posed by revelations that could undermine one's professional life, even in a literary political project meant to defy this very process. They may tell to live, but some also tell obliquely or anonymously to survive. Does visibility come with a price? Are their individual successes synonymous with an excessive excellence that hinges on the performative?

It seems that despite telling, they also know that negative labels and deflating stereotypes always precede them. At the same time that they are contesting the layers of power they regularly negotiate, they also understand that to keep their hard-earned space, they cannot reveal their own travails. Their successes are interpreted as singular achievements. With their testimonies, the group underscores isolation, recognizes the margins, asks for centrality, and reflects on the tensions inherent in this project. Through writing and publication, like Chicana and Latina feminists before them, they turn to the spaces of literature to create circles of community and support.[55]

Conclusion

The Latina/o authors of the 1990s created histories of universal importance, describing strategies of survival and empowerment rooted in the private confines of the home and the imagination. By presenting deeply personal stories revealing family life, the hardships of surviving extreme economic distress, and the need every individual has to belong to and thrive in their surrounding community, they countered long-standing narratives of dehumanization and dispossession. Their works responded to a new market need, focusing on diversity and multicultural curricula. As individual writers, however, they remember discrimination, continue fighting labels, and remain cautious of stereotyping. Latinas/os are the largest growing minority in the United States, yet they remain underrepresented in literary circles and the academy. Despite growing Latina/o star symbols in the media, they continue to be misrepresented. Nonetheless, it is fair to argue that, through fiction, autobiography, and *testimonio*, Latina/o writers and scholars have entered the literary market as individuals but have not abandoned their strong ethnic affiliations in forging pathways of understanding for their interrelated, vast communities. Much of the Latina/o literature of the 1990s connected individual histories to larger sociopolitical struggles and victories, thus resisting the expectations of the independent, neoliberal individual. Their writings highlight that individual lives are more than the negative portrayals that incite fear and xenophobia, and attest to the fact that Latina/o communities have a long-standing presence and significance in the United States.

Acknowledgments

Special thanks to Mari Castañeda for commenting on an early draft and to Ginetta Candelario and Ruth Behar for continued conversations on the subject.

Notes

1. The Latino population was 22,354,059 in 1990 and 35,305,818 in 2000, a 57.9% increase. U.S. Census Bureau, 'Population by Race and Hispanic or Latino Origin for the United States: 1990 and 2000,' online U.S. Census report (2001), http://www.census.gov/population/www/cen2000/briefs/phc-t1/tables/tab04.pdf. This data excludes the population of Puerto Rico. The Latino population of Puerto Rico was first measured in 2000, when it was 3,762,746, or 98.8% of the island's population. Betsy Guzmán, 'The Hispanic Population: Census 2000 Brief,' (U.S. Department of Commerce, 2001), https://www.census.gov/prod/2001pubs/c2kbr01-3.pdf. Guzmán's report contains national origin breakdown statistics for 2000 as well.
2. Juan Gonzalez, *Harvest of Empire: A History of Latinos in America* (New York: Viking, 2000), ix.
3. Harper and Row published the autobiographic fictions *Nilda* (1973) and *El Bronx Remembered* (1975) by Nicholasa Mohr.
4. Ann Hartness, *Latina and Latino Literature: Anthologies of the 1990s, A Selected Bibliography*, online BiblioNoticias, no. 95 (Austin: University of Texas, 1998), http://www.lib.utexas.edu/benson/bibnot/bn-95.html.
5. Audrey Smedley and Brian D. Smedley, *Race in North America: Origin and Evolution of a Worldview*, 2nd ed. (Boulder, CO: Westview Press, 1999).
6. Ibid., 69.
7. Ibid., 48.
8. Ibid., 58.
9. Ibid., 58–59.
10. Ibid., 42–71.

11 C. B. MacPherson, *The Political Theory of Possessive Individualism* (Oxford: Clarendon Press, 1962), 198 in Smedley, *Race in North America*, 49.
12 Smedley, *Race in North America*, 49.
13 MacPherson, *The Political Theory of Possessive Individualism*, 207 in Smedley, *Race in North America*, 49.
14 Smedley, *Race in North America*, 50.
15 Corrales, Javier, "Neoliberalism and Its Alternatives," in Peter K. Kingstone and Deborah Yashar (eds.), *Handbook of Latin American Politics*, Routledge Handbooks (New York: Routledge, 2012), 136.
16 Ibid., 138.
17 Ibid., 136.
18 Ibid., 137.
19 Ibid., 138.
20 Ibid., 139.
21 Ibid., 140.
22 Ibid.
23 Rosario Santos (ed.), *And We Sold the Rain: Contemporary Fiction from Central America* (New York: Four Walls Eight Windows, 1988).
24 Corrales, "Neoliberalism and Its Alternatives," 142.
25 Jon D. Rossini and Patricia Ybarra, "Neoliberalism, Historiography, Identity Politics: Toward a New Historiography of Latino Theatre," *Radical History Review*, vol. 2012 (2012), 163.
26 Ibid., 164.
27 Ibid., 163.
28 Ibid., 164.
29 Ibid., 163.
30 Ibid.
31 Ibid., 114.
32 Ibid.
33 Nicholasa Mohr, *Growing Up Inside the Sanctuary of My Imagination: A Memoir* (New York: Simon and Schuster, 1994), 45.
34 Ibid., 34.
35 Ibid., 78.
36 Ibid., 96.
37 Ibid., 111.
38 Esmeralda Santiago, *When I Was Puerto Rican* (New York: Vintage Books, 1994).
39 Ibid., 77.
40 Reinaldo Arenas, *Before Night Falls*, Trans. Dolores M. Koch, first English edition (New York: Viking, 1993). Cristina García, *Dreaming in Cuban* (New York: Knopf, 1992). Julian Schnabel directed a film version of *Before Night Falls*, released in 2000.
41 Invisibility is a major theme in the study of Latina/o literatures, memory, and representation: Julia Alvarez, *In the Time of the Butterflies* (Chapel Hill, NC: Algonquin Books, 1994); Julia Alvarez, *How the García Girls Lost Their Accents* (Chapel Hill, NC: Algonquin Books, 1991); Junot Díaz, *Drown* (New York: Riverhead Books, 1996); Loida Maritza Pérez, *Geographies of*

    Home (New York: Viking, 1999). See Ramona Hernández, Silvio Torres Saillant, and Lucía M. Suárez for more examples of treatment of the subject.
42 While stories of poverty abound in the newspapers, there is a wide array of class included in all of Latin American and Caribbean migrations. Many sociologists and historians pay careful attention to this. For example, Patricia Pessar, in *Visa for a Dream*, discusses this in her study of Dominicans; Alejandro Portes and Jorge Duany do so for Cubans; and Juan Gonzalez offers a thoughtful comparative study.
43 Díaz's subsequent books, human rights work, and interviews repeatedly admonish the trappings of machismo sparingly hinted at in his first book of short stories.
44 Loida Maritza Pérez, *Geographies of Home*, 71.
45 Sonia Saldívar-Hull, "Woman Hollering Transfronteriza feminisms," *Cultural Studies*, vol. 13, issue 2, 1999, 252.
46 Ibid., 251.
47 Ibid., 259.
48 Ana Castillo, *So Far From God* (New York: W.W. Norton, 1993).
49 Ibid.
50 Ibid., 3.
51 Ibid., 12.
52 Ibid., 3.
53 Ibid., 5.
54 Ibid., 1.
55 Groundbreaking titles include *This Bridge Called My Back*, *Cuentos*; *Bearing Witness/Sobreviviendo*; *In Other Words*; *Woman of Her Word*; *Nosotras: Latina Literature Today*; *Latina*; *Compañera: Latina Lesbians*; *Infinite Divisions*; the special issue of *Third Woman on The Sexuality of Latinas*; and *Making Face: Making Soul: Haciendo Caras*. This list of "pan-Latina anthologies" is adapted from the introduction of Latina Feminist Group's *Telling to Live: Latina Feminist Testimonios* (Durham, NC: Duke University Press, 2001), 5, which chronicles the creation of Latina feminist academic spaces. For more on the listed texts, see bibliography.

Bibliography

Alarcón, Norma, Ana Castillo, and Cherríe Moraga (eds.), "The Sexuality of Latinas," special issue of *Third Woman*, vol. 4 (1989).
Alvarez, Julia, *How the García Girls Lost Their Accents* (Chapel Hill, NC: Algonquin Books, 1991).
    In the Time of the Butterflies (Chapel Hill, NC: Algonquin Books, 1994).
Anzaldúa, Gloria (ed.), *Making Face, Making Soul: Haciendo Caras: Creative and Critical Perspectives by Feminists of Color* (San Francisco: Aunt Lute Foundation Books, 1990).
Arenas, Reinaldo, *Before Night Falls*, Trans. Dolores M. Koch, first English edition (New York: Viking, 1993).
Boza, María del Carmen, Beverly Silva, and Carmen Valle (eds.), *Nosotras: Latina Literature Today* (Binghamton, NY: Bilingual Review/Press, 1986).

Castillo, Ana, *So Far From God* (New York: W. W. Norton, 1993).
Castillo-Speed, Lillian (ed.), *Latina: Women's Voices from the Borderlands* (New York: Simon & Schuster, 1995).
Cisneros, Sandra, *Woman Hollering Creek and Other Stories* (New York: Random House, 1991).
Cochran, Jo, *Bearing Witness/Sobreviviendo: An Anthology of Writing and Art by Native American/Latina Women* (Corvalllis, OR: Calyx, 1984).
Corrales, Javier, "Neoliberalism and Its Alternatives" in Peter K. Kingstone and Deborah Yashar (eds.), *Handbook of Latin American Politics*, Routledge Handbooks (New York: Routledge, 2012), 130–57.
Díaz, Junot, *Drown* (New York: Riverhead Books, 1996).
Fernández, Roberta and Jean Franco (eds.), *In Other Words: Literature by Latinas of the United States* (Houston, TX: Arte Público Press, 1994).
García, Cristina, *Dreaming in Cuban* (New York: Knopf, 1992).
Gómez, Alma, Cherríe Moraga, and Mariana Romo-Carmona (eds.), *Cuentos: Stories by Latinas* (New York: Kitchen Table, Women of Color Press, 1983).
González, Juan, *Harvest of Empire: A History of Latinos in America* (New York: Viking, 2000).
Guzmán, Betsy, 'The Hispanic Population: Census 2000 Brief' (U.S. Department of Commerce, 2001), https://www.census.gov/prod/2001pubs/c2kbr01-3.pdf.
Hartness, Ann, *Latina and Latino Literature: Anthologies of the 1990s, A Selected Bibliography*, online BiblioNoticias, no. 95 (Austin: University of Texas Press, 1998), http://www.lib.utexas.edu/benson/bibnot/bn-95.html.
The Latina Feminist Group, *Telling to Live: Latina Feminist Testimonios* (Durham, NC: Duke University Press, 2001).
MacPherson, C. B., *The Political Theory of Possessive Individualism* (Oxford: Clarendon Press, 1962), in Smedley, Audrey and Brian D. Smedley, *Race in North America: Origin and Evolution of a Worldview*, 2nd ed. (Boulder, CO: Westview Press, 1999), 49.
Mohr, Nicholasa, *El Bronx Remembered* (New York: Harper and Row, 1975).
  Growing Up Inside the Sanctuary of My Imagination: A Memoir (New York: Simon and Schuster, 1994).
  Nilda (New York: Harper and Row, 1973).
Moraga, Cherríe and Gloria Anzaldúa (eds.), *This Bridge Called My Back: Writings of Radical Women of Color*, 2nd ed. (New York: Kitchen Table: Women of Color Pr., 1983).
Pérez, Loida Maritza, *Geographies of Home* (New York: Viking, 1999).
Pessar, Patricia R., *A Visa for a Dream: Dominicans in the United States* (Boston: Allyn and Bacon, 1995).
Ramos, Juanita (ed.), *Compañeras: Latina Lesbians, an anthology* (New York: Routledge, 1994).
Rebolledo, Tey Diana and Eliana S. Rivero (eds.), *Infinite Divisions: An Anthology of Chicana Literature* (Tucson: University of Arizona Press, 1993).
Rodríguez, Clara E. (ed.), *Latin Looks: Images of Latinas and Latinos in the U.S. Media* (Boulder, CO: Westview Press, 1997).
  Heroes, Lovers, and Others: The Story of Latinos in Hollywood (Washington, DC: Smithsonian Books, 2004).

Rossini, Jon D. and Patricia Ybarra, "Neoliberalism, Historiography, Identity Politics: Toward a New Historiography of Latino Theatre," *Radical History Review*, vol. 2012, 2012, 162–72.
Saldívar-Hull, Sonia, "Woman Hollering Transfronteriza feminisms," *Cultural Studies*, vol. 13, issue 2, 1999, 251–62.
Santiago, Esmeralda, *When I Was Puerto Rican* (New York: Vintage Books, 1994).
Santos, Rosario (ed.), *And We Sold the Rain: Contemporary Fiction from Central America* (New York: Four Walls Eight Windows, 1988).
Smedley, Audrey and Brian D. Smedley, *Race in North America: Origin and Evolution of a Worldview*, 2nd edition (Boulder: Westview Press, 1999).
Suárez, Lucia M., *The Tears of Hispaniola: Haitian and Dominican Diaspora Memory* (Gainesville: University Press of Florida, 2006).
U.S. Census Bureau, "Population by Race and Hispanic or Latino Origin for the United States: 1990 and 2000," online U.S. Census report (2001), http://www.census.gov/population/www/cen2000/briefs/phc-t1/tables/tab04.pdf.
Vigil-Piñón, Evangelina (eds.), *Woman of Her Word: Hispanic Women Write* (Houston, TX: Arte Público Press, 1987).

8

PAUL ALLATSON

From "Latinidad" to "Latinid@des": Imagining the Twenty-First Century

Now the United States' largest collective minority, the country's heterogeneous Latin@ population increased from 35.3 million (12.5 percent) in 2000 to 55.4 million (17.4 percent) in 2014 (Ennis, Ríos-Vargas, and Albert 2011; Colby and Ortman 2015). The figures – attributable to Latin@ population growth and immigration from the Spanish-speaking Americas – were paralleled by sizeable migrant intakes from other parts of the hemisphere, Asia and Africa. Numerous commentators interpret these demographic patterns as heralding two interrelated phenomena. First, they may be signaling the United States' evolution into a postracial age, exemplified by the election of the biracial President Barack Obama in 2008. Second, they may be signposting the irreversible "unwhitening" of the United States due to transnational migration patterns – which are also transforming immigrant receiver states across the "developed" world – and attendant ethno-racial transformations. In turn, these phenomena are often read by demographers, and institutions like the U.S. Census Bureau, as evidence of a twenty-first century in which the United States will have a Latin@ majority. Such speculations, moreover, are haunted by the epoch-changing temporal shift in global power and influence posed to the United States by the so-called "Asian century" and the emergence of powerhouse states across the "developing" world.

Albeit a blunt summation, these scenarios indicate why fundamental processes of transnational and transcultural change underwrite the remit of this chapter. Numerous literary and cultural critics have also argued that the United States' changing demographic contours – which coincide with an increasingly penetrative digitized communication age – modulate how Latin@ literary texts are being conceived, produced, received, and critiqued in the United States and across the world. In this chapter, accordingly, I focus on the literary consolidation and/or publishing debut in the early twenty-first century of selected Latin@ writers who appear to be responding to and/or emerging from such globally relevant changes. Their ranks, to select a few authors from many, include Maya Chinchilla, Roberto José

Tejada, Rodrigo Toscano, José Rivera, Edwin Torres, Justin Torres, Salvador Plascencia, Giannina Braschi, Oscar Casares, Nina Marie Martínez, and Susana Chávez-Silverman. Despite the continuing importance of literary production under Chican@, Puerto Rican, Cuban American, and other specific Latin@ rubrics, it is arguable that the aesthetic strategies of many twenty-first-century writers are generating new post-identitarian and transnational, often globally referential and informed, narratives. No unitary notion of the nation, (racialized, ethnicized, gendered, sexualized) identity, language, literary genre, or technological medium can encompass with any adequacy the work of such Latin@ cultural producers (Aldama 127–47). A baseline for this chapter, then, is that while many Latin@ writers may not disavow their Latin@ identities, their texts may be indicating to readers that such identities can no longer be conceived of as having ethno-national centers from which to measure Latin@ authenticity.

In this chapter I proceed with an overview of key critical positions that assist in recognizing new Latin@ literary aesthetics and in tracking how their authors challenge essentialist understandings of Latinid@d as the framework for interpreting their texts. Those critical positions underwrite my argument that while the authors' approaches may resist straightforward categorizations and neat comparisons, diverse aesthetic approaches are evident in literary representations of latinid@des in the twenty-first century. The authors may downplay, problematize, or sidestep specific Latin@ identity positions. Many authors deploy sophisticated genre disturbances, metafictional tropes, and experimental narratological approaches; this therefore delineates them from forebears whose cultural political aesthetic and references were anchored compellingly in ethno-nationalist readings of Latin@ marginalization – informed by Chican@ and Puerto Rican historical experiences – by virtue of the United States' imperial history. Many writers may deploy non-translational approaches to and intentional "misuses" of English, Spanish, and other languages. This has always been the case in Latin@ writing, but such linguistic choices are increasingly accompanied and bolstered by cosmopolitan, international typologies, references, and settings that either exceed homeliness in the United States, or imply a rejection of what an orthodox creative Latin@ text is, should be, and ought to contain in terms of its cultural references, settings, and context.[1] In short, numerous Latin@ writers are contributing to the emergence of new post-identitarian latinid@des that reflect the constant flux of transculturations and their potential to modulate the United States' twenty-first-century future.

Such aesthetic approaches, I argue, impel some conceptual adaptation on the part of readers and critics, as signaled in this chapter by the orthographic move from *latinidad* to latinid@d, which shifts the conventional placing of

"@" after "Latin." The move illustrates how latinid@d is being transformed in the digitized twenty-first century, and will continue to evolve in relation to as yet unforeseen techno-futures. The "@" recognizes that, like writers across the globe, Latin@ authors are using and gaining creative and fan base traction from digital and other platforms for their work, alongside traditional print media. The orthographic shift thus accepts that the technologies of literary production also influence how Latin@ writings are formulated and presented, read, and received.[2] In this context, moreover, latinid@d should be understood in its plural form of latinid@des, which emerge in and as multiple transcultural and transnational identifications, and attendant aesthetic practices.[3] That said, this orthographic move is risky, as Claudia Milian argues in the epilogue – subtitled, simply, "@" – to her 2009 study *Latining America*: "Slashes and *at* signs are far from trivial. These symbols communicate a genealogical trajectory of the field – an intellectual history. They should be treated as spaces of inquiry, possibility, and reconfiguration. The @, above all, is a Latin router, haltingly enunciating yet transporting us to a panoply of fragmented Latined lives" (158).

How, then, might we begin to read new literary aesthetics of latinid@des and the ways they embody consistently evolving transculturations that are local, transnational, and modulated by the contemporary digital information age? Possible responses are being signaled by scholars who have assessed Latin@ literature in relation to an historical moment that no longer invariably places faith in ethno-national centers. Here I am indebted to Marta Caminero-Santangelo's nuanced assessment in *On Latinidad: U.S. Literature and the Construction of Ethnicity* (2007) of critical approaches to what *latinidad* might signify, and for whom. I am especially compelled by her notion of latinid@d as an "elastic" set of phenomena harboring numerous potential Latin@ identifications, none of which may be in conceptual alignment or agreement (29). As she argues, with identity elasticity comes "[t]he possibility that no *one* understanding of the term [Latin@] might be sufficient to explain people's *various* identifications with it" (29, - italics in the original), to which I would add the possibility of Latin@ disidentification, and even the term's evaporation, when mediated in literary productions.

Caminero-Santangelo's articulation of Latin@ elasticity is helpful in understanding alternative approaches, including that of Claudia Milian, who places Latin@ and *latinidad* in dialogic relation to her preferred rivals, "Latin" and "Latineity." For Milian, the latter terms reflect how the migration north into the United States of "Latin" is symptomatic of unexpected shifts in "cultural signification" (1). That is, in the United States, "Latin" rubs up against Latin American *and* Latin@ *and* Latino/a or Latina/o, in the process giving rise to complex, but as yet not fully explored or understood, racialized configurations that are also involving African Americans and diverse Caribbean, Central American, and South American communities, including many indigenous peoples (1). For Milian, these terminological frictions demand our attention as transcultural signposts, as a "multiphasic something that is letting us know that whatever might be ascribable to blackness, Latinoness, and Latinaness is being dissolved" inside U.S. borders and beyond them (3). Evoking Caminero-Santangelo's notion of Latin@ elasticity, Milian's Latineity implies "copiousness." This operates "as a set of new possibilities in the referents and sources for Latinness, as a new understanding from which different types of Latinoness and Latinaness are redirected and picked up" (4). Indeed, Milian identifies new Latin-based identifications "that do not solely depend on a definite, firm color and national origin or that, in some cases, are even specific to the United States" (5). Further, she argues, those identifications "demand a distance from U.S. Latino and Latina authenticity and the ontological grammar of Latinidad" (6) when understood as singular or weighted by the historical experiences of particular communities.

These arguments are pertinent in relation to the emergence – first online and in live performance venues in California, then in print – of writers such as the Oakland-based Maya Chinchilla, a self-defined Central American/Guatemalan/*Chapina* queer poet, performer, and blogger. Chinchilla is the author of *The Cha Cha Files: A Chapina Poética* (2014), a collection of poems, stories, memoir fragments, and snapshots, and coeditor of *Desde el EpiCentro: An Anthology of US Central American Poetry* (2007). Both texts' titles, in effect, make specific aesthetic gestures – *chapina* poetics; the literal insertion of Central American Americans into the purported Latin@ literary centre, as captured orthographically in "EpiCentro" – to new latinid@des.[4] Writers from other communities are also contributing to this evolution. The story collection, *Vida*, from 2010, by the Colombian American Patricia Engel, for example, comprises interlinked stories featuring the character Sabina that move between New Jersey and Miami. The stories insert Colombianos into long-standing U.S. national and Latin@ literary archives about so-called "illegal immigrants" and/or immigrant hardship, archives that have been richly populated by Mexican and Puerto Rican historical experiences and representations.

Such elasticities and identitarian copiousness are by no means phenomena of the current century only. They are signposted in earlier cultural productions. One example derives from a scene in the "The Mission," a 1998 play by the Californian performance ensemble Culture Clash. The scene explores the tensions in San Francisco's Mission District and the literary ambitions of a character, Herbert, who is overwhelmed by the demands of the customers in the *taquería* that employs him. As an escape from his malaise he imagines himself in "Heaven," a reverie that prompts the following musing: "I said to myself, 'I'm an American.' And, in that same precious instant, I asked, 'What is an American?' I don't know. I don't remember. The population of Heaven is young, brown, and does not speak English. I have found very few 'Americans' here" (Montoya et al. 31). In this scene Culture Clash arguably provided post-Chican@ insights into the United States' twenty-first-century demographic future. European Americans are a minority in the face of an amorphously "browning" population. The United States' sense of itself as a nation, it is implied, now rests on complex relations between multiple ethno-racialized sectors. And the term Latin@ – understood as an indicator of a pan-ethnic group and identitarian stance in much of the critical literature in Latin@ Studies[5] – here seems to collapse in its "browned" relationship with other non-Latin@ communities.

Paralleling the above critical calls for a reflexive, flexible approach to *latinidades* is the "post-Sixties" generation – a creative temporal bridge of sorts – identified by Raphael Dalleo and Elena Machado Sáez in *The Latino/a Canon and the Emergence of Post-sixties Literature* (2007). For these critics, the post-Sixties generation of Latin@ writers emerged in the 1990s and differed from predecessors whose work was more often than not framed by civil rights enterprises, ambitions, and associated cultural politics. Moreover, the emergent writers were impelled to operate in a new publishing realm driven by market forces that completely transformed the authorial relationship to previous aesthetic and representational practices when understood within ethnic or nationalistic group limits and aspirations. This accords with Frederick Luis Aldama's recognition that since the 1990s Latin@ writers have been occupying a global publishing stage that affords many a genuinely international readership (148–52). This privileged global platform is often underestimated in U.S.-based readings of Latin@ literature in relation to particular ethno-national prisms of Latin@ identity and belonging that may not sit comfortably with broader transnational and cosmopolitan purviews.

A third critical approach, which again attends to identitarian elasticity as mediated through creative texts, derives from Ramón Saldívar's arguments in his 2013 essay, "The Second Elevation of the Novel: Race, Form, and the Postrace Aesthetic in Contemporary Narrative." Here Saldívar outlines four modes of "postrace aesthetics" in contemporary U.S. narrative, while also noting the capacities of some authors and texts to span and epitomize more than one mode (4). For example, Saldívar identifies Junot Díaz's *The Brief Wondrous Life of Oscar Wao* (2007) and other outputs as exemplifying all but the second mode. First, postrace aesthetics refers to narratives that are in "critical dialogue with the aesthetics of postmodernism," as evident, for example, in knowing uses of metafictional devices to reveal the narrative's constructedness, and the ironic playing with the purported disjunction between the fictional realm and the real (4). Second, postrace aesthetics are characterized by a willingness to play with generic traditions, conventions, and boundaries, and with such purported cultural binaries as high and low. Third, postrace aesthetics are typified by what Saldívar calls "speculative realism," which he describes as "a way of getting at the revisions of realism and fantasy into speculative forms that are seeming to shape the invention of new narrative modes in contemporary fiction" (3). Alongside Junot Díaz, Saldívar locates Yxta Maya Murray and her novel *The Conquest* (2002) in this category. And finally, Saldívar regards a postrace aesthetics as emphasizing the (again, elastic) "thematics of race in twenty-first century America" (5), as opposed to signaling a jettisoning of "race" altogether in narrative production.

Illustrating the critical complexities of assigning fixed or centered "Latin@" identities to authors and texts in the current postrace realm identified by Saldívar is the cult novel *Atomik Aztex* from 2005, by the Los Angeleno writer Sesshu Foster. As its opening lines indicate, the text is at once playful and confrontational, and already preparing readers to have their preconceptions toyed with: "I am Zenzontli, Keeper of the House of Darkness of the Aztex and I am getting fucked in the head and I think I like it. Okay sometimes I'm not sure. But my so-called visions are better than aspirin and cheaper" (1). The novel features parallel worlds, one ruled by Aztecs who long ago defeated the European invaders, the others involving Zenzontli being transported to such settings as the Battle of Stalingrad or a dystopian dream-induced vision of U.S. capitalist contemporaneity focused on a meat-packing factory in East Los Angeles. *Atomik Aztex* is named by Ramón Saldívar as a "minority" narrative – he does not define the novel further in relation to authorial ethnicity – that typifies the genre-blurring features of "postrace aesthetics" with its blending of speculative futurism and dirty realism. In Saldívar's formulation, the novel epitomizes how the "mixing of genres includes not just the canonic paradigms of classical, neoclassical, romantic, realist, and modernist origin, but also their outcast, lowbrow, vernacular, not to say kitschy varieties of what has come to be known as genre fiction, including the fantasy, sci-fi, gothic, noir, and erotic speculative writings of the postwar era" (4). It is of note, then, that within Latin@ studies *Atomik Aztex* has been described by at least one critic as "able to not just represent but formally mediate and rework the material forms with which it engages on its own formal terms and as a result of its own formal, Latino/a tradition" (Nilges 148). For his part Foster might beg to differ: "When people first meet me, they ask, 'Who are you? What's your background?' I have a white Dad and Nisei [second-generation Japanese American] mom and grew up in a Chicano barrio. I grew up with Asians, Chicanos and people with mixed heritage – but I've always had to simplify for people who come from outside that experience" ("Excerpts"). Foster is not a Latin@ author. Yet his upbringing in East Los Angeles, coupled with the novel's cultural and geospatial referents, and its uses of Chican@ and Mexican slang, as Nilges appreciates, mean that *Atomik Aztex* can be read otherwise. That possibility informs receptions of Foster's novel in some Latin@ constituencies; Aldama, for example, also discusses this novel in relation to "new Latino/a forms" (140–41).[6] But the possibility also confronts those constituencies with other receptions that could reject assumptions and faith in a Latin@ identity and a Latin@ literary tradition.

If the elastic inclusion of Foster in a "Latin@ tradition" is a critical and conceptual possibility, there is an obverse. The work of numerous Latin@ writers may defy and/or challenge the notion that there is such a thing as a "Latin@ tradition" and its presumed identity basis.[7] A case in point is *We the Animals* (2011), the debut novel from Justin Torres, a Brooklyn-raised writer with a Puerto Rican father and an Italian-Irish mother. Legible in relation to Saldívar's fourth mode of postrace aesthetics in its approach to race and ethnicity, *We the Animals* is an autobiographically modulated story of three brothers in a chaotic, at times violent, Puerto Rican and Anglo-American household in a white working-class town in upstate New York. Latinid@d does not emerge as a central narratorial concern in the novel. To their father the brothers are "mutts," his way of defining them ethnically as neither Anglo-American nor Puerto Rican. The novel does not pay further attention to such identitarian complexities aside from representing the brothers as a small grouping of ethnic "difference" that insulates itself from the surrounding "white" majority.

Other challenges to purported identity centers are evident in the work of the poet, performer, and playwright Rodrigo Toscano – author of such well-received texts as *Partisans* (1999), *The Disparities* (2002), *Platform* (2002), *To Leveling Swerve* (2004), *Collapsible Poetics Theater* (2007), and *Deck of Deeds* (2012). As Manuel Brito describes him, Toscano is a Chican@ writer raised in California, now resident of New York, with a career-long commitment to "progressive politics" that is global in gaze and application (51). At the same time, Toscano's experimental writing approach moves beyond understandings of Chican@ identity derived from the 1960s and 1970s Chicano Movement and associated symbolism, such as Aztlán. The transnational coordinates and transgressive metafictional properties of Toscano's aesthetic praxis are evident in his collection of some seventy short narratives, *Deck of Deeds* (2012), whose overarching frame derives from the Mexican card game *lotería*. In a 2013 interview with another noted Latin@ writer, Roberto José Tejada, Toscano says of this book that its inbuilt generic and narrative digressions are epitomized by the recurring "trope of the hotel room," a site inhabited by "trans-capital actors" and a setting for transgressive "exchanges": "Whether it's exchange values across the continents, or the exchange of body fluids. Or alien body fluids. Or alien beings swapping their identities with other alien beings. And by alien beings I don't mean extraterrestrials, I mean social alien beings" ("Rodrigo Toscano"). According to Tejada, moreover, those "social alien beings" are also portrayed by Toscano as bilingually "affable everyday personalities" who are "perplexed by the dynamics of technological, social, and economic change" of the twenty-first century ("Rodrigo Toscano").

That characterization of affable yet perplexed personalities could also be applied to the characters populating many other early twenty-first-century Latin@ literary works. As a result, those works appear to confirm the viability of the knowingly metafictional and genre-disturbing aspects of the postrace aesthetic identified by Ramón Saldívar. The Mexican-born Salvador Plascencia's 2005 novel, *The People of Paper*, merits attention here. Saldívar locates the novel in the first mode of his postrace aesthetics in that it embodies the "dialogic and critical relation between contemporary ethnic fiction and postmodern metafiction" as a "shared history" (4), and thus problematizes the idea of a "Latin@" tradition. Evoking Latin American magical realism, and indebted to the postmodern turn in U.S. and much fiction across the globe that began in the 1960s, *The People of Paper* revels in its own highly self-conscious narrative experimentation, the title iterating that the characters exist only on the page. One of the novel's narrative drives is a struggle against omniscient narration, cast as an astrological battle with Saturn – later revealed to be the author himself – that involves a character, Federico de la Fe, collaborating with a gang of flower pickers in the small town of El Monte in southern California. That location does evoke a "real world" site and associated history of Mexican immigration and labor exploitation, but that, arguably, is as far as the novel gets in gesturing toward historical veracity and realism.

The People of Paper calls attention to itself as a manufactured artefact that defies categorization given its insistent amplifications, digressions, and challenges to linearity. Contrasting columns of text in some chapters separate the experiences of particular characters, some text has been blocked out, and some names have been cut literally from the pages of the novel in its physical, printed form. Such devices evoke the late eighteenth-century novel, *The Life and Opinions of Tristram Shandy, Gentleman*, by Laurence Sterne. Federico de la Fe deals with his personal struggles and tragedies by applying burns to – and thus resurfacing or, more precisely, rewriting – his body, in a fictional parallel to the palimpsestic physical feel *and* readerly experience of the novel itself. That sensation is amplified in the character Merced de Papel, a woman made from origami whose lovers, the fathers of her legion progeny, bear her paper-cut scars on their bodies' private parts. The novel exemplifies a growing trend within Latin@ writing to deploy extensive and self-conscious intertextual references and metaphysical tactics, while also equally knowingly drawing on literary traditions that cannot be easily located within a Latin@ canon or literary tradition.

Another novel that invites scrutiny given its elastic postrace and post-Sixties relation to latinid@des is the Puerto Rican-born Giannina Braschi's *The United States of Banana* (2011). Her first "novel" to be written in English, the text forms a trilogy of sorts – given its shared characters and genre-mixing narrative devices – with her earlier *El imperio de los sueños* (1988; translated as *Empire of Dreams* in 1994), and the English-Spanish code-switching *Yo-Yo Boing* (1998). Implicitly anchored in the fraught Puerto Rican relationship with the United States since 1898, *The United States of Banana* nonetheless deals with the detonation – again literally – of that relationship into global terrain caused by the events of September 11, 2001, and subsequent declarations of the War on Terror by the George W. Bush administration. Cast in the novel as "a chicken with its head cut off" (45), the United States, now the sole imperial superpower, is represented entering the twenty-first century in a full-scale identity crisis, as announced by the novel's opening lines about the end of the world.

In a sense, as a novel, Braschi's *United States of Banana* is also in a formal identity crisis due to the fluidity of its generic framework. As Elizabeth Lowry argues, it "is in fact a mixed genre work: part memoir, part epic poem, part speculative fiction, part polemic, and, at times, a stage play" (156). The text relies heavily on numerous intertextual references, including the Spanish Golden Age play by Calderón de la Barca, *La vida es sueño* [Life is a Dream], which provides a structural basis for the theatricalized second part of the novel to make absurdist points about the Puerto Rican–U.S. relationship and U.S. global power alike. Moreover, a figure called "Giannini Braschi" herself appears in this polyglot, self-deprecatingly humorous text as both a character and the main narrator. That narratological ruse – again, a familiar postmodern trope – assists the author in bringing into literary representation a visceral sense of the cultural and geopolitical chaos that the events of 9/11 inaugurated, not just for New York and the United States but for the world (Lowry 156). An important trajectory in the novel lies in its musings about whether or not the post-9/11 twenty-first century will see a resurgence of Latin Americanism opposed to U.S. hegemony (18). But those musings grate against the speculative future of the text (in the second part) in which all Latin Americans are granted U.S. passports. The gesture does not provide them access to cosmopolitan mobility across the hemisphere, but rather to lives as worker-fodder for U.S. capitalist interests.

Literary attentions to hemispherical understandings of "America/ América" – an implicit geospatial frame for Braschi – have characterized the work of many writers now accorded status in Latin@ canons. But the works of Braschi and other writers are appearing to experiment and play much more deeply than previous generations with notions of hemispherical relevance, both on personal and literary levels. For example, the Los Angeles–born Roberto José Tejada approaches poetry as a preferred medium for exploring his sense of hemispherical belonging and meaningfulness – arguably as a cosmopolitan expansiveness attuned to displacements across the globe – that transcends national lines, identifications based on gender, sexuality, race, and ethnicity, and in his case, the binational record of U.S.-Mexican relations.[8] Tejada came to continental literary prominence in his mid-twenties as the founding editor in 1991 of the renowned bicultural and bilingual (English and Spanish) literary and visual art magazine *Mandorla* in Mexico City. As Tejada notes in a 2012 interview with Esther Allen, the magazine aimed to be transcontinental in its publication approach while also attending to the literary legacies of Anglophone and Hispanophone avant-garde traditions. Tejada also agrees with Allen that a hemispherical identity is much more important to him than any minority Latin@ identification when defined in relation to majoritarian national U.S. culture. However, Tejada also recognizes that his personal identification with an hemispherical identitarian position is risky: it emplaces him in an uneasy contrapuntal relationship with a neoliberal desire – as exemplified by the establishment of NAFTA in 1994 – for the end of economic borders and other national obstacles to the circulation of labor, commodities, and finance, to the benefit of multinational capitalism. Nonetheless, a personalized hemispherical anchor and an interest in connecting disparate historical moments of crisis, as with Braschi, are evident in such collections as *Mirrors for Gold* (2006), *Exposition Park* (2010), and *Full Foreground* (2012). The poems in *Full Foreground*, for example, like the *United States of Banana*, build from the events of 9/11, but move backward to contextualize that date in relation to other moments of violent upheaval: home-grown terrorism (McVeigh's bombing of the Federal Building in Oklahoma City in 1995); the ethnic cleansings that began in

1991 after the breakup of Yugoslavia; and the Gulf War of 1990–91 inaugurated by the first Bush administration (Allen).

Tejada is not alone among Latin@ writers who favor hemispherical identitarian parameters. Another example is provided by New York playwright José Rivera, the first Puerto Rican–born author to be nominated for an Oscar in recognition of his screenplay for *Diarios de motocicleta* (The Motorcycle Diaries), the 2004 film about Ernesto "Che" Guevara directed by Walter Salles. The screenplay and many of his theatrical works, from *The House of Ramon Iglesia* (1983) to *School of the Americas* (2006), the latter returning to Guevara to imagine his last day of life, confirm the description of Rivera by Caridad Svich as someone who "has established his theatrical voice at the intersection of the Old World and the New World, at the juncture of the Americas" (83). Svich notes that "the issue of cultural identity is not at the centre of Rivera's writing" as it is with many other Latin@ dramatists. Rather, that issue provides one piece in a broader set of dramaturgical, personal, and political concerns: "Environmental, moral, social and political decay in contemporary society is as much on Rivera's mind as how to syncretise a Latino (indigenous, African, Spanish, Creole) and 'American' identity" (83). Rivera himself refers to his sense of self as a collation of options that are at once doubled because of his Puerto Rican background and the rival aesthetic interests and demands of writing for the screen and for the stage: "Two loves. One lifetime of constant balance. Two sensibilities. Two audiences. Two languages. Two esthetic [sic] philosophies. Two ways to narrate a story. One pen, one hand, one hopelessly split brain" (Rivera 2006, 90).

Rivera's self-reflection could apply to Edwin Torres: poet, performer, collaborator with such groups as the Spanic Attack Artist Collective and the Poetry Project, self-designated "lingualisualist" (Poetry Foundation n. d.), and a highly anthologized stalwart of the Nuyorican Poets Café in New York. As befits that repertoire, he is responsible for diverse outputs including the CD "Holy Kid" (1998), the interactive website "Brainlingo," and such poetry collections as *Fractured Humorous* (1999), *The All-Union Day of the Shock Worker* (2001), *Onomalingua: Noise Songs and Poetry* (2002), *The PoPedology of an Ambient Language* (2008), *In the Function of External Circumstances* (2010), *Yes Thing, No Thing* (2010), *One Night for the Sleepy* (2012), and *Ameriscopia* (2014). As he says in "Sutra," from *Ameriscopia*, "I'm just a plaything / for judgement /a collection of entrances / arranged / by impossible history" (9). The poems respond to external events and personal events in equal measure – 9/11, new fatherhood, local performance spaces, food stalls – in a digressive nomadism that has always characterized Torres's writing, as was noted as early as 2000: "The nomad is a constant in Torres' work, an alter ego for this poet who is claimed by a diverse group of avant-garde factions" and, by implication, identifications (Coultas n. p.).

A number of the authors discussed in this chapter could also be read nomadically in relation to a trend identified by Claudia Sadowski-Smith as "U.S. fronteriza fiction." By this she means spatialized representations of the U.S.-Mexico borderlands – influenced as much by Mexican literary representations as U.S.-based ones – that are legible in hemispherical and global contexts as moving away deliberately from the "symbolic focus on the border as a terrain of Chicana/o identity formation (and largely beyond imagery associated with Aztlán) [in order] to locate Chicana/o border communities within debates about globalization in Mexican border towns" (719). As Sadowski-Smith elaborates, "U.S. fronteriza writing draws attention to the fact that as 'products to be used' and as 'means of production,' specific geographies, such as U.S. borders, embody and are transformed by social, political, economic, and topographic conditions that enable, shape, and sustain certain forms of social organization as well as cultural production" (723). This is an important, if controversial, insight: it suggests that certain canonical approaches to the "Borderlands" no longer carry the critical weight they once did, and that Chican@ authors in particular are no longer beholden to expectations that their narratives must deal with cultural identity and evoke the symbols of the Chicano Movement.

Two quite distinct authors exemplify this trend: the Texas-born Oscar Casares and the Californian Nina Marie Martínez. Casares's story collection, *Brownsville* (2003), and his novel *Amigoland* (2009) are both set in the city of Brownsville in deep South Texas, and as befits that setting are literally part of a long Borderlands literary tradition. Both *Brownsville* and *Amigoland* contain numerous references to border militarization and the U.S. immigration regime. The symbiotic relationship between Brownsville, Texas, and the Mexican city of Matamoros, Tamaulipas, across the Rio Grande is also a given for Casares. "Domingo" from *Brownsville*, for example, focuses on an undocumented migrant in Brownsville whose separation from his family in Mexico causes him great anxiety. *Amigoland* is the story of two estranged brothers, one of whom, Don Fidencio, is in a nursing home. The other, Don Celestino, is persuaded by his housekeeper and lover Socorro (who crosses the border bridge from Matamoros daily to work for him) to repair the relationship. They spirit Don Fidencio out of the nursing home and undertake a road trip into Mexico in a quest to find certain truths about their grandfather. However, Casares's narratives are not portrayals of Mexican American marginalization in relation to Anglo-American hegemony. Rather, they exemplify a narrative aesthetic that seeks to "move beyond cultural nationalist concerns with questions of Chicana/o identity formation and beyond the more metaphorical use of 'borderlands'" (Sadowski-Smith 735).

A second example of that trend is provided by Nina Marie Martínez's picaresque-like novel ¡Caramba! (2004), which also evokes the *telenovela* and magic realism, and has clear affinities with the rapidly developing genre of Chica or Latina Lit (Aldama 129–35). Like Toscano's *Deck of Deeds*, the novel is structured loosely around the game of *lotería*, with illustrated cards announcing each chapter. While most of the characters are Mexican Americans, none of these residents of the fictional town of Lava Landing, California, either refer to themselves in terms of that identity, or expend energy exploring the cultural politics of Chicano identity. The novel is also marked, as with so many Latin@ creative works, by an ear for code-switching, Spanglish, and Spanish slang, which are seamlessly embedded into the dominant English, and without apology.

Martínez's uses of Spanglish and Spanish-origin words and expressions in a predominantly English-language text is a shared feature of all the authors referred to in this chapter, but other Latin@ authors are going much further with their linguistic aesthetic. Susana Chávez-Silverman, for example, utilizes the Latin American literary form of the *crónica* or chronicle in two collections: *Killer crónicas: Bilingual memories/Memorias bilingües* (2004) and *Scenes from la cuenca de Los Angeles y otros natural disasters* (2010). The author constructs her *crónicas* out of e-mails that she has sent to individual and collective interlocutors across the world. The *crónicas* that result from this interactive regimen resist generic categorization as memoir, autobiography, prose poetry, epistolary writing, diary writing, fictocriticism, and even the chronicle itself, thus also evoking Saldívar's postrace aesthetic. But arguably the key characteristic of Chávez-Silverman's approach is her inventive intermixture of Spanish and English, or perhaps better said, Spanishes and Englishes, which may not conform to or replicate Spanglish (Lennon). But even that description falters given that the distinct accent and regional dialectical modalities of all the languages in which she writes are conveyed through unorthodox spellings, which evoke the specific places that concern the author: South Africa, California, Spain, Argentina. The cosmopolitan reach of such writing is increasingly common across Latin@ literatures, a point that was recognized in the 2005 *Los Angeles Times* review of *Killer crónicas* by Daniel Hernandez, which he described as "a testament to the maturing sense of global and pan-Latin citizenship being claimed by Chicanos and U.S.-born Latinos in the American West."

There is little doubt that "Latino/a literary forms in the ... early twenty-first century are a much more diverse terrain than in earlier epochs" (Aldama 127), and that this diversity is tied to a great extent to the demographic expansion of the Latin@ population. As catalogued in this chapter's opening, that expansion is paralleled by global shifts in U.S. power and the country's internalized sense of self as an immigrant-receiving state, both processes back-dropped by the rapid technological advances of the digital age. In those contexts, Latin@ literatures are not simply contributing to the new latinid@des, but are embroiled in their own identitarian elasticity and copiousness. However, the optimistic global outreach encoded above in Hernandez's reading of Latin@ cultural citizenship and in Aldama's recognition of Latin@ literary diversity continue to encounter certain limits within Latin@ literary studies.

Questions about Latin@ authenticity and who to include or not in the new latinid@des as mediated through Latin@ literary texts continue. One example will suffice as a way of closing: the case of Daína Chaviano, the biggest-selling living Cuban-born author of our epoch, and one of the most acclaimed authors of speculative fantasy and science fiction in the Spanish-speaking world. Despite an impressive back catalog of publications in Spanish, her sole novel available in English translation to date is *The Island of Eternal Love* (2008). Chaviano also brings to the Latin@ literary table a writerly preference for the English-language literary canon, and not the Hispanophone and Latin American canons. Chaviano is routinely described by critics and scholars as Cuban and Latin American, terms that thus fix her as always already outside ongoing debates about latinid@des, and that overlook her residency of Miami since 1991. This conceptual discrepancy has been recognized by Sabrina Vourvoulias who notes that Chaviano's "work is often left out of conversations about Latino/a speculative fiction in the United States." Chaviano is one of numerous Latin American–born authors now resident in the United States whose presence and literary outputs appear to indicate why Milian's plea for a critical distancing from the "ontological grammar of Latinidad" (6) is now emerging as a central debate in the evolution of latinid@des in the twenty-first century.

Notes

1 Even in the 1980s and 1990s cultural and intertextual references in diverse Latin@ literary texts often signposted surprising vectors of identification and disidentification that could radically re-signify, contradict, or disavow the purported Latin@ identification of the texts' protagonists and, by implication, of the authors themselves (Allatson 2002).
2 One example is provided by *Latino/a Rising*, an anthology of speculative and science fiction edited by Matthew David Goodwin, to be published by Restless Books in 2016. The collection is the outcome of a crowd-sourcing campaign initiated by the editor in 2014.

3 This pluralization reprises Frances Aparicio and Susana Chávez-Silverman's preference for Latinidades over the singular Latinidad due to the multiple and often contrapuntal identitarian weights the pluralized term can carry.
4 Milian discusses Central American American disruptions to latinid@des in terms of underlying assumptions about whiteness, blackness, and brownness. See also Alvarado for a comparative analysis of transcultural interchanges between U.S.-based Central American and Chican@ narratives, and Arias for a critical overview of the generation of Central American American writers that emerged since 2000.
5 See Oboler for the first analysis of the debates over Latinidad, and Caminero-Santangelo for her analysis of critical and literary approaches to Latinidades.
6 Foster's novel evokes numerous performance pieces by Guillermo Gómez-Peña and the speculative cyber-punk science fictions of Ernest Hogan, including his *Smoking Mirror Blues* (2001). That novel imagines a Californian future in which artificial intelligence software enables an Aztec trickster figure, the God Tezcatlipoca, to escape the virtual realm and run rampant through Hollywood. Hogan describes himself as "a recombocultural Chicano mutant" (Mondo Ernesto Blog).
7 These possibilities evoke discussions in Chican@ studies from the 1970s through to the 1990s over the ethnic authenticity of Chicanesque writing (La literatura chicanesca) or writing about Chican@s by non-Chican@s (Allatson 2007, 141).
8 Such approaches resonate with José David Saldívar's arguments about "transamericanity," his approach to U.S. narratives by authors from a range of ethno-racial backgrounds that emplaces the texts in a transcontinental framework, one that also underwrites his attempts to make broader comparative cognate-subaltern points between Latin@ writers and writers from the Global South such as the Indian author Arundathi Roy.

Works Cited

Aldama, Frederick Luis. *The Routledge Concise History of Latino/a Literature*. London and New York: Routledge, 2011.
Allatson, Paul. *Latino Dreams: Transcultural Traffic in the U.S. National Imaginary*. Amsterdam and New York: Rodopi Press, 2002.
  Key Terms in Latino/a Cultural and Literary Studies. Malden, MA: Blackwell Publishing, 2007.
Allen, Esther. "Roberto Tejada," *BOMB Magazine*: Artists in Conversation website (August 27 2012) <http://bombmagazine.org/article/6791/>.
Alvarado, Karina Oliva. "An Interdisciplinary Reading of Chicana/o and (US) Central American Cross-cultural Narrations," *Latino Studies* 11.3 (2013): 366–87.
Aparicio, Frances R. and Susana Chávez-Silverman, eds. "Introduction," in *Tropicalizations: Transcultural Representations of Latinidad*. Hanover, NH: University Press of New England, 1997. 1–20.
Arias, Arturo. "EpiCentro: The Emergence of a New Central American-American Literature," *Comparative Literature* 64.3 (2012): 300–15.
Braschi, Giannina. *United States of Banana*. Seattle, WA: AmazonCrossing, 2011.
Brito, Manuel. "Language Working to Uncover the Social and the Cultural: The Example of Rodrigo Toscano," *Critical Essays on Chicano studies*. Ed. Ramón Espejo *et al*. Bern: Peter Lang, 2007, 51–63.

Caminero-Santangelo, Marta. *On Latinidad: U.S. Latino Literature and the Construction of Ethnicity*. Gainesville: University Press of Florida, 2007.
Casares, Oscar. *Brownsville: Stories*. New York: Back Bay Books/ Little, Brown and Company, 2003.
Chaviano, Daína. *The Island of Eternal Love*. Trans. Andrea Labinger. New York: Riverhead Books, 2008.
Colby, Sandra L. and Jennifer Ortman. "Projections of the Size and Composition of the U.S. Population: 2014 to 2060," Current Population Reports, P25–1143, United States Census Bureau, Washington, DC, March 2015.
Coultas, Brenda. "*Fractured Humorous* Book Review," Electronic Poetry Center, April 2000 <http://epc.buffalo.edu/authors/torrese/fractured.html>.
Dalleo, Raphael and Machado Sáez, Elena. *The Latino/a Canon and the Emergence of Post-Sixties Literature*: New York: Palgrave Macmillan, 2007.
Díaz, Junot. *The Brief Wondrous Life of Oscar Wao*. New York: Riverhead, 2007.
Engel, Patricia. *Vida*. New York: Grove Press, 2010.
Ennis, Sharon R., Merarys Ríos-Vargas, and Nora G. Albert. "The Hispanic Population: 2010," 2010 Census Briefs, C2010BR-04, United States Census Bureau, Washington, D.C., May 2011.
"Excerpts from Sesshu Foster interviews," *Modern American Poetry*, no date. <http://www.english.illinois.edu/maps/poets/a_f/foster/interviews.htm>.
Foster, Sesshu. *Atomik Aztex*. San Francisco: City Lights, 2005.
Goodwin, Matthew David. Latino/a Rising. Kickstarter campaign, launched September 16, 2014. <https://www.kickstarter.com/projects/2019038492/latino-a-rising>.
Hernandez, Daniel. "Defining Life by Way of Blurring Language," *Los Angeles Times*, April 27, 2005. <http://articles.latimes.com/2005/apr/27/entertainment/et-book27>.
Hogan, Ernest. *Smoking Mirror Blues*. La Grande, OR: Wordcraft of Oregon, 2001. Mondo Ernesto Blog, 2015. <http://www.mondoernesto.com/>.
Lennon, Brian. "The Antinomy of Multilingual US Literature." *Comparative American Studies* 6.3 (Sep. 2008): 203–24.
Lowry, Elizabeth. "The Human Barnyard: Rhetoric, Identification, and Symbolic Representation in Giananina Brashci's *The United States of Banana*," in *Representing 9/11: Trauma, Ideology, and Nationalism in Literature, Film and Television*, ed. Paul Petrovic. London: Rowman and Littlefield, 2015, 155–64.
Martínez, Nina Marie.*¡Caramba! A Tale Told in Turns of the Card*. New York: Alfred A. Knopf, 2004.
Milian, Claudia. *Latining America: Black-Brown Passages and the Coloring of Latino/a Studies*. Athens, GA and London: University of Georgia Press, 2013.
Montoya, Richard, Ricardo Salinas, and Herbert Sigüenza. "The Mission." *Culture Clash: Life, Death and Revolutionary Comedy*. New York: Theatre Communications Group, 1998, 1–56.
Murray, Yxta Maya. *The Conquest: A Novel*. New York: Rayo, 2002.
Nilges, Mathias. "Marxist Literary Criticism," *The Routledge Companion to Latino/a Literature*. Ed. Suzanne Bost and Frances Aparicio. New York and London: Routledge, 2013, 143–51.
Oboler, Suzanne. *Ethnic Labels, Latino lives: Identity and the Politics of (re)presentation in the United States*. Minneapolis: University of Minnesota Press, 1995.
Plascencia, Salvador. *The People of Paper*. San Francisco: McSweeney's Books, 2005.

Poetry Foundation. "Edwin Torres," Poems and Poets, n.d. <http://www.poetryfoundation.org/bio/edwin-torres>.

Rivera, José. "Split Personality: Random Thoughts on Writing for Theater and Film," *Cinema Journal* 45.2 (2006): 89–92.

Sadowski-Smith, Claudia. "Twenty-First-Century Chicana/o Border Writing," *South Atlantic Quarterly* 105.4 (Fall 2006): 717–743.

Saldívar, José David. *Trans-Americanity: Subaltern Modernities, Global Coloniality, and the Cultures of Greater Mexico*. Durham, NC and London: Duke University Press, 2012.

Saldívar, Ramón. "The Second Elevation of the Novel: Race, Form, and the Postrace Aesthetic in Contemporary Narrative," *Narrative* 21.1 (2013): 1–18.

Salles, Walter (dir.) *Diarios de motocicleta* [The Motorcycle Diaries], feature film, screenplay José Rivera, 2004.

Svich, Caridad. "'An Urgent Voice for Our Times.' An Interview with Jose Rivera," *Contemporary Theatre Review* 14.4 (2004): 83–89.

Tejada, Roberto José. "Rodrigo Toscano." *Bomb Magazine* 125 (June 2013). <http://bombsite.com/issues/999/articles/7255>.

Torres, Justin. *We the Animals*. New York: Houghton Mifflin, 2011.

Vourvoulias, Sabrina. "Putting the I in Speculative: Looking at U.S. Latino/a Writers and Stories," TOR.com: Science fiction. Fantasy. The Universe. And Related Subjects. February 2, 2015. <http://www.tor.com/2015/02/02/looking-at-us-latino-latina-speculative-writers-and-stories/>.

PART III

Critical Methodologies and Themes

9

NORMA ELIA CANTÚ

Latin@ Poetics: Voices

> Even jade is shattered,
> Even gold is crushed,
> Even quetzal plumes are torn ...
> One does not live forever on this earth:
> We endure only for an instant!
> – Nezahualcoyotl (1402–72)

I begin with a memory of my father *declamando*[1] long poems in Spanish and of me as a three- or four-year-old being trained to do the same: memorize and perform poems in public. I clearly remember, at age five, *declamando* for a Mother's Day program at Mother Cabrini Catholic Church in Laredo, Texas. No doubt such early training started me on the path of poetry that led me to the writing of this essay where I seek to highlight the centrality of poetics to Latin@ literature and trace the shifts in themes and in modes of poetic expression in Latin@ literary history. I also seek to cover important poetry from a number of Latin@ poets while making the argument that literary production by Latin@s cannot be properly understood without considering poetics. It is mindful of a poet who lived more than 500 years ago on this continent, Netzahualcoyotl, it is mindful of his words that I write of, recall, and remember the poets and the poetry of our *antepasados* and our contemporaries. It is true that we "endure only for an instant," yet poetry endures, and I rejoice in that and celebrate the voices, a cacophony of poetry that spans more than 500 years and that shape-shifts with each generation.

Introduction

The legacy of Latin@ poets living and writing (in Spanish, English, or Spanglish) in the United States cannot be ignored. How can we talk of a Latin@ literary heritage without mention of José Martí, Sara Estela Ramírez, Julia de Burgos? How can we not mention Ricardo Sánchez, Sandra María

Estevez, Raúl Salinas, Pedro Pietri, Alurista, and other Chican@ and Latin@ poets who in the fervor of the 1960s ushered in an engaged poetry, a poetry of and by the people? In *Chicano Poetry: Response to Chaos*, the first full-length critical book on Chicano poetry, Juan Bruce-Novoa highlighted the work of Alberto Baltazar Urista Heredia (a.k.a. Alurista), Gary Soto, Bernice Zamora, José Montoya, and others who could be called the instigators of a "flowering of the Chicano Movement" and what the *floricantos* of the time celebrated, the poetry and song of the Movimiento Chicano. The poets Bruce-Novoa chose to include in his groundbreaking critical text – Abelardo Delgado, Sergio Elizondo, Rodolfo "Corky" Gonzales, Miguel Méndez, J. L. Navarro, Raúl Salinas, Ricardo Sánchez, and Tino Villanueva, as well as the already mentioned Alurista, Soto, Zamora, and Montoya – were not the only ones writing poetry at the time. Among those who were not included were Tejano poets José Antonio Burciaga, Evangelina Vigil, Nephtali de Leon, Reymundo "Tigre" Pérez, Inés Hernández (at that time Tovar), and José Montalvo, as well as Lorna Dee Cervantes and Barbara Brinson Curiel from California. Subsequent studies by literary critics such as Martha Sanchez, José Limón, and Rafael Pérez-Torres over the last forty years have dealt with a few more poets and have used different theoretical tools. A number of dissertations have explored Latin@ poetry as well. So the field is ever widening and being defined and charted in an ongoing process.

My focus in this essay, however, is more contemporary, although I do flash back to the poets of the late nineteenth and early twentieth centuries, but only briefly. I remain cognizant of how the choices affect the canon. A corollary to any conversation about a Latin@ poetic heritage must include a discussion of what constitutes a poetic canon: do we include works based on content or the poet's self-identification? First consider the poets themselves. For instance, would a survey of Latin@ poets include William Carlos Williams, whose mother was Puerto Rican? Would poems about the Latin@ experience by non-Latin@s be included? Would only poets born in the United States of Latino heritage be included? What about those who came to the United States as children? Or those who came as young adults or even older? Then also consider the genres. Would we include the folk poetic traditions found in our folk musical heritage, such as *corridos*, children's songs, *decimas*, or *alabanzas*? All these could be gathered under a category I would call "musipoesía," for they certainly possess poetic elements as well as musical elements found in the folk life of Latin@ communities. Limón has already shown the way that early Chicano poetry harkens back to the *corrido* tradition. And would we add rap and reggaeton as well as pop music to this category? While I conceive of these folk and popular poetic expressions equal to those that adhere to what most of us consider poetry – that is, what appears in print and with a decidedly "poetic" format – I will only briefly mention these poetic subgenres as I focus on a somewhat narrower definition of Latin@ poetics: the publication and performance by Latin@s of writing that is identified as poetry.

The poetic production of each *latinidad* brings with it a tradition that, although similar in roots (Spanish and indigenous), could be said to be vastly different. To paraphrase John Chávez and Carmen Giménez Smith, "the term 'Latin@ [poetry]' is as complex as each [poet's] varied life experience suggests" (2014). If we deign to trace the geographic origins of our *latinidades*, taking as a starting point what Aragón calls the "the bedrock of Latino poetry," or Chicano poetry (*Shifts* 1), we could lay out a map that indeed covers the entire continent and the Caribbean: from Cuban American poets, such as Richard Blanco, to Puerto Rican such as Martín Espada, to Dominican American Julia Alvarez, to Chilean American Marjorie Agosín, Argentinian American Alicia Partnoy, to Nicaraguan Americans Francisco Aragón and Roberto Vargas, and to countless other poets from the vast Caribbean and Latin American diasporas. To further complicate this mapping, we would then have to lay out the terrain of Chican@ poetry across the geography of the United States with the regional variants of Spanish and Spanglish from Nuevomejicano *decimas* to South Texas border poets, and Movimiento poets from California to Texas and Chicago and *pinto* (encarcerated) poets from all over the United States. Furthermore, we would need to account for the continuous and recent influx of poets from Mexico such as Xanath Carraza and Rossy Evelin Lima, and of particular identities within the diasporas such as Jewish Latin@ poets like Agosín and Uruguayan American Laura Cesarco Eglin. Our multilayered mapping would trace the poetic production diachronically back to 1848 and 1898 when the United States becomes the colonizing force in the present-day U.S. Southwest and the Caribbean, respectively. Moreover, our mapping would synchronically account for contemporary poetry by poets who identify as Chican@, Mexican American, and the myriad *latinidades*. By sheer numbers, Chican@ and Mexican American poets predominate. It is their work that is indeed the bedrock Aragón claims it to be, not just because it arises in a colonized space that houses the largest number of Latin@s but because of its scope and quantity to contain the largest number of poets and publications. However, Aragón and other scholars in gathering the work of contemporary poets have sought to widen the terrain. A recent volume of *Diálogo* (17:2), for instance, includes poets from various *latinidades* residing in the United States as well as poets living in Mexico and South America.

This vast territory, then, requires certain cartographic negotiations. So, in an effort to map out the terrain of Latin@ poetics, I have structured the essay to be as inclusive as possible around three major axis: Origins of a Latin@ poetic tradition, 1848–1950; Themes and Approaches to Latin@ Poetics (political, cultural, and linguistic considerations); and Contemporary Movements (CantoMundo, Border Poets, Spanish language poets, publications).

Origins of a Latin@ Poetic Tradition: 1848–1960

The year 1960 is what the Recovering the U.S. Hispanic Literary Heritage Project uses as a marker in its attempt to recover the literary production of Latin@s in the United States. It is a key year, to be sure, as it ushers in the decade that signals a significant shift in our literature; the 1960s then becomes the decade when we as a people turn to poetry and literature as a mechanism for articulating the salient political arguments of the time as a call to action.

Perhaps more than any other genre, poetry has inhabited the soul and minds of Latin@ writers in a deeper and more engaged fashion; it is a deeply rooted genre that manifests itself in poetic oral traditions such as the already mentioned *declamación*, *corridos*, *decimas*, and countless other subgenres from lullabies to dirges. From the various Latin@ home communities to the fervor of the political poetry of the 1890s and the Chicano Movement of the 1960s to today's experimental and slam poetry events, using words in a poetic fashion has been one of the most significant components of the motor that drives the Latin@ literary tradition. Poetry appears in late nineteenth- and early twentieth-century newspapers like *La Crónica de Laredo* or *La Prensa* in Texas and numerous others in New York City. Poet Sara Estela Ramírez's own newspaper, *La Corregidora*, like many other political publications, included poetry. Of course, along with the poetry that appears in these early newspapers, self-published poetry collections or those published in Mexico, Cuba, or Puerto Rico also appear. The Recovery Project has digitized Latina@ newspapers up to 1960 and in these we can find much of the poetry from before 1900 as well as the early part of the nineteenth century. We can claim that there was a lively poetic production that preceded the Chicano literary renaissance of the 1960s and 1970s, for in addition to the newspapers and self-published collections, we can refer to the publication in English such as Josefina Niggli's *Mexican Silhouettes* (1928) and in Spanish such as Américo Paredes's *Cantos de adolescencia* (1934). Similarly, in the other two major *latinidades*, Nuyorican and Cuban American poets engaged in a poetics of migration and of yearning for the homeland publishing in newspapers, literary journals, and small-run collections.

José Limón's exploration of the poetic production from 1965 to 1972 in *Mexican Ballads, Chicano Poems: History and Influence in Mexican*

American Social Poetry accurately locates the precursors to the political poetry of this period in the oral tradition, namely in the *corrido* (ballad), a "master poem" that, in literary critic Harold Bloom's terms, "as key symbolic action, powerfully dominates and conditions the later written poetry" (2). Deploying Américo Paredes's poetics "examined in an analysis of one of his formal poems and in the textuality of *With His Pistol in His Hand*, Paredes's classic study of the Mexican ballad," Limón focuses on "three long poems generated in the emergent American political culture of the 1960s known as the Chicano movement: José Montoya's 'El Sol y los de Abajo,' Rodolfo 'Corky' Gonzales's 'I Am Joaquin,' and Juan Gómez-Quiñones's 'Ballad of Billy Rivera'" (1). Martha Sánchez and Rafael Pérez-Torres also produced critical texts about Chicano and Chicana poetry; each bases the analyses on poets from the 1980s and 1990s, respectively.

Contemporary Poetics: 1960–Present

The recent anthology, *Beyond the Field: New Latin@ Writing* (2014), edited by John Chávez and Carmen Gimenez Smith, claims that "Over the last ten years, U.S. Latin@ writers have produced poetry and prose whose influence is yet to be seen, but whose cultural work is exceptional in its scope, variation, and vision," and that "the term 'Latin@ writing' is as complex as each member's varied life experience suggests." While this analysis reflects the reality of the literary production at the juncture between the twentieth and twenty-first centuries, it is no less true of earlier periods. Given the context of the times, namely the struggle for civil rights that the writers and poets of the 1960s and 1970s address, it is not surprising that the militant and fierce poetic voices of that time also clamored for social justice and whose cultural work was also "exceptional in its scope, variation and vision." Perhaps the poem that best illustrates this is Rodolfo "Corky" Gonzales's epic poem, *Yo Soy Joaquin* (1967), a classic that still speaks to readers who connect to its lineage and universality. Many poets come to mind from the three main *latinidades*: Nuyorican, Cuban American, and Chican@. Each group found that their poets led the literary movement of the times. A case in point is the central influence of Nuyorican poets Miguel Algarín, Miguel Piñero, Sandra Maria Esteves, Piri Thomas, Tato Laviera, and Pedro Pietri, whose collective vision and passion created a space for socially engaged poetry at the Nuyorican Poets Café. Olguín and Vásquez, in their introduction to *Cantos de adolescencia: Songs of Youth 1932–37*, a reprint of Américo Paredes's *poemario*, also note that in the 1930s and 1940s South Texas, Paredes belonged to a circle of trans-border writers and poets (xxxiv). It is the 1960s and 1970s poets in Texas, Arizona, New Mexico, and Colorado that we can look to for poetry engaged in the political work of the time, including works by Cecilio García Camarillo, Reymundo "Tigre" Pérez, raúlsalinas, Ricardo Sánchez, Evangelina Vigil, Inés Hernández Ávila (at the time Hernández Tovar), Lalo Delgado, Sabine Ulibarrí, Dorinda Moreno, and Bernice Zamora.

One way to glean the impact of the poetry produced during this tumultuous period is to look at the literary spaces where the poetry appeared: publications such as *Caracol* and *Tejidos* in Texas, *El Grito* and *Con Safos* in California, newspapers such as *La Prensa* in New York and in San Antonio. The more formal collections such as anthologies published at this time can also offer a view of the landscape. In the 1970s, several collections of Chicano and Puerto Rican literature appeared, including Chican@ anthologies such as Carlota Cárdenas de Dwyer's *Chicano Voices* and Dorothy E. Harth's *Voices of Aztlán: Chicano Literature of Today*. Anthologies of Puerto Rican poetry similarly highlighted the literary production of Puerto Rican poets in the mainland and on the Island: *The Puerto Rican Poets/Los poetas puertorriqueños* (1972), coedited by Alfredo Matilla and Iván Silén; and *Borinquen: An Anthology of Puerto Rican Literature* coedited by Iván Silén, María Teresa Babín, and Stan Steiner (1974). Julio Marzán's *Inventing a Word: An Anthology of Twentieth-Century Puerto Rican Poetry* (1980) gathered the work of poets such as Julia de Burgos and Luis Palés Matos, and is credited with being the first anthology to introduce the Afro-Latino poetic voice. Cuban American poetry was collected in early anthologies such as Angel Aparicio Laurencio's *Cinco poetisas cubanas 1935–1969* (1970) and the anthology *Veinte años de literatura cubano-americana: Antología 1962–1982* (1988), edited by Silvia Burunat and Ofelia García, gathered the work of Cuban and Cuban American poets and prose writers. It is not until the 1990s that we begin to see collections across *latinidades*, such as Martín Espada's *El Coro: A Chorus of Latino and Latina Poetry* (1997); more recently, El Museo del Barrio's *Me no Habla con Acento* (2011), a volume published to commemorate their fortieth anniversary that includes cotemporary poets across various *latinidades*: Edwin Torres, Rigoberto González, Maria Rodriguez-Morales, Erik Maldonado, Bonafide Rojas, Luz María Umpierre, Paul S. Flores, Roberto Vassilarakis, Caridad de la Luz "La Bruja," Nancy Mercado, Urayoán Noel, Chris "Chilo" Cajigas, Latasha N. Nevada Diggs, Roberto F. Santiago, Frank Perez, Sheila Maldonado, John "Chance" Acevedo, Machete Movement, Lisa Alvarado, A. B. Lugo, Jason Hernandez, Myrna Nieves, Tito Luna, and Carlos Andrés Gómez. Most of these poets have participated in the Museo's "Speak Up!" poetry series.

A few highlights emerge in the territory covered by this very brief historical overview: the increasingly complex nature of the poetry and of the poets within and across *latinidades*, especially in the anthologies; the dearth of critical studies of the poetic production, most of which has focused on Chican@ poets and poetry; and the need for collective and individual treatments of the histories and poetic output of the various *latinidades*.

Themes and Approaches to Latin@ Poetics

The varying poetic histories offer different themes and approaches; however, the defining moments center on politics, culture, and language. From the outset, Latin@ poetics involved a myriad of nuanced and well-pronounced differences across latinidades; after all, the differences lie in the already noted different historical trajectories and the different literary legacies the poets inherit. For instance, the romanticism of the nineteenth century found in the poetry published in Spanish-language newspapers and even in collections of the early twentieth century invariably harkens back to that of Spanish poets like Unamuno and to the Latin American poets such as Amado Nervo. And yet, political poetry, or what I would call activist poetics, existed even then alongside the sonnets to beauty. Published in 1911, Sara Estela Ramírez's "¡Surge!," a feminist call to women to resist, could be said to be the precursor of a Chicana/Latina feminist poetics that remains alive and well a hundred years after Ramírez published her poem in *La Crónica*. But the advent of the social turmoil of the mid-twentieth century invigorated the poetry of Nuyorican and Chicano poets. Similarities surface if we consider the larger picture. Individual poetic expressions may dwell on certain overarching themes such as language, identity, and cultural resistance to hegemonic U.S. popular culture and practices. Yet, the collective reach of the work surfaces in the unifying themes of solidarity, the search for linguistic freedom, and the political struggles on human and civil rights issues.

Pocho *Poetics*

The 1960s and 1970s brought an explosion of what Ben V. Olguín calls "*pocho* poetics," the poetry that idealizes and celebrates the figure of the "*pocho*" or the *pachuco*. Olguín claims that Paredes begins this practice and that the poetry, rife with Spanglish and caló, situates itself at the center of what Gloria Anzaldúa called "linguistic terrorism" that results from the oppressive conditions of language dominance that Chican@s experienced in what Rudy Acuña rightly proclaimed "Occupied America." The raw and often vernacular poetry that emerges in the 1960s and 1970s with José Montoya, Alurista, Ricardo Sánchez, Evangelina Vigil, and Lorna Dee Cervantes, along with the witty and brilliant wordplay of José Antonio Burciaga, decenters the previous generation's adherence to more European Spanish and English poetic forms such as sonnets. In his collection *Poxo*, Isaac Chavarria goes as far as changing the spelling of "*pocho*" in his rearticulation of the term. In keeping with the celebratory note of Paredes's poem that serves as an epigraph for Olguín and Vásquez, Chavarria also takes "pride" in declaring himself "*poxo*."

Identity, then, is a key theme of Latin@ poetry, and whether the poet is Boricua or Pocha, from East Harlem or East Los, geographical and ethnic identity surfaces in the poetry. Geography lends a clear nod to location, to what Emma Perez calls the *sitio y lengua*. In my view, it is a concern for poets everywhere. Neruda's *Isla Negra* is a case in point. So is Frost's poetry solidly situated in the landscape. Similarly, Lorna Dee Cervantes and José Antonio Burciaga locate their work in California and Texas, respectively. Yet another unifying theme based on geography may reside in the "border poetics" nestled within Gloria Anzaldúa's groundbreaking *Borderlands/La Frontera: The New Mestiza*, which blends prose and poetry but that also includes a section devoted to poetry. By deploying a borderlands sensitivity for analysis as well as for poetic expression, both Anzaldúa and Paredes use the metaphor of the geopolitical space of the U.S.-Mexico borderlands to articulate a poetics of space and identity. It is this same border poetics that Christopher Carmona, in his article "The Chican@ Nueva Onda as a Poetic Tidal Wave: The Revitalization Repoliticalization & Redefinition of 'Chican@' Through Poetry," explores. Poets along the U.S.-Mexico border attest to the *transfrontera* nature of a border poetics that was there with Paredes and Anzaldúa and continues with Pat Mora, Benjamin Alire Saénz, Alberto Ríos, Rigoberto González, Raquel Valle Senties, Lauren Espinoza, and Emmy Pérez among hundreds others, some who publish their poetry, and others whose poetry remains unpublished. I remember Mrs. Ramírez, our high school Spanish teacher at Martin High School in Laredo, Texas, always reciting poetry, writing her own verses witty and full of double entendres but always located in that "*sitio y lengua*" of the border. She exercised a border poetics that was local, to be sure, but that exemplifies hundreds of such voices, such as another Laredoan, Hilario Coronado Cuello, retired railroad worker, who wrote his autobiography in poetic form and titled it *Memorias*. Spoken word poet Amalia Ortiz's combines the border poetics with that of the oral performance and weaves in, as many other Chicanas and Latinas do, themes of sexuality and gender in her spoken word.

Women-Centered Poetics

The woman-centered poetics becomes what Tey Diana Rebolledo called "a woman's space" in her book, *Women Singing in the Snow: A Cultural Analysis of Chicana Literature*. "Loose Woman," the title poem of Sandra Cisneros's collection, is an excellent example of the feminist poetics I am talking about. Most recently, literary critic Larissa Mercado-López explored in Laurie Ann Guerrero's poetry what she calls maternal *facultad*, a poetics of motherhood, based on Gloria Anzaldúa's concept of *facultad*. The earliest work by Latinas explicitly and openly working with a poetics of gender and sexuality first appears in the 1970s with the work of Latina poets such as lesbian Puerto Rican poet Luz María Umpierre's *The Margarita Poems*. Additionally, Anzaldúa and Chicana poet Cherríe Moraga wove poetry and prose in their mixed-genre books, *Borderlands/la Frontera: The New Mestiza* (1987) and *Loving in the War Years: Lo que nunca pasó por sus labios* (1983) respectively. Other examples include Ana Castillo's *The Invitation* and Alicia Partnoy's *Volando Bajito/Low Flying*.

Along with lesbian and feminist poetics, the poetry by Rigoberto González, Pablo Miguel Martínez, and Eduardo Corral foregrounds a Latino sexual poetics that, beyond eroticism, explores what Mary Galvin refers to as a "queer poetics" in her book of the same name. I extend Galvin's claim that a queer poetics reaches beyond so the poet is freed from the heterosexist mindset that yields a certain poetics, positing Latin@ poets outside the white mindset and the normative whiteness associated with poetry in the United States. But the transitions Latin@ poetics is undergoing is akin to being in Nepantla, in that in-between space that Anzaldúa theorized. Rigoberto González's talk, "Latino Poetry: Pivotal Voices, Era of Transition," delivered at the U.S. Library of Congress in April 2014, lays out a contemporary poetics of transition that demands flexibility and accommodation by the larger hegemonic poetics. This flexibility would allow for difference, for poets of color and especially Latin@ poets, to express themselves in numerous poetic expressions that include formalist as well as experimental in a poetics that is inclusive and expansive and allows Spanish and English as well as indigenous languages. González focused on six poets, but the same would apply to hundreds of young voices that are setting the stage for the next phase in our trajectory, whether the poetry is in Spanish, English, or Spanglish.

Language

It is not just about the language, albeit language looms large as a theme and as a concern for Latin@ poetics. No. It is much more than just words, the choices of how to say what. It is about who we are as Latin@s in the

United States. The poetry of Mexican immigrants like Lucha Corpi, Liliana Valenzuela, and Rossy Evelin Lima remains rooted in the Mexican and morphs into Chicana aesthetics. This dynamic includes the daughter of an indigenous mother reclaiming her Nahuatl that surfaces in Xanath Caraza's poems, and the search for a totality of being that haunts Jewish Chicana Rosebud Ben Oni's experimental feminist poetry. The theme is not new. The search for an identity, the expression of one's identity, and the celebration of the group's identity are all themes that Latin@ poets have embraced.

The shifts noted by González exist at all levels and in all *latinidades*. Naomi Ayala, Carmen Giménez Smith, Leticia Hernández Linares, Mariposa, Lauro Hernandez, David Thomas Martinez, Carl Macum, Amy Sayre, and so many more create the shift with their words. And they write in all kinds of linguistic configurations. I thought that by now the issue of whether one writes in Spanish or English or Spanglish would have been resolved. Latin@ poets who live in communities that are truly bilingual, where the drastic measures to erase Spanish did not work, or where a continuous influx of Spanish speakers has not allowed English to conquer, know the beauty, the richness of the linguistic repertoire available. Rafael Pérez-Torres's chapter in *Movements in Chicano Poetry*, "Mouthing Off: Plyglossia and Radical Mestizaje," aptly explores the issue of language in the poetry of various Chican@ poets, but it is just as fitting when discussing Puerto Rican poets. He focuses on the poets who use Spanglish or Tex-Mex or interlingualism, a process that allows for the use of two or more languages, as Cuban writer Gustavo Pérez Firmat explains. It is clear that a poetics of silence emerges when the constraints of linguistic policing dominate, when linguistic terrorism will not allow for interlingualism. The linguistic tightrope that Latin@ poets must walk challenges their ability to balance and yet remain a poet.

Contemporary Movements

It was precisely this situation of not having a space to just be Latin@ poets, with all of our languages, all of our class statuses, all of our skin colors, all of our ways of being in the world, and especially the world of poetry and of the U.S. world of poetry, that motivated the establishment of CantoMundo, a summer workshop for Latin@ poets that nurtures and supports as it creates a community. Chicana poets Carmen Tafolla and Theresa Palomo Acosta had attempted to unite Chicana poets in the 1980s, but due to a number of factors, that movement never took off. Similarly, in the 1990s, there were attempts to unite Latin@ writers in a community; the most successful one, Macondo, started by Sandra Cisneros, continues to this day. Additionally, there are locally based groups such as Las Poetas, founded by Angela Cervantes in Kansas City in 2003, that has morphed into the Latino Writers Collective; and Mujeres Fuertes, a collective of Chicana poets founded in the 1990s in San Antonio and included Tejana Angela de Hoyos. Of course, other groups have gathered and continue to gather Latin@ poets: the Nuyorican Poets Café, founded in 1973, is one of the oldest and longest continuously running spaces for poets. But when Pablo Miguel Martínez, Celeste Mendoza, Deborah Paredez, Carmen Tafolla, and I met, we envisioned what CantoMundo could be and decided on a different structure, one modeled on Cave Canem and Kundiman, poetry workshops for African American and Asian American poets, respectively. We drafted our mission statement: "Through workshops, symposia, and public readings, CantoMundo provides a space for the creation, documentation, and critical analysis of Latina/o poetry." The first CantoMundo was held in Albuquerque, New Mexico; subsequently we have met at The University of Texas at Austin. Now in its fifth year, CantoMundo fellows number more than 60 Latin@ poets from all over the country and from all kinds of mixed race and mixed *latinidades*; we have formed a community of support, and plans are in the works for a poetry publication and an expansion to include more poets. Currently the acceptance rate is low given the space limitations. But it is not just in CantoMundo where poets have banded together.

Publications such as the special issue of *Diálogo* with more than 30 Latin@ poets from the Americas, and critical essays on contemporary issues such as the emergence of poetry in Mexico by indigenous poets, attest to the very active Latin@ poetic world. In small groups like the Latino Writers Collective in Kansas City, or the highly competitive Macondo Workshop in San Antonio, poets are coming together to work on their craft, to publish their work, and to ensure that Latin@ poetry is not subsumed, or erased, by the larger world of poetry in the United States.

In the lower Rio Grande Valley of South Texas, a group of Border Poets in what is commonly called El Valle have come together, as they did when Paredes was a young poet there, and are publishing and actively promoting their Chican@ poetry. The increase in Latin@ poets writing in Spanish and publishing heartens me. A few journals publish work in Spanish and they are thriving; of course, with the Internet, and social media, the venues for Latin@ poetics to reach ever wider audiences are also thriving.

At various times in our literary history, a Latin@ poetics has emerged that answers the call for a literary art that is at once political and relevant. At least at three points in time, we can identify such activity: at the end of the nineteenth century and the beginning of the twentieth century; during the 1960s and 1970s; and the current moment in the early twenty-first century. Francisco X. Alarcón's call for poets to unite against the atrocities committed by the passage of anti-immigrant and anti-ethnic studies laws in Arizona was an overwhelming success, indicating that the movement is still alive and well.

One publisher told me that they did not publish poetry because it does not sell. I can understand that. But if our own publishers only publish what sells, we are doomed. Yet, there is always hope. I remain optimistic as I see new venues like Aztlan Libre Press take on the service of publishing Latin@ poets. However, the obvious need for more spaces for our poetry – publications, both electronic and print, new journals, slam poetry and spoken word venues, prizes and awards – remains. I look forward to a continued renaissance, to a Latin@ poetics that is inclusive, that embraces and celebrates poets like Grisel Acosta and Vincent Toro, Sheryl Carolina Ebed, and Millicent Acardi alongside the veteran@s.

Conclusion

As Rigoberto González proclaimed in his 2014 talk at the U.S. Library of Congress:

> I am not proclaiming the Chicano voice as the most important or even the most audible, but rather, the most frequently heard by those who are listening to the varied tenors and tones of Latin@ poetry. And it becomes particularly pressing today, when the pitch of the debates over immigration reform and the need for Mexican American Studies has reached such intensity, that the Chicano voice–that Chicano voices–must continue to speak in order assert the Chicano community's relevance to American society and culture. Poetry today, as in the past, will write the way.

The contemporary Latin@ literary scene is an occasion for celebration, as Latin@ poets are taking their place in the mainstream world of poetry. More and more Latin@ poems are appearing in publications such as *Poetry Magazine*, where a recent issue included Deborah Paredez's poems. Latin@ poets are receiving poetry awards: CantoMundo fellow Barbara Brinson Curiel won the Philip Levine prize in 2013, for instance. The ConTinta gatherings at the annual meeting of the Association of Writing Programs feature poetry reading. The poets Tino Villanueva and Jesús Flaco Maldonado were the honored in 2013 and 2014, respectively. Literally hundreds of poetry readings and slam poetry contests happening all over the country attest to the power of this new old movement. And what is perhaps most encouraging is the return of *declamación* contests to certain schools with a large Spanish-speaking population. Drawn to hip-hop and rap, many young poets are attending and competing in slam poetry events. As the Nuyorican Poets Café celebrated its fortieth year of operation, we can proudly point to the renaissance and continued celebration of Latin@ poetic tradition that extends back to pre-contact with European poetic traditions. A Latin@ poetics is one that is fiercely alive and that is an instrument for change. We can rest assured that regardless of Netzahualcoyotl's warning, that "one does not live forever," at least for now Latin@ poetry is alive and well.

Notes

1 The art of "declamación" is a staple of Mexican oral tradition that seeped into the U.S. cultural milieu of the 1950s and 1960s. Even in the 1980s and 1990s, contests were held in schools along the U.S.-Mexico borderlands.

Works Cited

Acuña, Rudy. *Occupied America: A History of Chicanos*. New York: Harper & Row, 1981. 8th edition. New York: Pearson, 2014.

Algarín, Miguel and Miguel Piñero. *Nurorican Poetry: An Anthology of Puerto Rican Words and Feelings*. New York: William Morrow & Co., 1975.

Anzaldúa, Gloria. *Borderlands/La Frontera: The New Mestiza*. 1987. 4th edition. San Francisco: Aunt Lute Books, 2012.

Aragón, Francisco, Ed. *The Wind Shifts: New Latino Poetry*. Tucson: University of Arizona Press, 2007.

Burunat, Silvia and Ofelia García, *Veinte años de literatura cubanoamericana: Antología 1962–1982*. First publication, Havana. Tucson, AZ: Bilingual Review, 1988.

Cárdenas de Dwyer, Carlota. *Chicano Voices*. Boston: Houghton Mifflin, 1975.

Carmona, Christopher. "The Chican@ Nueva Onda as a Poetic Tidal Wave: The Revitalization Repoliticalization & Redefinition of 'Chican@' Through Poetry." *Diálogo*, vol. 17, no. 2 (Fall 2014): 49–56.

Chavarria, Isaac. *Poxo: Poems*. College Station, TX: Slough Press, 2013.

Chávez, John and Carmen Gimenez Smith, Eds. *Beyond the Field: New Latin@ Writing*. Denver, CO: Counterpath Press, 2014.

Coronado Cuello, Hilario. *Memorias*. 2nd ed. Laredo, TX: Printed in Mexico, 1988.

Corpi, Lucha. *Poemas de Mediodía/Noon Words*. Fuego de Aztlan, 1980. Houston: Arte Público Press, 2001.

Fireflight: Three Latin American Poets. Berkeley, CA: Oyez, 1976.

Variaciones sobre una tempestad / Variations on a Storm. Berkeley, CA: Third Woman Press, 1990.

Eglin, Laura Cesarco. *Llamar al agua por su nombre*. El Paso, TX: Mouthfeel Press, 2010.

Sastrería. Montevideo, Uruguay: Yauguru, 2011.

Tailor Shop: Threads, translated by Teresa Williams. Georgetown, Kentucky: Finishing Line Press, 2013.

Espada, Martín. *El Coro: A Chorus of Latino and Latina Poetry*. Amherst: University of Massachusetts Press, 1997.

Galvin, Mary E. *Queer Poetics: Five Modernist Women Writers*. Westport, CT: Praeger, 1999.
González, Rigoberto. "Latino Poetry: Pivotal Voices, Era of Transition." Library of Congress Website. http://www.loc.gov/today/cyberlc/transcripts/2014/140410plc1830.txt Accessed May 5, 2015.
Harth, Dorothy E. *Voices of Aztlán: Chicano Literature of Today*. New York: New American Library, 1974.
Limón, Jose E. *Mexican Ballads, Chicano Poems: History and Influence in Mexican-American Social Poetry* (The New Historicism: Studies in Cultural Poetics). Oakland: University of California Press, 1992.
Mercado-López, Larissa. "Laboring Histories: The 'Reconciliation' of Maternity in the Poetry of Laurie Ann Guerrero." *Diálogo*, vol. 17, no. 2 (Fall 2014): 57–63.
Moraga, Cherrie L. *Loving in the War Years: Lo que nunca pasó por sus labios*. Boston: South End Press, 1983.
Olguín, Ben V. "Reassessing Pocho Poetics: Américo Paredes's Poetry and the (Trans) National Question." *Aztlán: A Journal of Chicano Studies*, 30, 1 (Spring 2005): 87–121.
Paredes, Américo. *Cantos de Adolescencia, Songs of Youth: 1932–1937*. Translated with an introduction and annotation by Ben V. Olguín and Omar Vásquez Barbosa. Houston, TX: Arte Público Press, 2007.
Pérez-Torres, Rafael. "Mouthing Off: Plyglossia and Radical Mestizaje." In *Movements in Chicano Poetry: Against Myths, Against Margins*. New York: Cambridge University Press, 1995, pp. 208–44.
  Movements in Chicano Poetry: Against Myths, against Margins. New York: Cambridge University Press, 1995.
Umpierre, Luz María. *The Margarita Poems*. Bloomington, IN: Third Woman Press, 1987.

10

ISABEL DÚRAN

Latina/o Life Writing: Autobiography, Memoir, *Testimonio*

It is a dangerous thing/ to forget the climate of your birthplace,/ to choke out the voices of dead relatives/ when in dreams they call you/ by your secret name./It is dangerous/ to spurn the clothes you were born to wear/ for the sake of fashion; ... dangerous/ to disdain the plaster saints/ before which your mother kneels/ praying with embarrassing fervor/ that you survive in the place you have chosen to live:/ a bare, cold room with no pictures on the walls,/ a forgetting place where she fears you will die/ of loneliness and exposure./ Jesús, María, y José, she says,/ el olvido *is a dangerous thing.* "El Olvido" – Judith Ortiz Cofer

Introduction

Many intentions, motivations, reasons, and means that aim at ends have been provided by critics of autobiography to explain why men and women of all times and places, of all origins, creeds, cultures, and nationalities, one day decide to write about themselves. The search for one's identity and roots, coming to terms with one's traumas and ghosts from the past, presenting a communal portrait of one's milieu or group, curative and cathartic reasons, sharing experiences of conversion, confessing one's beliefs, vices, or sins, giving testimony of a successful or a painful state or experience, denouncing situations of injustice, presenting an apology for one's stances – the list could go on and on, and each and every one of those reasons or motivations would be true. But what lies behind all of those reasons to write an autobiography is an act of remembrance; a desire to escape forgetfulness, as Judith Ortiz Cofer beautifully explains in her poem quoted above, because "*el olvido*" is a dangerous thing. And no human being is more exposed to forgetting his/her heritage and ancestry and less safe from acculturation than the one who has abandoned his/her former existential landscape, culture, language, and mode and has had to adapt to and integrate or assimilate into a new one. That is the case of the bicultural being, of the Latina/o in the United States. That is the case of the "divided self" where the inherited cultural traditions collide with the alternative standards of an adopted country. In other words, the "them" vs. "us," or the "here" vs. "there" of practically every Latina/o autobiography.

"My book is necessarily political," states Richard Rodriguez in the first chapter of his autobiography, *Hunger of Memory*, and indeed, this sentence could be applied to almost every autobiography – and certainly to every Latinoa/o autobiography (7). This literary form has historically been a space full of political consequence because it allows what is normally disallowed: the voicing of silenced or repressed ideas and values. In a culture in which minoritized citizens have often had to struggle for their rights, ethnic autobiography proclaims the value of the ethnic self. It is no wonder, then, that the ethnic school considers autobiography an excellent index of sociopolitical reality, since it often recreates a collective past, and therefore it is a particularly useful means of understanding cultural history (Hokenson 97).

In the beginning, autobiography criticism was interested in the author per se, but then more sophisticated questions of referentiality, mimesis, and the issue of the ontology of the self began to dominate the inquiries. If, in the past, one could distinguish between two main tendencies, namely the defenders of the historical veracity of autobiography versus those who admitted fiction or "design" in the form, today that old and stale question of autobiographical truth versus the inevitable fiction necessary for the genre has stopped being a concern of the critics. But at the same time, things have become rather more complicated. The more traditional, historically oriented critics proceeded to study autobiography as a genre based on the notion of a preexisting ontological self that provided a neat referent that the writer could capture and translate into words. That is, according to their view, there existed a verifiable relationship between the text and the extratextual referent. Contrary to these traditional views, an alternative literary theory emerged in the late 1960s and 1970s attacking such premises: the deconstructionists postulated a textual self and stripped autobiographical discourse of referential truth. The result is that there exist two opposing critical views of the nature of the self and its relation to language: Is it self-autonomous and transcendent, or is it contingent and provisional, dependent on language for its very existence?

Between the warring factions of humanist and deconstructionist formulations, certain conciliatory positions did emerge as these critics wondered, "Why do writers persist in trying to find and discover their selves through autobiography?" The answer to this question was provided by those critics who approached autobiography, not so much with rhetorical intentions, but in the spirit of the cultural analyst, asking what such texts can teach us about the ways in which individuals in a particular culture experience their sense of being "I." These critics subscribe to the idea that the autobiographical "I," however fugitive and unreliable, is indeed the textual double of a real person, as much as it is a self-evident textual construct. In this line of thought, Latina/o writers have challenged what disables them in both humanist and poststructuralist poetics, and have taken what enables them. They have appropriated the postmodern project of decentering the universal subject, for precisely such decentering has made space for the experience of ethnic minorities; at the same time, they have refused to relinquish the possibility of a unified self: why give up a visibility and a position from which to act, a visibility and a position only just beginning to become available to them?

Latina/o Life Writing: Authors, Themes, Texts

It is not my intention to provide a comprehensive overview of Latina/o life writing produced since the 1970s, for that project would either occupy several volumes or be reduced to some name-dropping, followed by one or two descriptive lines. I have instead chosen to focus on some key authors and on unifying issues, themes, texts, and "panethnic" (Caminero-Santangelo 21) concerns, broached by most Latina/o authors belonging to the four largest subgroups (Mexican, Cuban, Puerto Rican, and Dominican), that will provide a rigorous portrait of the genre. Moreover, following Frederick Aldama's approach, I use the term "Latina/o life writing" as a category to identify a "dialectal variation of world literature" that coexists in the United States alongside other literary dialects, including the so-called literary mainstream (Aldama xvi). The period I cover (except for one or two exceptions) corresponds to writers whose coming of age as writers happened in or after the 1970s, a period during which "discussions of Latino identity focus on concepts such as Latinidad, *mestizaje*, and brownness" (Stavans 2011, vi), since I am most interested in texts that foreground the problematic nature of the "panethnic, transracial and transnational" identities (Caminero-Santangelo 32). Finally, I tend to reduce to a minimum the discussion of cases of autobiographical fiction. There are many cases of Latina/o narratives that powerfully invite the reader to "connect the life of the living author with the fictional life represented in the book" (Torres-Saillant 74). However, given space restrictions, I focus only on texts in which the author, narrator, and main character bear the same name and whose authors aim at telling their *own* life story, testimony, or memoir, in whatever generic form they may find most suitable to their communicative aims (narrative, poetry, essay, or a mixture thereof).

The Bicultural Self

James Olney, in his comparative study of Western and African autobiographies, explained how, if we look at African autobiography, we shall not find *"autoautography"* (Olney 1993, 218), the kind of text that features a Rousseauian portrait of "myself"[1]; but what he calls *autophylography*. This can be expanded to most Latina/o autobiography, where what we shall find is *not* a portrait where the subject makes a claim of absolute uniqueness and imagines that his experience is unrepeated and unrepeatable à la Rousseau; instead, the Latina/o autobiographer often executes a collective portrait of the life shared by the group, and presents, in Velasco's words, a portrait of the "Total self" as opposed to the "individual I" (Velasco 330), thus raising the question of how group identities constitute an essential quality of self-definition. What critic Genaro Padilla has said about Chicano autobiography applies more generally to Latinos: "individual experience and collective historical identity are inextricably bound" (6), as Gustavo Pérez Firmat admits in his memoir *Next Year in Cuba*, a text that develops his thesis of the one-and-a-half generation to describe the identity of those Cubans who came to the United States in their early adolescence, after their exile prompted by Fidel Castro's revolution:

> The portrait is also a group picture ... Although the narrative relies on the circumstances of my life in a foreign and familiar land, I share these circumstances with countless other immigrants. I can't presume to speak for all Hispanic Americans, or even for all the Cuban-Americans; yet it would be disingenuous for me to think that my words, my feelings, my experiences, are mine alone. The truth is that they emerge from a choral or *communal setting* and resonate with shared experiences and expectations. (Pérez Firmat 1995, 13; italics added)

The "communal setting" often entails two shared experiences: bilingualism and biculturalism. Whereas some earlier immigrant autobiographers (usually European) were eager to tell an assimilationist story of becoming an American, a majority of Latinas/os write as a conjunction of cultures, working in the very "interzone" where their different languages and cultural ideologies of self overlap, for it is there that identity must be discovered and a compromise negotiated (Hokenson 100).

Speaking of postcolonial literatures, Homi Bhabha provides an excellent description of the ironically privileged positionality "at the break" that can be applied to Latina/o life writing. He speaks of the possibilities of being *in between*, of occupying an interstitial space that is not fully governed by the recognizable traditions from one's place of origin. This third space is skeptical of traditional notions of identity that depend for their authority on being geographically "originary," or concepts of culture that depend for their value on being pure:

> What is theoretically innovative, and politically crucial, is the need to think beyond narratives of originary and initial subjectivities and to focus on those moments or processes that are produced in the articulation of cultural differences. These 'in-between' spaces provide the terrain for elaborating strategies of selfhood – singular or communal – that initiate new signs of identity, and innovative sites of collaboration, and contestation, in the act of defining the idea of society itself. (Bhabha 1–2)

We could position Puerto Rican writers Esmeralda Santiago and Judith Ortiz Cofer alongside the majority of recent exiled or immigrant memoirs or *testimonios* written by Latinas/os, where the authors write at a conjunction of cultures, working from their in-betweenness where their different languages and cultural ideologies of the self overlap. Esmeralda Santiago's *When I Was Puerto Rican* (1993) and Judith Ortiz Cofer's *Silent Dancing* (1990) depict the bicultural condition of their Puerto Rico–born authors, who migrated to the United States as children and struggled to become the successful writers they are today. But we are not just reading two childhood memoirs. We are also reading two bicultural coming-of-age stories of migration that present lives lived between English and Spanish, between *Los Nuevayores* and *la Isla*, between being a *jíbara* or a modern *americana*. That is why both Santiago and Ortiz Cofer find it difficult to speak of any particular "national identity," because their projects articulate how migration shapes and redefines gender and national identities. While traditional immigrant literature in the United States is defined by its boundaries between here and there and the distinctiveness of the two places, Ortiz Cofer and Santiago locate themselves in a hybrid space whose stance, according to Carmen Faymonville, can be described as "transnational," neither assimilationist nor necessarily oppositional.

A similar transnationalist perspective that does not require a quasi-linear movement from exile to U.S. citizen, but that expresses no absolute loyalty to either the culture of origin or U.S. culture as a life in-between, is again provided by Gustavo Pérez Firmat's *Next Year in Cuba*:

> Where am I most me? Which of these two locales that I have described is my true place?.... Miami or North Carolina? Cuba or America? This book grows out of my need to find an answer to these questions, or at least to understand

more completely why I cannot answer them ... I write to become who I am, even if I'm more than one, even if I'm *yo* and you and *tú* and two. (1995, 270)

If Pérez Firmat says in his book "I didn't grow away from Cuba, for I'm as Cuban now as I ever was. I'd rather say that I grew out of Cuba" (1995, 255), the same can be applied to Santiago and Ortiz Cofer. For the three authors, Cuba and Puerto Rico have become a transnational space that transcend the geographic boundaries of the "Island" – a symbolic space that may be felt and experienced in the United States, where the exiled citizen learns to live surrounded by multiple manifestations of cultural syncretism. For Santiago and Ortiz Cofer, Puerto Rico is their motherland, and the United States is their adopted country. But they do not mourn their acculturation (the loss of their language, culture, history, and tradition). On the contrary, their memoirs are exercises in transculturation in the sense that they seek to overcome the partial loss of their land of origin by mutual interchange of language and culture, by representing a series of complex processes of adjustment and re-creation – cultural, literary, linguistic, and personal – that allow for new, hybrid configurations to arise out of the clash of cultures.

But the lesson about transculturation is not learned without difficulties. Both Puerto Rican authors share with other women's autobiographies the painful mother-daughter conflict that Silvia Schultermandl has called "transnational matrilineage," a term we could adopt to refer to the distance and sense of disconnectedness that daughter protagonists feel as they investigate their matrilineal Puerto Rican heritage from within a U.S. perspective. "My mother," reflects the young Judith, "was so different from my classmates' mothers that I was embarrassed to be seen with her. While most of the other mothers were stoutly built women with dignified gray hair who exuded motherliness, my mother was an exotic young beauty, black hair down to her waist and a propensity for wearing bright colors and spike heels. I would have died of shame if one of my classmates had seen her sensuous walk and the looks she elicited from the men on our block" (*Silent Dancing* 126). And yet, both Puerto Rican women pay homage in their memoirs to their brave, warrior mothers who fought against poverty, racism, and marital abandonment (in Santiago's case) or against homesickness and cultural estrangement (in both cases), to give their daughters what they could not embrace and enjoy themselves: the American dream.

Borders, Hybridity, and Brown Selves

Since the 1960s, the general celebration of cultural diversity has had a huge impact on the way historians study frontiers, so much so that there is a strong tendency now to define the frontier concept with such phrases as meeting place, contact point, and middle ground; that is, the borderlands are figured as a contested territory in which cultural interaction takes place. As Velasco explains (317), whereas a frontier is the space that separates the zone of civilization from that which is beyond, the Spanish word *la frontera*, as used by Latina/o writers, conveys the idea of the borderlands as a positive, enriching zone of cross-cultures, contact, and interaction. In order to illustrate this type of re-theorization of *la frontera*, we could compare Mexican American writers Gloria Anzaldúa and Richard Rodriguez and their use of the *mestiza* and "brown" metaphors, respectively. Both Anzaldúa's *Borderlands/La Frontera* (1999) and Rodriguez's *Brown: The Last Discovery of America* (2002) are compilations of essays, digressions, soliloquies and disquisitions private and historical that do not have a narrative continuity, in which, if Rodriguez tries to formulate how Hispanics are browning an America that has always defined itself as black or white, then Anzaldúa also tries to discover the nature of the *mestiza*, and the process of *mestizaje* that she and her kinfolk embody within the United States. And their presentation of ethnic identity in terms of a metaphorically brown or *mestiza* in-betweenness is what creates a bridge between these two texts (Durán 2007). Their autobiographies propose a brown or *mestiza* "inter" space for a new ethnic and cultural identity to exist (Bruce-Novoa 1990, 31).

"I write of a color that is not a single color … I write of blood that is blended … I write about race in America," writes Richard Rodriguez in *Brown* (xi). And, while writing about race, he in fact undermines the notion of race and proclaims the idea of a "brown" – blended, impure, *mestiza*, and contradictory – America. Rodriguez is positioning himself against essentialist visions of pure Mexicanness, very much in line with Werner Sollors's theorizations of race. In *The Invention of Ethnicity*, Sollors reminds us that, while ethnic groups are typically imagined as if they were natural, real, eternal, stable, and static units, the ethnogenetic studies that result from such premises typically lead to an isolationist, group-by-group approach that emphasizes authenticity and cultural heritage within the individual group, at the expense of dynamic interaction and syncretism (xiv). That syncretism is, arguably, what both Rodriguez and Anzaldúa seek, because the same lack of racial purity, expressed as a borderlands identity, is also celebrated by Anzaldúa in one of the poetic proclamations included in *Borderlands*: "To live in the Borderlands means you/ Are neither hispana indígena negra española/ Ni gabacha, eres mestiza, mulata, half breed/ Caught in the crossfire between camps/ While carrying all five races on your back" (Anzaldúa 216).

Moreover, Anzaldúa's inclusion of the mythical and religious aspects of Chicana/o life in what has been called "automitografía" (Velasco 326) becomes a type of generic border crossing that achieves a new experimental voice for a higher sense of the cultural self. This new voice aims at rehearsing an identity that enables her to reject all those binary oppositions or frontiers between black/white, American/Mexican, man/woman, English/Spanish that she sees as simplistic products of Western thought. As a lesbian Chicana, she has to find her own race in an amalgamated identity: "as a *mestiza* I have no country, my homeland cast me out; yet all countries are mine because I am every woman's sister or potential lover. As a lesbian I have no race, my own people disclaim me; but I am all races because there is the queer of me in all races" (102).

Another Chicano autobiography that also proposes a "brown" identity is Oscar Zeta Acosta's *The Autobiography of a Brown Buffalo*, the account of some months in the life odyssey of a writer, an activist, and a civil rights attorney who became a leading figure in the Chicano rights movement of the 1960s. When *Brown Buffalo* begins, Acosta quits his job as a legal adviser in an Oakland legal clinic because his life seems empty and without purpose, and begins a cross-country, existential journey to find his true self. When his voyage through the disillusion of the American Dream finally takes him to the end of his exodus, he returns to Mexico to confront himself with his own truth. Back in his ancestral homeland, he discovers his true identity; that of a brown buffalo: "[W]hat is clear to me after this sojourn is that I am neither a Mexican nor an American. I am neither a Catholic nor a Protestant. I am a Chicano by ancestry and a Brown Buffalo by choice" (199). Why a Brown Buffalo? Because it is "the animal that everyone slaughtered" (both the cowboys and the Indians) and "because we do have roots in our Mexican past, our Aztec ancestry, that's where we get the brown from" (198). So, if, against the cultural normalcy of a white America, Oscar Acosta grew up hating his brown body because it did not conform to the normative ideal, Oscar *Zeta* Acosta[2] undergoes an empowering metamorphosis that leads him to choose the identity of a symbolic "Brown Buffalo."

The Bilingual Self

The issue of bilingualism and its metaphors has occupied almost all Latina/o life writers whose lives are divided between the two logos, very often using Spanish as their private tongue and English as their public language. One clear example would again be Anzaldúa's bilingual *Borderlands/La Frontera*, in which she jumps from one language to another without feeling compelled to translate or apologize for her bilingualism: "the switching of 'codes' in this book from English to Castilian Spanish to the North Mexican dialect to Tex-Mex to a sprinkling of Nahuatl to a mixture of all of these, reflects my language, a new language –the language of the Borderlands" (Anzaldúa iv).

Ilan Stavans, Mexico-born Jew who immigrated to the United States in 1985, captured his existential and linguistic journey (from Yiddish to Spanish and English) in his 2001 memoir, *On Borrowed Words: A Memoir of Language*, where he weaves personal reminiscences with an investigation into language acquisition and cultural code switching. In fact, Stavans has devoted a large part of his intellectual life to reflecting on the status of Hispanics/Latinos in the United States, and on the border language called Spanglish. In his previous autobiographical book of essays, *The Hispanic Condition*, Stavans discusses bilingual education and concludes that "what is applauded in today's multicultural age is a life happily lost and found in Spanglish ... a round trip from one linguistic territory and cultural dimension to another, a perpetual bargaining" (Stavans 1996, 13–14)

A very different view of Spanglish as a solution to intercultural and interlingual "vertigo" (Pérez Firmat 1995, 249) is offered by Cuban American Gustavo Pérez Firmat in his autobiographical book *Cincuenta lecciones de exilio y desexilio* (2000). In this particular book, written entirely in Spanish, Firmat does not believe that the two languages can merge into an amalgam called Spanglish. Rather, the bilingual person, Firmat thinks, lives in a constant shaking between each language, depending on the circumstances: "If my life depended on a sentence, I would write it in English ... if my life depended on a *spoken* sentence, I'd die if I couldn't speak it in Spanish" (1995, 53). Without explicitly saying it, in this sentence he is in fact telling us that his professional or public language is English, while his private and emotional language is Spanish. When he turned fifty, though, the time came when he felt he had to "unlearn English" (2000, 9) and work in Spanish as well, as he did in *Cincuenta lecciones*, an autobiographical experiment that melts essays and maxims with poems and nostalgic confessions, which in various manners convey the feeling of the linguistic rupture, disjunction, and "dyslexia" that exile brings along.

Another Latino autobiography that partly offers itself to an analysis from the point of view of issues of bilingualism is Richard Rodriguez's first book of autobiographical essays, *Hunger of Memory*, published in 1982 to both critical acclaim and heated controversy. It is one of the most vilified Mexican American texts, having gained its notoriety among Chicana/o critics from its author's apparent rejection of his ancestral Mexican roots. Yet, upon its publication, *Hunger of Memory* received remarkable praise in the mainstream media from non-Chicana/o reviewers. As a child of immigrants, Rodriguez presents the choices available to him as a series of polarities that must be resolved in favor of assimilation (Spanish versus English, Catholic versus Protestant, Mexican versus American), and probably the most central of these polarities is the one between the public and private spheres, as defined by the two languages he speaks (Paravisini-Gebert 84). Rodriguez presents Spanish as the most powerful obstacle to assimilation for Mexican Americans, and hence the importance given in the text to the process of his education as the necessary path that will lead him from Spanish to English, and, thus, from a private to a public life as an assimilated American:

> My awkward childhood does not prove the necessity of bilingual education. My story discloses instead an essential myth of childhood – inevitable pain. If I rehearse here the changes in my private life after my Americanization, it is finally to emphasize the public gain. The loss implies the gain. (27)

One need not contradict Rodriguez's claim that the gain outweighed the loss, but the fact of the matter is that his own narrative sometimes suggests otherwise. Because *Hunger of Memory*, as many critics have pointed out, is a somewhat contradictory text: an autobiography that celebrates the American education that transformed its author, but whose dominant tone is one of nostalgia for his lost, private world from which English uprooted him (Couser 223).

One cannot write about bicultural, bilingual selves without at least mentioning Dominican American voices. The two most highly acclaimed authors are Julia Alvarez and Junot Díaz, whose fiction is now a sine qua non if one wishes to approach the immigrant experience of the Dominicans in the United States. Even if they are not autobiographies, Alvarez's novels, *How the García Girls Lost Their Accents* (1991) and its sequel *¡Yo!* (1997), present life stories that resemble so much Alvarez's life that some friends and relatives recognized themselves in the books' pages. Both novels tell the story of an immigrant's search for identity and both have Yolanda García (Yo) as the protagonist who finds her identity while immersing herself into the history of her native island. The more autobiographical *Something to Declare* (1995) is Alvarez's first book of essays: a writer-on-writing book, in which she relates her life as the member of an exiled family who had to escape from the dictatorship of Trujillo, and in which the issue of language is also given special prominence. In the essay "My English," for example, she describes how English went from being the mysterious language that her parents spoke to keep secrets from her and her sisters in Santo Domingo (both her parents spoke fluent English) to her passport into a new world and a future as a writer in the United States.

On the other hand, the ten stories that comprise Junot Díaz's volume *Drown* (1996) also lend themselves to autobiographical readings, and Díaz himself has declared that he likes to play with autobiography, but "no matter how hard I try to be autobiographical, the demands of fiction transform the material" (Torres-Saillant 74). It seems, then, that memoir and autobiography have not emerged as the preferred modes of literary expression in the work produced by Dominican American authors.

The Latino Version of Conversion Narratives

Religion is not only a crucial element of autobiography; it is *the* inspirational matrix of life writing, even if the word did not exist when Saint Augustine wrote his *Confessions*, the account of his conversion from sin to grace. Since then, one of the most recurring patterns in autobiography from different periods and places is precisely the story of (de)conversion because it represents an aspect of the maturing process and a move toward self-discovery. One could examine some Latina/o coming-of-age narratives as examples of secular conversions. Chicano author Luis Rodriguez, for example, in his memoir *Always Running. La Vida Loca: Gang Days in L.A.* (1993), narrates his conversion from being a gang member to reaching the "grace" of becoming just the opposite of what he was. Luis was a veteran of East L.A. gang warfare from the age of twelve, witnessing countless shootings, acts of street crime, rape, scenes of police abuse, imprisonment, beatings, arrests, revenge murders, drug addiction, and suicide attempts. At fifteen he started to see a way out of the *barrio* through activism, education, and the power of words. His is a success story from violence and desperation to fighting for peace and hope, from *la vida loca* to the life of poetry, journalism, and social activism.

Of course, it could be argued that every autobiography depicts a kind of conversion or radical change of some sort. Indeed, as Jean Starobinski has put it, "one would hardly have sufficient motive to write autobiography had not some radical change occurred in his life-conversion, entry into a new life, the operation of grace" (78). But Luis Rodriguez follows the pattern of religious conversions almost step by step. If we take the conversion moment of St. Augustine's, or of any spiritual autobiography, that moment (or moments) will be described as having been incited by a sudden apparition or the hearing of a voice; or by the "sortes" or opening of a book at random, where one happens to read the precise revelatory lines that foster the conversion. Very similar rhetorical strategies are used by Luis Rodriguez to describe his various moments of conversion. The "sudden apparition" at the Community Center of Chente Ramírez, a young activist who struggles to convert young Luis to the "religion" of social activism, fosters the first signals of change in the almost-criminal teenager. The second moment of conversion takes the "sortes" formula for what he reads in a book will play a paramount role in his conversion. The book that will become a living bible for him was *Down These Mean Streets*, the autobiography of Puerto Rican

Piri Thomas. Soon thereafter, Luis starts to write, gets his first literary prize for some stories, graduates, continues with his social activism in favor of the disinherited, and goes to university. The conversion has finalized successfully: "I began a new season of life. Intellect and body fused, I now yearned to contribute fully, embodied with conscious energy, to live a deliberate existence dedicated to a future humanity ... without injustice, coercion, hunger and exploitation" (243).

"Conversion narratives" are very often testimonial acts. The definition of the Spanish word *testimonio* (testimony) that Smith and Watson propose is the kind of life writing whose narrator "intends to communicate the situation of the group's oppression, struggle, or imprisonment, to claim some agency in the act of narrating, and to call upon readers to respond actively in judging the crisis" (206). This definition is perfectly applicable to some other works such as Piri Thomas's *Down These Mean Streets* (1967), a work that presents a similar story of the Puerto Rican son of immigrants set in the context of extreme poverty and racial discrimination. We also learn about his dealing with gangs, self-hatred, drugs, crime, incarceration, and ultimate rehabilitation. We even perceive a sort of "religious" conversion at the end of his prison days, when he turns to God and to his aunt's church for consolation. It is no wonder, then, that Luis Rodriguez identifies with its author, since both texts epitomize the harsh life of poverty, delinquency, and social injustice that so many Latinas/os have shared, and "the angst of the immigrant experience as it afflicts the young" (Torres-Saillant 72). Likewise, the harshness and injustices of *barrio* life, and education as the road to rehabilitation, are also the main focus of Chicano Jimmy Santiago Baca's prison memoir, *A Place to Stand* (2001). Long considered one of the best poets in the United States today, Baca was still illiterate at the age of twenty-one. And yet, *A Place to Stand* is the remarkable tale of the making of a poet, after many years spent in a maximum-security penitentiary, thanks to reading and to his discovered passion for writing.

The Personal Essay: Returns and Re-Encounters

The "personal essay" is that genre of life narrative that is literally a self-trying-out, a testing of one's own intellectual, emotional, and psychological responses to a given topic. As Smith and Watson put it, "since its development by Montaigne as a form of self-exploration engaging received wisdom, the personal essay has been a site of self-creation" (200). We have already spoken of some texts not written as a single life narrative, but as a compilation of essays or thoughts (Anzaldúa's *Borderlands/La Frontera*, Richard Rodriguez's volumes, Stavans's *The Hispanic Condition*, or Julia

Alvarez's *Something to Declare*). We shall now argue that the "personal essay" is a genre very much in line with the Latina/o writer's necessity to express private and individual thoughts, arguments, and beliefs while at the same time providing a cultural critique or a sociopolitical commentary on the situation of their kinfolk. This is the case of Mexican American Dagoberto Gilb's *Gritos* (2004), an interesting collection of essays that sound like strong explosions of personal thoughts and emotions ("gritos") around various issues. Each of the four sections of the book is focused on a particular cluster of themes, including racism, life on the border, being a teacher and a writer, *la familia*, and national identity. After all, Gilb's "shouts" articulate the necessity to return to one's past and to ruminate about one's roots, to fight forgetfulness, to express the sense of belonging that breathes inside every autobiographical expression.

The same necessity of return and recovery of one's lost heritage lies at the heart of Richard Rodriguez's second book of essays, *Days of Obligation: An Argument with my Mexican Father*. A book that can be read as the story of the biblical prodigal son who, after turning his back to his Mexican cultural and linguistic parental legacy in his obsessive quest for total assimilation, now returns to a triple father: Mr. Rodriguez, Mexico, and the God of his Catholic faith. The book constitutes an expanded dialogue of the adult son with his Mexican father around various issues and obsessions. But now the son is not just the assimilated American of *Hunger of Memory* trying to convince himself of the gains that his departure from his Mexican heritage entailed; now he is rather the Mexican son who has returned to his fatherland to observe it as an insider, and feels that the "days of obligation" to also return to God the Father of his Mexican Catholicism cannot be procrastinated, since his religious upbringing constitutes an integral part of his ethnic patrimony.

A recent autobiographical piece published by Ilan Stavans is also structured around the idea of returning to one's roots, so important in bicultural selves who have lost or neglected a part of their history. In his 2012 *Return To Centro Histórico: A Mexican Jew Looks for His Roots*, Stavans searches for his Jewish roots through photographs using pictures as "engines" (7). Ilan Stavans, like Richard Rodriguez, decides to revisit his hometown, Mexico City, but he heads to the *Centro Histórico*, the downtown area where the hidden Jews escaping the Inquisition were burned at the stake. In his pictorial meditation, Stavans not only undertakes a personal journey, but merges with an entire culture in his exploration of the important role that Jews have played in the development of the Hispanic world. Inevitably, the first pages of this mental autobiography are devoted to questioning the purity of his Mexican identity and, using the pronoun "we" that speaks of a communal sense of identity, admits that the effort of finding one's roots involves the entire community, because "the search for roots is a way to look back at a page in history that explains our love for *el país Azteca*, the Aztec homeland. The imperative is to explain to ourselves not how far we've traveled in our journey of assimilation but how truthful we've remained to our origins" (102).

The same technique of using a photographic cartography was used by Chicana writer and critic Norma Cantú in *Canícula: Snapshots of a Girlhood en la Frontera*, a book that she has described as a "fictional autobioethnography" (xi), and that, not unlike the fictional *The House on Mango Street* by Sandra Cisneros, is a collection of fictional portraits (snapshots) of representative Hispanic characters, neighbors, and *barrio* dwellers that the reader can identify with.

Since the 1980s, Chicana autobiographical production has introduced gender and sexuality into the racial discourse, and has radically reworked Chicana/o identity politics. Cherríe Moraga's *Loving in the War Years: lo que nunca pasó pos sus labios* (1983) proposes a similar project to that presented by Anzaldúa, insofar as it also brings a new emphasis to the configuration of a liminal subject: the lesbian woman within the ethnic context (Velasco 314). Moraga's eclectic volume, which unites essays, political thoughts, journal entries, and poetry, strikes the reader with a title that, again like *Borderlands/La Frontera*, mixes English and Spanish. But the title is just a first glimpse of the constant code-switching that we shall find in "este libro [which] covers a span of seven years of writing" (i), where Moraga compiles new and old writings gathered from previous publications. The book constitutes, in many ways, an open declaration of her lesbianism, which she had to keep secret and unpronounced ("nunca pasó por sus labios"), and hence the simile between her love for women and the harassed love relationship that Bogart and Bergman live in "the war years" of *Casablanca* (29). But, linking sexism and racism, Moraga equates the sexual oppression that she felt within her community for being a "dyke" (52) with the racist oppression felt by non-whites in the United States. In this line of thought we hear in *Loving in the War Years* the voice of a Chicana with a white complexion (a "güera") who needs to come to terms with her sexual identity, but also with her "Chicano heritage" (96), after having "lost herself to the gavacho" (iii): "What I never quite understood until this writing," the author explains in an essay entitled "Las Vendidas," is that "to be without a sex – to be bodiless – as I sought to be to escape the burgeoning sexuality of my adolescence ... means also to be without a race ... as I grew up sexually, it was my race, along with my sex, that was being denied me at every turn" (125). Being the daughter of a Mexican mother and a white father,

Moraga confesses that "I grew white. Fought to free myself from my culture's claim on me" (ii), and thus the need to recover and re-encounter her long-neglected bicultural identity (51). Thanks to the cathartic act of writing autobiographically, Moraga emerges from feeling torn between two worlds to embracing both worlds, uniting them in poetic harmony.

Conclusions

Life writing may be regarded as the most important form in Latina/o literature, since its practice epitomizes the main sociocultural compulsions that have fed Latina/o writing from the outset of the tradition (Torres-Saillant 64–65). In the lines above we have seen how Latina/o autobiographers combine personal story with cultural critique; that is, they subscribe to a process of life writing that links communal truth and personal narrative that may serve as a declaration of freedom from the perspective of the dominant culture, a celebration of the importance of group identity and its significance in one's personal identity, a demand for respect for one's group, an attempt to recapture a neglected or lost cultural heritage, and an acceptance or celebration of diversity from the wider society (Bjorklund 154). While each writer will champion a construction of identity informed by his or her individual personality, it will have repercussions at a collective level, because more often than not, the Latina/o writer feels responsibility of telling about group history as part of her/his personal histories.

My aim in presenting a number of shared themes, concerns, narrative strategies, and communal "metaphors of the self," to use James Olney's expression (Olney 1972), has been to provide a transatlantic reading of Latina/o life writing that approaches its Cuban, Mexican, Dominican, or Puerto Rican creators as a few of the many voices that compose the chorus of American literature. Immigrant, exiled, bicultural, and at times bilingual voices that, in their stylistic innovation, in their adaptation of traditional models of life writing, or in their creation of alternative, hybrid and experimental modes of self-expression, have elevated the genre to the most interesting limits of writing in the first person.

Notes

1 The often-quoted first two sentences of Rousseau's *Confessions* (1782) are eloquent enough: "I have entered upon a performance which is without example, whose accomplishment will have no imitator. I mean to present my fellow-mortals with a man in all the integrity of nature; and *this man shall be myself*. I know my heart, and have studied mankind; I am not made like any one I have been acquainted with, perhaps like no one in existence; if not better, I at least claim originality, and whether Nature did wisely in breaking the mould with which she

formed me, can only be determined after having read this work" (Book I, emphasis added).
2 Acosta added "Zeta" to his name when he became a political activist in the late 1960s. He says that he took his name because it was the name of a Mexican revolutionary he heard about in a movie.

Works Cited

Acosta, Oscar Zeta. *The Autobiography of a Brown Buffalo*. New York: Vintage Books, 1989.
Aldama, Frederick: *A Routledge Companion to the History of Latino Literature*. New York: Routledge, 2013.
Alvarez, Julia. *How the García Girls Lost Their Accents*, 1991.
  Something to Declare. Chapel Hill, NC: Algonquin Books of Chapel Hill, 1995
  ¡Yo!. Chapel Hill, NC: Algonquin Books, 1997
Anzaldúa, Gloria. *Borderlands/La frontera* (1987). San Francisco: Aunt Lute Books, 1999.
Baca, Jimmy Santiago, *A Place to Stand: The Making of a Poet*. New York: Grove Press, 2001.
Bhabha, Homi K. *The Location of Culture*. New York: Routledge, 1994.
Bjorklund, Diane. *Interpreting the Self: Two Hundred Years of American Autobiography*. Chicago: University of Chicago Press, 1998.
Bruce-Novoa, Juan. *Retrospace: Collected Essays on Chicano Literature, Theory and History*. Houston, TX: Arte Público Press, 1990.
Caminero-Santangelo, Marta. *On Latinidad: US Latino Literature and the Construction of Ethnicity*. Gainesville: University Press of Florida, 2007.
Cantú, Norma. *Canícula: Snapshots of a Girlhood en la Frontera*. Albuquerque: University of New Mexico Press, 1995.
  "Memoir, Autobiography, Testimonio." Suzanne Bost and Frances R. Aparicio (eds.), *The Routledge Companion to Latino/a Literature*. New York: Routledge, 2013, 310–22.
Cofer, Judith Ortiz. *Silent Dancing: A Partial Remembrance of a Puerto Rican Childhood* Houston, TX: Arte Público Press, 1990.
Couser, G. Thomas. *Altered Egos: Authority in American Autobiography*. New York: Oxford University Press, 1989.
Díaz, Junot. *Drown*. New York: Riverhead Books, 1996
Durán, Isabel: "The Brown/*Mestiza* Metaphor, or the Impertinence against Borders." A. Manzanas (ed.), *Border Transits: Literature and Culture across the Line*. Amsterdam and New York: Rodopi, 2007, 119–45.
Faymonville, Carmen: "New Transnational Identities in Judith Ortiz Cofer's Autobiographical Fiction." *Melus*, 26.2 (2001): 129–59.
Gilb, Dagoberto, *Gritos: Essays*. New York: Grove Press, 2003.
Hokenson, Jan Walsh, "Intercultural Autobiography." *Auto/Biography Studies*, 10.1 (1995): 92–113.
Moraga, Cherríe. *Loving in the War Years: lo que nunca pasó por sus labios*. Boston: South End, 1983.
Olney, James. *Metaphors of Self; the Meaning of Autobiography*. Princeton, NJ: Princeton University Press, 1972.

"The Value of Autobiography for Comparative Studies: African vs. Western Autobiography." William Andrews (ed.), *African American Autobiography: A Collection of Critical Essays*. Upper Saddle River, NJ: Prentice Hall, 1993, 212–23.

Padilla, Genaro. *"My History, Not Yours": The Formation of Mexican American Autobiography*. Madison: University of Wisconsin Press, 1993.

Paravisini-Gebert, Lizabeth. "Richard Rodriguez's Hunger of Memory and the Rejection of the Private Self." *U.S. Latino Literature: A Critical Guide for Students and Teachers*. Westport, CT: Greenwood Press, 2000, 81–92.

Pérez Firmat, Gustavo. *Next year in Cuba: A Cuban Emigre's Coming of Age in America*. New York: Anchor Books, 1995.

Cincuenta lecciones de exilio y desexilio. Miami, FL: Ediciones Universal, 2000.

Rodriguez, Luis. *Always Running: La Vida Loca, Gang Days in L.A.* Willimantic, CT: Curbstone Press, 1993.

Rodriguez, Richard. *Hunger of Memory: The Education of Richard Rodriguez*. Boston: D.R. Godine, 1982.

Days of Obligation: An Argument with My Mexican Father. New York: Viking Penguin, 1992.

Brown: The Last Discovery of America. New York: Viking, 2002.

Rousseau, Jean-Jacques. *The Confessions of J. J. Rousseau*. The Project Gutenberg EBook, 2006. http://www.gutenberg.org/files/3913/3913-h/3913-h.htm

Santiago, Esmeralda. *When I Was Puerto Rican*. New York: Vintage Books, 1994.

Schultermandl, Silvia. *Transnational Matrilineage: Mother-Daughter Conflict in Asian American Literature*. Berlin: Lit, 2009.

Smith, Sidonie and Watson, Julia (Eds.). *Reading Autobiography: A Guide for Interpreting Life Narratives*. Minneapolis: University of Minnesota Press, 2001.

Sollors, Werner (Ed.). 1989. *The Invention of Ethnicity*. New York: Oxford University Press, 1989.

Starobinski, Jean. "The Style of Autobiography." James Olney (ed.), *Autobiography: Essays Theoretical and Critical*: Princeton, NJ: Princeton University Press, 1980, 73–83.

Stavans, Ilan. *The Hispanic Condition: Reflections on Culture and identity in America*. New York: Harper Perennial, 1996.

On Borrowed Words: A Memoir of Language. New York: Viking, 2001.

Return to Centro Histórico: A Mexican Jew Looks for His Roots. New Brunswick, NJ: Rutgers University Press, 2012.

(ed.). *The Norton Anthology of Latino Literature*. New York: W.W. Norton & Co., 2011.

Thomas, Piri. *Down These Mean Streets*. New York: Knopf, 1967.

Torres-Saillant, Silvio. "The Latino Autobiography." Alan West-Durán (ed.), *Latino and Latina Writers*, Vol. I. New York: Thomson Gale, 2004, 61–79.

Velasco, Juan. "Automitografías: The Border Paradigm and Chicana/o Autobiography." *Biography*, 27.2 (Spring 2004): 313–38.

11

LAWRENCE LA FOUNTAIN-STOKES

Queering Latina/o Literature

To Sandra K. Soto

There are multiple ways (and multiple challenges) to understand the phrase "queering Latina/o literature." One way (perhaps the dominant one, certainly the one most popular in Latina/o and lesbian and gay literary surveys) is as an invitation to see how the identity, biography, life experiences, or body of a Latina/o author (particularly related to their sexual orientation, sexual practices, reproductive or sexual anatomy, and/or gender expression) maps onto or impacts their (her, his, hir) literary production, particularly (but not exclusively) for self-identified non-heterosexual or non-cisgender writers, be they lesbian, gay, bisexual, transgender, and/or intersex (LGBTI).[1] In this conception, queer Latina/o literature is defined as literature by LGBTI Latina/o authors, particularly by ones who are out of the closet (that is to say, have publicly disclosed their sexual orientation) and who openly thematize this experience in their literature, bringing together a discussion of ethnicity and sexuality.

Several immediate challenges come to mind. One is what we mean by Latina/o, and if it refers exclusively to people of Latin American descent, including those of indigenous, African, European, Middle Eastern, and/or Asian and Pacific Islander heritage, who write predominantly or exclusively in English in the United States, or if the category is expansive enough to account for authors based in the United States who are writing predominantly or exclusively in Spanish or in another language, whether currently or in the past, or to other individuals (for example, from Spain) writing in the United States about Latinas/os. Another challenge is historical: how far back are we willing to consider Hispanic experience in the United States, and when to begin. With the culmination of the U.S.-Mexican War in 1848 and of the U.S.-Spanish War of 1898? Or only as recently as 1965, which some sources identify as the "beginning" of Chicana/o literature in the United States? A final challenge is the bind of identity, and the assumption (or expectation) that it will always translate into a meaningful literary representation of a particular topic, accompanied with the occasional recrimination from fellow scholars, writers, or readers when this does not occur.

A second way to interpret "queering Latina/o literature" is to offer an analysis of the themes or subject matter discussed in varied literary works, for example, acceptance or rejection of sexual diversity or gender nonconformity, which may or may not coincide with the known identity of an author. A third is to provide a critical lens or framework to interpret a text, employing queer theory or LGBTI reading strategies (as Sandra K. Soto proposes in her study *Reading Chican@ Like a Queer*), the result of more than forty years of scholarship on this topic; by "queer theory" I wish to reference the entire spectrum of queer critical studies, including the queer-of-color critique and queer diaspora studies, as Michael Hames-García explains in his essay "Queer Theory Revisited" included in *Gay Latino Studies: A Critical Reader*.[2]

These aforementioned practices (the three options I list above) benefit from the revalorization of the term "queer," which has come to represent a political, cultural, and academic stand that actively works toward the recognition, destigmatization, and decriminalization of marginalized genders and sexualities, on the one hand, but that also seeks to offer a broader analysis of the workings of power and sexuality in society, offering readings and theorizations that go beyond identitarian concerns, on the other. In the case of the queer-of-color critique, the analysis of sexuality is insistently linked to that of race and ethnicity, partaking of women-of-color feminist theoretical contributions such as the concept of intersectionality, a commitment to see the interrelation between gender oppression and other social factors such as race and class.[3] This holistic commitment to expansive social analysis marks a wide range of queer Latina/o critical volumes such as Cherríe Moraga and Gloria Anzaldúa's anthology *This Bridge Called My Back: Writings by Radical Women of Color* (1981), José Esteban Muñoz's *Disidentifications: Queers of Color and the Performance of Politics* (1999), Juana María Rodríguez's *Queer Latinidad: Identity Practices, Discursive Spaces* (2003), and Michael Hames-García and Ernesto Javier Martínez's *Gay Latino Studies: A Critical Reader* (2011).[4]

The apposition between the gerund "queering" (from the verb "to queer") and the noun phrase "Latina/o literature" might also suggest a distance or opposition, an effect that can be regarded positively (in terms of integrating a new perspective) or negatively: as the *Oxford Dictionary* indicates, "queer" is an informal, offensive term for homosexual; "to queer" (informal) is defined as "spoil or ruin (an agreement, event, or situation)," a threat

I would like to take quite seriously, particularly as a critical stance that challenges orthodoxies.⁵ Ultimately, the apposition suggests that there is a "before" (a Latina/o literature that exists outside of queerness, previous to it), a polemical proposition for those of us who would insist that there is no outside (inherent) exclusion: queerness (call it what historically appropriate term you may) is not new to Latinas/os; it is constitutive and foundational, as Arnaldo Cruz-Malavé has argued in his discussion of the work of Luis Rafael Sánchez, Piri Thomas, Miguel Piñero, Miguel Algarín, Edwin Torres, and Pedro Pietri in his appropriately titled article "'What a Tangled Web!'"⁶ If Latina/o literature has always been queer (particularly as a marginalized, outsider tradition, an internal colonial cultural formation in a white supremacist, heteronormative, patriarchal, imperialist country), what would "queering" it mean, short of the wordplay with yet another verb, to query, in which case "queering" becomes nothing more than a playful written variation of its homophone "querying"?

Queer Latina/o literature is intrinsically yet at the same time paradoxically not marginal; to only argue for its marginality is to have a limited vision of the current status of the culture industries (particularly publishing) and of the advances and significant impact of queer Latina/o literary studies. To phrase it differently: queer Latina/o literature is doing extremely well, and so are long-range, historical queer readings of Latina/o culture (in English, Spanish, and Spanglish), broadly construed. An important number of contemporary queer Latina/o writers and scholars have been recognized at the national level with diverse prizes, including Lambda Literary Awards (also known as "Lammys"), the leading prize in the United States for LGBT book publishing since 1989 (although not totally free of controversy).⁷ Winners range from Chicano detective novel writer Michael Nava (for *Goldenboy* in 1989, *Howtown* in 1991, *The Hidden Law* in 1993, and *Rag and Bone* in 2002) and novelist and editor Carla Trujillo (for her anthology *Chicana Lesbians: The Girls Our Mothers Warned Us About* in 1992) to Cuban American physician and poet Rafael Campo (*What the Body Told* in 1997; *The Poetry of Healing* in 1998), Cuban American novelist Achy Obejas (*Memory Mambo* in 1997; *Days of Awe* in 2002), Chicano novelist Erasmo Guerra (*Between Dances* in 2001), and Chilean American writer Mariana Romo-Carmona (*Conversaciones: Relatos por padres y madres de hijas lesbianas y hijos gay* in 2002). More recent winners include young adult literature writer Alex Sánchez (*So Hard to Say* in 2005 and the Dr. James Duggins Outstanding Mid-Career Novelist Prize in 2011), Chicana novelist and scholar Alicia Gaspar de Alba (*Desert Blood: The Juarez Murders* in 2006), Chicana memoirist and activist Jeanne Córdova (*When We Were Outlaws: A Memoir of Love & Revolution*), and Chicano coeditors Michael

Hames-García and Ernesto Javier Martínez (*Gay Latino Studies: A Critical Reader*) in 2012. In 2013, *nuevomexicano* novelist Benjamin Alire Sáenz (*Everything Begins and Ends at the Kentucky Club*), Puerto Rican scholar Ramón Rivera-Servera (*Performing Queer Latinidad: Dance, Sexuality, Politics*), and Chicana/o authors Cherríe Moraga and John Rechy (Lambda Literary Pioneer Awards) won awards. (It is somewhat disheartening, however, to note that no Latina/o received a Lambda Literary Pioneer Award before that year.) These wins complement the recognitions bestowed in 2014 on Puerto Rican short story author Luis Negrón (*Mundo Cruel*), Chicano poet Rigoberto González (*Unpeopled Eden*), and African American–Puerto Rican novelist, playwright, and editor Charles Rice-González (Dr. Betty Berzon Emerging Writer Award); Negrón's win is notable in that, as Clare Swanson notes, "*Mundo Cruel* is the first translated work to ever win in the General Gay Fiction category" (the book was originally published in Spanish in Puerto Rico; Negrón has lived in Boston and discusses queer migration to the United States).[8] In addition, since 2009, the director of the Lambda Literary Foundation has been a Latino gay author, Tony Valenzuela, who first came to notoriety due to his unpopular positions on safe sex and HIV (consenting to unprotected intercourse without condoms), later developed in his performance piece *The (Bad) Boy Next Door*.[9]

As this rich list suggests, one could write a fascinating essay "queering Latina/o literature" simply by discussing Latina/o "Lammy" Award winners over the last twenty-five years. Moreover, several Latino authors that explore queer topics or issues related to homoeroticism and homophobia have won Pulitzer Prizes (Nilo Cruz in 2003; Junot Díaz in 2008), albeit not for works that focus on this theme.[10] One would not know from this enumeration how contested and challenging the process of recognition and validation of queer Latina/o literature has been, or the difficulties that some LGBTI Latina/o authors still face in writing and publishing their works. In this sense, it is of crucial importance not to overgeneralize the success of specific authors, widespread as it might be, and assume it represents the experience of every single member of the group. One would also not know that this literature extends well beyond the contemporary period; critical accounts rarely mention any references that antecede the 1960s.[11]

As recently as forty years ago (in the mid- to late 1970s), there was a widespread perception that there was no such thing as lesbian and gay Latina/o literature, and if there was, it was completely marginal to the broader project of an ethnic community literature; scholars such as Juan Bruce-Novoa and Efraín Barradas were crucial in recognizing pioneering authors.[12] A good number of academic battles have been waged precisely about whom to include and when to date this literature's origins: the 1963 publication of John Rechy's *City of Night* seems for many critics as far back as they are willing (or able) to go, unless it is to mention anxiety or homophobia, in which case critics go as far back as the 1959 publication of José Antonio Villarreal's novel *Pocho*.[13] Indeed, many scholars have profound reservations about Rechy's early work and prefer to start in 1981 with *This Bridge Called My Back*, dismissing Rechy's contributions on the grounds that he did not thematize queer Chicano experience explicitly enough, an opinion shared by people as disparate as Tomás Almaguer, Cherríe Moraga, and Frederick Aldama.[14] Most Chican@/Latin@ critics also frequently ignore the rich Spanish-language and bilingual literary production of openly gay authors such as the Puerto Ricans Víctor Fragoso (*El reino de la espiga, Ser islas/Being Islands*) and Manuel Ramos Otero (*Concierto de metal y otras orgías de soledad, La novelabingo, El cuento de la mujer del mar*), both of whom lived and published extensively in the New York/New Jersey area in the 1970s, explicitly discussed homosexuality in their works, and organized community events for Latina/o constituencies.

While very limiting, it is understandable that some scholars start their conceptualizations after 1960, particularly if, following sociologist Manolo Guzmán's discussion in *Gay Hegemony/Latino Homosexualities*, we understand the term "gay" as a historically specific social formation consolidated predominantly among white men in the United States in the 1950s, which replaced earlier conceptualizations such as "fairy" that were more prevalent in the earlier twentieth century, not to mention even older terms such as "sodomite," "invert," "uranist," "nellie," "pansy," "Mary," or the nineteenth-century German-language scientific term "homosexual" invented by Karl-Maria Kertbeny in 1869, more than a decade before the introduction of the term "heterosexual" in 1892.[15] Yet this discussion does not even consider Latino-specific terms in Spanish such as *maricón, marimacha, joto, tortillera, cachapera, loca, pájaro, pato, pata*, and *puto*, which have been of crucial importance in the articulation of queer Latina/o sensibilities and cultural formations; it ignores the explosion of homosexual literature in Latin America by men and women dating as far back as the late nineteenth century; and it also reduces "queer" to be the equivalent of gay, and strangely presents the term "lesbian" as ahistorical, universal, and timeless.[16]

"Gay and lesbian" is not the equivalent of queer or of queering or of reading like a queer; it does not stand in for the complexity of Latina/o sexual diversity and gender expression as portrayed in literature in a transhistorical and comparative framework. For this reason, it is crucial to look before 1963 (and even before 1959) to avoid a presentist attitude that limits literary debates to our contemporary period, and that by extension suggests that there were no gender transgressions, anxieties, same-sex loving Latina/o authors or representations worthy of our analysis before this time. Scholars who propose this longer queer timeline include Emilio Bejel (discussing José Martí), María Cotera (discussing Jovita González), and Sandra K. Soto, who provocatively analyzes the work of Américo Paredes, highlighting this foundational figure's sensitivity to matters of gender and sexuality, particularly in his little-known short story "Over the Waves Is Out" (1953).[17]

What would reconsiderations of our dominant chronologies for queer Latina/o literature look like? Where to start? One possibility is by considering Cuban-born Loreta Janeta Velázquez's U.S. Civil War cross-dressing adventures, described in her memoir *The Woman in Battle: A Narrative of the Exploits, Adventures and Travels of Madame Loreta Janeta Velázquez, Otherwise Known as Lieutenant Harry J. Buford, Confederate States Army* (1876), which has been discussed by Jesse Alemán.[18] Another is by focusing on exiled Cuban writer José Martí's outrage about the accusations of Cuban men's effeminacy published in the Philadelphia *Manufacturer* on March 6, 1889, to which he responded effusively in the *New York Post* on March 25 of that year, as chronicled by Emilio Bejel in his *Gay Cuban Nation*. (For a discussion of Martí's extended exile in the United States and his voluminous analysis of American culture and society in relation to Latin America, see Laura Lomas's important *Translating Empire: José Martí, Migrant Latino Subjects, and American Modernities*.)

Another way to queer Latina/o literature is by looking at three early twentieth-century Puerto Rican cases: that of the anarchist (and pants-wearing gender transgressor and free-love advocate) Luisa Capetillo, who condemned lesbianism and prostitution in *Mi opinión sobre las libertades, derechos y deberes de la mujer* [*My Opinion on the Liberties, Rights and Duties of Women*], which she self-published in 1911; that of the avowedly heterosexual tobacco worker and labor leader Bernardo Vega, specifically his mention in his *Memoirs* of throwing his watch overboard in 1916 as he approached New York City for fear of being considered effeminate; and that of the married, heterosexual Puerto Rican writer José Isaac de Diego Padró, particularly his complex portrayal of the adventures of the effeminate bisexual Cuban sadist Sebastián Guenard in New York City, published in 1924 in an eponymous novella that shares Decadent elements with the work of Joris-Karl Huysmans and Oscar Wilde and that was later expanded in the novel *En babia*, published in Puerto Rico in 1940.[19] All three authors spent important periods of their lives in New York City; Capetillo also lived in Ybor City (now a neighborhood in Tampa), Florida.[20]

For some people (for example, my students), the fact that Capetillo was simultaneously a nonconformist gender-radical pant-wearing feminist anarchist and a lesbophobe is paradoxical. In her mind, wearing pants (which she defended in her 1911 book and for which she was incarcerated in Cuba in 1915) was about having the freedom to work with the same comfort as men; espousing free love between a man and a woman and challenging the power of the Catholic Church and of the state was about having rights as a law-abiding heterosexual adult who engaged in monogamous, consensual relationships marked by mutual respect that did not have to be sanctioned by a judge or a priest. None of these were tied to sex work as a legitimate form of employment or to same-sex relationships between women. Clearly, what we have is an example of how a radical defense of an alternative gender expression (engaging in what was perceived to be a "masculine" practice, that is to say, wearing pants) and of sexual autonomy (challenging state- and church-sanctioned marriage) did not have to go hand in hand with advocacy for sexual variance, at least not in 1911. This in spite of the fact that the defense of homosexuality and the condemnation of anti-sodomy laws date back as far as 1869, precisely to the time of Karl-Maria Kertbeny.

Bernardo Vega's 1916 anxieties about male effeminacy (perhaps highlighted by his editor, César Andreu Iglesias) indicate that the public presentation of masculinity was different in Puerto Rico than in New York; these anxieties coincide with de Diego Padró's 1924 representation, but with an important difference: while the former is concerned with not being perceived in a certain way, the later actually created a complex literary character that grips our attention and makes us aware of a particular queer Hispanic New York City world. Padró's at-times unsympathetic, anxiety-ridden, and pathological (yet also complex, detailed and for me, moving, and important) portrayal of Sebastián Guenard as an eccentric, queer, and tortured soul includes mentions of his strident, nervous loud laughter; his predilection for unusual clothing; his penchant for collecting antiques bought at orientalist bazaars; his proximity to madness; his friendship with a nameless Puerto Rican narrator; and their mutual visits to Mott Street to eat frog legs at Chinese restaurants frequented by New York socialites where African American jazz bands and Chinese classical ensembles play. There is something extraordinary in Guenard's representation, particularly in the narrator's simultaneous attachment to and repugnance toward him, a contradiction that is resolved narratively by killing the character, even if he is resurrected in the later novel. Guenard's cosmopolitanism, his mannerisms, and what is described as his *locura* (or rather, his *delirio* or *invisible fantasma*) feel very familiar, easily identifiable with a particular ideation of homosexuality as cultural affectation and pathology.

Padró antedates the observations of the much better known homosexual Spanish poet Federico García Lorca (1898–1936), who lived in New York City in 1929–30 and wrote memorable verses about his experience. Specifically, Padró anticipates Lorca's crisis over effeminateness, which will lead the Spaniard to his comparative discussion of stigma in his "Ode to Walt Whitman" (published in *Poet in New York*), where Lorca denounces the "Faeries of North America/Pájaros of Havana/Jotos of Mexico/... Maricas of the whole world" (my translation).[21] It is clear that transgressing gender and sexual norms in 1920s and 1930s Hispanic New York was a complex matter (but perhaps no more complex than a Latina woman fighting for the Confederacy dressed as a man, as in the case of Loreta Janeta Velázquez).

Lorca's multilingual assessment of what we could call the competing stigmatized homosexualities of modernity (most profoundly represented for him in the term "marica," the diminutive of Mary), generated as a Spanish-speaker in New York City that reflects on the legacy of an American poet (Whitman) and on the difference between his "wholesome" masculine fraternal camaraderie and the effeminate homosexuality of the late 1920s, raises the fascinating question of what it would mean to consider Lorca as an honorary Latino (or a particular work, say *Poet in New York*, as a part of the Latina/o literary canon), particularly if we take "queering" seriously, as an act of making strange, of reading expansively and of challenging orthodoxies. This possibility is conjured by a whole series of works by contemporary Latina/o authors such as Víctor Fragoso's *El reino de la espiga: Canto al coraje de Walt y Federico* (1973); Manuel Ramos Otero's poem "Lorca" from his series "Epitafios" in *El libro de la muerte* (1985); Jaime Manrique's book of essays *Eminent Maricones: Arenas, Lorca, Puig, and Me* (1999), in which the New York-based Colombian American author discusses the Spaniard's inner turmoil; and by Cuban-American playwright Nilo Cruz's *Lorca in a Green Dress* (2003), which begins with Lorca's murder in 1936 and imagines the poet's afterlife in surrealist tones.[22]

Perhaps this is the kind of queer reading operationalized by Chicana critic Catrióna Rueda Esquibel in her important scholarly work, *With Her Machete in Her Hand: Reading Chicana Lesbians* (2006), with her inclusion of Sor Juana Inés de la Cruz (1651–95) as a Latina antecedent.[23] To many, the inclusion of a seventeenth-century Novohispana or Mexican nun as a Latina lesbian cultural icon can seem somewhat strange. Esquibel highlights how Chicanas such as Alicia Gaspar de Alba have been inspired to write about her, for example in her 1999 novel *Sor Juana's Second Dream*; scholar Laura G. Gutiérrez shows how contemporary Mexican lesbian performers such as Jesusa Rodríguez also engage her legacy.²⁴ The influence is not limited to Mexicanas and Chicanas; in 1987, in her poem "Título: En que trata de lo que es y no hay mah ná'" (from *The Margarita Poems*), Luz María Umpierre had envisioned Sor Juana (identified by her birth name, Juana de Asbaje) sending a memo to contemporary Chicana author Ana Castillo.²⁵ In addition, the Cuban American lesbian performance artist Carmelita Tropicana has also found inspiration in the Mexican nun in her performance *Sor Juana: The Nightmare* included in *I, Carmelita Tropicana: Performing Between Cultures* (2000).²⁶

What both of these examples (Federico García Lorca and Sor Juana Inés de la Cruz) suggest is that the category of Latina/o can be productively challenged, reconceptualized, and expanded, whether by virtue of linguistic affinities (the Spanish language), country of origin (Spain and Mexico), or historical anachronism; queer Latina/o cultural archives include multiple, uncontainable sources. In fact, in 1935, in her (until recently) unpublished short story "Shades of the Tenth Muse," the heterosexual Tejana folklorist and novelist Jovita González will also appeal to Sor Juana and to the early British North American poet Anne Bradstreet (1612–72) in her conceptualization of a coming together of literary and cultural influences, staged as a conversation between women writers, as scholar María Cotera has discussed; Cotera is also interested in the politics of women's collaborations and how they challenges heteronormative assumptions, particularly in the case of González's and Margaret Eimer's coauthorship of *Caballero* (also written in the late 1930s and early 1940s, but not published until 1996), a novel set during the time of the signing of the Treaty of Guadalupe Hidalgo (1848) that includes a sympathetic portrayal of a nonconventional, effeminate artistic male character, Luis Gonzaga, who is harassed by his father (who calls him a marica) and who abandons his family and develops an intimate emotional friendship with an older man.²⁷ If we go on to consider Nicole Guidotti-Hernández's scathing critique in her book *Unspeakable Violence* of Jovita González's perceived anti-Indian prejudice, we end up with an even messier, inassimilable, and simultaneously fascinating queer situation.²⁸

These incidental or more fully fleshed out literary treatments are in counterpoint to other early portrayals, many of which are barely acknowledged by Latina/o scholars. The openly (and scandalously) lesbian upper-class Cuban-Spanish-American poet, novelist, and playwright Mercedes de Acosta (1893–1968), who published prolifically and whose plays *Jehanne d'Arc* (1922) (written for her lover Eva Le Gallienne) and *Jacob Slovak* (1923) were produced in New York in the 1920s, has only rarely been acknowledged as a Latina lesbian precedent, in spite (or perhaps because) of the scandal provoked by the publication of her memoir, *Here Lies the Heart* (1960), in which she wrote openly about her numerous relationships with women.²⁹ Perhaps part of the resistance has to do with de Acosta's consistent self-identification as "Spanish," a practice that reflect her family's complex background but that was not at all uncommon among Latinas/os. Her detailed discussion in *Here Lies the Heart* of her father's participation in the Cuban wars of independence does indicate his profound Caribbean identification.³⁰ One notable recuperation of de Acosta's legacy is Odalys Nanin's play *Garbo's Cuban Lover*, which showcases de Acosta's relationship with Greta Garbo; the play was written and performed by a Cuban American lesbian (Nanin), co-directed by Puerto Rican actress Ivonne Coll, and presented by MACHA Theater Company in Los Angeles in 2001.³¹

What would a serious reconsideration of Mercedes de Acosta's life and work mean for queer Latina/o literature? For one, it would give us a clear precedent for and interpretive framework to understand wealthy, upper-class, and/or avant-garde Hispanic Caribbean women authors in New York City who write in English, such as the Cuban American playwright María Irene Fornés (*Fefu and Her Friends*, 1977) and the contemporary Puerto Rican author Giannina Braschi, who also explores questions of women's same-sex attractions in her books *Asalto al tiempo* (1981), *La comedia profana* (1985), *El imperio de los sueños* (1988), *Empire of Dreams* (1994), *Yo-yo Boing!* (1998), and *United States of Banana* (2011). Clearly, an awareness of de Acosta's romantic preferences allows for differential readings of de Acosta's 1920s poetry, filled with for the most part undetermined (genderless) love objects, insistently referred to in the second person or in the abstract; it also allows for a new interpretation of her poems in which she professes love toward all humans: men, women, children, immigrants, rich and poor, as evidenced in books such as *Moods* (1919), *Archways of Life* (1921), and *Streets and Shadow* (1922). It also suggests points of contact between her work and that of eminent Latin American lesbian authors from the same period such as the Nobel Prize–winning Chilean Gabriela Mistral (1889–1957), whose complex biographical negotiations have been explored by scholars such as Licia Fiol-Matta.³² Mentions such as these suggest the crucial importance of archival research (which now might mean simply accessing the Internet), and how it will continue to unearth early literary portrayals of Latina/o queer experience, ones that antedate the 1960s by decades.

So far, I have presented a rather unorthodox account of queer Latina/o literature, one that has little in common with most widely available narratives, including those by AnnLouise Keating (1995), David Román (1995), Ilan Stavans (1995), Manuel de Jesús Hernández-G. (1999), Harold

Augenbraum and Margarite Fernández Olmos (2000), Yolanda Retter Vargas (2005), Guillermo de los Reyes and John Pluecher (2008), and Frederick Luis Aldama (2013), and that is perhaps closer to the visions offered by Gabriel Estrada (2005), Michael Hames-García and Ernesto Martínez (2011), and Sandra Soto (2013). Most of these narratives typically exalt the 1980s and early 1990s as key decades for the consolidation of queer Latina/o literature in the United States, specifically identifying the publication of the anthology *This Bridge Called My Back: Writings by Radical Women of Color* (1981) as a watershed moment, at times almost as a *Deus ex machina*, practically coming out of nowhere, with no historical precedents, particularly no long-range ones.[33] Many of these scholars highlight the subsequent work of Chicana writers Cherríe Moraga (*Loving in the War Years*, 1983) and Gloria Anzaldúa (*Borderlands/La frontera: The New Mestiza*, 1987), less frequently mentioning the work of the Puerto Rican poet and scholar Luz María Umpierre (*The Margarita Poems*, 1987).[34] They also call attention to the importance of anthologies such as *Compañeras: Latina Lesbians*, edited by Juanita Ramos (the pseudonym of Juanita Díaz-Cotto) in 1987 and *Chicana Lesbians: The Girls Our Mothers Warned Us About* by Carla Trujillo in 1991, and lament the paucity of male equivalents to these authors and works.[35]

Contrary to this dominant view, I would like to once again insist that the 1960s, 1970s, and 1980s were also extremely rich for openly gay authors, for example the previously mentioned Puerto Ricans Víctor Fernández Fragoso and Manuel Ramos Otero, the Cuban American Reinaldo Arenas (who arrived in the United States in 1980 and wrote about his experiences in Miami and New York in his memoir *Before Night Falls*), and Chicanos John Rechy and Michael Nava.[36] For example, as early as 1971, Ramos Otero was already publishing explicitly homoerotic fiction in Spanish, such as his short story "Hollywood Memorabilia" (in *Concierto de metal y otras orgías de soledad*), which focuses on a gay Puerto Rican character wandering the streets of New York City, meeting men in movie theaters around Times Square and having sex.[37] This was also a period of great artistic creativity for Nuyorican authors such as Miguel Algarín ("A Mongo Affair") and Miguel Piñero (*Short Eyes*), whose complex sexualities and literatures have barely been explored except by scholars such as Arnaldo Cruz-Malavé ("'What a Tangled Web!'"), and for more discreet or closeted Chicano authors such as Arturo Islas and Richard Rodriguez. Recognition of the pioneering status of Ramos Otero and Fragoso was immediate in articles and book reviews by scholars such as Efraín Barradas. The reception of queer Chicano authors was much more reserved, in part due to the politics of cultural nationalism, which demanded an explicit commitment to *la causa* (and to a very specific set of politics) in order to be considered a legitimate Chicana/o author worthy of recognition; authors who failed to comply were dismissed as irrelevant or deficient.

As Frederick Aldama notes, Juan Bruce-Novoa and other scholars celebrated Rechy as a pioneering gay Chicano author as early as 1979.[38] Nevertheless, as scholar Antonio Viego highlights, in the early 1990s Cherríe Moraga and Tomás Almaguer aggressively criticized Rechy and other authors such as Islas and Rodriguez for not being more forthright about their sexuality and/or ethnicity.[39] According to Moraga and Almaguer, these gay Chicano authors failed to interlink these identity categories in a clear and direct way and did not highlight the homophobia of Chicana/o communities as part of a politics of resistance and transformation. This critique of 1980s Chicano writers is reproduced by David Román in his otherwise insightful assessment of the status of Latino gay literature published in *The Gay and Lesbian Literary Heritage* (1995), a volume that also includes an enthusiastic review about Latina lesbian literature by AnnLouise Keating; in his work Frederick Aldama will repeat the critique of Rechy, but not of Islas.[40] Yet, as Viego argues, Moraga and Almaguer (and, we could add, Román) criticize Rechy, Islas, and Rodriguez for not being gay *in a certain way*: one that is easily recognizable, that clearly states the oppression (some) Chicano gay men experience within the context of a repressive, traditional, patriarchal, and homophobic Chicano culture. Román contrasts Colombian writer Jaime Manrique and his best-selling novel *Latin Moon in Manhattan* (1992) to what he portrays as the more limited portrayals of Rechy and Islas.[41]

In a lovely response to Viego's article, Luz Calvo and Catrióna Rueda Esquibel discuss how in fact not only are there many ways to be Chicano and gay; there are many ways to be Chicana and lesbian (or same-sex loving).[42] What none of these writers or critics seem to be paying attention to are the more subcultural 1970s queer Chicano manifestations of members of the Los Angeles–based arts collective ASCO such as Gronk. While this discussion of the differences in the development of Latina/o gay and lesbian literature might seem like a thing of the past, it is crucial to understand this historical polemic, as it explains initiatives such as Hames-García and Martínez's *Gay Latino Studies* anthology (the need and urgency that the editors felt) as well as narratives that continue to be repeated in assorted literary histories.

I would like to conclude by highlighting the important role of queer U.S. literary anthologies, many of which have been written or view themselves in opposition to each other, for example, Carla Trujillo's *Chicana Lesbians* as a Southwestern or West Coast, Chicana corrective to Juanita Ramos's East Coast, pan-ethnic *Compañeras: Latina Lesbians*, which Trujillo felt was not "Chicana enough" (see her introduction), and Jaime Cortez's *Virgins, Guerrillas, and Locas* (1999), perceived as an edgier, more cutting edge, West Coast version of Jaime Manrique and Jesse Dorris's New York–oriented *Bésame Mucho: New Gay Latino Fiction* (also of 1999).⁴³ More recent projects such as Emanuel Xavier's *MARIPOSAS: A Modern Anthology of Queer Latino Poetry* (2008), Charles Rice-González and Charlie Vázquez's *From Macho to Mariposa: New Gay Latino Fiction* (2011), and Lázaro Lima and Felice Picano's *Ambientes: New Queer Latino Writing* (2011) – not to mention volumes in Spanish such as the Puerto Rican anthology *Los otros cuerpos: antología de temática gay, lésbica y queer desde Puerto Rico y su diáspora*, coedited by David Caleb Acevedo, Moisés Agosto Rosario, and Luis Negrón in 2007, which included pieces translated from English into Spanish – are not simply additive endeavors, but in fact reflect competing notions and different visions for Latina/o queer literature.⁴⁴ An exhaustive comparison of these anthologies and a discussion of the important role of literary journals is beyond the purview of my article, but it promises to shed even more light about the current status and future direction of the ever growing queer Latina/o literary field.

Notes

1. "Hir" is a third-gender article that is not marked as masculine or feminine. Cisgender refers to a non-transgender or non-transsexual person. The Intersex Society of North America (ISNA) defines "intersex" as "a general term used for a variety of conditions in which a person is born with a reproductive or sexual anatomy that doesn't seem to fit the typical definitions of female or male" (http://www.isna.org/faq/what_is_intersex).
2. Sandra K. Soto, *Reading Chican@ Like a Queer* (Austin: University of Texas Press, 2010); Michael Hames-García, "Queer Theory Revisited," in *Gay Latino Studies: A Critical Reader*, eds. Michael Hames-García and Ernesto Javier Martínez (Durham, NC: Duke University Press, 2011), pp. 19–45.
3. See Kimberlé Williams Crenshaw, "Mapping the Margins: Intersectionality, Identity Politics, and Violence Against Women of Color," *Stanford Law Review* 43 (July 1991): 1241–99; Chela Sandoval, *Methodology of the Oppressed* (Minneapolis: University of Minnesota Press, 2000); José Esteban Muñoz, *Disidentifications: Queers of Color and the Performance of Politics* (Minneapolis: University of Minnesota Press, 2009).
4. Cherríe Moraga and Gloria Anzaldúa, eds., *This Bridge Called My Back: Writings by Radical Women of Color*, 2nd ed. (New York: Kitchen Table; Women of Color Press, 1983); Muñoz, *Disidentifications*; Juana María Rodríguez, *Queer Latinidad: Identity Practices, Discursive Spaces* (New York: New York University Press, 2003); Hames-García and Martínez, *Gay Latino*.
5. See "queer," *Oxford Dictionaries*, http://www.oxforddictionaries.com/us/definition/american_english/queer.

6. Arnaldo Cruz-Malavé, "'What a Tangled Web!': Masculinity, Abjection, and the Foundations of Puerto Rican Literature in the United States," in *Sex and Sexuality in Latin America*, eds. Daniel Balderston and Donna J. Guy (New York: New York University Press, 1997), pp. 234–49.
7. See *Lambda Literary*, http://www.lambdaliterary.org/; Tony Valenzuela, "Op-ed: The Lambda Literary Awards Are as Essential as Ever," *Advocate.com* (October 09, 2012), http://www.advocate.com/commentary/2012/10/09/op-ed-lambda-literary-awards-are-essential-ever.
8. See Clare Swanson, "A Landmark Win for 'Mundo Cruel,'" *Publisher's Weekly* (13 June 2014), http://www.publishersweekly.com/pw/by-topic/industry-news/publisher-news/article/62875-a-landmark-win-for-mundo-cruel.html.
9. See Stephen Gendin, "They Shoot Barebackers, Don't They?" *POZ Magazine* (February 1999), http://www.poz.com/articles/211_1459.shtml.
10. The openly gay playwright Nilo Cruz explores queer themes in works such as *Dancing on Her Knees* (1994) and *Lorca in a Green Dress* (2003); he won a Pulitzer for *Anna in the Tropics*. Junot Díaz's debut collection *Drown* (1996) includes discussions of homophobia; he won a Pulitzer for *The Brief Wondrous Life of Oscar Wao*. On Díaz, see Danny Méndez, *Narratives of Migration and Displacement in Dominican Literature* (New York: Routledge, 2012), pp. 139–44; Sandra K. Soto, "Queerness," in *The Routledge Companion to Latino/a Literature*, ed. Suzanne Bost and Frances R. Aparicio (New York: Routledge, 2013), pp. 80–82.
11. Regarding U.S. Latina/o lesbian and gay literature, see Frederick Luis Aldama, *Brown on Brown: Chicano/a Representations of Gender, Sexuality and Ethnicity* (Austin: University of Texas Press, 2005) and *The Routledge Concise History of Latino/a Literature* (New York: Routledge, 2013), pp. 98–126; Harold Augenbraum and Margarite Fernández Olmos, "Appendix B: Latino Gay and Lesbian Authors and Their Works," in *U.S. Latino Literature: A Critical Guide for Students and Teachers* (Westport, CT: Greenwood Press, 2000), pp. 203–04; Juan Bruce-Novoa, "Homosexuality and the Chicano Novel," *Confluencia: Revista Hispánica de Cultura y Literatura* 2.1 (1986): 69–77, and "In Search of the Honest Outlaw: John Rechy," *Minority Voices* 3.1 (Fall 1979): 37–45; Guillermo de los Reyes Heredia and John Pluecher, "Gay and Lesbian Literature," in *The Greenwood Encyclopedia of Latino Literature*, ed. Nicolás Kanellos (Westport, CT: Greenwood Press, 2008), vol. 2, pp. 507–16; David William Foster, *El Ambiente Nuestro: Chicano/Latino Homoerotic Writing* (Tempe: Bilingual Press/Editorial Bilingüe, 2006); Gabriel Estrada, "Gays," in *The Oxford Encyclopedia of Latinos and Latinas in the United States*, eds. Suzanne Oboler and Deena J. González (Oxford: Oxford University Press, 2005), vol. 2, pp. 188–92; Manuel de Jesús Hernández-G., "Building a Research Agenda on U.S. Latino Lesbigay Literature and Cultural Production: Texts, Writers, Performance Artists, and Critics," in *Chicano/Latino Homoerotic Identities*, ed. David William Foster (New York: Garland, 1999), pp. 287–304; AnnLouise Keating, "Latina Literature," in *The Gay and Lesbian Literary Heritage*, ed. Claude J. Summers (New York: H. Holt, 1995), pp. 432–35; Ricardo L. Ortíz, *Cultural Erotics in Cuban America* (Minneapolis: University of Minnesota Press, 2006) and "Sexuality Degree Zero: Pleasure and Power in the Novels of John Rechy, Arturo Islas, and Michael Nava," in *Critical Essays: Gay*

and Lesbian Writers of Color, ed. Emmanuel S. Nelson (New York: Haworth Press, 1993), pp. 111–26; Yolanda Retter Vargas, "Lesbians," in *The Oxford Encyclopedia of Latinos and Latinas in the United States*, vol. 2, pp. 545–49; David Román, "Latino Literature," in *The Gay and Lesbian Literary Heritage*, pp. 435–37; Soto, "Queerness," pp. 75–83; Ilan Stavans, *The Hispanic Condition* (New York: HarperCollins, 1995), pp. 113–15.

12 See Bruce-Novoa ("Homosexuality" and "In Search") and Efraín Barradas, "*Concierto de metal para un recuerdo y otras orgías de soledad*," *Sin nombre* 3 (1972): 108–10, "Fragoso, Víctor, *El reino de la espiga: Canto al coraje de Walt y Federico*," *Ventana* 12 (1974): 35–40, and "Fragoso, Víctor, Ser islas/Being Islands," *Sin nombre* 9.4 (1979): 91–93.

13 See Daniel Enrique Pérez, *Rethinking Chicana/o and Latina/o Popular Culture* (New York: Palgrave Macmillan, 2009); Jennifer Domino Rudolph, "Masculinities," in *The Routledge Companion to Latino/a Literature*, pp. 67–74.

14 See Tomás Almaguer, "Chicano Men: A Cartography of Homosexual Identity and Behavior," *differences: A Journal of Feminist Cultural Studies* 3.2 (Summer 1991): 75–100; Cherríe Moraga, "Queer Aztlán: The Re-Formation of Chicano Tribe," *The Last Generation* (Boston: South End Press, 1993), pp. 145–74; and Frederick Luis Aldama (*Brown on Brown* and *Routledge*).

15 See Manolo Guzmán, *Gay Hegemony/Latino Homosexualities* (New York: Routledge, 2006). On the use of fairy, see George Chauncey, *Gay New York: Gender, Urban Culture, and the Makings of the Gay Male World, 1890–1940* (New York: Basic Books, 1994).

16 On Latin American queer literature, see David William Foster, *Gay and Lesbian Themes in Latin American Writing* (Austin: University of Texas Press, 1991); Emilie L. Bergmann and Paul Julian Smith, eds., *Entiendes?: Queer Readings, Hispanic Writings* (Durham, NC: Duke University Press, 1995); and Sylvia Molloy and Robert McKee Irwin, eds., *Hispanisms and Homosexualities* (Durham, NC: Duke University Press, 1998).

17 See Emilio Bejel, *Gay Cuban Nation* (Chicago: University of Chicago Press, 2001); María Cotera, *Native Speakers: Ella Deloria, Zora Neale Hurston, Jovita González, and the Poetics of Culture* (Austin: University of Texas Press, 2008); and Soto, *Reading*.

18 See Loreta Janeta Velázquez, *The Woman in Battle: The Civil War Narrative of Loreta Janeta Velazques, Cuban Woman and Confederate Soldier*, introduction by Jesse Alemán (Madison: University of Wisconsin Press, 2003).

19 Luisa Capetillo, *A Nation of Women: An Early Feminist Speaks Out (Mi opinión sobre las libertades, derechos y deberes de la mujer)* (1911) (Houston, TX: Arte Público Press, 2004); Bernardo Vega, *Memoirs of Bernardo Vega: A Contribution to the History of the Puerto Rican Community in New York*, ed. César Andreu Iglesias, trans. Juan Flores (New York: Monthly Review Press, 1984); José I. de Diego Padró, "Sebastián Guenard," in *Relatos* (San Juan: Instituto de Cultura Puertorriqueña, 1997), pp. 59–85.

20 On Luisa Capetillo, see Nancy Hewitt, "Luisa Capetillo: Feminist of the Working Class," in *Latina Legacies: Identity, Biography, and Community*, ed. Vicki Ruíz and Virginia Sánchez Korrol (New York: Oxford University Press, 2005), pp. 120–34, and Lisa Sánchez-González, *Boricua Literature: A Literary History of the Puerto Rican Diaspora* (New York: New York University Press, 2001). On

Bernardo Vega, see La Fountain-Stokes, "Gay Shame, Latina- and Latino-Style," in *Gay Latino Studies* (pp. 55–80), and *Queer Ricans: Cultures and Sexualities in the Diaspora* (Minneapolis: University of Minnesota Press, 2009). On De Diego Padró, see Pedro Juan Soto et al., *En busca de J.I. de Diego Padró* (Río Piedras: Editorial de la Universidad de Puerto Rico, 1990).

21 Federico García Lorca, "Oda a Walt Whitman" (from *Poeta en Nueva York*), http://writing.upenn.edu/library/Lorca-García_oda-a-walt-whitman.html.

22 Víctor Fragoso, *El reino de la espiga: Canto al coraje de Walt y Federico* (New York: Nueva Sangre, 1973); Manuel Ramos Otero, "Lorca," in *El libro de la muerte* (Río Piedras: Editorial Cultural; Maplewood, NJ: Waterfront Press, 1985), pp. 45–46; Jaime Manrique, *Eminent Maricones: Arenas, Lorca, Puig, and Me* (Madison: University of Wisconsin Press, 1999); Nilo Cruz, *Lorca in a Green Dress* (Ashland: Oregon Shakespeare Festival, 2003).

23 Catriona Rueda Esquibel, *With Her Machete in Her Hand: Reading Chicana Lesbians* (Austin: University of Texas Press, 2006).

24 See Laura G. Gutiérrez, *Performing Mexicanidad: Vendidas y Cabareteras on the Transnational Stage* (Austin: University of Texas Press, 2010).

25 Luz María Umpierre, *The Margarita Poems* (Bloomington, IN: Third Woman Press, 1987), pp. 27.

26 See Alina Troyano, *Sor Juana: The Nightmare*, in *I, Carmelita Tropicana: Performing Between Cultures* (Boston: Beacon, 2000), pp. 123–36.

27 See Cotera, *Native Speakers*.

28 Nicole Guidotti-Hernández, *Unspeakable Violence: Remapping U.S. and Mexican National Imaginaries* (Durham, NC: Duke University Press, 2011).

29 Mercedes de Acosta, *Here Lies the Heart* (New York: Reynal, 1960). Also see Nicole Trujillo-Pagán, "De Acosta, Mercedes (1893–1968)," in *Latinas in the United States: A Historical Encyclopedia*, eds. Vicki L. Ruiz and Virginia Sánchez Korrol (Bloomington: Indiana University Press, 2006), pp. 189–90; Robert A. Shanke, *"That Furious Lesbian": The Story of Mercedes de Acosta* (Carbondale: Southern Illinois University Press, 2003).

30 De Acosta, *Here*, pp. 11–16.

31 See *Garbo's Cuban Lover*, http://www.machatheatre.org/reel/reel_garbo.php.

32 See Licia Fiol-Matta, *A Queer Mother for the Nation: The State and Gabriela Mistral* (Minneapolis: University of Minnesota Press, 2002).

33 See Almaguer, "Chicano Men"; De los Reyes Heredia and Pluecher, "Gay"; Keating, "Latina"; Retter Vargas, "Lesbians"; Román, "Latino"; Soto, "Queerness."

34 On Umpierre, see La Fountain-Stokes, *Queer Ricans*, pp. 64–92; Soto, "Queerness," pp. 79–80.

35 Ramos, Juanita, ed., *Compañeras, Latina Lesbians* (New York: Latina Lesbian History Project, 1987); Carla Trujillo, ed., *Chicana Lesbians: The Girls Our Mothers Warned Us About* (Berkeley, CA: Third Woman Press, 1991).

36 On Fragoso and Ramos Otero, see La Fountain-Stokes, *Queer Ricans*, pp. 19–63. On Arenas, see Bejel, op.cit., pp. 140–55; Ortíz, *Cultural Erotics*, pp. 43–61; Stavans, *Hispanic Condition*, pp. 114–15.

37 Manuel Ramos Otero, "Hollywood Memorabilia," in *Concierto de metal para un recuerdo y otras orgías de soledad* (San Juan: Editorial Cultural, 1971), pp. 77–85.

38 Aldama, *Routledge*, p. 120.

39 Antonio Viego, "The Place of Gay Male Chicano Literature in Queer Chicana/o Cultural Work," *Discourse* 21.3 (1999): 111–31, reprinted in *Gay Latino Studies*, pp. 86–104.
40 Aldama, *Brown on Brown*, chapters 2 and 3; Aldama, *Routledge*, p. 123.
41 Román, "Latino," p. 436–37.
42 Luz Calvo and Catrióna Rueda Esquibel, "Comment: Our Queer Kin," in *Gay Latino Studies*, pp. 105–12.
43 See Carla Trujillo, *Chicana*; Ramos, *Compañeras*; Jaime Cortez, ed., *Virgins, Guerrillas, and Locas: Gay Latinos Writing on Love* (San Francisco: Cleis Press, 1999); Jaime Manrique and Jesse Dorris, eds., *Bésame Mucho: New Gay Latino Fiction* (New York: Painted Leaf Press, 1999).
44 Emanuel Xavier, ed., *MARIPOSAS: A Modern Anthology of Queer Latino Poetry* (Mountain View, CA: Floricanto Press, 2008); Charles Rice-González and Charlie Vázquez, eds., *From Macho to Mariposa: New Gay Latino Fiction* (Maple Shade, NJ: Tincture, 2011); Lázaro Lima and Felice Picano, eds., *Ambientes: New Queer Latino Writing* (Madison: University of Wisconsin Press, 2011); David Caleb Acevedo, Moisés Agosto Rosario, and Luis Negrón, eds., *Los otros cuerpos: antología de temática gay, lésbica y queer desde Puerto Rico y su diáspora* (San Juan: Editorial Tiempo Nuevo, 2007).

12

CLAUDIA MILIAN

Latinos and the Like: Reading Mixture and Deracination

A striking scene from the 2009 Academy Award–nominated film, *Precious*, sets up the entangled workings and dilemmas of the white, brown, dark brown, black, and mixed-race Latina/o economies illuminating this study. In it, the titular protagonist, an African American teenager portrayed by Gabourey Sidibe, attempts to understand how a "whiteness" that looks "of color" bands together with blackness. She asks Mariah Carey, who plays an ethno-racially indeterminate caseworker, "So are you Italian, or what color are you, anyway? Are you some type of black or Spanish?" Not only this, but also perplexing is the social worker's name, Mrs. Weiss. Precious does not know what to call her on several grounds. Weiss is a homonym for "wise," and Carey is erringly addressed onscreen as "Ms. White" – occasioning a wise nonwhite moment of pensive measure. Eventually, Carey's character quips, "What color do you think I am? No, I'd like to know. What color do you think I am?" Precious fails to streamline Mrs. Weiss. Her evasive but no less symptomatic answer turns to "My throat is dry." A dry, sore, or scratchy throat is a general indication of fatigue sometimes attributed to bad weather or wind. In this instance, however, it is running through an inventory of Mrs. Weiss's puzzling colors that provokes it. "Ms. White's" off-whiteness does not provide, as Blas Falconer and Lorraine M. López have it, "fast access and easy comprehension" of a U.S. body with a panoply of dangling ontological categories (1). Carey's familial composition, off-camera, includes a white mother and Venezuelan father, biographical details that allow her to metamorphose into the filmic Ms. White (or, on equal footing, a hypothetical missed white).[1] Lacking one fitting definition, Mrs. Weiss's *visual cacophony* proves cinematically irritating. It highlights an unfamiliar American affect of classificatory discomfort. How the multilayered placelessness of Latina/o bodies is situated within the long-ingrained U.S. spectrum of black-white relations, paired with the wide array of *latinidad*, lies at the core of these pages, for as George Reid Andrews reminds us, "quietly elided" in U.S. discussions about Latinos and African Americans "is the fact that 'blacks' and 'Hispanics' are not necessarily separate groups" (3).

For starters, numerous and revisionist clusters are coevally appended to the rapidly changing Latina/o genus. Latina/o cultural practices and ethnoracialized identities have transitioned into such affirming and distinguishable approximations as Afro-Latinos, binational Latinos, biracial Latinos, and Other Latinos. Miriam Jiménez Román and Juan Flores put across that Afro-Latinos and Latinas – "Latin@s of visible or self-proclaimed African descent" (4) touch on "the anti-Black racism within the Latin@ communities" (2). Binational Latinos – "the product of two cultural and national identities" (Rúa 129) – broaden the perceived singularity of Latina/o, laying out prospective formations in inter-Latino spaces. The intermingling of Puerto Ricans and Mexicans in Chicago has fostered, considering Mérida Rúa's take on an enhanced Latinidad, PortoMex, and MexiRican sartorial subjectivities that negotiate nationalist tensions. Biracial Latinos face questions of acceptance and excisions within a label that, as Falconer and López assess it, is an "impossibly narrow" and "fictive categorization" (1). Latinos become as such through a false initiation – an ersatz beginning that administers this preliminary grouping. The dominant referents of the Latina/o carapace inscribe collective belonging through the Spanish language and marginal migrant experiences that operate as the salient traits in these "expected cultural narratives" (4).

Other Latinos generate a heterogeneity that exceeds the historically situated triad of Mexican American/Chicana/o, Puerto Rican, and Cuban American. José Luis Falconi and José Antonio Mazzotti's focal strand, *The Other Latinos*, gives prominence to Central and South Americans. Falconer and López's commitments submit another comprehensive name, *The Other Latin@*, as a means to challenge *a* – but, more concretely, their quest troubles *the* – "Latino 'narrative' " from a domain that debunks "the illusion of cultural cohesion" (4; 1). A panoptic Latinoness coalesces with the multiplicity of otherness touching on the strains and alienation from the U.S. experience and the commanding parameters of Latina/o. Not to be overlooked in these overlapping maps is, as Luis Urrieta, Jr. calls to mind, "an ignored issue by most academics who study Latinos": the "racist and genocidal attitude toward *indígenas*.... Indigenous people are forced to be Hispanic or Latino, under a largely *mestizaje* discourse" (322).[2] Of importance to the provenance of Latina/o Studies is also its intersection with the sociocultural histories of the Chinese *fronterizos*, as Grace Peña Delgado (2012) has explored.

The chain that connects these flourishing and conjoined strategies is the reappearance of the crucial and comparative medium: "Latina/o." These divergent distinctions counter the accepted wisdom surrounding Latinos.

Each categorical departure from this intellectual mix suggests that they are not "fully" Latina/o, as this classification has already been predetermined. It is worth inquiring for whom the insulated subject in question, the Latina/o heading, is so facile, adequate, and legible. Who claims and embraces it with such accuracy and certitude? How this group's protean story has been drafted and contested in the fashioning and rumination of a divided (Latina/o) self and in the narrative practices that search for a ("right") type of (omitted) Latina/o to arrive at a "rightly" studied (Latina/o) subject is surveyed here. The clashing logic that engulfs embodied Latina/o designations is probed through a graphological scope concentrating on Latina/o writing systems of ambiguity, ambivalence, and distanciation. But while the state of Latina/o is suspect, the all-encompassing promise of Latina/o knowledge – even if we have been pointed to this unstable panorama's errors and omissions – is not. Does migrating from – and altering the meanings of – Latina/o unfailingly bring us back to a Latina/o being? Can these subjects be disarticulated from the ideological attachments, sociocultural practices, and political memberships that revolve around it? What are the new epistemological arrangements, analytic experimentations, and conjectural questions in the multipositioning and rethinking of Latina/o sociopolitical bodies?

Another plot line necessitates evaluation and incites us to take up this query: What is the Latina/o course in contemporary African American literature? To turn to Sapphire's debut novel, *Push*, which was adapted into the motion picture just mentioned, *Precious*, the presence of "coffee-cream-colored" people from "Spanish talk land" (16) is not as marginal as it may initially seem. Sapphire pushes for the widest possible range of a "community" of Spanish speakers in this work about physical and sexual abuse, incest, illiteracy, HIV infection, homelessness, and urban decay during Ronald Reagan's presidency.[3] Sapphire's Spanish talk land – or Latin *patria* – can be amended to what Ed Morales regenerates as "living in Spanglish." Morales proposes that "the working definition for Latinos (or Hispanics) should be 'everything.' All races, all creeds, all possible combinations" (2). Spanglish enunciates "what we are doing, rather than where we [come] from" (ibid).[4] Sapphire's protagonist, Claireece Precious Jones – or, as she prefers it, Precious, as "my name mean something valuable" (69) – is a cartographer of a Spanglish omnium-gatherum that is doing, undoing, and reinventing Latina/o "normalcy."

Precious describes a Spanish guy, in EMS uniform, who helps deliver her firstborn child, Little Mongo. This Latino is the source of the verb advancing Sapphire's title. He counsels the teenager on how to exert force during the pushing stage of labor, signaling how Latins make their way through life's hardships. "Precious, it's almost here," he urges. "I want you to push, you hear me momi, when the shit hit you again, go with it and push, Preshecita. *Push*" (10). Precious gives birth to and immortalizes this relationality by naming her daughter Mongo, declaring, "sound Spanish don't it? Yeah, thas why I chose it, but what it is is short for Mongoloid Down Sinder, which is what she is; sometimes what I feel I is" (36). Mongo's denomination resonates with anthropologist Robin Nagle's focus on the upcycling of useful junk, valuable rummage otherwise called "mongo." Mongo and mongoing are a noun and a verb, punctuating that "we are all implicated in the process of creating garbage" (Carp 2010). "People who take things from the trash to keep," Nagle amplifies, "are mongoing." Precious's Latined Mongo works through, as Arturo Arias and I delineated in another venue, a nonexpendable "'mongo collection' [of] 'bad' American 'objects'" that cobble together "excessive" and "grotesque" differences as cultural salvage (141). Our precious Mongo, for his name means and is something valuable, effectuates everyday "Spanish speakers" that are subject to change.

Sapphire fractures the assumed neat flow of Latina/o by delivering a cornucopia of differences in a black-white-Latina/o triangulation to literary constituencies that are processing categorical slippages too. The black-and-white dyad is not so unyielding, fluctuating as it is to brownness and dark brownness. I lay, as follows, a fundamental inquiry with huge implications that tell a thing or two about the proliferation of Latina/o in ways that are not simply additive but that heighten formidable displacements, for these emissions of Latinness cannot head "home." How is mixture read and where is it moving, colliding with the normative identifiable signifiers of black, white, and brown? The nucleus of deracinated bodies interweaves with deracinated mixtures and their ostensible proper embodiments. Latina/o gradations unfurl multidirectional forms of subjectivation that prompt us to reread and rethink bodily, epistemological, historic, and geographic deracination.

Pantheons of Non-Whiteness, Genealogical Latin Odysseys, and the Latin "Diaspora" Diaspora

Let us now invoke early interlocutors – Evelio Grillo and Piri Thomas, for the most part – to canvass the course of Latina/o articulation and identifications that were previously available. From there, I give attention to Raquel Cepeda's *Bird of Paradise: How I Became Latina* and its commitment to the untapped aspects and accretions awaiting this population, as they, to paraphrase James D. Watson, rely on DNA testing not "to set the" – but really *a mixed* – "record straight" (286). These figures expedite another *analogous goal*: to chart shades of brownness and how this "same" brown "data" is broken down, included or excluded, and cataloged in Latina/o writing. I take stock of a literary brown palette – tabulating a brown lot, so to say, and pinning on the grammar codifying brown and dark brown worlds. We may (or may not) see "Latina/o" bodies through these pictorials. But as these maps lead us to like-minded people, the typical characteristics and collective perception of Latinos and Latinas requires reshuffling as we seize upon other critical liaisons that heed comparative ethno-racial discourse.

I obligingly begin with Grillo's germane Latin contacts in *Black Cuban, Black American*. His story was retrieved through Arte Público Press's Recovering the U.S. Hispanic Literary Heritage Project, a national archival undertaking that documents and preserves this group's written culture from the sixteenth century to the 1960s. Grillo backtracks to the 1920s, an era when Afro-Latinos sought to establish American roots (12). He depicts a Latin community in Ybor City, Florida as one inhabited by a mixture of "white Cubans, Italians, black Cubans, black Americans, Spaniards, and not a very visible number of white Americans of European extraction" (6). His reference to a lack of tangible white Americanness of European extraction keys into how whiteness fluctuates among Latin communities. Grillo recites his experiences as a black Cuban facing "discrimination along racial lines and separation along social and economic lines" (7). A split had black Cubans and white Cubans living apart (9). On the whole, however, Grillo conveys that their "identity as black Americans developed strongly," forging an epistemological nexus with African American literary and intellectual thought (16). "My heart and mind," he records, "belonged to Nat Turner, Frederick Douglass, Harriet Tubman, Sojourner Truth, Paul Laurence Dunbar, John Brown, Paul Robeson, Langston Hughes, W. E. B. Du Bois, Allison Davis, Alain Locke, and the two brothers, James Weldon Johnson and James Rosamond Johnson, who wrote the song very dear to my heart 'Lift Every Voice and Sing' " (17). Considering the rigidity of Jim Crow, a black-white gaze informs Grillo's outlook, as his contemporaries culturally become black Americans "to be an integral part of American life" (12). Grillo's optic spans black, white, Latin, colored, Negro, mulatto, "brown-skinned," "very dark," and "beautiful dark bodies" (68; 75; 106). This visual index textures and "retouches" the Jim Crow story beyond black and white.

Thomas sets *Down These Mean Streets* in motion through stentorian shouts that emit his desire for acknowledgment from his broken-down building's rooftop in Spanish Harlem. In his pursuance of recognition, he gestures toward a vocabulary that haphazardly performs motley phases of misrecognition.[5] "I'm a skinny, dark-face, curly haired, intense Porty-Ree-can," he claims, charting an out-of-the-ordinary name for his national origins (x).[6] He proceeds to smile and narratively avow, "I'm a Porty Rican" (121) in respect to a group that is characterized by historian Lorrin Thomas as "the United States' first and only citizen-immigrants" (3). The assortment of familial gazes give rise to, as his mother sees him, a *morenito*, *negrito*, and brown son (18; 19; 135). To his brother, Thomas is an "Indian" (145). Strangers appraise him as a "dirty fuckin' spic," "a nigger," or a "black spic" (24; 32; 241). Thomas wonders if he is a "black bastard," albeit one who tries "to be a Negro, a colored man, a black man, 'cause that's what I am" (119; 124). He likewise materializes as *tregeño* [sic], a "Puerto Rican Negro," and a "Puerto Rican black bastard" (147; 173; 234).

The torrent of inconsistent and unwieldy terms reveal that Thomas could be anything but white, what Lorrin Thomas bids as an "'excess visibility' [that] produced a new form of invisibility" (11). These extensive problematic appellations stand for his efforts to come into being throughout his life stages, which may shift to a different self-description and evaluative selfhood. A politics of a probable panethnic horizon emanates when Thomas's family moves to Long Island, and he asks if the neighborhood has "a lotta *Latinos*" and *morenos* (82). This is the book's single manifest expression of Latina/o subjects. Partnered with *morenos*, Latinos are a source of a difference that lives together or nearby – inducing a narrative of affiliation that engenders new patterns of recognition. Latina/o is local: the Latin world has come to New York, and Thomas places it on terra firma. Latino evolves into a speculative site, something around the corner from the mean streets.

Spreading out Thomas's Latinness, Cepeda's Manhattan demonstrates that the contours of this ethno-racial assemblage are unsettled and invite porous topographies and kinships. "While America will always, I think, feel foreign to me," she declares, "New York City is my home. This is where I can construct my own identity freely and reject labels imposed on me" (259). Manhattan is the capital of a network of bodies that have been fukú'd – or, to reword, fucked by the deracination brought by the Cold War. Fukú is a spoken and embodied act, Junot Díaz has alerted us, since it mirrors, "fuck you" (304). It is auditory for the deracinated migrant, too, as Cepeda enhances Díaz's cultural theory by turning it into a larger unit of migratory comparisons. She recalls a moment when her father's car inched into Manhattan from John F. Kennedy International Airport and the world passes them by. In New York City's "sad mixture of rust brown and slate," this fukú'd bunch is "yelling all kinds of 'fuck yous' and throwing gestures of what feels like *fukú* in different languages" (44). Cepeda talks about her building being "like a *barrio* within a *barrio*," wherein one could stumble upon a "little quiet man" who has been "described as being Dominican, Cuban, Puerto Rican, and sometimes Mexican" (45). The memoirist does not provide a clear-cut answer to this man's nationality, which surges as a new type of americano partaking in the multilingual tumult of the fukú genus.

Manhattan facilitates the yoking of two islands vis-à-vis Cepeda's "dominiyorkian" becoming as "a trasnational who isn't all the way American or Dominican but travels between both worlds" (177; 120). These interfacing double islands, where the restrictive "American" mainland melds American regions, erect a global geography of Latinness. It is not only Cepeda's DNA that is being mixed but also the political boundaries shaping the fukú'd dwellers of the American landmass, searching for a progeny of knowers. The standard names of spaces have been outgrown, requiring us to know individual tendencies and "originary" preferences through some other names that match these unprecedented kinships. Cepeda's rewritten project, dominiyorkian, circles around and pulls along other local features and spatial narratives.

The dominiyorkian writer draws on a mélange of interactions among ethno-racial conglomerations, the spirit's limitlessness, the supernatural, and the power of dreams (255). Cepeda's itinerant strivings for belonging and recognition through her mixture begin anew with the search for a personalized genetic history, or in Alondra Nelson's parlance, "genealogical journeys" that can be traced to Alex Haley's *Roots: The Saga of an American Family*.[7] The allure of ethnic lineage testing, Nelson gets across, is that it is "less taxing and seemingly more authoritative than conventional genealogical research ... for some root-seekers of African descent" (253). I leave to the side scientific details on the methods for gathering and analyzing genetic codes and chromosomes, as well as the skepticism on the validity of the testing technologies that determine genetic markers in these DNA evaluations. I focus, rather, on the promise of a global family tree that propels Cepeda's course of action. Unlocked by ancestral DNA, Cepeda becomes Latina. If an imperative solicitude for biracial Latinas has been, as Stephanie Greist (2011) unearths, whether they are Latina/o enough, we cross paths, once more, with a rendition of an incomplete (Latina/o) "whole." It is prudent to revisit Greist's question through scientific technology: at what point is the DNA Latino "Latina/o enough"?

There are copious concerns that DNA testing biologizes race, that it is a pseudoscience, and that it is, to cite Troy Duster's title, a "Backdoor to Eugenics." DNA indisputably assists in family configurations, as conspicuously proven through paternity tests, and in the rewriting of foundational American history, as is the case with, as Annette Gordon-Reed has briefed us, "The Hemingses of Monticello" (cf. Foster et al. 1998; Smith and Wade 1998).[8] *Bird of Paradise* chisels Latinos as "prototypical new Americans," since they are "the products of European immigration, colonialism, and slavery." Of provocative interrogation is this disclosure: "being Latino means being from everywhere" (260). Inasmuch as Latina/o is all over the map, DNA genealogies come into sight as a reflection on – and a component for "homing" – this ubiquitousness. DNA studies pave the way for recording the diverse races that Latinos and Latinas inhabit, elaborating that "we carry New World history in our genes" (235). Scientific diagnostics establish, with definite assurance, a Latina/o multiraciality "scattered around the world," one that transcends nations, for Cepeda belongs to Mother Earth (244). Her expeditions to Morocco and the Dominican Republic empower her connection with an international body politic that "is slightly older, in a New World way, than the United States." Cepeda's Latin odysseys allow her to find "characteristics of my face in the faces of the people in my global community" (154).[9]

While DNA results broadcast her planetary unions, Cepeda leans on a methodological log that zooms in on Latina/o physiognomy to arrive at a differently organized ethno-racial project. This mixed Latin background's phenotypes and color preferences expose apprehensions on the operations of these greater human relations as they measure scales of import around appearance. Cepeda's traits harvest inconclusiveness – observe the number of likes tallied below to indicate semblance and approximations based on rough calculations of existence – crossing over to "Puerto Rican and something, or, like, Black and white" (85). To be Dominican is to embody an interrogative form, eliciting such confounding topics of conversation as, "Is that biracial? Or like a Puerto Rican?" (117). The Dominican simulacrum looks like dark caramel and *indio* tones that have "golden skin like fried ripe *maduros*" (xiv; 4). Crumbling brown-dark brown qualifiers – or "gorgeous brown ball[s] of flesh" running the gamut "from *leche condensada* to espresso" (34; 16) – are allied with Africa. Someone with "thick brown skin, a wide nose, and almond-shaped eyes *como una africana*" is synchronized as a *"negra haitiana"* (16; 13). A woman is facetiously dubbed Blanca "as a joke, because she's mad dark-skinned" (90). Cepeda's "Mami looks like the funny Indian lady on TV who sings about being something called a 'half-breed.' On other days she looks like a *china*, especially when she smiles" (23–24). Her father's "skin looks like dark butter," whereas her paternal grandmother "is very brown, a *trigueña*" (47). A *prieta*, a *mulata áspera*, a juicy *morena*, the color of brown sugar, and a tobacco-colored maternal grandfather also populate Cepeda's memoir (12; 14; 15; 33; 211).[10]

Cepeda lays open, as David Howard puts it, the Dominican Republic's "multiplicity of colors." Dominicans "describe race with a plethora of color-coded terms, ranging from coffee, chocolate, cinnamon, and wheat, to the adoption of *indio/a*, a device that avoids using *mulato/a* or *negro/a*" (3).[11] Yet Cepeda's nonwhite composite is not free from interpretive error and affect. In redefining and re-envisioning race – alluded to as "extra-genetic forms of 'kinship'" by Nelson (255) – will differentiated physical features still be setup and interpreted as such, walking side-by-side with scientific documentation? The legacy of these imprecise and unscientific qualifiers seems like a racialized inheritance that is hard to extirpate. But Cepeda intimates that the transmission of these taxonomies will not be passed on through ethnic lineage analysis, since Latina/o will be worked on in another way. Cepeda's Latin gathering for the DNA age can be approached through what Nelson designates as the "factness of diaspora," which "denotes the imbrication of the 'biogenetic facts' of genealogy testing *and* aspirations for African affiliation against the backdrop of histories of forced displacement" (255). DNA testing "presents consumers with the paradox of *imprecise pedigree*." It provides provisional alliances that neglect to "associate a root-seeker with specific persons at precise spatial-temporal locations" (260).

As Cepeda routes Latina/o in myriad environs, she constructs a conjectural yet fixed "factness" around understudied twenty-first-century continents of knowledge.[12] This prospect directs "genetic" Latinness to a Latin "diaspora" diaspora overlay. Borrowing from Rogers Brubaker's "'diaspora' diaspora" insight, where "a dispersion of the meanings of the term in semantic, conceptual and disciplinary space" (1), leads to this notion's simultaneous universalization and disappearance, a Latin "diaspora" diaspora branches outside America. A discrepant Latina/o "diaspora" diaspora broaches a climate of unforeseen expansion. It is an off-the-map Latin "diaspora" diaspora that becomes Latino and Latina through unfinished circulations of alternative terrains, "genetic 'homelands,'" new sources, and embodiments for self-reformations. "A consideration of dispersion involves being able to name a common point of departure for it," postulates Stéphane Dufoix. "People can't be dispersed without first having been together. But who is dispersed? What dispersed population(s) are we talking about?" (35). Latina/o status may be the common extent of Latin transmission – the "factual" necessity – that gets to a neoteric place with a greater accessibility to being.

James Clifford imparts that "Diasporic populations do not come from elsewhere in the same way that 'immigrants' do" (250).[13] But there is something else conceptually swerving to, as Brubaker shares, an "application of the term diaspora to an ever-broadening set of cases: essentially to any and every nameable population category that is to some extent dispersed in space." Latina/o, as a floating Latin signifier, is already dispersed in bounteous spaces. "The problem with this latitudinarian, 'let-a-thousand-diasporas-bloom' approach," Brubaker cautions, "is that the category becomes stretched to the point of uselessness.... If everyone is diasporic, then no one is distinctively so. The term loses its discriminating power – its ability to pick out phenomena, to make distinctions. The universalization of diaspora, paradoxically, means the disappearance of diaspora" (3). That disintegration may be whether Latina/o, as we "know" it, will continue to work in the same way. Take cognizance that I frame this dispersion as a *Latin* "diaspora" diaspora, a diffusion that is not immobile – or tidily assimilated – in the United States. A Latin "diaspora" diaspora, to gather from Clifford, is "loose in the world" (249).[14]

In this Latin "diaspora" diaspora, the root seeker delves for and piles up genetic beginnings – flexibly spreading Latina/o outside the American milieu. Could it be that Latina/o mixtures have already been so exhausted in "America" that these ethno-racial arrangements warrant, once again, mobilities, imaginations, and alignments with other "displaced" populations? It is as though Latina/o can only be actualized through different instantiations: the body moves, internationally, depending on DNA ancestral geographic areas. The Latin "diaspora" diaspora multiplies, molding a Latina/o stock of unknown kindred and affinities. It affords being, at all times, *like* Latino and Latina, or of keeping company with Latinos and the like. If prior correlations for Latin mixture have been colloquially sized up through such culinary ingredients as fried ripe *maduros*, dark butter, and brown sugar, the next ensuing stage likely promises a more "accurate" being through another economy of likenesses. Cepeda admits to becoming Latina through modification. Latinaness gravitates toward absence, propelled by finding and quantifying the presence of Latins in the world. Without shifting processes, Latina/o appears run-down and uninhabitable. The Latin "diaspora" diaspora attempts to bring a change of pace to Latina/o bodies, for there are more Latins to be made. Each likely Latin is predicated on forms of defying legibility and localization. Latin orients toward unexpected places wherein such identities are tinkered with, making these Latina/o life practices paradoxically un-Latina/o Latina/o. Lest we forget, this new worldly Latin – the un-Latina/o Latina/o steered by DNA to assume Latina/o form – cannot emerge without its elemental matrix, the likes of the Latino and Latina. The Latin "diaspora" diaspora is a new adaptation and with the perspective of constantly being "away."

These three takes dramatize an active wait and reception for something that is like Latina/o. Latina/o is a pursuit, a hereafter, a mutation.

Double-Crossings

"I don't know how far I'm gonna go with this story," Precious tells us from the novel's onset (3). But her routes and observations have taken us to this investigation's epistemic strands: cartography, history, and personhood. Precious was not a long way off from Latina/o pursuits that cleave apart and take charge of unitary discourses of being. These forays into ethno-racial identity do not offer an explanatory account or an ordered, synoptic Latina/o chronology and genealogy. These thematic approaches, more readily, spotlight political events that bring about a Latino or Latina. Analytic care should be accorded to knotty points that reckon with the processes through which a far-reaching set of Latin relations turn up. These blueprints rehearse Latin encounters that cut the umbilical cord on a "pure" Latina/o discourse, buckling it to other likely subjects.

To make use of Jacalyn D. Harden's judicious stance, augmented from W. E. B. Du Bois's twentieth-century prognosis, the problem at this juncture of "the twenty-first century is the problem of double-crossing the color line" (2). This mapping of the double-cross doubtlessly nears closer to Latina/o crossings of many color lines – *moving* lines and borders. Double-crossing puts to the test notions of betrayal, bringing to the fore the crossing and recrossing of physical and intellectual borders. Can any of the abovementioned clusters in the "shared" Latina/o space – Afro-Latinos, binational, biracial, and Other Latinos, the indígena Latina/o, the Spanglish Latina/o, the DNA Latina/o, and profuse forms of unbelonging and deracination – work without migration? Owing to the maxim, "We didn't cross the border, the border crossed us," we can extrapolate an epistemology of bodies. As ideological and reinforced borders have crossed and cut across bodies, what become bodies of knowledge are a spatial shift – a new geography – that places being as a source countering how these bodies have been structured. Mobility and double-crossing are the nodal points delivering us to the instability of the U.S. Latina/o foundation and its discursive migrations.

Notes

1. Much gratitude is owed to my invaluable and incomparable community of first readers: John Morán González, Miguel Segovia, Marc Schachter, and Tanya L. Shields. Equally stimulating is this other possibility: that the Venezuelanness of Carey's father – an "invisible" Latinness – erases her "race." It is not U.S. whiteness, which has been accessed, conquered, recalibrated, and domesticated by many folks "of color," that is in question, but Venezuelan *off*-whiteness.
2. Urrieta adjusts the annals of Latina/o consciousness by asking: "What does it mean to be an indígena Latina/o in the United States" (324)? This preoccupation is urgent, as 2013 news items disclosed that, per a 2010 U.S. Census brief,

"Mexican-American Indians" now constitute "the fourth largest tribal group in the United States" (Ojeda 2013). The *New York Times* headlined this burgeoning demographic, reporting in 2011 "an explosion in respondents of Hispanic descent who also identified themselves as American Indians" (Decker 2011).

3 Sapphire's theming of the silence around HIV, homelessness, and a rundown city shows the internal abandonment of American citizens during the Cold War and its overlaps with foreign and domestic foes. Jacqueline Foertsch speculates that the Cold War "spawned a plague, not of communism or of bomb-related illness, but of paranoia, xenophobia, and red-baiting that took in witch-hunt proportions" (9). The HIV/AIDS crisis during the Reagan-Bush era's governing practices brought a "'plague upon' multiple populations deemed deserving of such punishment" (4; cf. Shilts 1987; Brier 2011). Communism, gays, ethno-racialized peoples, the working classes, and HIV/AIDS infection brought ideological reactions against "the infectious enemy" (18).

4 Morales's Spanglish paradigm, as a verb, models alternative Latina/o maps. While "Spanglish" may be centered in the United States, a "Spanglish Latina/o" can pop up anywhere. In my first monograph (2013), I drifted toward the tenet of Latin@, with the "at" sign, for subjects who enact "Latined" significations. Forms of Latin@ness – Latin-*at*-ness – are not Latina/o specific, as these referents walk out of the presupposed brown/Spanish-speaking body. Latin@ness gears toward Latined living inasmuch as the Latin signifier hosts a free flow of people that stir with or without the easily assumed subject in *latinidad*. Spanglish is not a monolithic block. Junot Díaz has submitted that Spanglish is "sloppy," a perception that coincides with a clumsy and awkward Latin being. A massive bilingual community borrows from their "Latin" vocabulary. "You have Colombians being influenced by Venezuelans in the United States," Díaz elaborates. "You have Salvadorans being influenced by Puerto Ricans, you have Mexicans. We have multiple Spanishes and I think people are becoming multiply fluent" (Ratner-Arias 2013). Just as there are several Latina/o assemblages, there are prodigious Spanglishes also.

5 Lorrin Thomas's proposition on Puerto Rican recognition merits attention: "During the revolutionary anticolonial explosions of the sixties, Puerto Rican activists, along with African Americans and Chicanos, began to appropriate the sensibility, if not the precise meanings, of recognition as a 'grammar of social conflict.' In this context, *recognition* took on precisely the idea of demanding a voice, of insisting on acknowledgment as valid and legitimate social actors" (13).

6 The Thomas patriarch invokes Frantz Fanon's *The Wretched of the Earth*, or to recall the original French title, *Les Damnés de la Terre*, for what is at stake in reintroducing the Martiniquan thinker is the condemnation to failure captured under the declaration "The Damned of the Earth." Thomas hears his father sound off on life as a living hell through a sequence "full of damns." "My father kept talking to the walls. Some of the words came out loud, others stayed inside. I caught the inside ones – the damn WPA, the damn depression, the damn home relief, the damn poorness, the damn cold, the damn crummy apartments, the damn look on his damn kids, living so damn damned and his not being able to do a damn thing about it" (11). Damnation, Lewis R. Gordon expounds, "means witnessing concrete instances of arbitrary death and social practices that demonstrate that one group of people's lives are less valuable than others' to the point

of their not being considered to be really people at all" (11). Thomas's clumsy "Porty Ricanness" drags with it his immense roster of "arbitrary death" and Latin darkness. Lorrin Thomas reminds us that, "Unlike other immigrant groups that would become known as 'hyphenated Americans' over time – Italian-American, Japanese-American – Puerto Ricans in the United States were never referred to as Puerto Rican-Americans.... For most of the twentieth century, though, this was an impossible category, suggesting quietly the unresolvable tension between its two terms: *Puerto Rican* and *citizen* fit together only when mediated by the United States" (3).

7 In *Roots*' thirtieth anniversary edition, Michael Eric Dyson renders that "Haley's comet of a book" afforded "a touchstone for alternative history" (x; ix). He started a dialogue "about black roots that continues to this day," as "DNA tests to determine black ancestry are more popular than ever. Scientific advance is part of the explanation, but the cultural impetus for such an agenda of racial discovery lies with Haley's inspiring book. It is also fitting that *Roots* appeared the same year that Black History Week was officially extended to Black History Month" (xi). Henry Louis Gates, Jr. also contributed to the making of DNA tests more palatable through his PBS specials and companion books: the 2006 *African American Lives*, the 2008 *African American Lives 2*, and the 2010 *Faces of America* miniseries. Gates aspires to "get into the DNA of American culture" in each one-hour episode, transporting audiences to a "journey with one celebrity pair bound together by an intimate, sometimes hidden link, trek[king] through layers of ancestral history, uncover[ing] secrets and surprises of their family trees and shar[ing] life-altering discoveries" (PBS.org). Some of Gates's guests have included Margaret Cho, Stephen Colbert, Robert Downey Jr., Quincy Jones, Eva Longoria, Condoleezza Rice, Ruth Simmons, Martha Stewart, Barbara Walters, and Oprah Winfrey. The *Wall Street Journal* reported that Gates is a "founding partner of African DNA, which offers African-American clients a method of tracing their history beyond 1870, the year where federal census records end in the 'black hole of slavery.'" But to refrain from a conflict of interest, "his company isn't used for the analyses on the PBS shows. He says he donates most of the profits he generates from African DNA." Given the frisson around genetic history, Gates gauged that "his ancestral pursuits now occupy nearly half of his professional time" (Jurgensen 2013).

8 Some individuals administer genetic tests that may reveal illness, disorders, and diseases. Alondra Nelson notifies us that "other subjects, citizens, or social groups" resort to these tests "in the hope of repairing injury and rectifying injustices committed by states, institutions, or other entities." The Innocence Project is an example of a "U.S. initiative 'dedicated to exonerating wrongfully convicted people through DNA testing and reforming the criminal justice system.'" In Argentina, DNA analysis is used "to examine the remains discovered in mass graves and determine the identities of persons suspected to have been abducted by agents of a repressive seven-year military dictatorship that began in 1976. More recently, now adult children suspected to have been taken from their 'disappeared' mothers and placed in adoptive families are now being compelled by the Argentinean government to undergo genetic testing, whether or not the adoptees desire this information. Genetics is in these ways being put to the use of mending of what has been 'smashed'" (Nelson 2012, 21).

9 Jennifer L. Hochschild and Maya Sen indicate that "The relationship between a Latino racial identity and DNA ancestry testing is much more complicated than that between a black (or white or Asian) identity and DNA ancestry testing. The reason is that autosomal DNA tests do not include a region of 'Latin America;' Latinos will learn the proportion of their ancestry that is European, Asian, Native American, or African" (22). Kim Tallbear finesses this point of Latin American exclusion from DNA profiles, as primacy is given to "founder populations." She states: "In the genomes of the living and the dead, scientists look for molecular sequences – the 'genetic signatures' of ancient peoples whom they perceive as original as original continental populations: for example, Indo-Europeans, Africans, Asians, and Native Americans. Native American DNA, as a (threatened and vanishing) scientific object of study, can help answer what are, for these scientists, pressing human questions" (3).

10 Racial hierarchies are apparent through hair textures, which as Ginetta E. B. Candelario contends, are "the principle bodily signifier[s] of race, followed by racial features, skin color, and, last ancestry" that tailors Dominican social identity (223). Cepeda describes these hair distinctions as "*un poco duro*," (4–5; 25) "*lacio*," (13), and "*bueno*" (43).

11 Candelario points out that discourses on Dominican identity formation have maintained that this group is "racially Indian and culturally Hispanic" (2). She explicates: "To the extent that the mulata has been semantically erased in favor of the *India* (who is understood to be representative of Dominican 'in-betweenness'), the *India* operates as an iconographic stand-in for Dominican women" (240). Dominicans "use language that affirms their 'Indian' heritage – Indio, Indio oscuro, Indio claro, trigueño [sic] – and signals their resistance to foreign authority, whether Spanish or Haitian, and their autochthonous claims to sovereignty while accounting for the preponderance of medium to dark skin tones and complexions in the population" (5).

12 *Bird of Paradise* facilitates Latina/o becomings through privatization, as corroborated by an exclusive cutout promotion for "10% off any DNA test" in the book's penultimate page. By redeeming Cepeda's coupon, a reader inaugurates her own DNA voyage. This offer advertises a transactional ethno-racial identity in tune with U.S. consumerism. Cepeda's readerly bonds further sediment through fixed biological "facts" bolstered by the DNA testing and literary markets. Moving in sync to a commodified direction, Cepeda's memoir strengthens an intimacy with familiar strangers, in a manner of speaking, as her coupon drives at a Latin special treatment. *Bird of Paradise* appears to break open a space for a "truthful" DNA community of Latinness, what Anthony Elliott adverts to as "a near universal consumerism and DIY life politics." The acronym for "do it yourself" is not altogether suitable in this case in point, for it hints at "DIYer" who creates or repairs a self-identity, but with the help of professionals. A DIY life politics, as spearheaded for Latinos in pursuit of global ("Latina/o") DNA, manifest a scientific family tree, a DNA "selfie," if you wish, where the picture is not the self-portrait taken with a digital device. The DNA selfie, much like the social media selfie, hints at the branding and recognition of the self through one's unique profile. "In privatized, postmodern society," Elliott proceeds, "the individual is recast, first and foremost as a *consumer identity*.... Privatization sets itself against all traditional ways of living and conduct

at the level of daily life" (xxi). A DIY Latinness flows out from this consumer-led understanding of buying one's lineage and arriving at a stylized subjectivity. *Bird of Paradise* reprints the "Frequently Asked Questions" (283–91) and the "DNA Test Kit Instructions" from the DNA website Cepeda nudges readers to visit. Cepeda's DNA Latina arises through a consumerism that possesses the means and global traits to produce personal identity.

13 Clifford draws out this idea thus: "In assimilationist national ideologies such as those of the United States, immigrants may experience loss and nostalgia, but only en route to a whole new place. Such ideologies are designed to integrate immigrants, not people in diasporas" (250).

14 The Latin "diaspora" diaspora's loose end is fed through – bundled up – by DNA, other global technological platforms, and biological systems that are routine such as, say, in vitro fertilization (IVF). Present-day questions that are opening the door to new modes of reorganization and recognition entail: What is Latina/o life? How is Latina/o produced and reproduced through these technological processes? And what does one mean by this type of coming together through scientific "Latinidad"? This "diaspora" diaspora kinship institutes, as Sarah Franklin presses, "Biological Relatives" (2013). If assisted human reproduction through IVF has "changed scientific understandings of what life is," it also thrusts us into the realm of redefining it, as technology is becoming more biologized (3). IVF "both recapitulates and personalizes a wider process through which biology is not only denaturalized but 'cultured up.' " "While continuing to function as an experimental tool, IVF technology is embedded in a naturalized and normalized logic of kinship, parenthood, and reproduction: it is pursued in the hope of alleviating childlessness" (4). Is DNA *latinidad* also a hope in alleviating "Latinolessness"? IVF is considered with the DNA Latina/o because it highlights embodiments assisted and predicated through technology. We may well join Franklin in wondering about the obvious and "normal" future kinship of Latina/o. "IVF is a technique that replicates a well-known biological process, namely fertilization, and confirms the ability to stimulate this process technologically," writes Franklin. "It is thus doubly reproductive: it successfully reproduces reproduction, and its reproductive success biologically is what confirms, or proves, that it works technologically" (6).

Works Cited

Andrews, George Reid. *Afro-Latin America, 1800–2000*. New York: Oxford University Press, 2004.

Arias, Arturo, and Claudia Milian. "Introduction: U.S. Central Americans: Representations, Agency, and Communities." *Latino Studies* 11.2 (Summer 2013): 131–49.

Brier, Jennifer. *Infectious Ideas: U.S. Political Responses to the AIDS Crisis*. Chapel Hill: University of North Carolina Press, 2011.

Brubaker, Rogers. "The 'Diaspora' Diaspora." *Ethnic and Racial Studies* 28.1 (January 2005): 1–19.

Candelario, Ginetta E. B. *Black behind the Ears: Dominican Racial Identity from Museums to Beauty Shops*. Durham, NC: Duke University Press, 2007.

Carp, Alex. Robin Nagle. *The Believer*. September 2010. <http://www.believermag.com/issues/201009/?read=interview_nagle>, accessed September 1, 2013.
Cepeda, Raquel. *Bird of Paradise: How I Became Latina*. New York: Atria Books, 2013.
Clifford, James. *Routes: Travel and Translation in the Late Twentieth Century*. Cambridge, MA: Harvard University Press, 1997.
Decker, Geoffrey. "Hispanics Identifying Themselves as Indians." *New York Times*, July 3, 2011. <http://www.nytimes.com/2011/07/04/nyregion/more-hispanics-in-us-calling-themselves-indian.html?_r=0>, accessed November 1, 2013.
Díaz, Junot. *The Brief Wondrous Life of Oscar Wao: A Novel*. New York: Riverhead Books, 2007.
Dufoix, Stéphane. *Diasporas*. Translated by William Rodarmor. Berkeley: University of California Press, 2008.
Duster, Troy. *Backdoor to Eugenics*. New York: Routledge, 2003.
Dyson, Michael Eric. "Haley's Comet." *Roots: The Saga of an American Family*. By Alex Haley. New York: Vanguard Press, 2007 [1974], ix–xi.
Elliott, Anthony, ed. "Editor's Introduction." *Routledge Handbook of Identity Studies*. New York: Routledge, 2011, xii–xxiv.
Falconer, Blas, and Lorraine M. López. "Introduction." *The Other Latin@: Writing Against a Singular Identity*. Edited by Blas Falconer and Lorraine M. López. Tucson: The University of Arizona Press, 2011, 1–7.
Falconi, José Luis, and José Antonio Mazzotti, eds. *The Other Latinos: Central and South Americans in the United States*. Cambridge, MA: Harvard University David Rockefeller Center for Latin American Studies, 2007.
Foertsch, Jacqueline. *Enemies Within: The Cold War and the AIDS Crisis in Literature, Film, and Culture*. Urbana: University of Illinois Press, 2001.
Foster, Eugene A., M. A. Jobling, P. G. Taylor, P. Donnelly, P. de Knijff, Rene Mieremet, T. Zerjal, and C. Tyler-Smith. "Jefferson Fathered Slave's Last Child." *Nature* 396 (November 5, 1998): 27–28.
Franklin, Sarah. *Biological Relatives: IVF, Stem Cells, and the Future of Kinship*. Durham, NC: Duke University Press, 2013.
Gordon, Lewis R. "*Through the Hellish Zone of Nonbeing*: Thinking through Fanon, Disaster, and the Damned of the Earth." *Human Architecture: Journal of the Sociology of Self-Knowledge* 5.3 (Summer 2007): 5–12.
Gordon-Reed, Annette. *The Hemingses of Monticello: An American Family*. New York: W. W. Norton & Company, 2008.
Greist, Stephanie Elizondo. "Latina Enough." *The Other Latin@: Writing Against a Singular Identity*. Edited by Blas Falconer and Lorraine M. López. Tucson: The University of Arizona Press, 2011, 15–20.
Grillo, Evelio. *Black Cuban, Black American: A Memoir*. Houston, TX: Arte Público Press, 2000.
Haley, Alex. *Roots: The Saga of an American Family*. New York: Vanguard Press, 2007 [1974].
Harden, Jacalyn D. *Double Cross: Japanese Americans in Black and White Chicago*. Minneapolis: University of Minnesota Press, 2003.
Hochschild, Jennifer L., and Sen, Maya. "Singular or Multiple? The Impact of Genomic Ancestry Testing on Americans' Racial Identity." April 15, 2013.

<scholar.harvard.edu/files/msen/files/hochschild_sen_reification.pdf>, accessed September 12, 2013.
Howard, David. *Coloring the Nation: Race and Ethnicity in the Dominican Republic.* Oxford: Signal Books, 2001.
Jiménez Román, Miriam, and Juan Flores, eds. *The Afro-Latin@ Reader: History and Culture in the United States.* Durham, NC: Duke University Press, 2010.
Jurgensen, John. "Doubling Down on DNA." *Wall Street Journal*, March 22, 2012. <http://online.wsj.com/article/SB10001424052702304636404577297502843 4834 54.html>, accessed October 2, 2013.
Morales, Ed. *Living in Spanglish: The Search for Latino Identity in America.* New York: LA Weekly Books, 2002.
Nelson, Alondra. "Reconciliation Projects: From Kinship to Justice." *Genetics and the Unsettled Past: The Collision of DNA, Race, and History.* Edited by Keith Wailoo, Alondra Nelson, and Catherine Lee. New Brunswick, NJ: Rutgers University Press, 2012, 20–31.
——. "The Factness of Diaspora: The Social Sources of Genetic Genealogy." *Revisiting Race in a Genomic Age.* Edited by Barbara A. Koenig, Sandra Soo-Jin Lee, and Sarah S. Richardson. New Brunswick, NJ: Rutgers University Press, 2008, 253–68.
Ojeda, Esmeralda. "Mexican-American Indians Now Make Up the Fourth Largest Tribal Group in the United States." *Newspaper Tree*, October 24, 2013. <http://newspapertree.com/articles/2013/10/24/mexican-american-indians-now-make-up-fourth-largest-tribal-group-in-the-united-states>, accessed November 1, 2013.
PBS. "About: Finding Your Roots with Henry Louis Gates, Jr." PBS.org. <http://www.pbs.org/wnet/finding-your-roots/about/>, accessed October 2, 2013.
Peña Delgado, Grace. *Making the Chinese Mexican: Global Migration, Localism, and Exclusion in the U.S.–Mexico Borderlands.* Stanford, CA: Stanford University Press, 2012.
Precious. Directed by Lee Daniels. DVD. Santa Monica: Lionsgate, 2010 [2009].
Ratner-Arias, Sigal. "Junot Díaz On Immigration: 'I'm Not Certain that Anyone Stops Being an Immigrant.'" *Huffington Post*, September 19, 2013. <http://www.huffingtonpost.com/2013/09/19/junot-diaz-immigration_n_3954792 .html>, accessed September 19, 2013.
Rúa, Mérida. "*Colao* Subjectivities: PortoMex and MexiRican Perspectives on Language and Identity." *CENTRO Journal* xiii.2 (Fall 2001): 116–32.
Sapphire. *Push.* New York: Borzoi, 1996.
Shilts, Randy. *And the Band Played On: Politics, People, and the AIDS Epidemic.* New York: St. Martin's Press, 1987.
Smith, Dinitia, and Nicholas Wade. "DNA Test Finds Evidence of Jefferson Child by Slave." *New York Times*, November 1, 1998. <http://www.nytimes .com/1998/11/01/us/dna-test-finds-evidence-of-jefferson-child-by-slave .html?pagewanted=all&src=pm>, accessed September 12, 2013.
Tallbear, Kim. *Native American DNA: Tribal Belonging and the False Promise of Genetic Science.* Minneapolis: University of Minnesota Press, 2013.
Thomas, Lorrin. *Puerto Rican Citizen: History and Political Identity in Twentieth-Century New York City.* Chicago: The University of Chicago Press, 2010.
Thomas, Piri. *Down These Mean Streets.* New York: Vintage Books, 1997 [1967].

Urrieta, Jr., Luis. "Las Identidades También Lloran, *Identities Also Cry*: Exploring the Human Side of Indigenous Latina/o Identities." *Comparative Indigeneities of the Américas: Toward a Hemispheric Approach*. Edited by M. Bianet Castellanos, Lourdes Gutiérrez Nájera, and Arturo J. Aldama. Tucson: University of Arizona Press, 2012, 321–35.

Watson, James D. *DNA: The Secret Life*. New York: Alfred A. Knopf, 2003.

13

THEA PITMAN

Mestizaje and Cyborgism on Either Side of the Line

The concept of a human organism integrated with man-made components is nothing new in the history of the human imagination (González 2000a). However, the very real possibilities of combining human bodies and machines, especially (networkable) computer systems, via ever more advanced prosthetics and implants have increased exponentially in the developed world since the term "cyborg" itself was coined in 1960 by Clynes and Kline (Borst 2009, 14). As Donna Haraway observes in "A Cyborg Manifesto: Science, Technology, and Socialist-Feminism in the Late Twentieth Century," a seminal piece of writing that began appearing in different versions from the mid-1980s onward, "by the late twentieth century, our time, a mythic time, we are all chimeras, theorized and fabricated hybrids of machine and organism; in short, we are cyborgs" (Haraway 1991, 150).[1]

In Haraway's view then, modern science turns us all into cyborgs through technological appendages, implants, interventions, and interfaces that enhance and maintain us (crowns, artificial limbs, pace makers, IVF treatments, or even just access to computers and other high-tech gadgets). While popular discourse has often championed the emancipatory potential of new technologies to enhance and extend fallible human bodies, offering at least partial liberation from the "meat" of material existence, the proliferation of cyborgs also brings with it fears of the monstrous, and raises questions about the nature of our very humanity (Dixon 2007, 306). Furthermore, Haraway also warns that with the growth in nanotechnology in particular, "The ubiquity and invisibility of cyborgs is precisely why these sunshine-belt machines are so deadly. They are as hard to see politically as materially" (Haraway 1991, 153). Much cyborg-related technology, then, is

---

The introduction and sections concerning the work of Guillermo Gómez-Peña and Los Cybrids are abridged versions of a chapter of mine entitled 'Mestiz@ Cyborgs: The Performance of Latin American-ness as (Critical) Racial Identity', originally published in Claire Taylor and Thea Pitman, *Latin American Identity in Online Cultural Production* (New York: Routledge, 2012).

very reactionary in nature: it is simply an extension of hegemonic control over us in order to ensure the maintenance of a smooth-running and compliant, productive, and reproducible workforce.

Nevertheless, what Haraway hopes for in her manifesto is that "liberation rests on the construction of the consciousness, the imaginative apprehension, of oppression, and so of possibility" (Haraway 1991, 149). What she wants to identify and promote is a "cyborg consciousness" that, despite being the product of powerful interests, can critique and challenge that paradigm of control: "The main trouble with cyborgs, of course, is that they are the illegitimate offspring of militarism and patriarchal capitalism, not to mention state socialism. But illegitimate offspring are often exceedingly unfaithful to their origins" (Haraway 1991, 151). According to Haraway, it is those unfaithful ones that will be most resistant/conscious and it is to cultural production that she looks for examples.

Representations and performances of cyborgic personae have proliferated in science-fiction literature and film since the 1960s. They have also appeared in increasing numbers in (performance) art and, more recently, in cultural products designed specifically for circulation online (cf. Hables Gray 1995; Dixon 2007; Borst 2009). It goes without saying that these cyborg figures may be charged with a whole array of different meanings corresponding to the discussion of the significance of the cyborg outlined above. Nevertheless, there are certain parameters to the meanings that such cyborgs can express. Much of the discourse of early Cyborg Theory assumed a universal "us" as its subject – "we are [all] cyborgs" – yet overlooked the fact that only in the West do a majority of "us" have access to cyborg technologies. Other critics were at least more explicit in their judgment that cyborgs expressed "existential and spiritual uncertainties and crises within *late industrial Western societies*" alone (Dixon 2007, 306; emphasis added). As a whole, Cyborg Theory seemed incapable of conceiving the existence of other subject positions that might be deemed "cyborgic."

It is no surprise, then, to find that the vast majority of the cyborgs in cultural production are white and located in (the fantasy worlds of) the West. Where the occasional nonwhite body is depicted as cyborgic, such figures are typically presented as both eroticised and exoticised commodities for consumption or representations of the "other" that must be eliminated at all costs. In a brief overview of those few cyborgs that were 'racially "marked" as not "white"' to be found in contemporary Western popular culture which Jennifer González first published in 1995, she argued that the cyborg was a figure heavily laden with meaning: "I do not see the cyborg body as primarily a surface or a simulacrum which signifies only itself; rather the cyborg is like a symptom – it represents that which cannot otherwise be represented" (González 2000b, 541); it represents our unspoken fears and desires, particularly with regard to questions of race and the tug-of-war between discourses of racial purity versus those of race mixture. She went on to judge that the nonwhite cyborg-as-symptom in Western popular culture typically corresponded to "(mostly male) cyborg fantasies" of "a powerful, yet vulnerable, combination of sex toy and techno-sophisticate," an eroticised, exotic commodity. She concluded with the damning assessment that "Cyborg bodies [... do not] – as yet – function as radical alternatives. It may be that the cyborg is now in a new and progressive phase, but its 'racial' body politics have a long way to go" (González 2000b, 548–50).

It is now nearly twenty years since González so rotundly critiqued the "'racial' body politics" of the cyborg in Western popular culture and what I want to explore in this chapter is the growing number, and possible significance, of representations of noticeably Latina/o, that is, *mestiza/o*, cyborgs by Latina/o cultural producers from the early 1990s to the early 2000s. There is an obvious parallelism or sense of continuity between the figure of the *mestiza/o* and that of cyborg. Discourse on the subject of the mixing of humans and machines clearly echoes that about the mixing of different "races" of humans: if the discourse of *mestizaje* was a combination of hope for a "cosmic race" working to overcome a fear of the racial "other" by "consuming" it, the discourse on cyborgism, as noted above, similarly negotiates between utopianist hopes and fears of dystopia. Nevertheless, what I should like to underscore here is that contemporary Cyborg Theory not only has points of interesting comparison with *mestizaje*; it is derived in part from the discourse of *mestizaje* as it had been resemanticised by U.S. *latinidad*.

In the latter sections of "A Cyborg Manifesto," Haraway used Chicana cultural theory as a key support for her own theorisations, comparing the resistant "cyborg" with the subject of Third World feminism, with prominent references to the figure of La Malinche. In so doing she drew heavily on the work of Chela Sandoval, whose doctoral thesis focused on Chicana/Latina/Third World feminisms and made judicious, grounded use of Anzaldúa's theorisations of "*mestiza* consciousness." In particular Haraway identified Sandoval's work on "oppositional consciousness" and the resistant methodologies ("technologies") of "women of color" as having strong parallels with her formulation of "cyborg consciousness." This link between *la mestiza* of "*mestiza* consciousness" and the cyborg of Cyborg Theory or cyberfeminism has been made repeatedly, for better or for worse, by subsequent theorists who have drawn on her formulations.

There is no doubt that the production of identifiably *mestiza/o* cyborgs by Latina/o cultural producers that has come about in the last twenty years seeks in some way to respond to Haraway's drawing of parallels between *mestiza* and cyborg consciousnesses. It should be noted that most of the Latina/o cultural producers studied in this chapter were closely involved in the Southern Californian academic world that was the birthplace of Cyborg Theory in the late 1980s and early 1990s and they would have undoubtedly been aware of Donna Haraway's work and quite possibly of the co-optation of Anzaldúa's "*mestiza* consciousness" therein.

But how exactly have Latina/o cultural producers responded? Perhaps, given all the parallelisms, this is a field where Latina/o cultural producers will seek to trump Haraway et al. and reclaim a position for themselves as "world leaders" in all kinds of mixing, within and beyond the parameters of humanism. Their enthusiasm for the figure of the *mestiza/o* cyborg will therefore underscore their a priori aptitude for a *continual process* of revitalised mixing, their ongoing commitment to the kind of "critical mestizaje" that Rafael Pérez-Torres has argued for: "Only a constantly critical and questioning deployment of mestizaje – a mestizaje on the margins, so to speak – can move processes of identification beyond established and disabling social scripts" (Pérez-Torres 2006, 66).

Nevertheless, the prevalence of a racial discourse in the United States which focuses in particular on questions of hypodescent and phenotype, or even just skin colour, has worked to propagate an ever-more reified form of the discourse of *mestizaje* among and about today's Latino communities in which *mestizaje, raza, latinidad,* "Latin looks," and even "brownness" are all interchangeable: Marilyn Miller argues that this reified conceptualisation of *mestizaje* "now becomes a synonym for all Latino expression *in* the United States" (Miller 2004, 142; emphasis in the original). Instead of an ongoing process where *mestizaje* is "produced through a series of concrete *practices* that can never be reduced to a type of *body*" (González 2000a, 47; emphasis in the original), "real" *mestizaje* is lost to view and substituted by an a priori thing, an "essential" brown body. This reification of *mestizaje* may combine unhelpfully with the tendencies already noted above in relation to the mainstream depiction of nonwhite cyborgs, to emphasise the exotic, erotic, consumable, and expendable nature of the *mestizo* body, whatever the intentions of the cultural producer concerned. Alternatively, representations may play more on the tensions implicit in the *mestiza/o* cyborg figure than on the parallelisms, positing the cyborg as the impure other of a now purified and naturalised *mestiza/o* body that seeks to ally itself more closely with nature and hence rejects technology.

In order to put some flesh on the bones – to use a rather *démodé* humanist metaphor – of this theoretical outline, this chapter will examine the presence of cyborgism in a Latina/o literary work in traditional print form (Alejandro

Morales's *The Rag Doll Plagues*) before moving on to consider Guillermo Gómez-Peña's influential work on the figure of the "ethno-cyborg," and, by way of a coda, the online manifestation of a *mestiza/o* cyborg "principle" in the work of performance and multimedia artists Los Cybrids. This use of materials from both offline and online media constitutes the literal reference to discourses of *mestizaje* and cyborgism "on either side of the line" of my title, in addition to the relevance of borders to both discussions of cyborgism and Chicano/Latino Studies in particular. Taking up Jennifer González's earlier arguments about the meaning of cyborg figures in art and popular culture, this chapter contends that, although in some early, typically offline, examples the cyborg figure functions as a "symptom" signalling both a Latino rejection of cyborgism and new technology per se, in tandem with a more ambivalent and essentialist attitude to the discourse of *mestizaje* than the author is ostensibly willing to admit, in its most radical online manifestations it functions as a pathogen, an active agent of a specifically "viral" and resistant form of critically *mestizo latinidad*.

Gabriela Chung and Her Robotic Right Arm

Despite admitting in interview his qualms about the potential for discourse about identity to be "a trap" resulting in no real answers despite one's best efforts (Gurpegui 1996, 8), the Chicano writer and academic Alejandro Morales clearly sets the question of identity formation centre-stage in his overall assessment of his own work which he encapsulates in the essay "Dynamic Identities in Heterotopia" (Morales 1996). Nevertheless, a tension remains in Morales's assessment of his subject matter over whether he is describing a multicultural "heterotopia" in Southern California composed of "a profusion of cultural enclaves, a multitude of othernesses' with 'literal and metaphorical borders" between them, or whether he intends to suggest a process of (cultural) mixing in tune with Pérez-Torres's concept of "criticial mestizaje" where these cultural enclaves "develop[...] together" and where the "dynamic identities" such co-development spawns are engaged in "an unending, unfinished process of continuous movement, of ceaseless change, of always becoming" (Morales 1996, 24). This tension between ethnic essentialism and "critical mestizaje" lies at the heart of Morales's fifth novel, *The Rag Doll Plagues* (1992).

The novel is divided into three sections focusing on a different historical era and geographical location. The first is set in and around Mexico City on the eve of independence from Spain. The second is set in Southern California in the 1980s. The third is set in the late twenty-first century in a dystopian state known as the Lamex Coastal Region of the Triple Alliance, an area stretching from central Mexico to the Pacific Coast and embracing the key urban centres of Mexico City and Los Angeles. In each case the main protagonist is a doctor (Gregorio/Gregory) whose job it is to help tackle a different plague, and in each case the question of *mestizaje*, both cultural and more often racial, is key to the dénouement of the section. In the second section the main character's AIDS is caused by contamination of blood products given to her as a haemophiliac, yet there is some sense that in her wake she has encouraged greater cultural mixing as she, a Jewish American, has embraced Mexican/Chicano culture. In the first and third sections the plague only abates after different ethnic groups start to mix with each other, either by sexual reproduction and the creation of *mestiza/o* subjects in the first section, or by blood transfusions from 'MCMs' (or 'Mexico-City-Mexicans') to 'Euranglos' in the final section. The novel therefore sets great store on what John Gamber, in his more detailed study of the novel as a whole terms "positive cultural, ethnic, racial, and gender pollutions" (Gamber 2012, 86). Other critics have also praised the dynamic nature of *mestizaje* in Morales's narrative: "What *Plagues* celebrates is continuous *mestizaje* ... But this *mestizaje* ... no longer stems from the notion of an eventual product, Vasconcelos's *raza cósmica*. Rather, the emphasis is on the process" (Martín-Rodríguez 1996, 94; emphasis in the original).

Given this focus on *mestizaje* as a never-ending, constantly mutating process, and given the futuristic setting of the third section of the novel, it is no real surprise to find a cyborg as one of the main characters. Gabriela "Gabi" Chung is the personal assistant and lover of the Medical Director of the Lamex Health Corridor of the Triple Alliance who has accepted her employer's request to replace her right arm with a high-tech prosthesis – "a robotic arm" comprising "a computerized knowledge bank whose fingertips were laser surgical instruments and knowledge cylinders" (Morales 1992, 136) – to enhance her productivity as a medic. Even if almost entirely compliant with hegemonic (and very masculinist) interests, Gabi would appear at first sight to be the epitome of "critical mestizaje": the possible Asian-Hispanic mix apparent in Gabi's name and the increasing popularity of "cross-cultural, racial marriages" between Mexicans and Asians in this fictitious region since circa 2020 (Morales 1992, 148), may be read as indicating that she represents a further stage of racial mixing that moves beyond the potential essentialisms of *mestizaje* as traditionally conceived in the U.S. Southwest. We are also told that Gabi has studied and worked extensively in Latin America and has a penchant for spending her free time in Mexico City (Morales 1992, 135, 169), so she may be taken to be an example of an ongoing trend in cultural *mestizaje* at the very least.

In this context, then, Gabi Chung's cyborg status may be seen be a logical high-tech continuation of this discourse of "critical mestizaje" which might even signal a deliberate reclamation of *la mestiza* from appropriation by Cyborg Theory.

However, as Gamber notes, "Gabi's cyborg identity could be portrayed as a positive formation within *The Rag Doll Plagues*, but it is not" (Gamber 2012, 85). Like the nonwhite cyborgs of so much Western popular culture, Gabi is the "other" that every aspect of the novel directs us to reject. Gabi is (part of) an "experiment" and the compliant lover/assistant of each successive male Medical Director of the Lamex Health Corridor; she is there simply to serve men's purposes, like a high-tech prostitute pimped by her employers. And, as with so many misogynistic descriptions of women, she is described as excessive: the space dedicated to the Medical Director's fascination with her arm and her compliant attitude to her cyborgic status is equalled by the space dedicated to her sexual attributes and her penchant for emotional outbursts and "old-style" partying. And these contradicting excesses are what cause her downfall: her cyborgic status is unstable/discursively unacceptable; her too human body rejects her prosthetic arm; she is demoted and, as a result, commits suicide. The mixing of human and machine is, therefore, rejected in the novel.

But Gabi stands for rather more than the limits of humanism per se. She also represents the limits of Morales's discourse on *mestizaje*. While earlier I indicated all the ways that Gabi might be read as *mestiza*, most critics settle for Morales's laconic description of "her Asian face" (Morales 1992, 135) and identify her in contemporary racial terms as Asian American. I would argue that the reason why Gabi is more easily interpreted as "Asian" or "Asian American" is that it distances her from the attempt to resemanticise the discourse of *mestizaje* elsewhere in the novel. She does not represent the dizzying complexity of future *mestizajes*, but reminds us that the novel's "real" understanding of *mestizaje* is rather more essentialist in conception.

Gabriela Chung stands in stark comparison to the Medical Director, Gregory Revueltas, the real *mestizo* who defines himself explicitly in relation to "the brown faces" of "*mi raza*" (Morales 1992, 143–44). He notes that he has personally resisted sacrificing an arm to have a high-tech prosthesis added, despite the threat to his professional standing, and, as the narrative progresses, he charts his gradual (re-)awakening to human emotions and values that professional success in contemporary Lamex preclude. Given that the narrative ends with Gabriela dead and the doctor, now a *curandero*-figure in a "Lower Life Existence" neighbourhood, "transfigured into all those that have gone before me: my progenitors, my hopeful ever-surviving race" (Morales 1992, 200), one can only judge Morales's work as revealing the tensions of the confluence of *mestizaje* and cyborgism where the cyborg functions as the impure other of a now purified and naturalised, essential *mestizo* body that looks to the past and to nature for sustenance and is content to live in the bounded "cultural enclaves" of Morales's Southern California.[2] In the context of the novel's sustained discourse around viruses, symptoms of disease and agents that can protect against such diseases, it is perhaps ironic that Gabi, the cyborg – the character who has the most technologically advanced resources "on hand" with which to actively define and defeat the plague of the final section – must be interpreted, in the terms of Jennifer González's arguments about the meaning of cyborgs in cultural production, not as an agent that has the power to move the argument about race mixing on a stage, but rather as a symptom that reveals the limits of Morales's discourse of *mestizaje*.

Ethno-Cyborgs and Hyper-Racialised Replicants

Guillermo Gómez-Peña (along with his performance troupe La Pocha Nostra and sundry other collaborators) has played a seminal conscience-raising role with respect to the relationship of race and technology, particularly the Internet. Since the mid-1990s, he has sought to play out some of the issues raised in relation to this topic via composite performance personae that he terms "ethno-cyborgs," evidencing a critical awareness in his work of the writings on cyborgism and posthumanism of Haraway and Allucquère Rosanne Stone, for example.[3] The argument that I would like to advance with regard to Gómez-Peña's work is as follows: Gómez-Peña's statements on race and *mestizaje* fluctuate between essentialism and a more critical approach. In particular, his approach to the relationship between Latinas/os and new technologies/the internet, although suggesting a healthy challenge to mainstream (white) American assumptions on the subject based on this group's racialised and racist approach to *latinidad* (in Gómez-Peña's estimation) and hence evidencing Gómez-Peña's desire to move beyond mainstream society's essentialist approach to race, also clearly relies on an amount of strategic essentialism to define both groups. His performance of "ethno-cyborg" subjects and their subsequent circulation in online "galleries" ostensibly seeks to challenge the prevalent reification of raced bodies in visual culture through their articulation of a "disturbing" and unstable combination of raced bodies and technology in tandem with discourse of Latino virality that endorses "critical mestizaje," but Gómez-Peña's recourse to (strategic) essentialism mean that these figures are perhaps too easily reincorporated into the fears and desires of the mainstream (racist) imaginary that he purports to challenge.

In terms of Gómez-Peña's attitude to race and *mestizaje*, in his own view his approach is clearly anti-essentialist. As he has commented with reference to traditional, reified conceptualisations of *mestizaje*,

> *Mestizaje* is a thing of the past. Binary models are no longer operative.... What do you do with Post-Mexicanos? We're the product of several racial mixtures and many overlapping subcultures. What are we then? Post-mestizos? Meta-mestizos? ... Our identities are in permanent flux.... More than mestizos, our multiracial and multicultural kids are poly-cultural (and poly-gendered) cyborgs. (González and Gómez-Peña 2009, 253)

Despite his rejection of *mestizaje* per se, these comments are entirely consonant with Pérez-Torres's definition of "critical mestizaje," and arguably, cyborg figures are where this kind of approach to race should be in evidence.

However, in terms of Gómez-Peña's approach to new technologies, where he attempts to appropriate and infiltrate the world of high technology on behalf of Latinas/os, there is almost always a rather more polarised racial dynamic to his thinking. In his much re-edited essay, "The Virtual Barrio @ The Other Frontier; or, The Chicano Interneta" (1995–97),[4] he challenged the utopianist conceptualisation of a "cyberspace" that was purportedly raceless but tacitly white and anglophone, arguing that, "forced to assume the unpleasant but necessary roles of web-backs, cyber-aliens, techno-pirates, and virtual *coyotes*," Chicana/o artists would attempt "to 'brownify' virtual space; to 'spanglishize' the net, and 'infect' the *linguas francas*" (Gómez-Peña 2000, 258–59). This racial, as well as linguistic, polarisation is also apparent in a slightly later performance piece, Tech-illa Sunrise (.txt dot con Sangrita)," co-authored with Rafael Lozano-Hemmer, where the explicitly white frontiersman (of so much of the early rhetoric of cyberspace) ironically recalls "the Cambrian era of cyberspace": "We were young, ambitious and white, / & there was no one else around to bother us." He then goes on to narrate the loss of that cyber-Eden: "Then came the Others, / brown people, tar people, e-mongrels of sorts, / speaking bizarre linguas polutas" (Lozano-Hemmer and Gómez-Peña 2001).

What is evident in all of the above is Gómez-Peña's direct challenge to what he sees as the hegemonic conceptualisation of new technology as white and pure. Instead he attempts to reverse the dynamics of the new medium point for point. He hence challenges the dazzling whiteness and the frontiersman/colonialist rhetoric of early anglophone cyberspace with a determination to "pollute" and "brownify" those spaces via a process of "unauthorised" colonisation (the creation of a "virtual barrio" of "web-backs" and "e-mongrels"). It is this point-for-point approach that substitutes white for brown, pure for mongrel, and hegemonic colonisation for subaltern infiltration which has the potential to be the Achilles' heel of Gómez-Peña's approach. He might articulate opposition to hegemonic positions but, in the (strategic) essentialism of his approach, he still remains bound by hegemonic paradigms of thought themselves. He still works within the binaristic racialised discourse of mainstream U.S. society.

Nevertheless, Gómez-Peña's stance on race in/and cyberspace is not quite so easily dismissed as just a simple politics of inversion which actually delivers more of the same. In "Tech-illa Sunrise" Lozano-Hemmer and Gómez-Peña posit "brown" not so much as the opposite of white as might elsewhere appear to be the case, but as a contrast to the U.S. racial polarities of black and white: it is a third position. They propose that Lupita, a (voracious) Latina service provider,

> has long ago dropped the binary code in favour of a recombinant self-organizing system of neural nets interconnected via EMR fields that allow for complex emergent phenomena, lighter and deeper shades of brown.
> El ciberespacio es café, no blanco ni negro, remember ... (Lozano-Hemmer and Gómez-Peña 2001)

While this kind of tactic might essentialise black and white bodies and subject positions, it provides a more radical conceptualisation of brown ones. The brown bodies that Gómez-Peña wants to see infiltrating cyberspace are also implicitly not (just) attractive, aspirational Latina/o bodies with smooth, coffee-coloured skin as commodified by corporate America as the "generic pan-Hispanic" (cf. Dávila 2002, 272–73). The invented verb "to brownify" and the reference to "brown people, tar people, e-mongrels of sorts" suggest distaste and dirtiness. These terms are semantically unappealing, unassimilatable by mainstream culture, and hence suggest that Gómez-Peña is invoking a radical form of *mestizaje*, one that mutates and recombines to keep up its challenge to unsettle the binaries of hegemonic culture: if coffee-coloured mixtures are now acceptable, an invocation of more disturbing and complex mixtures follows.

The potential to mutate and propagate exponentially also chimes with Gómez-Peña's championing of virality as modus operandi. In "The Virtual Barrio," Gómez-Peña argued that Latina/o "Web-backs" should aim to constitute "el nuevo virus virtual" (Gómez-Peña 2000, 260); in "Tech-illa Sunrise," Lozano-Hemmer and Gómez-Peña scripted a parodic virus alert for what they called "QuetZalcoat-82L or simply 'The Mexican Bug'" (Lozano-Hemmer and Gómez-Peña 2001), made more realistic by the fact that so many known computer viruses have stemmed from Latin America.[5]

These positive invocations of Latino virality seek to challenge the popular imaginary and its hasty association of race with infection and disease, contamination, and dirtiness. They also seek to turn on its head the history of (self-)conceptualisations of Latin America as more passively, congenitally diseased, in large part on account of its racial make-up (cf. Trigo 2000). In Gómez-Peña's work the dynamics of racial mixing are thus articulated as a mutant, recombinant bug, and they are conceived as extremely efficient in their functioning as such. Furthermore, the association of *mestizaje* with virality helps Gómez-Peña keep *mestizaje* critical: virality is a dynamic that is much less easily reified into a resultant body than *mestizaje* because it is more a question of an unseen agent or principle than an identifiable body in itself.

While such theoretical discussion of *mestizaje* and virality in Gómez-Peña's writing might sound very promising; the visual representation and performance of such theories via "ethno-cyborg" personae arguably presents more challenges. Ethno-cyborgs were engendered in Gómez-Peña's work as a response to the materials gathered from an online questionnaire linked to *The Temple of Confessions*, subsequently *The Ethno-Cyberpunk Trading Post and Curio Shop on the Electronic Frontier* (1994), a project which sought to gather mainstream "white" fears and desires regarding the racialised Latina/o other. This data was used to create the ethno-cyborgs of the *Mexterminator* project such as El Mad Mex (performed by Gómez-Peña himself, and also referred to as El Mexterminator or El Ethnographic Loco in other versions) and Cyber-Vato (performed by Roberto Cifuentes). Photographs of these ethno-cyborgs have subsequently been disseminated online, on the first *Pocha* website (see, for example, "Ethno-Techno: A Virtual Museum of Radical Latino Imagery and Fetishized Identities" [1998–c. 2000]), and newer ethno-cyborgs have been created for some of the more fully internet-based work on the current website (see, for example, *The Chica-Iranian Project* [2005]).

Gómez-Peña's most instantly recognisable ethno-cyborg figures combine clearly raced human bodies (via the exposure of expanses of naked brown flesh, as well as significant amounts of luxuriant brown hair) and technological elements which are deliberately low-tech, "techno-rascuache" additions – El Mad Mex's prosthetic right arm is a plastic toy painted silver, for example (Dixon 2007, 328). And this emphasis on both (spoof) technology and even more importantly the *mestizo* body is key: Gómez-Peña describes his "new pantheon of mighty robo-Mexicans" as being "armed with mysterious shamanic artifacts and sci-fi automatic weapons, their bodies enhanced with prosthetic implants and their *brown skin* decorated with Aztec tattoos" (Gómez-Peña 2000, 50; emphasis added), and as "refracting fetishized constructs of identity through the spectacle of [their] *'primitive,' eroticized bodies on display*" (Gómez-Peña 2000, 49; emphasis added). These personae are also referred to interchangeably as "hyper-racialised replicants,"[6] borrowing the term "replicant" from *Blade Runner* (dir. Ridley Scott 1982) where it was coined to designate a cyborg that is all machine on the inside with only the form/the skin of a human. This works to further underscore the centrality of the visible display of race to Gómez-Peña's articulation of these personae.

These ethno-cyborgs, with their insistence on the visibility of the *mestizo* body, seem to want to flag up the "congenital" predisposition of *mestizas/os* to mixing, including mixing human and machine, and hence suggest that they are destined to reproduce rapidly and more suited to life in (dialogue with) cyberspace than those who would conceive of themselves as racially pure. In a tongue-in-cheek riff on Haraway's most contentious statement Lozano-Hemmer and Gómez-Peña claim, "Nosotros, los otros… / We are all ethno-cyborgs, chiborgs, cyBorges, ciboricuas y demás […] / We R slowly corrupting your default configuration. / […] / We are reverse engineering your ass" (Lozano-Hemmer and Gómez-Peña 2001). *Mestiza/o* cyborgs are threatening to take over cyberspace. Furthermore, as Thomas Foster points out, the image of the ethno-cyborg's prosthesis may, in the light of Allucquère Rosanne Stone's discussion of the role of the prosthesis as opposed to the instrument or tool, signify a positive "process of incorporation without assimilation" that keeps *mestizaje* critical and messy by challenging binaristic either/or logic (Foster 2002, 53).

However, there are a number of caveats that accompany such a positive assessment of Gómez-Peña's interpretation of ethno-cyborg figures. In particular what remains of the performance of such figures in the images that circulate online is less convincingly resistant. El Ethnographic Loco is depicted with his toy prosthetic right hand clawing at his own mouth suggesting a conflicted, non-assimilated, unstable cyborgic identity, but one where the (fake) technology is rebelling against the (raced) human who would otherwise direct it. There is an ironic reference here to Australian performance artist Stelarc's high-tech third arm and his exploration of how technology can enhance human capabilities – Gómez-Peña's low-tech prosthesis suggests that it will more likely cause disability in "the wrong hands" than overcome any natural or accidental limitations to human ability. This reading thus evokes mainstream conceptions of Latinas/os as unsuited to handling technology. And while the technology is depicted as turning against Gómez-Peña in this image, the potential is also there (and released in other similar images) for the violence to be turned outwards. Gómez-Peña's literal ethno-cyborg figures thus also explore mainstream U.S. society's fear and outright rejection of the (almost always male) racial other: they are dystopian, disturbing images of the unhinged Latino male made more threatening via prosthetic limbs and weapons.

Clearly, in Gómez-Peña's view, these images are meant to be read as a critique of the mainstream fears, fantasies, and prejudices evoked (Gómez-Peña 2000, 49–50). Yet there is no guarantee that just reflecting that material back to the same audience, even with a bit of exaggeration, will mean that the images will be perceived as critiquing mainstream perceptions of Latinas/os. Arguably, without a willing assumption of criticality on behalf of the viewer, they run the risk of being seen as simply indulgent of both racist and sexist stereotypes of *latinidad*. Other critics have also expressed concern that "the decision to put forward stereotypes can have the effect of immunizing the audience from careful reflection about what they are seeing" (McGahan 2008, 79). Furthermore, these images circulate online alongside those on pornography websites, for example, where sadomasochism and racial fetishes are amply indulged, and those on gaming sites where the player can combine cross-racial desire and consumerism in the construction and collection of hybrid avatars (cf. González 2000a), and this may well mean that, "taken out of context," they will be neutralised in their impact by the dominance of these other graphic regimes in cyberspace. Only when viewed in their intended artistic context where the cyborg personae are part of a repertoire of ever-mutating ethno-cyborg figures and where the images are components of "photo-performances" that reference the "process of production as much as ... the final result" (González and Gómez-Peña 2009, 238) can his ethno-cyborgs circulating online avoid indulging mainstream expectations of raced bodies and continue to articulate a discourse of "critical mestizaje."

Warning! Cybrid Ideological Bacteria Downloading!

Whereas Gómez-Peña and colleagues present their viewers with an ever-mutating array of images of hyper-racialised cyborgs which contrive to retain the power to unsettle the viewer and provoke a revision of racial paradigms, the work of a group of Latino artists known as Los Cybrids, though clearly influenced by Gómez-Peña's ground-breaking work from the late 1990s, offers a rather different, potentially more radical approach to the subject, particularly with reference to the way in which they seek to perform a *mestiza/o* cyborg identity online.

Los Cybrids was made up of three Latina/o artists: Praba Pilar, John Jota Leaños and René Garcia. Active from 1999 until 2003, they defined themselves as "a junta of three poly-ethnic cultural diggers of the Latino sort dedicated to the critique of cyber-cultural negotiation via techno-artístico activity,"⁷ working to challenge some of the early postulations of Cyborg Theory/posthumanism, and in dialogue with more recent critical cybercultural studies. Their work included (predominantly offline) performance, installation and digital art designed to "undermine the passive acceptance and unacknowledged overarching social, cultural and environmental consequences of Information Technologies."⁸ They were generally very negative about the potential for a productive relationship between Latinas/os and new technologies, particularly the internet, arguing that the digital revolution was marginalising Latinas/os in low-paid service jobs or being used by those in power to conduct surveillance of ethnic others more effectively (Gonzalez 2001). Yet despite this stance on new technology, they had their own website from mid-2001.⁹

The concept of the *mestiza/o* cyborg lies at the heart of Los Cybrids' endeavours. The use of the term "cybrid" in their name, although a real scientific term used in the field of stem cell research, clearly indicates their identification with the concept of a mixed-race cyborg, combining as it does the "cy-" prefix with the term "hybrid." Their use of the Spanish masculine plural definite article ("Los" Cybrids), as well as the epithet used to define the group that appears in the title of their website (La Raza Techno-Crítica Collective), also focuses attention on their laying claim to the term "cybrid" on behalf of Latinas/os, and this comes articulated as a *critical*, self-aware statement of identity, thus challenging the depoliticising conflation of *mestizas/os* and cyborgs in Cyborg Theory.

Figurative images of *mestiza/o* cyborgs are also prominent in their work. On their website, the changing self-portraits at the top of the "Artists" page gestured towards the group members' identities as *mestiza/o* cyborgs in their combination of anthropological images of racial "specimens" mixed with the patterns and textures of digital material. This was particularly clear in the image of Praba Pilar. Furthermore, the group is perhaps best known for a series of digital murals featuring *mestiza/o* cyborg figures that they produced for display on a reclaimed billboard outside the Galería de La Raza in San Francisco in 2001–02 and which have subsequently continued to circulate online. These murals aimed to provoke viewers to grasp what negative implications new technologies might have for people of colour and they met with critical acclaim in the context of their original display (cf. Latorre 2008, 238).

While such images in circulation online, like the stills of ethno-cyborg performance personae on Gómez-Peña's website, may also have managed to provoke critical awareness of the issues in themselves primarily through their framing and the accompanying commentaries, Los Cybrids also moved beyond figurative representations of the *mestiza/o* cyborg, to the performance of what I term a *mestiza/o* cyborg "principle" that more convincingly achieves the above aims. The group's website achieved this by simulating a particularly Latina/o viral infection when one tried to access a site that defined itself in terms of its *mestiza/o* cyborgic nature. Before reaching the group's homepage, viewers would see a series of black screens with text in white, green and yellow which simulated the programming commands of pre-Windows computing. The first screen was headed by the statement: "<– ¡ORALE, WE'RE GONNA LAY DOWN A DOWNGRADE," and other revealing terms embedded in the commands on this and the following two screens included "cybrid," "jotascript," and "te chingas." These screens would seem to flash rapidly on and off[10] before a pop-up appeared saying: "WARNING! Los Cybrids Ideological Bacteria version 3.1 has been released into the neural network! The Global Inequality Virus has infected all systems. Downgrade now!," with an "OK" or "Cancel" option.[11] (Earlier versions of the pop-up simply said: "WARNING! Cybrid Ideological Bacteria Downloading! WARNING!") Clicking "Cancel" would take users on a loop back to the flashing screen, thus making them think they had really got a viral/bacterial infection and their computer had seized up. Clicking "OK" would take users to Los Cybrids' website itself. Only those in the know and with a real interest in accessing Los Cybrids' website would have been likely to dare to click "OK." As Pilar has noted, "We were hoping to get web hits from people outside of activist/artist circles, who would not be in on the 'joke' of the ideological virus. It was interventionist in nature".

It is this performance of viral infection on behalf of a racialised minority group in their website's opening sequence that most succinctly expresses Los Cybrids' political agenda. Taking issue with the mindset of mainstream Anglo-American society that posits cyberspace as pure (and white) and in need of protection, and simultaneously associates the concept of race – and particularly racial hybridity – with impurity, pollution, and disease, Los Cybrids were determined to act out these fears. They thus performed the viral infection of race and more generalised subalternity online. Moreover, the principle of the *mestiza/o* cyborg – *el cybrid* – was what underpinned and authorised this endeavour: this was a *mestiza/o* cyborgic form of performance.

Viral *Latinidad*: *Mestiza/o* Cyborg Bodies as Symptom or Pathogen?

I would like now to return to Jennifer González's contention that "the cyborg is like a symptom [representing] that which cannot otherwise be represented" (González 2000b, 541). González's assessment is helpful in the case of Alejandro Morales's depiction of Gabriela Chung where she signifies the inadmissible limits of the *The Rag Doll Plagues*'s discourse of *mestizaje*, and its reliance on an essentialist conceptualisation of the *mestizo* body as whole and as allied with humanity, spirituality, and the natural world, and therefore a rejection of technology and the messier more critical potential of the discourse of *mestizaje*. However, what we may conclude from an examination of *mestiza/o* cyborg figures and in particular the more performative ways in which they have been invoked in more recent online work, is that for some Latina/o artists, more than a symptom, the *mestiza/o* cyborg is conceived as a pathogen, an active agent; not simply a rash or an inflammation signalling malaise about racial boundaries and their crossing but also a cipher for the deployment of (a particularly hybrid form) of racial identity as a principle of bacterial or viral contamination. As such, with its threat that it can spread racial hybridity, literally through bodily contact or metaphorically through the corruption of files and hard drives, the *mestiza/o* cyborg and its discourse has much greater power to disturb those who would chance upon it and to challenge the reifying tendency of the visual power system that is race. Furthermore if, in its contemporary form, *latinidad* is found to be more "contagious" than ever, "circulating through the most diverse of networks" (Beasley-Murray, 2003:223) and hence may be described, loosely, in today's computer-savvy terminology as "viral," it is the more self-possessed and deliberately challenging virality of the *mestiza/o* cyborg in online cultural production, created explicitly to challenge U.S. conceptions and "pop cultural images of Latinos" and the contemporary global dissemination of such (Gómez-Peña 2000, 51), that is arguably the best expression of this messy, unsettling and critical "viral *latinidad*."

Notes

1 For the purposes of this chapter, the 1991 version of the essay from *Simians, Cyborgs, and Women* has been used.
2 López Lozano reads Morales as "highlighting the fear of intercultural contact and the shortcomings of concepts such as *mestizaje* to resolve social inequalities" and as "advocating instead a multicultural agenda able to address the socioeconomic complexities of contemporary society" (López Lozano 2003, 39). Priewe also lets Morales off the charge of a completely "essentialist return-to-roots," arguing simply that the novel "achieves a satiric tension that remains unresolved" (Priewe 2004).
3 Gómez-Peña's most significant writing on the subject of "ethno-cyborgs" is the essay "Ethno-cyborgs and Genetically Engineered Mexicans: Recent Experiments in 'Ethno-Techno' Art" (Gómez-Peña 2000, 45–57).
4 It is the latter version, as reproduced in *Dangerous Border Crossers* (2000), that has been consulted here.

5 See Beasley-Murray's conceptualisation of "viral *latinidad*" and his anchoring of this concept in the origin of the SirCam virus in Latin America (Beasley-Murray 2003).
6 Cyber-Vato and El Mad Mex are referred to as both cyborgs and as replicants (Gómez-Peña 2000, 44).
7 "Manifesto," Los Cybrids' website.
8 "Manifesto," Los Cybrids' website.
9 The site was last updated in 2003 and was finally taken offline in late 2007.
10 In fact, they would switch repeatedly between the screen with a black background and the same screen with a light grey background.
11 This is the final 2003 version.

Works Cited

Beasley-Murray, Jon. 2003. 'Latin American Studies and the Global System', in *The Companion to Latin American Studies*, ed. Philip Swanson (London: Arnold), pp. 222–38.

Borst, Elizabeth M. 2009. Cyborg Art: An Explorative and Critical Inquiry into Corporeal Human-Technology Convergence. Unpublished doctoral thesis. University of Waikato, NZ. Available at: http://researchcommons.waikato.ac.nz/bitstream/handle/10289/3976/thesissequence=1. Accessed: 13 November 2013.

Dávila, Arlene. 2002. 'Culture in the Ad World: Producing the Latin Look', in *Media Worlds: Anthropology in New Terrain*, ed. Faye D. Ginsburg, Lila Abu-Lughod and Brian Larkin (Berkeley: University of California Press), pp. 264–80.

Dixon, Steve, with contributions by Barry Smith. 2007. *Digital Performance: A History of New Media in Theater, Dance, Performance Art, and Installation* (Cambridge, MA: MIT Press).

Foster, Thomas. 2002. 'Cyber-Aztecs and Cholo-Punks: Guillermo Gómez-Peña's Five-Worlds Theory', *PMLA*, 117:1, 43–67.

Gamber, John Blair. 2012. *Positive Pollutions and Cultural Toxins: Waste and Contamination in Contemporary US Ethnic Literatures* (Lincoln: University of Nebraska Press).

Gómez-Peña, Guillermo. 2000. *Dangerous Border Crossers: The Artist Talks Back* (London: Routledge).

—— 2005. *The Chica-Iranian Project: Orientalism Gone Wrong in Aztlán*, http://www.pochanostra.com/chica-iranian. Accessed 27 March 2012.

Gómez-Peña, Guillermo, and La Pocha Nostra. 1998-c.2000. 'Ethno-Techno: A Virtual Museum of Radical Latino Imagery and Fetishized Identities', *La Pocha Nostra*, http://www.pochanostra.com/antes/rene/galeria/gallery.html. Accessed 22 March 2012.

Gonzalez, Angel. 2001. 'A Disturbing, Latino View of Tech', *Wired*, 27 June, http://www.wired/com/culture/lifestyle/news/2001/06/44799. Accessed 29 January 2009.

González, Jennifer. 2000a. 'The Appended Subject: Race and Identity as Digital Assemblage', in *Race in Cyberspace*, ed. by Beth E. Kolko, Lisa Nakamura, and Gilbert B. Rodman (New York: Routledge), pp. 27–50.

—— 2000b. 'Envisioning Cyborg Bodies: Notes from Current Research', in *The Cybercultures Reader*, ed. by David Bell and Barbara M. Kennedy (London: Routledge), pp. 540–51. [First published 1995]

González, Jennifer, and Guillermo Gómez-Peña. 2009. 'Pose and Poseur: The Racial Politics of Guillermo Gómez-Peña's Photo-Performances', in *Race and Classification: The Case of Mexican America*, ed. by Ilona Katzew and Susan Deans-Smith (Stanford, CA: Stanford University Press, pp. 236–63).

Gray, Chris Hables, ed. 1995. *The Cyborg Handbook* (New York: Routledge).

Gurpegui, José Antonio. 1996. 'Interview with Alejandro Morales', in *Alejandro Morales: Fiction Past, Present, Future Perfect*, ed. by José Antonio Gurpegui (Tempe, AZ: Bilingual Review/Press), pp. 5–13.

Haraway, Donna J. 1991. *Simians, Cyborgs, and Women: The Reinvention of Nature* (London: Free Association Books).

Latorre, Guisela. 2008. *Walls of Empowerment: Chicana/o Indigenist Murals of California* (Austin: University of Texas Press).

López Lozano, Miguel. 2003. 'The Politics of Blood: Micegenation and Phobias of Contagion in Alejandro Morales's *The Rag Doll Plagues*', *Aztlán*, 28:1, 39–73.

Los Cybrids (John Jota Leaños, René Garcia and Praba Pilar). 2001–07. *Los Cybrids: La Raza Techno-Crítica Collective*, http://www.cybrids.com/. 2003 version available from http://prabapilar.com/pages/projects/los_cybrids/index.html. Accessed 30 March 2012.

Lozano-Hemmer, Rafael and Guillermo Gómez-Peña. 2001. 'Tech-illa Sunrise (.txt dot con Sangrita)', http://www.pochanostra.com/antes/jazz_pocha2/mainpages/techilla.htm. Accessed 18 February 2008.

Martín-Rodríguez, Manuel M. 1996. 'The Global Border: Transnationalism and Cultural Hybridism in Alejandro Morales's *The Rag Doll Plagues*', in *Alejandro Morales: Fiction Past, Present, Future Perfect*, ed. by José Antonio Gurpegui (Tempe, AZ: Bilingual Review/Press), pp. 86–95.

McGahan, Christopher L. 2008. *Racing Cyberculture: Minoritarian Art and Cultural Politics on the Internet* (New York: Routledge).

Miller, Marilyn Grace. 2004. *Rise and Fall of the Cosmic Race: The Cult of Mestizaje in Latin America* (Austin: University of Texas Press).

Morales, Alejandro. 1992. *The Rag Doll Plagues* (Houston, TX: Arte Público Press).

—— 1996. 'Dynamic Identities in Heterotopia', in *Alejandro Morales: Fiction Past, Present, Future Perfect*, ed. by José Antonio Gurpegui (Tempe, AZ: Bilingual Review/Press), pp. 14–27.

Pérez-Torres, Rafael. 2006. *Mestizaje: Critical Uses of Race in Chicano Culture* (Minneapolis: University of Minnesota Press).

Priewe, Marc. 2004. 'Bio-Politics and the ContamiNation of the Body in Alejandro Morales' The Rag Doll Plagues', *MELUS*, 29:3/4, available from *Literature Online*, http://lion.chadwyck.co.uk. Accessed 24 July 2013.

Taylor, Claire, and Thea Pitman. 2012. *Latin American Identity in Online Cultural Production* (New York: Routledge).

Trigo, Benigno. 2000. *Subjects of Crisis: Race and Gender as Disease in Latin America* (Hanover, NH: Wesleyan University Press).

14

MARTA CAMINERO-SANTANGELO

Historias Transfronterizas: Contemporary Latina/o Literature of Migration

Since the 1990s, contemporary Latina/o writers increasingly highlight transnational migratory circuits as a constitutive aspect of the Latino/a experience, contesting prior paradigms of unidirectional "immigration" and assimilation to a new culture. Authors such as Julia Alvarez, Cristina García, Francisco Goldman, Reyna Grande, Esmeralda Santiago, Héctor Tobar, Achy Obejas, Ana Castillo, Graciela Limón, Josefina López, Helena María Viramontes, Angie Cruz, Junot Díaz, and Ana Menéndez, among many others, demonstrate the contemporary heterogeneity of migratory experiences as ideas, stories, and people travel from Latin America to the United States and back again, as well as from – and to – other points of origin, including Spain, China, and the African continent, and even between Caribbean islands. Whether focusing on historical or contemporary Latino migration, these writers imagine identities as not just bicultural (as is common in "ethnic" American literature) but insistently transnational, marked by behaviors such as return visits home, remittances, lingering political allegiances and involvement with home country politics, and even return migrations. In the process, these texts also often pose significant challenges to the dominant cultural U.S. narrative of the "American Dream," in which immigrants who arrive in the United States can work hard, climb a ladder of social mobility, and achieve success to a degree unimaginable at "home."

A recent study by the *Washington Post* and the Miller Center at the University of Virginia found that Latinos are still largely invested in the American Dream, and, in particular, the notion that they will rise rather than fall in social class, thanks to hard work and education, and that their children will do even better (Constable and Clement). Yet the realities for Latinos are much more complex. Latinos still lag far behind non-Latino whites in college graduation rates or household income, for instance, and social and economic betterment tends to fall off in the third generation after improving from the first to the second. Further, the dramatic intensification of border militarization, marked by the implementation of Operation Gatekeeper in 1994, along with the attendant escalation of nativist and anti-immigrant rhetoric, the increase in raids, deportations, and anti-immigrant legislation (such as Arizona's SB 1070), and the failures of substantive immigration reform at the national level in the early part of the new millennium, have dimmed prospects substantially for newer Latino immigrants and made Latino communities increasingly wary.

In the two decades since Operation Gatekeeper, some Latina/o literature has begun specifically to examine what becomes of "the American dream" for migrants in the face of an increasingly transnational reality. The typical immigrant American Dream narrative is complicated by the realities of transnationalism in several ways. For one thing, the American Dream narrative assumes a one-directional movement from country of origin to the United States, along with a trajectory of incremental assimilation. Arrival in the United States signals the commencement of a trajectory, and the achievement of the American Dream is reached both by economic prosperity in the new land and by becoming culturally "American." But literary narratives of transnationalism, both fictional and nonfictional, reflect that the movement of people and cultures is decidedly more tangled than a unidirectional flow. Transnational lives are often marked by multiple returns to cultures of origin and by identities that are profoundly shaped by and in both cultures. Indeed, "progress" in many transnational stories is marked not by metaphorical "arrival" in the United States but by the healthy and successful integration of multiple and complicated national identities. Further, literal arrival in the United States no longer necessarily marks the beginning of a transnational or bicultural story: many literary texts increasingly depict lives which are already profoundly influenced by U.S. culture and economic or political domination even while in the home country, and in some texts the "home country" has itself been a point of destination and arrival for multiple and complex cultures. Finally, in the face of sometimes vitriolic nativist rhetoric in public discourse, such that the Latino "immigrant" has come to signify absolute "otherness" to the national narrative of "American" values, some authors write stories depicting the grim failures of the American Dream of success and prosperity. A theme common to a plethora of contemporary Latino/a literary production is that the Dream, it turns out, is indeed not reality. Latina/o literary scholars, then, increasingly approach these texts through the lens of a complex and often tangled transnationalism, rather than through the prior lens of assimilation or even of bicultural ethnicity.

"Minority" Literature

Prior to the early 1990s, Latina/o literature was arguably characterized, in large part, by the sense of being a "minority" ethnic population within the United States. While the most prominent fiction, poetry, drama, and memoirs published from the Chicano Movement of the 1960s to roughly 1990 was highly attuned to the cultural origins *elsewhere* of the author and his/her characters, the works themselves tended to be firmly set in the United States, giving evidence of a developing Chicano/a or Nuyorican sensibility, even while gesturing toward the impact of those cultural origins. The "present" of the literary texts, as it were, was predominantly "here" rather than "there"; and "here," for better or for worse, was "home." Consider, for instance, Luis Valdez's classic Chicano play *Zoot Suit* (first performed in 1978), which enacts a key moment in the ethno-racial memory of Chicanos: the Zoot Suit riots and the Sleepy Lagoon murder trials of several Mexican American youth, trials notorious for their abrogation of legal protections and civil rights. But all the Chicanos in Valdez's play are U.S. citizens, and the play's focus is squarely on their experience as an oppressed and "second-class" minority *within* the United States, rather than as an immigrant population *from* somewhere else.

Rudolfo Anaya's classic Chicano novel *Bless Me, Ultima* (1972) shares this sensibility; while the New Mexican town he portrays is infused with the culture of its Mexican-origin inhabitants, who bear Spanish surnames, sometimes speak in Spanish, and practice a strong folk Catholicism, the migrant patterns portrayed in the story are from the plain to the fertile farmland closer to town, not from Mexico to the United States. Likewise, the migration of the narrator's parents from Puerto Rico in Piri Thomas's classic memoir *Down These Mean Streets* (1967) is only an implicit subtext to the internal migrations – from Spanish Harlem, to Long Island, to the South, and back again – of Piri himself. Even in *Pocho* (1959) by José Antonio Villarreal, a very early Mexican American narrative published before the beginning of the Chicano movement, the historical migration of the family patriarch to the United States in the wake of the Mexican Revolution is just a prelude to the main focus of the novel, which is about the tensions of assimilation and cultural preservation that ultimately drive the Rubio family apart.

New Migrations and Transnationalism

The last two decades of Latina/o literary production certainly continue to narrate the draw of the United States as a destination for immigrants;

indeed, in many cases this aspect of migration is only magnified in recent texts. In Graciela Limón's novel *The River Flows North* (2009), a coyote-led group of migrants from Mexico and Central America share their stories propelling migration, including accounts of grueling poverty, economic displacement due to competition from U.S. corn imports, the suppression of the Zapatista movement, and the pull of the mythical American Dream, all urging them North. The migrants are following *la Ocho* [Highway 8], which will "take them to steady jobs and the good life"; the migrant version of the American Dream narrative is that "Life would be hard for a time, [but] ... there would be shelter, maybe a little house, and soon a family" (38). The novel thus becomes a collective representation of the forces driving the movement of people, which is repeatedly represented through the image of the river: "The flow of people moves to where jobs wait" (2–3). As one character Doña Encarnación, describes it, "At first it was only a trickle of people, many of them who said they came from such distant places as Guatemala and El Salvador ... in constant movement, always al norte. In time the trickle became a river that flowed north, most of those people headed for the United States" (99; 101). Like a river, migration is depicted in Limón's novel as a natural and to some degree uncontrollable force that cannot be contained by nation-state borders or legislation and that, furthermore, simply reverses the historical flows southward of prior migrations.

Helena María Viramontes's novel *Under the Feet of Jesus* (1995) recounts the life of a family of migrant workers as they follow the harvest season from crop to crop in order to survive. But unlike earlier Chicano/a literature with farmworkers as its subject – such as Tomás Rivera's classic text *... y no se lo tragó la tierra* (1971; translated as *And the Earth Did Not Devour Him* ...) – the community of workers in Viramontes's novel is apparently composed of both U.S. citizens and undocumented immigrants, with a deliberate textual ambiguity about characters' legal statuses. The mother, Petra, for example, worries about "la migra" (60–61), while the young, adolescent protagonist Estrella tries "to remember which side she was on and which side of the wire mesh she was safe in" (59–60), suggesting that she and her family might be undocumented. It is only near the novel's conclusion that it is revealed that she and her siblings are actually U.S. citizens, with birth certificates concealed under a statue of Jesus to prove it (166). The very care with which these particular "documents" are treated by Estrella's mother suggests their importance for the family members, who are on some level aware that they might be called upon to prove their right to be here. The ambiguity and confusion underscore the ways in which Latina/o migrant workers are regarded as foreigners who are excluded from narratives of American belonging, no matter what their actual legal status. This particular complication seriously undermines a notion that immigration, arrival, and citizenship are the first steps in a "Dream" of achievement.

Beginning in the 1990s, a wave of Latina-Caribbean writers also considerably altered the landscape of Latina/o literature by thematizing recent waves of migration from Cuba, the Dominican Republic, and Puerto Rico. Most notably, Julia Alvarez's *How the García Girls Lost Their Accents* (1991) and Cristina García's *Dreaming in Cuban* (1992), as well as, to a somewhat lesser extent, Achy Obejas's debut collection of short stories *We Came All the Way From Cuba So You Could Dress Like This?* (1994), brought attention to the narratives of what Rubén Rumbaut has termed the "1.5 generation," those who immigrated as children to the United States with their parents, as well as shifting attention to Caribbean migratory circuits (65). In Dominican American writer Angie Cruz's novel *Let It Rain Coffee* (2006), outmigration is a recognized and accepted fact of Dominican life. Headlines in New York remind immigrant Dominicans of both the frequency and the potential costs of migration:

> U.S. LURES DOMINICANS TO THE CRUEL SEA
> DOMINICANS FIND BACK DOOR TO NEW YORK IN PUERTO RICO
> ANOTHER NATIVE GOES HOME TO DOMINICAN REPUBLIC IN COFFIN (25).

The implication in all these cases is that the outward flow of migration toward the United States cannot be staunched.

Yet, all the texts above are insistently transnational rather than unidirectional in their sensibilities, and pose some significant challenges to prior progress narratives of arrival followed by assimilation and achievement. In Alvarez's and García's debut novels, both authors stress the perseverance of transnational ties marked by return visits home and even the possibilities of return migration. Alvarez's *García Girls* opens with Yolanda (a transparent author figure, Yolanda's nickname is "Yo" or "I") returning "home" to the Dominican Republic as an adult for a visit and contemplating whether she will stay there to live; in Alvarez's sequel of sorts, *¡Yo!* (1997), the same character is featured in multiple stories that take place in the Dominican Republic. García's *Dreaming in Cuban* ends with Cuban exile Lourdes Puente and her daughter Pilar returning to Cuba and to Lourdes's mother Celia (who stayed in Cuba) for a visit; the return trip is meant to reconcile Lourdes to her traumatic past at the hands of Castro's rebels and to reconnect Pilar to a lost Cuba that she knew only as a young child. The trip, however, makes Pilar realize (in one of the most often cited passages from the novel) that she belongs in New York, "not instead of here [Cuba], but more than here" (236); the return journey ends with her helping her Cuban cousin Ivanito leave Cuba by way of the Peruvian Embassy, in what will become known as the "Marielitos" exodus of 1980. In both Alvarez and García, travel back and forth from the place of origin marks a much more transnational sensibility than was evident in narratives of unidirectional immigration, assimilation, and "ethnic" existence played out within the boundaries of the United States.

Esmeralda Santiago is a writer often discussed in terms of her embrace – at least to a certain degree – of an "American Dream" narrative of economic and educational uplift. In her first and still most often cited memoir, *When I Was Puerto Rican* (1994), Santiago details a life of both rural and urban poverty in Puerto Rico until her mother left her father to bring the children to New York. While life in New York is hardly a paradise or even a safe haven for the young Negi (short for Negrita, Santiago's nickname as a child), and while the adolescent Negi is subjected to predatory encounters, educational discrimination (the principal assumes she is unintelligent because she does not speak fluent English and therefore places her in a remedial classroom), and the continuing shame of poverty in the face of the welfare system, she does manage to earn admission to The High School of Performing Arts in New York – and eventually, the epilogue tells us, to Harvard – thus reaffirming a narrative of ultimate triumph over hardships and obstacles. Indeed, as more than one reading has pointed out, in the memoir's prologue Santiago describes turning away from the guavas of her childhood, despite their nostalgic value, toward the apples and pears of her adulthood – thus underscoring the title's suggestion that she *was* Puerto Rican but is no longer.

Santiago's memoir is complicated, however, in that it seems to highlight the notion that Puerto Rico was always already infused with the influence of U.S. culture and economy. In other words, the memoir suggests that Santiago's childhood in Puerto Rico was already in some sense "transnational," even while the narrating persona Negi seems quite committed to the notion of discrete and non-overlapping national identities, with Puerto Rico and the United States represented as separate and bounded even when the narrative itself shows how they seep into each other. The same dynamic is true of Alvarez's *How the García Girls Lost Their Accents* and García's *Dreaming in Cuban*. In *García Girls*, American beauty magazines are found in the homes of the wealthy but spark the dreams of the domestic servants, who fantasize about shedding the trappings of service to start new lives in New York. ("Yo tiro la cuchara / Yo tiro el tenedor / Yo tiro to' lo' plato' / Y me voy pa' Nueva York" [257]). American toys from F.A.O. Schwartz are brought home from traveling Dominicans as seemingly marvelous gifts for children, thus beginning early on the cultivation of desire for U.S. products. In *Dreaming in Cuban*, the effect of the U.S. presence in Cuba is felt in the fault lines dividing those with ties to U.S. business and those who are aligned with a nationalist Cuban vision, even prior to Castro's revolution.

Circular and Global Migrations

Other writers have ushered in a new transnational sensibility by depicting repeating returns to the home country or actual return migration. In Cuban American writer Achy Obejas's novel *Days of Awe* (2001), the narrator, Ale, works as a translator who makes repeated visits to Cuba, becoming increasingly reconnected to her Cuban history and heritage, as well as to Cuban nationals and their current lives, through her return travels. In Sandra Cisneros's short story "Woman Hollering Creek" (1991), from her collection by the same name, the main character Cleofilas travels north to the United States with her husband, but flees the oppressive and abusive marriage to return south to Mexico to live with her father and brothers. In Luis Alberto Urrea's *Into the Beautiful North* (2009), a group of migrants embark on a quest to the United States to find Mexican men to repopulate their village, which has been decimated by the outmigration of the male population. Thus the quest is by definition a circular one, in which migration north is conjoined with migration "home."

Several contemporary Latino/a writers also reach back to historical movements that were more circuitous or complex – indeed, more "global" – trajectories than simple, one-way immigration. Alvarez's novel *In the Name of Salomé* (2000), about the Dominican national poet Salomé Ureña, reveals that Salomé's husband received his medical training in France and eventually was repeatedly exiled from (and returned to) his home country; Salomé's daughter Camilla teaches at Vassar College in the United States, but eventually goes to Cuba, inspired by Castro's revolution. Alvarez's novel *Saving the World* (2006) intertwines the narrative of an expedition from Spain to bring a smallpox vaccine to the New World – via orphan boys serving as live carriers – with a philanthropic medical project from the United States to the Dominican Republic for the treatment of AIDS in a health center. Cristina García's novel *Monkey Hunting* (2003) shifts the much more common emphasis in prior Cuban American literature from a focus on migration *out* of Cuba (to the United States) to antecedent migration circuits *into* Cuba. One of the novel's characters, Chen Pan, the forefather of the family portrayed in the novel, comes from China to Cuba under the impression that he will be paid for his labor. Once there, he is enslaved, but escapes and weds an Afro-Cuban slave, Lucrecia, whom he frees through purchase. Their descendants migrate to the United States (and from there to Vietnam during the war) but also back to China. In these cases and others, contemporary writers are challenging the construction of the United States as the final destination or "dream" of a one-directional migration from the Latin American country of origin.

In Achy Obejas's novel *Days of Awe*, the United States is again decentered from the more expected immigrant narrative as the point of final destination; instead, Cuba itself is a palimpsest of much older migrations, including those of the Jewish diaspora. Thus the sense of unbelonging and forced performances of assimilation and accommodation faced by immigrants in the United States is shown to have its historical precedent in the Jews who overtly became Christian while clandestinely practicing their faith in Cuba. In all these cases, migration across oceans and land borders, rather than life-long residence within a geographically bounded nation, is represented as the fundamental pattern of human existence.

Versions of the American Dream

Narratives of migration that do involve the United States as "destination point" increasingly contest and question the "American Dream" achievement narrative, underscoring the ways in which the United States fails to live up to its ideals or to this promised future. Limón's *The River Flows North* highlights the fact that the migrants, referred to as "dreamers" because they make the perilous journey across the border in search of dreams of various kinds, so frequently never reach their goal (either geographical or metaphorical); "the road that takes them to a better life" bears the double meaning suggestive of both economic prosperity in the United States and the peace and painlessness of death (1). The spirits of those who have died attempting to cross the border "stay behind with their dreams of the good life, and they haunt the pathway that might have taken them to *la Ocho*" (4). While the policies of Operation Gatekeeper and border militarization are not directly implicated in Limón's *The River Flows North*, the focus on migrant deaths suggests the ways in which restrictive immigration policies have closed the formerly "open doors" to immigrants and turned their dreams into nightmares. In Limón's rendering, then, border crossing deaths are a visceral reminder of the ways in which, for many, the promise of the American Dream itself has failed.

Cuban fictions of arrival tend to be somewhat less overtly contestatory of the possibilities of success in the United States, thanks to an easier reception on the whole, but even they can be deeply aware of the ways in which a new "American" existence is circumscribed by the treatment of Latinos as foreign "others." Achy Obejas's short story "We Came All the Way From Cuba So You Could Dress Like This?" (1994), from her collection of the same name, is self-conscious about the privileged access routes of Cuban immigration. The narrator, who arrives in the United States as a child, recalls that "this is 1963, and no Cuban claiming political asylum actually gets turned away" (113), but nonetheless she still remembers the sting of exclusion, "things that can't be told," that relegate her and her family to the edges of a national narrative (124). The old Cuban exiles of Ana Menéndez's story "In Cuba I Was A German Shepherd" (2001), also from her collection of the same name, play dominoes in a park in Miami with Dominican immigrants and tell jokes, many of them bitter. The punch line of the title joke, for instance – uttered by a "mutt" trying to pick up a poodle – points attention to how status has been deflated by migration from Cuba to the United States in a trajectory that moves opposite to the presumptions of the American success story. All four men understand themselves to be reduced to the status of spectacle, akin to animals in a zoo, for the tourists who drive through the park.

Several critics have noted the ongoing persistence in Dominican American literature – one might even say obsession – with the looming figure of dictator Rafael Trujillo, who controlled the Dominican Republic from 1930 to 1961; as Vanessa Pérez Rosario writes in *Hispanic Caribbean Literature of Migration*, "During the twentieth century Dominican literature has been particularly concerned with the Trujillo dictatorship" even decades after his assassination (13). Trujillo is inscribed as the direct or indirect cause of Dominican migration in much Dominican American literature, including Alvarez's *How the García Girls Lost Their Accents* and Junot Díaz's Pulitzer Prize–winning *The Brief Wondrous Life of Oscar Wao* (2007). Some recent Dominican American literature, however, illustrate the diversity of migration pulls. Díaz's collection of short stories, *Drown*, represents the Dominican patriarch as coming to the United States, at least ostensibly, to make a better life for his family on the island. Yet the father's precise motivations are unclear, since he forgets and (temporarily) abandons his Dominican family in pursuit of the American Dream, beginning a new family in his new land. Papi's absence is the haunting presence of several of the stories in *Drown*, characterizing the ways in which economic outmigration becomes encoded as abandonment of home and family; as John Riofrio points out, the opening story of the collection, "Ysrael," reveals "an important detail about Dominican life: the poverty which plagues the island has created a situation in which survival depends upon fathers leaving the island to try and carve out a better life for themselves and their families ... [leaving] an entire generation of Dominican boys forced to grow up without fathers" (26).

In Angie Cruz's novel *Let It Rain Coffee*, a Dominican woman named Esperanza dreams of going to Dallas, which she knows by way of the popular 1980s television series. She travels to Puerto Rico by *yola*, leaving her family behind in the Dominican Republic, replicating the theme of familial migration as abandonment, although eventually her husband joins her in New York. Later, Esperanza points out to her father-in-law, "How else would you have survived in that campo without us sending checks back home every month?" (48), underscoring the transnational existence of those participating in the newest migration circuits and perhaps even stretching the geographical boundaries of the American Dream. (When there *are* no remittances from the United States, desertion is often assumed, as in Reyna Grande's *Across a Hundred Mountains*). Even after his arrival in the United States the father-in-law, Santo, dreams of going "back home" for a visit (47), but – as with some of the characters in Francisco Goldman's *The Ordinary Seaman* – his journey "home" becomes a metaphor for his actual death (77–78).

Francisco Goldman's 1997 novel depicts a crew of men recruited from various Central American countries to serve aboard the *Urus*, a ship under Panamanian registry docked at the Brooklyn harbor. The ship, however, turns out to be unusable, so the men are caught in a watery limbo where there is no transnational movement at all as they conduct repairs without pay. In some ways, then, this novel depicts the opposite of global migration flows; capturing the stillborn dreams of its crewmen, the grounded ship symbolizes stagnation and limbo in a nationless existence of non-belonging. The men cannot go off board since they will be "illegal" in the United States, and they cannot return home (except through death). The promise of the American Dream calling immigrants to its shores has – like the bereft hulk of ship at novel's end – been turned on its side (see Caminero-Santangelo, "Central Americans").

Indeed, in contemporary Latina/o literature that recounts Central American migrations of the 1980s and early 1990s, the promised American "Dream" is a vision decimated by the U.S. involvement in repressive regimes of terror from which many migrants were fleeing, as well as by the U.S. denial of the vast majority of asylum applications from nations whose governments, however violent, were supported by the United States. Helena María Viramontes's short story "Cariboo Café," from the collection *The Moths and Other Stories* (1985), was one of the earliest of this genre, representing the intersecting stories of a Central American woman, who flees to the United States after her young son disappears at the hands of state terror, and two young siblings (of unspecified but probably Mexican origin) who become lost in Los Angeles while their undocumented parents work. Viramontes's story is notable for the way in which it brings together multiple forces driving migration, including the economics of exploited labor that pulls unauthorized migrants from South of the border but also the oppressive governments, backed by the U.S. government, that served as a "push" for so many refugees who were then unable to obtain asylum in the United States. The two storylines intersect with the third, that of a short-order cook in a café serving a largely undocumented clientele from the nearby factory; the cook's own son was killed in Vietnam. The intersection of the three narrative lines and perspectives – with open-ended pronouns colliding against each other and shifting in their references at the story's conclusion – underscores how violent U.S. foreign policies combined with heightened nativism and restrictive immigration laws "at home" have resulted in "lost" children in all three cases. In Graciela Limón's novel *In Search of Bernabé* (1993), the Salvadoran Civil War and assassination of Archbishop Romero result in a chaos in which the protagonist, Luz Declano, loses her son Bernabé; she travels to Mexico, across the border to the United States and back in search of her son. Once again, the circular migratory route undermines the notion that the United States is the final, desired destination, instead serving to highlight the repressive Salvadoran regime that assassinated its citizens with the tacit support and approval of the U.S. government.

Demetria Martínez's novel *Mother Tongue* (1994) examines the Sanctuary Movement (though it is never named as such within the novel), and its effort to come to the aid of these Central American refugees, both by providing literal sanctuary within the United States (since most asylum applications were rejected, many refugees were "illegally" present and subject to deportation) and by offering a platform for migrant refugees to tell their stories, which often implicated U.S. cooperation with the repressive regimes the refugees were fleeing. In order to carry out his own work on behalf of the Salvadoran resistance, José Luis eventually returns "home," in yet another example of circular migration that rejects the "immigration, assimilation, and American Dream" paradigm.

In Mario Bencastro's novel *Odyssey to the North* (1998), a variety of Central American immigrants find their way north, where they work together in a restaurant in Washington, DC, making use of the nation's capital as a symbol for a narrative unrealized in the lives of these characters. One character laments, 'Who would want to leave his family to go to a strange country? ... "No one, not even a crazy person. Unless you're in a desperate situation, like I am" (26). The question invokes what some have termed the right *not* to migrate, emphasizing the ways in which dire economic or political conditions force migration; the ability to make a sustainable living while remaining in one's home country is in fact a privilege only available to some. Another character in the novel, a Salvadoran woman, is deported to her home country because she fails to fit the criteria for asylum laid out by U.S. law ("The Oppressed" 65). Specifically, she cannot establish that she is individually at risk of persecution, since the entire country is subject to such persecution. As Susan Coutin has elaborated, Central American asylum cases were challenged by the difficulty of reshaping a situation of generalized repression and terror into a narrative that fit the requirements of U.S. asylum law, which required evidence of *individual* persecution.

Héctor Tobar's novel *The Tattooed Soldier* (1998) follows the current trajectories, interspersed with histories told in flashback, of a Guatemalan death squad soldier who has migrated to Los Angeles, and that of a young former student, also a migrant to southern California, whose family the soldier murdered. The American Dream has most clearly failed Antonio, the former student, who finds himself evicted from his apartment in Los Angeles and living in a makeshift, ramshackle "community" of the homeless, many of them other Latino and African American men. The horrifying living conditions and lack of availability of a sanitary water supply remind him of the *colonias* for peasants in Guatemala, suggesting that for the poor and disenfranchised of society, not much has changed. Indeed, the Los Angeles riots triggered by the Rodney King verdict in 1992, which take place near the conclusion of the novel, signal the widespread and barely controlled outrage over poverty, deprivation, and disenfranchisement. But even for the soldier, Longoria, trained in part by the U.S. military at the School of the Americas and Fort Bragg, the United States proves to be a hollow dream; he imagined order and cleanliness (because of his military training), but finds that the chaos and disorder caused by poverty exists in Los Angeles as well, which confuses him.

Undocumented Immigration

In the two decades since the escalation of border militarization, raids, and deportations during the late 1990s and early 2000s, writers have also turned their attention to the trauma of undocumented immigration on families and communities left behind in home countries, on communities in the United States who fear deportation of their members, and on the undocumented migrants in the process of their migration. In Ana Castillo's novel *The Guardians* (2007), an undocumented man goes missing while migrating between Mexico and the United States, leaving behind his undocumented teenaged son, in the care of the boy's aunt (the man's sister) who has become a U.S. citizen. The novel suggests that the trauma of disappearance affects both the undocumented and "documented" alike, including those whose families have been U.S. citizens for generations. In Reyna Grande's *Across a Hundred Mountains* (2006), a father migrates to the United States but disappears, leaving his family back in Mexico assuming his abandonment of them and therefore leaving them vulnerable to malicious gossip and exploitation. Years later his daughter, now grown, comes to the United States to look for him, where she eventually learns the truth about his death. But the disappearance and loss, coupled with the lack of knowledge about what happened to him, has caused irreparable damage to the family.

In the play *Detained in the Desert* (2011), Josefina López targets Arizona's SB 1070, a law that purported to crack down on illegal immigration but came under fire for encouraging racial profiling by state authorities. A Hispanic woman, Sandi Belen, who is a U.S. citizen, is stopped, "profiled," and put under removal proceedings, while her white Canadian boyfriend, who is undocumented, is allowed to pass a checkpoint unquestioned. The play is also a scathing critique of virulent anti-immigrant rhetoric for inciting oppression and racism. A racist talk radio announcer, Lou Becker, who hosts the show *Take Back America*, has a change of heart in the course of the play when he himself is kidnapped and abandoned in the desert by Latino men avenging the death of their brother in a hate crime. The play works to counter the expectations addressed and inflamed by Arizona's SB 1070 and similar anti-immigrant legislation in other states clearly targeting Latinos; the only actual immigrants in the play are the Canadian undocumented boyfriend and the white radio host, who turns out to be a naturalized citizen originally from Scotland.

Julia Alvarez, whose previous fictions focused on Dominican characters and migrations, turns in her young adult novel *Return to Sender* (2009) to the plight of a young, adolescent undocumented girl whose father has been hired to work on a farm in Vermont; as the novel opens, her mother, who returned to Mexico to visit her own dying mother, has gone missing on her journey back north across the border. The novel, told through the alternating perspectives of the Mexican girl and the teenaged boy whose family owns the farm where her father has been hired, tries to redefine "America" for its young readers according to the more expansive and inclusive vision of its ideals, rather than according to the dominant nativism of current anti-immigrant discourse. Thus, during a visit to Washington, DC near the novel's conclusion, Mari realizes that "this was not just the capital of one country, but the home of everyone who loves freedom" (245), deploying the ideal of "freedom" as a justificatory trope for the expansion of the American Dream.

As this sheer variety of literary production establishes, U.S. Latina/o writers have moved well beyond a binary of country of origin/country of destination, or a dynamic of cultural preservation versus assimilation and cultural loss. Return migrations, transnational and global migration circuits, and tangled new identity formations that are more complex than mere (dual) "hybridity" are the mark of the last two decades of literature representing the movement of peoples. At the same time, since the "American Dream" narrative relies on the premise of re-rooting and re-territorializing, many Latino/a writers depicting migratory subjects are extending a literary legacy in which the dominant narrative of the "American Dream" is exposed as one that is available only to a very few.

Works Cited

Alvarez, Julia. *How the García Girls Lost Their Accents*. 1991. New York: Plume / Penguin, 1992.
　¡Yo! Chapel Hill, NC: Algonquin Books of Chapel Hill, 1997.
　In the Name of Salomé. Chapel Hill, NC: Algonquin Books, 2000.
　Saving the World. Chapel Hill, NC: Algonquin Books, 2006.
　Return to Sender. New York: Alfred A. Knopf, 2009.
Bencastro, Mario. *Odyssey to the North*. Trans. Susan Giersbach Rascon. Houston, TX: Arte Público Press, 1998. Published in original Spanish as *Odisea del Norte* in 1999.
Caminero-Santangelo, Marta. "Central Americans in the City: Goldman, Tobar, and the Question of Panethnicity." *LIT: Literature, Interpretation, Theory* 20.3 (July 2009): 173–95.
Castillo, Ana. *The Guardians*. New York: Random House, 2007.
Cisneros, Sandra. *Woman Hollering Creek*. New York: Random House, 1991.
Constable, Pamela and Scott Clement. "Hispanics Often Lead the Way in their Faith in the American Dream, Poll Finds." *Washington Post*, January 30, 2014. Available online, http://campaign.r20.constantcontact.com/render?ca=f290e2f1-6fdd-4bb3-a782-6e22897817a0&c=23af9190-32a8-11e3-80df-d4ae52753a3b&ch=24925070-32a8-11e3-81f8-d4ae52753a3b, accessed February 1, 2014.
Coutin, Susan Bibler. "The Oppressed, the Suspect, and the Citizen: Subjectivity in Competing Accounts of Political Violence." *Law and Social Inquiry* 26.1 (Winter 2001): 63–94.
Cruz, Angie. *Let It Rain Coffee*. New York: Simon & Schuster, 2006.
Díaz, Junot. *The Brief Wondrous Life of Oscar Wao*. New York: Riverhead, 2007.
García, Cristina. *Dreaming in Cuban*. New York: Ballantine Books, 1992.
　Monkey Hunting. New York: Alfred A. Knopf, 2003.
　A Handbook to Luck. New York: Alfred A. Knopf, 2007.
Goldman, Francisco. *The Ordinary Seaman*. New York: Grove Press, 1997.
Grande, Reyna. *Across a Hundred Mountains*. New York: Atria, 2006.
Limón, Graciela. *In Search of Bernabé*. Houston, TX: Arte Público Press, 1993.
　The River Flows North. Houston, TX: Arte Público Press, 2009.
López, Josefina. *Detained in the Desert and Other Plays*. Dillon, MT: WPR Publishing, 2011.
Martínez, Demetria. *Mother Tongue*. New York: Ballantine, 1994.
Menéndez, Ana. *In Cuba I Was a German Shepherd*. New York: Grove Press, 2001.

Obejas, Achy. *We Came All The Way From Cuba So You Could Dress Like This?* Pittsburgh, PA: Cleis Press, 1994.
Days of Awe. New York: Ballantine Books, 2001.
Rivera, Tomás. *... y no se lo tragó la tierra / ... And the Earth Did Not Devour Him.* Trans. Evangelina Vigil-Piñón. 1971 (orig. Spanish). Houston, TX: Arte Publico Press, 1992.
Rosario, Vanessa Pérez. *Hispanic Caribbean Literature of Migration.* New York: Palgrave Macmillan, 2010.
Rumbaut, Rubén and Alejandro Portes, ed. *Ethnicities: Children of Immigrants in America.* Berkeley: University of California Press, 2001.
Santiago, Esmeralda. *When I Was Puerto Rican.* New York: Vintage, 1994.
Thomas, Piri. *Down These Mean Streets.* 1967: New York: Vintage / Random House, 1991.
Tobar, Héctor. *The Tattooed Soldier.* New York: Penguin, 1998.
Valdez, Luis. *Zoot Suit and Other Plays.* Performed 1978. Houston, TX: Arte Público Press, 1992.
Villarreal, José Antonio. *Pocho.* 1959. New York: Anchor Books, 1989.
Viramontes, Helena María. *The Moths and Other Stories.* Houston, TX: Arte Público Press, 1985.
Under the Feet of Jesus. Penguin, 1995.

INDEX

Abingdon Square (María Irene Fornés 1988), 101
abolition, 13, 19
"Absence" (Pedro Juan Soto 1956), 50–51
Acardi, Millicent, 158
Acevedo, David Caleb, 190
Acevedo, John "Chance," 152
Acheson, Dean, 72, 73
Acosta, Grisel, 158
Acosta, Oscar "Zeta," xix, 60, 168, 176n2
Across a Hundred Mountains (Reyna Grande 2006), xxi, 240, 242–243
Acuña, Rudy, 153
administrative colonialism, xxviii, 52
Adventures of Juan Chicaspatas, The (Rodolfo Anaya 1985), 107
aesthetics of politics, 58, 64. See also cultural nationalism
affirmative action, 108–109
African Americans, 37, 131, 195–196
African American women, xxx
Afro-Latinos, 152, 196, 199, 205
Agosin, Marjorie, 149
Agüero Sisters, The (Cristina García 1997), 84
AIDS crisis, xxx, 77–78, 93, 108, 206n3
Alarcón, Francisco X., 157–158
Alarcón, Norma, 96–97
Albizu Campos, Pedro, 44, 58–59, 62
Aldama, Frederick Luis, 132, 134, 141, 163, 182, 188, 189
Alemán, Jesse, 183
Algarín, Miguel, xx, 67–68, 104, 151, 180, 188
Alire Saénz, Benjamin, 154, 181
Allatson, Paul, xxxi–xxxii
Allen, Elizabeth, 137
Allende, Salvador, 73

Alliance for Progress, 75
All-Union Day of the Shock Worker, The (Edwin Torres 2001), 138
Almaguer, Tomás, 182, 189
Alurista, xx, 64, 104, 148, 154
Alvarado, Lisa, 152
Alvarez, Julia: and 1990s, xxxi; and bicultural, bilingual selves, 170; on class and immigration, 119; and Cold War themes, 79–80, 81, 82, 86, 87; and education, 94; fiction of, xx; and invisibility, 124–125n41; and migration narratives, 231, 235–236, 237, 239, 243; and multicultural canon, 111; personal essays of, 172–173; poetry of, 149
Alvarez de Toledo, José, 4
Always Running (Luis Rodriguez 1993), xxi, 171–172
Ambientes: New Queer Latino Writing (2011), 190
American Dream: Latina/o perspectives on, 26–29; and migration narratives, 234, 236–237, 238–242, 243, 244; and minority literature, 231–232; and 1990s, 119; and Puerto Rican diaspora, 45, 48–49; and reverse migration, 168; underside of, 108; and U.S. Latina/os, 112
American Renaissance, 8
American Studies, xxiv–xxv, 17
América's Dream (Esmeralda Santiago 1997), xxi
Americas Review, The, 95
Ameriscopia (Edwin Torres 2014), 138
Amigoland (Oscar Casares 2009), xxii, 139–140
"A Mongo Affair" (Miguel Algarín), 188

247

Anaya, Rudolfo: and anthologies, 98, 99; fiction of, xix, 60, 67, 107, 233; and mainstream publishing, 91; memoir of, 109; on Puerto Rican–Chicana/o relations, 68
Andrews, George Reid, 195–196
And the Earth Did Not Devour Him (Tomás Rivera 1987), 105
And We Sold the Rain (Rosario Santos), 115
Anna in the Tropics (Nilo Cruz 2003), xxi
Another Land (Richard Vasquez 1982), 107
anthologies, 98–100
anti-Black racism, 196
anti-immigrant rhetoric, 232, 243
anti-Mexican sentiment, 37
Anzaldúa, Gloria: and autobiography, 174; and border poetics, 153–155, 167–168; and education, 94; as essayist, 172; and intersectionality, 92; and Latina identity, 96; and *mestiza* consciousness, 215–216; and 1990s, xx, 109; and queer-of-color critique, 179; and queer scholarship, 182, 188; on sexism and homophobia, xxx
Aragón, Francisco, 149
Arango Manzano, Pepilla, 14n1
Arbenz, Jacobo, 73, 85
Archila, William, 88
Archways of Life (Mercedes de Acosta 1921), 187
Arenas, Reinaldo, xxi, 77–78, 87, 118–119, 188
Argentina, 74, 115
Arias, Arturo, 198
Arizona's SB 1070, 232, 243
Arte Público Press, 91, 95, 199
Art of Exile, The (William Archila 2009), 88
Asalto al tiempo (Giannina Braschi 1981), 187
ASCO, xix, 189
"A Son of the Tropics" (María Cristina Mena), 30
Atomik Aztex (Sesshu Foster 2005), xxi, 133–134
"A Town Sets a Black Man on Fire" (José Martí 1892), 21–22
Augenbraum, Harold, 188
autobiography, xxxii, 161–163, 171–172. *See also* life writing
Autobiography of a Brown Buffalo, The (Oscar Zeta Acosta 1972), xix, 60, 168
Ayala, Naomi, 156
Aztlán, 66, 98–99. *See also* Chicano Movement

Aztlán: An Anthology of Mexican American Literature (Luis Valdez and Stan Steiner 1972), 67
Aztlán: Essays on the Chicano Homeland (1989), 98
Aztlan Libre Press, 158

Babín, María Teresa, 67, 152
Baca, Jimmy Santiago, 104–105, 172
"Backdoor to Eugenics" (Troy Duster), 201
(Bad) Boy Next Door, The (Tony Valenzuela), 181
Bad Boys (Sandra Cisneros 1980), 105
Balaguer, Joaquín, xix, 79–80
"Ballad of Billy Rivera" (Juan Gómez-Quiñones), 151
Banana Wars, 30
Bandido (Luis Valdez 1981), 102
Bantam Books, 67
Barradas, Efraín, 181, 188
Batista, Fulgencio, xix, xxix
Battle of Algiers (Gino Pontecorvo), 62
"Bayaminiña" (Pedro Juan Soto 1956), 48–49
Before Night Falls (Julian Schnabel 2000), 124n40
Before Night Falls (Reinaldo Arenas 1993), xxi, 77–78, 118–119, 188
Bejel, Emilio, 183
Beltrán, Cristina, 57–58
Bencastro, Mario, xxi, 241–242
Ben Oni, Rosebud, 156
Bésame Mucho: New Gay Latino Fiction (Jaime Manrique and Jesse Dorris 1999), 190
Between Dances (Erasmo Guerra 2001), 180
Beyond Stereotypes: The Critical Analysis of Chicana Literature (1985), 98
Beyond the Field: New Latin@ Writing (2014), 151
Bhabba, Homi, 164–165
biculturalism, 164–165
bilingualism, xxix, 168–169
Bilingual Review / La Revista Bilingüe, 95
Bilingual Review Press, 95
Binder, Wolfgang, 100
biracial Latinos, 196, 205
Bird of Paradise: How I Became Latina (Raquel Cepeda 2013), xxii, xxxiii, 198–199, 200–203, 208–209n12
Birds (Lisa Loomer 1986), 102
"Birth of the God of War" (María Cristina Mena), 31

248

INDEX

Black Cuban, Black American (Evelio Grillo), 199
Black Hair (Gary Soto 1985), 106
Black Mesa Poems (Jimmy Santiago Baca 1989), 105
Blackwell, Maylei, 66
Blade Runner (Ridley Scott 1982), 224
Blaine, James G., 22
Blanco, Richard, xxii, 149
Bless Me, Ultima (Rudolfo Anaya 1972), xix, 60, 67, 107, 233
Bloom, Harold, 151
Blue Horse of Madness (Olivia Castellano 1983), 105
Blue Mandolin, Yellow Field (Olivia Castellano 1980), 105
Bodega Dreams (Ernesto Quiñonez 2000), xxi
Border Culture: The Multicultural Paradigm (Guillermo Gómez-Peña 1989), 104
Borderlands/La Frontera (Gloria Anzaldúa 1987): and border poetics, 154; and code switching, 174; and identity, 92; and Latina/o literary studies, 109; and life writing, 167–168, 172–173; publication of, xx; and queer scholarship, 188; and woman-centered poetics, 155
Borderlands literary tradition, 139–140
border militarization, 238
Borders (Pat Mora 1986), 105
Boricua Movement, xxix, xxxii, 52, 59–60, 69n4. *See also* cultural nationalism
Borinquen, 66–67
Borinquen: An Anthology of Puerto Rican Literature (María Teresa Babín and Stan Steiner 1974), 67, 152
Boza, María, 100
bracero program, xviii
Bradstreet, Anne, 186
Braschi, Giannina, xxi, xxxii, 129, 136–137, 187
Brazil, 76
Breaking Boundaries: Latina Writing and Critical Readings (1980), 99
Breath, Eyes, Memory (Edwidge Danticat 1994), xxi, 82
Brickhouse, Anna, 17
Brief Wondrous Life of Oscar Wao, The (Junot Díaz 2007), xxii, 82, 132–133, 239
Brinson Curiel, Barbara, 148, 158
Brito, Manuel, 134
Broadway theater, 103, 116
Broken Eggs (Eduardo Machado 1984), 103

Brooks, Gwendolyn, 57
Brother, I'm Dying (Edwidge Danticat 2007), 83
Brown, John, 199
Brown Berets, 61–62
Brownsville (Oscar Casares 2003), xxi, 139
Brown: The Last Discovery of America (Richard Rodriguez 2002), 167
Brubaker, Rogers, 203–204
Bruce-Novoa, Juan, 99, 148, 181, 189
Burciaga, José Antonio, 103–104, 107, 148, 154
Burton, Henry S., 11
Burunat, Silvia, 152
Bush, George H. W., 93
Bush, George W., 136
By Lingual Wholes (Victor Hernandez Cruz 1982), 106

Caballero (Jovita González and Margaret Eimer/Eve Raleigh 1996), xviii, 38–40, 186
Cajigas, Chris "Chilo," 152
Calderón, Héctor, 100
Calderón de la Barca, 136
caló, 91–92, 153
Calvo, Luz, 189, 194n42
Caminero-Santangelo, Marta, xxxiii–xxxiv, xxxvn13, 130–131
Campo, Rafael, xxi, 180
Campos, Pedro Albizu. *See* Albizu Campos, Pedro
Candelaria, Cordelia, 100
Candelaria, Nash, 107
Canícula: Snapshots of a Girlhood en la Frontera (Norma E. Cantú 1995), xxi, 174
CantoMundo, 156–157, 158
Cantos de adolescencia (Américo Paredes 1934), 150, 151
Cantú, Norma E., xxi, xxxii, 174
Capetillo, Luisa, 51–52, 183–184
Capsule Course in Black Poetry Writing (Gwendolyn Brooks 1975), 57
"Captive" (Pedro Juan Soto 1956), 50
Caracol, 152
¡Caramba! (Nina Marie Martínez 2005), xxi, 140
Caramelo (Sandra Cisneros 2002), xxi
Caraza, Xanath, 156
Cardenas de Dwyer, Carlota, 152
Carey, Mariah, 195
"Cariboo Café" (Helena María Viramontes 1985), 240–241

249

Carmona, Christopher, 154
Carrasco, Barbara, 96
Carraza, Xanath, 149
Casares, Oscar, xxi, xxii, xxxii, 129, 139–140
Castañeda, Antonia, 98
Castellano, Olivia, 94, 105
Castillo, Ana: in Luz María Umpierre's poem, 186; and migration narratives, 70n15, 231, 242; and multicultural canon, 111; in 1980s, xx, xxxi, 91, 97, 108; and 1990s, 120–121; poetry of, 105; and woman-centered poetics, 155
Castro, Fidel, 73, 76, 78, 118, 164
Cave Canem, 157
Celso (Leo Romero 1985), 106
Central America, xxx, 5. *See also specific countries*
Central American migration, xxvii, xxxiii–xxxiv, 240, 241–242
Cepeda, Raquel, xxii, xxxiii, 198–199, 200–201, 204
Cervantes, Angela, 156–157
Cervantes, Lorna Dee, xx, xxx, 65–66, 105, 148, 154
Cesarco Elgin, Laura, 149
Cha Cha Files, The: A Chapina Poética (Maya Chinchilla 2014), 131
Chambers, Henry Kellett, 30
"Champs" (Pedro Juan Soto 1956), 49–50
Changing our Power: An Introduction to Women's Studies (1988), 97
Chants (Pat Mora 1984), 105
charros, 27
Chavarria, Isaac, 154
Chávez, Denise, xx, 91, 94, 103, 106
Chávez, John, 149, 151
Chávez-Silverman, Susana, xxxii, 129, 140, 142n3
Chaviano, Daína, 141
Chiapas, xxxi
Chicago Boys, 115
Chica Lit, 140
Chican@s, 134–135, 139, 148, 149, 153, 156. *See also* Chicana/os
Chicana Lesbians: The Girls Our Mothers Warned Us About (Carla Trujillo 1991), 180, 188, 189–190
Chicana/os, xxxiii–xxxiv, 69n4, 139, 174, 178. *See also* Chican@s; Chicano Movement
Chicana Voices: Intersections of Class, Race and Gender (1986), 99

Chicano Authors: Inquiry by Interview (1980), 99
Chicano in China, A (Rudolfo Anaya 1986), 109
Chicano Literature (1982), 99
Chicano Literature, A Reference Guide (1985), 99
Chicano Movement: and Cold War themes, 76–77; and feminism, 66; and *floricantos*, 148; and Latina/o literature, xxix; and literary settings, 233; and masculinist identification, 65; and poetics, xxxii, 150–151; and poetry, 63–64, 104; symbolism of, 98–99, 134–135. *See also* Aztlán; Chicana/os; cultural nationalism
"Chicano Nationalism: The Key to Unity for La Raza" (Rodolfo "Corky" Gonzales), 63–64
Chicano Nations: The Hemispheric Origins of Mexican American Literature (Marissa López 2011), 69
Chicano Poetry, A Critical Introduction (1986), 100
Chicano Poetry: A Response to Chaos (1982), 99, 148
Chicanos: Antología histórica y literaria (1980), 99
Chicano Struggle, Analysis of Past and Present Efforts (1984), 99
Chicano studies, xxiv, 41–42, 59, 77
Chicano Theater: Themes and Forms (1982), 102
Chicano Voices (Carlota Cardenas de Dwyer), 152
Chile, xxix
Chinchilla, Maya, xxxii, 128, 131
Chinese Exclusion Act (1882), 23
ChismeArte, 95–96
CIA-sponsored coups, xxix
Cinco poetisas cubanas 1935–1969 (1970), 152
Cincuenta lecciones de exilio y desexilio (Gustavo Pérez Firmat 2000), 169
Cisneros, Sandra: and Arte Público Press, 95; and autobiographical fiction, 174; and education, xxx, 94; and Macondo, 156; and Midwest Latina Writers Workshop, 97; and migration narratives, 237; and multicultural canon, 111; in 1980s, 91; in 1980s and 1990s, xx; and 1990s, xxxi, 120; poetry of, 105, 155; short stories of, 106; in 2000s, xxi
City of Night (John Rechy 1963), xix, 182

class: and Afro-Latino-Caribbean-diasporic identity, 82; and HIV/AIDS infection, 206n3; and Internet, xxxiii; and intersectionality, 179; and Latina/os, 231–232; and Latina/o writers, xxviii; and 1990s, 111; and queer Latina/o literature, xxxii; and María Amparo Ruiz de Burton, 10–11; structuration of, xxxii–xxxiii
Clemente Chacón: A Novel (José Antonio Villarreal 1984), 108
Clifford, James, 203–204
code-switching, 91–92, 105, 136, 140, 168–169, 174
Cofer, Judith Ortiz, xx, 94, 95, 105, 108, 161, 165, 166
Cold War: and Cristina García's books, 84–85; and exiles, 75–76; and Guatemala, 81–82; and Latina/o literary studies, xxvii; and Latina/o literature, xxix; and migrant flows, xxiv; and U.S. policy toward Latin America, 72–73
Coll, Ivonne, 187
Collapsible Poetics Theater (Rodrigo Toscano 2007), 134
Colombia, 76
Colombian Gold (Jaime Manrique 1983), 108
Colón, David, 32
Colón, Jesús, 25, 51–52
"Colonel, The" (Carolyn Forché 1978), 87, 88
colonial modernity, 48, 52–53
Columbian Quincentenary, xxiv–xxv, xxxi
Comiendo Lumbre: Eating Fire (Gina Valdés 1986), 105
Compañeras: Latina Lesbians (Juanita Ramos/Juanita Díaz-Cotto 1987), 100, 188, 189–190
compontes, 24–25
Concierto de metal y otras orgías de soledad (Manuel Ramos Otero), 182, 188
Conduct of Life (María Irene Fornés 1985), 101
"Coney Island" (José Martí 1880), 21
Conquest, The (Yxta Maya Murray 2002), 133
Con Safos, 152
Contemporary Chicana Poetry: A Critical Approach to an Emerging Literature (1985), 100
Contemporary Chicano Poetry: An Anthology (1986), 100
ConTinta, 158

Conversaciones: Relatos por padres y madres de hijas lesbianas y hijos gay (Mariana Romo-Carmona 2002), 180
Córdova, Jeanne, 180–181
Córdova, Teresa, 99
Coronado Cuello, Hilario, 154
Corpi, Lucha, xx, 95, 108, 156
Corral, Eduardo, 155
Corrales, Javier, 114–115
Corretjer, Juan Antonio, 25
corridos, 40, 148, 150, 151
Corridos (Luis Valdez 1982), 102
Cortes, Hernán, 65
Cortez, Jaime, 190
Coser y Cantar (Dolores Prida 1981), 103
Cota-Cárdenas, Margarita, 99, 108
Cotera, María, 66, 183, 186
Cotto-Thorner, Guillermo, 26
Country Between Us, The (Carolyn Forché 1981), 87
Coutin, Susan, 242
Crazy Love (Elías Muñoz 1989), 108
Create Dangerously: the Immigrant Artist at Work (Edwidge Danticat 2010), 82–83
Creativity and Criticism: Charting New Frontiers in American Literature (1988), 98
Criticism in the Borderlands (1991), 100
crónica, 140
Crusade for Justice, 61–62, 63, 68
Cruz, Angie, xxi, 231, 235, 239–240
Cruz, Migdalia, 101
Cruz, Nilo, xxi, xxx, 101, 116, 181, 185
Cruz, Victor, 95
Cruz González, José, 101–102
Cruz-Malavé, Arnaldo, 180, 188
Cuatlicue, 31
Cuba: and filibustering expeditions, 5; and independence, 19, 118; and Jewish diaspora, 238; and migration to United States, xxvii, xxx; and Ostend Manifesto, xvii; and repression, 78; and U.S. intervention, xxix; and U.S. relations, xix, xxii; and U.S.-Spanish War, xviii, xxviii
Cuba and His Teddy Bear (Reinaldo Povod 1986), 103
Cuban Americans, xxiv, 92, 118–119, 164, 199. *See also specific writers*
Cuban American Writers: Los Atrevidos (1988), 99
Cuban exiles, 11, 13, 239
Cuban Revolution, xix, 84–85, 118

251

Cuba y los Estados Unidos (José Martí 1889), 20–21
Cuentos Chicanos: A Short Story Anthology (1984), 99
Cuentos: Stories by Latinas (1983), 96
cultural nationalism, 61, 63–65, 68–69, 188–189. *See also* aesthetics of politics; Boricua Movement; Chicano Movement
Culture Clash, 92, 103–104, 131–132
Culture Wars, 93, 94–95
Curandera (Carmen Tafolla 1983), 105
Cyborg Theory, 213–214, 215, 220, 226

Dalleo, Raphael, 132
Danticat, Edwidge, xxi, 82–84, 87
Danube, The (María Irene Fornés 1982), 101
Darío, Rubén, 30
Davis, Allison, 199
Daydí-Tolson, Santiago, 100
Days of Awe (Achy Obejas 2001), 180, 237, 238
Days of Obligation: An Argument with my Mexican Father (Richard Rodriguez), 173
Day the Cisco Kid Shot John Wayne, The (Nash Candelaria 1988), 107
de Acosta, Mercedes, 186–187, 193n29
debt peonage, 27, 39
de Burgos, Julia, xviii, 17, 25, 147, 152
Decade of Hispanic Literature, A: An Anniversary Anthology (1982), 95
decimas, 149, 150
Deck of Deeds (Rodrigo Toscano 2012), 134–135
declamación, 147, 150
"Declaration 1968" (Miguel Piñero), 63
de Hoyos, Angela, 108, 157
de la Luz, Caridad "La Bruja," 152
de la Selva, Salomón, xviii, 17, 18–19, 20, 22, 29–31, 32
de Leon, Nephtali, 148
Deleuze, Gilles, 8
Delgado, Abelardo, 148
Delgado, Lalo, 152
Delia's Song (Lucha Corpi 1989), xx, 108
Delille, Jacques (L'Abbé), 3
de los Reyes, Guillermo, 188
Denver Youth Conference, 68
Desde el EpiCentro: An Anthology of US Central American Poetry (2007), 131
Desert Blood: The Juarez Murders (Alicia Gaspar de Alba 2006), 180
Detained in the Desert (Josefina López 2010), xxii, 243

Dew Breaker, The (Edwidge Danticat 2004), 82–84
Diálogo, 157
Diarios de motocicleta (The Motorcycle Diaries, Walter Salles 2004, screenplay by José Rivera), 138
"Diary of a Martyr" (Juan Clemente Zenea 1871), 14
diaspora: Central American, xx; concept of, xxxiii; Cuban, xix; Hispaniolan, xxvn8; Jewish, 238; Latin American, 18, 149; Latin "diaspora," 198–204, 209n14; in literature, xxiii; Mexican, 41–42; Puerto Rican, xxviii, xxvn10, 25, 31, 45–52, 60; queer, 179; and status identifications, 112–113
Díaz, Junot: and Cold War themes, 82–84; and Dominican American life stories, 119, 170; and education, 111; and fukú, 200; and invisibility, 124–125n41; and migration narratives, 231, 239; and 1990s, xxi, xxxi; and postrace aesthetics, 132–133; and Pulitzer, xxii, 116, 181, 191n10; on Spanglish, 206n4
Díaz, Porfirio, 18
Díaz-Cotto, Juanita, 188
Díaz Guerra, Alirio, xviii
"Dictatorships and Double Standards" (Jeane Kirkpatrick 1979), 74
Dictionary of Literary Biography, The (1989), 99
digital natives, xxxiii
Dirty Girls Social Club, The (Alisa Valdes-Rodriguez 2003), xxi
disidentification, xxxi–xxxii, 130, 141n1
Disidentifications: Queers of Color and the Performance of Politics (José Esteban Muñoz 1999), 179
Disparities, The (Rodrigo Toscano 2002), 134
DNA testing, 201–202, 207n8, 208n9, 208–209n12
Dominican Republic: and migration to United States, xxiv, xxvii, xxx; and Puerto Rican communities, xxxiii–xxxiv; and U.S. intervention, xviii, xxix, 79–80; and U.S. occupation, xix. *See also specific writers*
Don Chipote, Or When Parrots Breast-Feed (Daniel Venegas 1928), 25, 26–27
Douglass, Frederick, 199
Down These Mean Streets (Piri Thomas 1967), xix, 59–60, 171–172, 199–200, 233

INDEX

Downtown (Jimmy Santiago Baca 1981), 105
Dreaming in Cuban (Cristina García 1992), xx, 84, 118–119, 235–236
Drown (Junot Díaz 1996), xxi, 82, 119, 170, 239
Du Bois, W. E. B., 199, 205
Dufoix, Stéphane, 203
Dunbar, Paul Laurence, 199
Dúran, Isabel, xxxii, xxxvn9
Duster, Troy, 201
Duvalier regimes, 74, 76, 82–84

Ebed, Sheryl Carolina, 158
Editorial Bilingüe / Bilingual Review, 91
Eimer, Margaret, xviii, 186
El Bronx Remembered: A Novella and Stories (Nicholasa Mohr 1986), 106
El Cóndor and Other Stories (Sabine Ulibarrí 1988), 107
El Coro: A Chorus of Latino and Latina Poetry (1997), 152
El cuento de la mujer del mar (Manuel Ramos Otero), 182
Elements of San Joaquin, The (Gary Soto 1977), xix, 106
El Filibusterismo (José Rizal 1891), 22–23
El Grito: A Journal of Contemporary Mexican American Thought, 67, 152
El imperio de los sueños (Giannina Braschi 1988), 136, 187
Eliot, T. S., 31
Elizondo, Sergio, 148
El laúd del desterrado (1858), xvii, 7, 12–13, 14
El libro de la muerte (Manuel Ramos Otero 1985), 185
El Louie (José Montoya 1970), xix
El Mensagero Semanal (Philadelphia and New York 1828-29), 6, 8–9
El Mundo Zurdo, 96
El Museo del Barrio, 152
El Plan Espiritual de Aztlan (Rodolfo "Corky" Gonzales, Alurista, and Juan Gómez-Quiñones), 64
El reino de la espiga (Víctor Fragoso 1973), 182, 185
El Salvador: and exiles, 76; and migration to United States, xix–xx, xxx; and repression, 87–88; and U.S. intervention, xxix, 74, 75
El Soldado Desconocido (*The Unknown Soldier*) (Salomón de la Selva 1922), 30
"El Sol y los de Abajo" (José Montoya), 151

El Teatro Campesino, 102
"El Vendido" (José Montoya 1969), 65
Eminent Maricones: Arenas, Lorca, Puig, and Me (Jaime Manrique 1999), 185
Empire of Dreams (Giannina Braschi 1994), 136, 187
Emplumada (Lorna Dee Cervantes 1981), xx, 105
En babia (José Isaac de Diego Padró 1940), 183
Enclave (Tato Laviera 1981), 104
Engel, Patricia, 131
English language: and assimilation, 169–170; and Latina/o literary studies, xxv; and literature, 42–43; and LULAC, 38–39; and Mexican American writers, xxix; and María Amparo Ruiz de Burton, 10
English-only laws, 94
"Escape" (Margarita Virginia Sánchez 1973), 64–65
Espada, Martín, xx, 106, 149, 152
Espinoza, Dionne, 66
Espinoza, Lauren, 154
Esquibel, Catrióna Rueda, 185, 189, 194n42, 195
essentialism, 68, 129, 167, 217–219, 220–222, 228
Estampas del Valle y otras obras (Rolando Hinojosa-Smith 1973), xix, 60, 67
Esteves, Sandra María, 104, 147–148, 151
Estrada, Gabriel, 188
ethnicity, 10–11, 179. *See also specific ethnicities*
ethno-cyborgs, 217, 220–225, 226, 228n3
"Ethno-Techno: A Virtual Museum of Radical Latino Imagery and Fetishized Identities" (1998-2000), xxi
Everything Begins and Ends at the Kentucky Club (Benjamin Alire Sáenz 2013), 181
exiles: and Cold War, 75–76; and Cristina García's books, 84–85; Cuban, xxviii, 4, 11–13, 92, 239; and El Salvador, 87; and 1990s, 112–113; and Spanish language, 8; and trans-American writing, 14
Exiles of Desire (Juan Felipe Herrera 1983), 106
Exposition Park (Roberto José Tejada 2010), 137

Fábregas, Virginia, 33n3
facultad, 155
Falconer, Blas, 195
Falconi, José Luis, 196

Family Installments: Memories of Growing Up Hispanic (Edward Rivera 1982), xx, 109
Famous All Over Town (Daniel James/ Danny Santiago 1983), 92
Fanon, Frantz, 57, 120, 206–207n6
Farming of Bones, The (Edwidge Danticat 1997), 82
Farolitos of Christmas, The (Rodolfo Anaya 1987), 107
Father Is a Pillow Tied to a Broom (Gary Soto 1980), 106
Faymonville, Carmen, 165
Fefu and Her Friends (María Irene Fornés 1977), xix, 187
feminism: Chicana, 31, 66, 120–121, 153; and cyborgs, 215; and Latina/o literature, xx, xxvii, xxx, 96–97; and poetry, 104
Fernandez, Evalina, 104
Fernández, Roberto, 95, 108
Fernández Olmos, Margarite, 188
Ferrá, Max, 101
Ferrer, Ada, 24
Fifth Horseman, The (José Antonio Villarreal 1984), 108
Figueroa, Sotero, 24
Fiol-Matta, Licia, 187
Five Indiscretions: A Book of Poems (Alberto Ríos 1985), 106
Five Poets of Aztlán (1985), 100
Flaco Maldonado, Jesus, 158
Flores, Juan, 24, 25, 196
Flores, Paul S., 152
Floricanto, 95
Flor y Canto IV and V (1980), 99
Forché, Carolyn, 87, 88
Fornés, María Irene, xix, xxx, 100–101, 187
Foster, Sesshu, xxi, 133–134, 142n6
Foster, Thomas, 224
Fractured Humorous (Edwin Torres 1999), 138
Fragoso, Víctor, 182, 185, 188
Friedman, Milton, 114, 115
From Macho to Mariposa: New Gay Latino Fiction (2011), 190
From the Restless Roots (Ray González 1986), 106
Full Foreground (Roberto José Tejada 2012), 137
Fusco, Coco, xx

Galería de La Raza, 226
Galvin, Mary, 155

Gamber, John, 218
Garbo, Greta, 187
Garbo's Cuban Lover (Odalys Nanin 2001), 187
García, Cristina: and Cold War themes, 84–87, 88; and Cuban American writing, 118–119; and education, 94; and migration narratives, 231, 235, 237; and multicultural canon, 111; and 1990s, xx, xxxi
García, John, 99
García, Ofelia, 152
Garcia, René, 225–226
Garcia Camarillo, Cecilio, 152
García Lorca, Federico, 185, 186
Gaspar de Alba, Alicia, 98, 105, 180, 185
Gay and Lesbian Literary Heritage (David Román 1995), 189
Gay Cuban Nation (Emilio Bejel), 183
Gay Hegemony/Latino Homosexualities (Manolo Guzmán), 182
Gay Latino Studies: A Critical Reader (Michael Hames-García and Ernesto Javier Martínez 2011), 179, 180–181, 189
gender: and American dream, 29; and cyborgs, xxxiii, 221; and Hispaniola, 82; and Latina identity, 96, 97; and *latinidades*, 5; and life writing, 174; and Mexican American culture, 38–39, 42–43, 66; and migration, 165; and 1980s, 92–93, 107; and 1990s, 111; and Nuyoricans, 48, 60; and poetry, 105, 137, 154, 155; and queer scholarship, xxxii, 178–180, 183–185, 187; in *Rag Doll Plagues*, 218
Generacíon del '40, 51–52
Geographies of Home (Loida Maritza Pérez 1999), xxi, 119–120
George Washington Gómez: A Mexicotexan Novel (Américo Paredes 1990), xviii, 40–42
Getting Home Alive (1986), 105
Gilb, Dagoberto, xxi, 107, 173
Gilded Age, xxviii, 19
Giménez Smith, Carmen, 149, 156
Giving Up the Ghost: Teatro in Two Acts (Cherríe Moraga 1986), xx, 104
"God in Harlem" (Pedro Juan Soto 1956), 50–51
Goldenboy (Michael Nava 1988), 108, 180
Golden Glass (Alma Villanueva 1981), 105
Goldman, Francisco, xxi, 231, 240
"Gold Vanity Set, The" (María Cristina Mena), 31
Gómez, Alma, 96

INDEX

Gómez, Carlos Andrés, 152
Gomez, Marga, 103–104
Gómez-Peña, Guillermo, xx, xxi, xxxiii, 104, 217, 220–225, 226
Gómez-Quiñones, Juan, 64, 151
Gonzales, Rodolfo "Corky," xix, 63–64, 148, 151
Gonzales-Berry, Erlinda, 100
González, Genaro, 95, 108
González, Jennifer, 214–215, 217, 227–228
González, John Morán, xxxivn4, 15n14
González, Jovita, xviii, xxviii, 36, 38–40, 183, 186
González, Ray, 106
González, Rigoberto, 152, 154, 155–156, 158, 181
Good Neighbor Policy, xviii, 75
Gordon-Reed, Annette, 201–202
Grande, Reyna, xxi, 231, 240, 242–243
Great Depression, xviii, 36–37, 42, 52
Grillo, Evelio, 198–199
Gritos (Dagoberto Gilb 2004), 173
Gronk, 189
Growing Up Inside the Sanctuary of My Imagination (Nicolasa Mohr 1994), 117
Gruesz, Kirsten Silva, 4, 17, 18
Guam, xviii
Guardians, The (Ana Castillo 2007), 242
Guatemala: and exiles, 76; and migration to United States, xix–xx, xxx; and repression, 77–78; and U.S. intervention, xxix, 73–74, 75
Guattari, Félix, 8
Guerra, Erasmo, 180
Guerrero, Laurie Ann, 155
Guevara, Ernesto "Che," 138
Guidotti-Hernández, Nicole, 186
Gutiérrez, Laura G., 185–186
Guzmán, Manolo, 182

Haiti, xviii, xxix, xxx
Haley, Alex, 201, 207n7
Hames-García, Michael, 179, 180–181, 188, 189
Handbook to Luck, A (Cristina García 2007), 84–85
Haraway, Donna, 213–214, 215, 216, 220, 224
Harden, Jacalyn D., 205
Harth, Dorothy E., 152
Heredia, José María, 3–4, 8–10, 12–13
Here Lies the Heart (Mercedes de Acosta 1960), 187

Hernandez, Daniel, 140–141
Hernandez, Jason, 152
Hernandez, Lauro, 156
Hernandez, Leticia, 156
Hernández Ávila, Inés, 148, 152
Hernández Cruz, Victor, 106
Hernández-G, Manuel de Jesús, 187
Hernández Tovar, Inés. *See* Hernández Ávila, Inés
Herrera, Brian, 116
Herrera, Juan Felipe, 106
Herrera-Sobek, María, 98, 105
Hidden Law, The (Michael Nava 1993), 180
Hijuelos, Oscar, xx, xxx, xxxi, 94, 107
Hinojosa, Rolando. *See* Hinojosa-Smith, Rolando
Hinojosa-Smith, Rolando, xix, 60, 67, 95, 107
Hispanic Caribbean Literature of Migration (Vanessa Pérez Rosario), 239
Hispanic Condition, The (Ilan Stavans), 169, 172
Hispanic Playwright Laboratory at INTAR, xxx, 101–102, 103
Hispanics in the United States: An Anthology of Creative Literature (1980), 98
Hispaniola, xxx, 82
Hoffnung-Garskof, Jesse, 24
Hoheb, Elena, 31–32
"Hollywood Memorabilia" (Manuel Ramos Otero), 188
homophobia, xxx, 181–182, 189, 191n10
Honduras, xix–xx, xxx
Horno-Delgado, Asución, 99
Hospital, Carolina, 99
House of Ramon Iglesia, The (José Rivera 1983), 103, 138
House on Mango Street, The (Sandra Cisneros 1984), xx, 91, 106, 174
Howard, David, 203
How Else Am I Supposed to Know I'm Still Alive (Evalina Fernández 1989), 104
How Junior Got Throwed in the Joint (Denise Chávez 1981), 103
How the García Girls Lost Their Accents (Julia Alvarez 1991), xx, 79, 119, 170, 235, 239
Howtown (Michael Nava 1991), 180
Huerta, Jorge, 102
Hughes, Langston, 199
Hunger of Memory: The Education of Richard Rodriguez (1981), xx, 108–109, 162, 169–170, 173

Huxley, Aldous, 31
Huysmans, Joris-Karl, 183

I, Carmelita Tropicana: Performing Between Cultures (Alina Troyano 2000), xxi, 186
I, Rigoberta Menchú (1982), 77–78
I Am Joaquin (Rodolfo "Corky" Gonzales 1967), xix, 63–64, 151
identity, xxv, 92, 113, 175, 178–179. See also specific identities
I Don't Have to Show You No Stinking Badges (Luis Valdez 1986), 102
Iglesias, César Andreu, 184
Iguana Killer, The: Twelve Stories of the Heart (Alberto Ríos 1984), 107
Immigrants in Our Own Land & Selected Early Poems (Jimmy Santiago Baca 1982), 105
immigration reform, xix, xx, 232
"Impressions of America (By a Very Fresh Spaniard)" (1880), 21
In Cuba I Was a German Shepherd (Ana Menendez 2001), xxi, 239
indigenous languages, xxiv, xxv, 155
inequality, 22, 60, 113, 115–116
Inheritance of Strangers (Nash Candelaria 1985), 107
"Innocents, The" (Pedro Juan Soto 1956), 49
In Nueva York (Nicholasa Mohr 1988), 106
In Search of Bernabé (Graciela Limón 1993), xxi, 241
interlingualism, 156
International Monetary Fund (IMF), 115
Internet, xxi, xxvii, xxxiii, 157, 187, 220–226
intersectionality, 179
intertextual references, 136, 141n1
In the American Grain (William Carlos Williams 1925), xviii, 32
In the Eye of the Hurricane (Eduardo Machado 1989), 103
In the Function of External Circumstances (Edwin Torres 2010), 138
In the Name of Salomé (Julia Alvarez 2000), 79, 237
In the Time of the Butterflies (Julia Alvarez 1994), 79–80, 119
Into the Beautiful North (Luís Alberto Urrea 2009), 237
Inventing a Word: An Anthology of Twentieth-Century Puerto Rican Poetry (1980), 152
Invention of Ethnicity, The (Werner Sollors), 167
Invitation, The (Ana Castillo), 155
Island of Eternal Love, The (Daína Chaviano 2008), 141
Islas, Arturo, xx, 108, 188–189

Jacob Slovak (Mercedes de Acosta 1923), 186
James, William, 19
Jehanne d'Arc (Mercedes de Acosta 1922), 186
Jewish diaspora, 238
Jicoténcal (1826), xvii, 7
Jim Crow, 199
Jiménez, Francisco, 98
Jiménez Román, Miriam, 196
Johnny Tenorio (Carlos Morton 1983), 103
"John of God, the Water-Carrier" (María Cristina Mena 1928), 31
Johnson, James Rosamond, 199
Johnson, James Weldon, 199
Jones-Shafroth Act, xviii, 44
Juana de Asbaje. See Sor Juana Inés de la Cruz
Juárez, Benito, xvii, 12

Kanellos, Nicolás, 26–27, 29, 95, 102
Kazan, Elia, 62
Keating, AnnLouise, 187, 189
Keller, Gary, 95, 98
Kennan, George F., 72–75, 87
Kertbeny, Karl-Maria, 182, 184
Killer crónicas: Bilingual memories/Memorias bilingües (Susana Chávez-Silverman 2004), 140
King, Rodney, 80, 242
King of Cuba (Cristina García 2013), 84
Kirkpatrick, Jeane, 74–75, 87
Kitchen Table: Women of Color Press, 96
Klail City (Rolando Hinojosa 1987), 107
Krik? Krak! (Edwidge Danticat 1996), 82
Kundiman, 157

La Bamba (Columbia Pictures 1987), 102
La Bodega Sold Dreams (1980), 103
La carreta (René Marqués 1954), xix, xxviii–xxix, 45–47
La Carreta Made a U-Turn (Tato Laviera 1984), xx, 52, 104
La comedia profana (Giannina Braschi 1985), 187
La Corregidora, 150

INDEX

La Crónica, 153
La Crónica de Laredo, 150
Lady Matador's Hotel, The (Cristina García 2010), 84–87, 88
La Fountain-Stokes, Lawrence, xxxii–xxxiii, xxxvn10
La Malinche, 65, 215
Lambda Literary Awards, 180, 191n7
Lambda Literary Foundation, 181
La novelabingo (Manuel Ramos Otero), 182
La Patria (New Orleans 1846–50), 6
La Pocha Nostra, xxi, xxxiii, 220
La Prensa, 150, 152
La Raza Techno-Crítica Collective, 226
La República (San Francisco 1885), 6
Las Aventuras de Don Chipote, o Cuando los pericos mamen (Daniel Venegas 1928), xviii, 25, 26–29
Las Mujeres Hablan: An Anthology of Nuevo Mexicana Writers (1988), 100
Las Poetas, 156–157
Last of the Menu Girls, The (Denise Chávez 1986), xx, 106
Latin@: authors, 130, 140; dramatists, 138; literature, xxxi–xxxii, 141, 147; poetics, 149, 153, 159, 161; poets, 148, 154–158; population, 128, 141
Latina feminism. See feminism
Latina Feminist Group, 121–122
Latin America, xxvii–xxviii, 18, 192n16
Latin American Studies, xxiv–xxv
Latina/o identity, 94, 196–197
Latina/o literature: in 1980s, 109–110; in 1990s, 122–123; and anthologies, 98–100; and criticism, 97–98; and Culture Wars, 93, 94; and feminism, 96–97; and history, 14; and journals, 95–96; and life writing, 163; and literary studies, xxiv, 17, 77; and neoliberalist individualism, xxxi; and 1980s, 91–92; and poetics, xxxii; and queer literature, 189
Latina/o migrant workers, 234–235
Latina/o playwrights, 100–104
Latina/o Studies, xxiv–xxv, 196
Latina/o writers: and art versus politics, 101–102; and Cold War themes, 77–78; and cultural nationalism, 68; and life writing, 122–123, 163–164, 167; and migration narratives, 231, 243–244; and modernism, 29–32; and 1980s, xxx, 91, 94; and 1990s, xxxi; and pioneers, 60–61; and queer literature, 180; and symbolic homelands, 66–67; and trans-American writing, 17, 19–22. See also specific writers
latinidades: and identity, xxxi–xxxii, 5–6, 132, 142n1; and Latin@ literatures, 129–130, 141; and Latina/o literary studies, xxiv; and migration, xxiii, xxvii, xxx, xxxiii–xxxiv, 17–19; and poetry, 149–153, 156–157; and race, 24, 142n4
Latining America (Claudia Milian 2009), 130
Latin Jazz (Virgil Suárez 1989), xx, 108
Latin Moon in Manhattan (Jaime Manrique 1992), 189
Latino/a Canon and the Emergence of Post-sixties Literature, The (2007), 132
Latino Writers Collective, 157
Laurencio, Angel Aparicio, 152
La Verdad (New York 1848–60), 6
La vida es sueño (Calderón de la Barca), 136
Laviera, Tato, xx, xxx, 52, 95, 104, 151
La Voz de la América (New York 1865–67), 6
Lawrence, D. H., 31
Lazo, Rodrigo, xxvii, xxxivn2
League of United Latin American Citizens (LULAC), 38, 40–42, 52
Leal, Luis, 98
Leaños, John Jota, 225–226
Lebrón, Lolita, 44
Legend of La Llorona, The: A Short Novel (Rodolfo Anaya 1984), 107
Let It Rain Coffee (Angie Cruz 2006), xxi, 235, 239–240
LGBTI Latina/o authors, 178, 181. See also queer U.S. Latina/o literature
Life and Opinions of Tristram Shandy, Gentleman, The (Laurence Sterne), 136
Life Span (Alma Villanueva 1984), 105
life writing, xxvii, xxxii, xxxvn9, 163–165, 171–172, 175. See also autobiography; memoir; testimonio
Lima, Lázaro, 190
Lima, Rossy Evelin, 149, 156
Limón, Graciela, xxi, 231, 234, 238, 241
Limón, José, 148, 150
Line of the Sun, The (Judith Ortiz Cofer 1989), 108
Literature Chicana – Creative and Critical Writings Through 1984 (1985), 100
Little Death (Michael Nava 1986), 108
Living Up the Street: Narrative Recollections (Gary Soto 1985), 109
Locke, Alain, 24, 199

Loida Pérez, Maritza, xxi, 119–120, 124–125n41
Lomas, Laura, xxviii, xxxivn3, 183
Lomelí, Francisco, 98, 99
Loomer, Lisa, 102
"Loose Woman" (Sandra Cisneros), 155
López, Antonio, 24
López, Josefina, xxii, 102, 104, 231, 243
López, Lorraine M., 195
López, Marissa, 69
López, Tiffany Ana, xxx
"Lorca" (Manuel Ramos Otero 1985), 185
Lorca in a Green Dress (Nilo Cruz 2003), 185
Lorde, Audre, 96
Lord of the Dawn: The Legend of Quetzalcóatl (Rodolfo Anaya 1987), 107
Los Angeles Latino Writers Association, 95–96
Los Cybrids, xxi, xxxiii, 217, 225–227
Los otros cuerpos: antología de temática gay, lésbica y queer desde Puerto Rico y su diáspora (2007), 190
los sediciosos, xviii, 38
Los Vendidos (Luis Valdez 1967), xix, 65
lotería, 140
Loving in the War Years (Cherríe Moraga 1983), xx, 92, 109, 155, 174–175, 188
Lowry, Elizabeth, 136–137
Lozano-Hemmer, Rafael, 221, 222, 224
Lucas Guevara (Alirio Díaz Guerra 1914), xviii
Lugo, A. B., 152
Luna, Tito, 152
lynching, 23
"Lynching of the Italians, The" (José Martí 1891), 21–22

Maceo, Antonio, 23
Machado, Eduardo, 102, 103
Machado Sáez, Elena, 132
MACHA Theater Company, 187
Macho Camacho's Beat (Luis Sánchez 1980), 107
Macondo, 156, 157
MacPherson, C. B., 114
Macum, Carl, 156
Madero, Francisco I., 18
Magic of Blood, The (Dagoberto Gilb 1993), xxi
Mainstream Ethics: Etica Corriente (Tato Laviera 1988), 104
Maldonado, Erik, 152
Maldonado, Sheila, 152
Mambo Kings Play Songs of Love, The (Oscar Hijuelos 1990), xx, xxxi, 107
Manifest Destiny, xxvii, 11
Manrique, Jaime, 108, 185, 189
Many Deaths of Danny Rosales, The, and Other Plays (Carlos Morton 1983), 103
Margarita Poems, The (Luz Maria Umpierre 1987), xx, 105, 155, 186, 188
María Irene Fornés: Plays (1986), 101
Mariel exodus, xx, 118, 236
Marín, Francisco Gonzálo, 24
MARIPOSAS: A Modern Anthology of Queer Latino Poetry (Emanuel Xavier 2008), 190
Marqués, René, xix, xxviii–xxix, 36, 45–47
Márquez, Antonio, 99
Márquez, Teresa, 100
Martí, José: on inequalities, xxviii; as literary figure, 7; and "Nuestra América," xvii; and poetic legacy, 147; and queer scholarship, 183; and trans-American writing, 17, 18–19; and transculturation, 20–23, 33n2; and U.S. expansionist ideology, 5
Martín: &, Meditations on the South Valley (Jimmy Santiago Baca 1987), 105
Martinez, David Thomas, 156
Martínez, Demetria, xxi, 98, 105, 241
Martínez, Ernesto Javier, 180–181, 188, 189
Martínez, Julio, 99
Martínez, Nina Marie, xxi, xxxii, 129, 139–140
Martínez, Pablo Miguel, 155, 157
Martínez-Echazabál, Lourdes, 23
Marzán, Julio, 152
Matilla, Alfredo, 152
Mayer, Oliver, 102
Mazzotti, José Antonio, 196
Melendez, Miguel "Mickey," 62
memoir, xxxii, 108–109. *See also* life writing
Memorias (Hilario Coronado Cuello), 154
Memory Mambo (Achy Obejas 1997), xxi, 180
Mena, María Cristina, xviii, 17, 18, 20, 22, 25, 29–31
Menchú, Rigoberta, 77–78, 81, 85–86, 87
Méndez, Miguel, 60, 148
Mendoza, Celeste, 157
Menéndez, Ana, xxi, 231, 239
Mercado, Nancy, 152
Mercado-López, Larissa, 155

mestizaje: discourse of, 196, 215–219, 228; and Latino identity, 69n4, 163; and life writing, 167; and virality, 220–225

mestiza/o cyborgs, 215–216, 226, 228

Mexican American literature, xxix, 36–37, 52–53. *See also specific writers*

Mexican Ballads, Chicano Poems: History and Influence in Mexican American Social Poetry (José Limón), 150–151

Mexican Revolution, xviii, 42, 59

Mexican Silhouettes (Josefina Niggli 1928), 150

Mexico: and American dream, 168; and Chicana/o movement, 66–67, 98; and Chicano literature, 60–61; and fronteriza fiction, 139; and Latina/o literature, 17–18, 22, 29–30; and life writing, 173; and LULAC, 38, 41; and *mestizaje*, 217–218; and Mexican American literature, 37, 40; and migration, xviii, 3–4; and migration narratives, 11–12, 28, 233–234, 237, 241–243; and NAFTA, xxi, xxx–xxxi, 115; and 1990s, 111; and poetry, 149, 150, 154, 157, 159n1; and queer literature, 185–186; and U.S.-Mexican War, xvii, xxvii, 5, 10, 39

Midwest Latina Writers Workshop, 97

migration: and American dream, 238–244; and "double-crossing," 205; and *latinidades*, xxx–xxxiv, 17–18, 128, 130; and life writing, 165; narratives of, 118–119; and 1990s, 111; and poetics, 150; and poverty, 116–117, 125n42; and queer literature, 181; and transnational identities, 231, 233–235, 237

Milian, Claudia, xxxiii, xxxvn11, 130–131, 141, 142n4

Millay, Edna St. Vincent, 30

Miller, Marilyn, 216

minor literature, 8, 10, 14, 20

Mi Opinión Sobre las Libertades, Derechos y Deberes de la Mujer (Luisa Capetillo 1911), 183–184

Mirrors for Gold (Roberto José Tejada 2006), 137

Mission, The (Culture Clash 1988), 104

Mission Street Manifesto: For All Varrios (Juan Felipe Herrera 1983), 106

Mistral, Gabriela, 187

Mixquiahuala Letters, The (Ana Castillo 1986), xx, 108

modernism, 17, 29–32, 37, 46–47, 52

modernismo, 17

Modern Ladies of Guanabacoa, The (Eduardo Machado 1983), 103

Mohr, Nicholasa, xix, 59–60, 106, 117–118

Monkey Hunting (Cristina García 2003), 84, 237

Monroe Doctrine, xvii, xxvii

Montalvo, Jose, 148

Monthly Criterion, The, 31

Montoya, José, xix, 65, 94, 104, 148, 151, 154

Montoya, Richard, 92, 103–104

Moods (Mercedes de Acosta 1919), 187

Mora, Pat, 105, 154

Moraga, Cherríe: on Chicano nationalism, 68; drama of, 104; and education, 94; and intersectionality, 92; and Kitchen Table: Women of Color Press, 96; and María Irene Fornés, xxx, 101; memoir of, 109, 174–175; in 1980s, xx; poetry of, 155; and queer scholarship, 179, 181, 182, 188, 189; and South Coast Repertory's Hispanic Playwrights Project, 102; and Third Woman Press, 97

Morales, Alejandro, xx, 216–218, 228

Morales, Aurora Levin, 105

Morales, Ed, 197

Morales, Rosario, 105

Morán González, John. *See* González, John Morán

Moreno, Dorinda, 152

Morton, Carlos, 102, 103

Mother Tongue (Demetria Martínez 1994), xxi, 241

Moths and Other Stories, The (Helena María Viramontes 1985), xx, 106, 240–241

Movement, Machete, 152

Movements in Chicano Poetry, 156

Mud (María Irene Fornés 1983), 101

Mujeres Fuertes, 157

Mundo Cruel (Luis Negrón 2010), xxii, 181

Muñoz, Carlos Jr., 63–64

Muñoz, Elías, 95, 108

Muñoz, José Esteban, 179

Muñoz, Manuel, xxi

Muñoz Marín, Luis, 45

Murray, Yxta Maya, 133

My Father Was a Toltec (Ana Castillo 1988), xx, 105

"My Protocol for our Sister Americas" (María Cristina Mena 1943), 22

"My Race" (José Martí), 23

My Visits with MGM (My Grandmother Marta) (Edit Villareal), 102
My Wicked, Wicked Ways (Sandra Cisneros 1987), xx, 105

Nagle, Robin, 198
Nanin, Odalys, 187
Nava, Michael, 108, 180, 188
Navarro, J. L., 148
Necessary Theater: Six Plays About the Chicano Experience (1989), 102
"Negro Digs up his Past, The" (Arturo Alfonso Schomburg 1925), 24
Negrón, Luis, xxii, 181, 190
Negrón Muntaner, Frances, 24
Nelson, Alondra, 201, 203, 207n8
neoliberalism, xxvii, xxix, xxx–xxxi, 112–113, 114, 115
Nervo, Amado, 153
Nevada Diggs, Latasha N., 152
New Negro, The (Alain Locke 1925), 24
New York publishers, xxxi
Next Year in Cuba (Gustavo Pérez Firmat), 164
Nicaragua: and Salomón de la Selva, 29–32; and exiles, 76; and migration to United States, xix–xx; and U.S. intervention, xvii, xxix, 73–75; and U.S. occupation, xviii, 18, 30
Nieves, Myrna, 152
Niggli, Josefina, 150
Nilda (Nicholasa Mohr 1973), xix, 59–60
Noel, Urayoán, 152
North American Free Trade Agreement (NAFTA), xxi, xxx, 115, 137
Norton Anthology of Latino Literature, xxiv
Nosotras: Latina Literature Today (1986), 100
Not by the Sword (Nash Candelaria 1982), 107
Novena Narrative (Denise Chávez 1987), 103
"Nuestra América" (José Martí 1891), xvii
Nuevos Pasos: Chicano and Puerto Rican Drama (1989), 102
Numbers (John Rechy 1981), 108
Nuyorican literature, xxix–xxx, 37, 44–52, 59, 76–77, 92, 188, 233. *See also* Nuyorican Poets Café; Puerto Rican literature; *specific writers*
Nuyorican Poets Café, 67–68, 71n29, 104, 138, 151, 157, 158–159. *See also* Nuyorican literature

Obejas, Achy, xxi, 180, 231, 235, 237, 238–239
"Ode to Walt Whitman" (Federico García Lorca), 185
Odyssey to the North (Mario Bencastro 1998), xxi, 241–242
Off and Running (Gary Soto 1986), 106
"Of Time and Song" (Salomón de la Selva), 32
Olguín, Ben V., 153, 154
Olivares, Julián, 100
Olney, James, 164, 175
On Borrowed Words: A Memoir of Language (Ilan Stavans 2001), 169
On Call (Miguel Algarín 1980), 104
Once Removed (Eduardo Machado 1986), 102
One Night for the Sleepy (Edwin Torres 2012), 138
One Today (Richard Blanco 2013), xxii
On New Ground: Contemporary Hispanic American Plays (1987), 103
Onomalingua: Noise Songs and Poetry (Edwin Torres 2002), 138
Operation Bootstrap, xix, 37, 45, 117
Operation Gatekeeper, 232, 238
Operation Wetback, xix
Ordinary Seaman, The (Francisco Goldman 1997), xxi, 240
Ortiz, Amalia, 154
Ortiz, Fernando, 20
Ortiz, Richard, xxix, xxxvn7
Ortiz Cofer, Judith. *See* Cofer, Judith Ortiz
Osborn, M. Elizabeth, 103
Ostend Manifesto, xvii
O'Sullivan, John L., 11
Other Latinos, The (José Luis Falconi and José Antonio Mazzotti), 196
Other Man Was Me, The (Rafael Campo 1994), xxi
"Our America" (José Martí 1891), 18–19, 22–23
Our House in the Last World: A Novel (Oscar Hijuelos 1983), 107
Outrageous: One Act Plays (Miguel Piñero 1986), 103
"Over the Waves Is Out" (Américo Paredes 1953), 183

Padilla, Genaro, 164
Padró, Diego, 183–185
Padró, José Isaac de Diego. *See* Padró, Diego
Palacios, Monica, 103–104

Palante: The Young Lords Party (1971), 62
Palés Matos, Luis, 152
Palomo Acosta, Theresa, 156
Panama, xx, xxix
Pantallas (Dolores Prida 1986), 103
Papoleto Meléndez, Jesús, 68
Paradise Lost, 3
Paredes, Américo, xviii, xxviii, 36, 40–42, 150, 151, 153–154, 183
Paredez, Deborah, 157, 158
Parsley Massacre, xviii
Parsons, Lucy, 24
Partisans (Rodrigo Toscano 1999), 134
Partners in Crime (Rolando Hinojosa 1985), 107
Partnoy, Alicia, 149, 155
Passion (Ana Maria Simo 1987), 102
Patchwork Colcha (Carmen Tafolla 1980), 105
Peña Delgado, Grace, 196
People of Paper, The (Salvador Plascencia 2005), xxi, 135–136
Peregrina (Judith Ortiz Cofer 1986), 105
Peregrinos de Aztlán/Pilgrims of Aztlán (Miguel Mendez 1974), 60
Pérez, David, 62
Pérez, Emma, 154
Perez, Frank, 152
Pérez, Reymundo "Tigre," 148, 152
Pérez Firmat, Gustavo, 164, 165–166, 169
Pérez Rosario, Vanessa, xxxvn5, 239
Pérez-Torres, Rafael, 148, 151, 156, 216
Performing Queer Latinidad: Dance, Sexuality, Politics (Ramón Rivera-Servera 2013), 181
periodization, xxv–xxvi, xxvii
Philippines, and U.S.-Spanish War, xviii
Picano, Felice, 190
Pietri, Pedro, xix, 62–63, 67–68, 104, 148, 151, 180
Pilar, Praba, 225–226, 227
Piñero, Miguel, xix, xxx, 63, 67–68, 95, 102–103, 151, 180
Pinochet, Augusto, 73, 115
Pita, Beatrice, 11–12
Pitman, Thea, xxxiii, xxxvn12
Place to Stand (Jimmy Santiago Baca 2001), 172
Plascencia, Salvador, xxi, xxxii, 129, 135–136
Platform (Rodrigo Toscano 2002), 134
Platt Amendment, xviii

Plessy vs. Ferguson (1896), 23
Pluecher, John, 188
Pocho (José Antonio Villarreal 1959), xix, xxviii, 42–44, 61, 153–154, 182, 233
Poema en Veinte Surcos/Poems in Twenty Furrows (Julia de Burgos 1938), 25
Poems Across the Pavement (Luis J. Rodriguez 1989), 106
Poems Taken from My Yard (Jimmy Santiago Baca 1986), 105
Poesías (José María Heredia 1825), 9
poetics, xxxii, 61–62, 147
Poet in New York (Federico García Lorca), 185
Poetry Magazine, 158
Poetry of Healing, The (Rafael Campo 1998), 180
Poetry Project, 138
police brutality, 37, 46
Ponce, Mary Helen, 91, 95, 107, 108
Ponce, Puerto Rico, massacre, xviii, 44
Pond, The (La Charca) (Manuel Zeno Gandía 1894), 24–26
PoPedology of an Ambient Language, The (Edwin Torres 2008), 138
Portillo Trambley, Estela, 67, 103
possessive individualism, 112–113, 114, 115–116
postrace aesthetics, 132–135, 140
Pot, Pol, 74
Pound, Ezra, 30, 32
poverty, and stereotypes, 118, 125n42
Poxo (Isaac Chavarria), 154
Pratt, Mary Louise, 20
Precious (Sapphire), 197–198, 205
Premio Quinto Sol, 67
Prida, Dolores, 103
Promenade and Other Plays (María Irene Fornés 1987), 101
Promise, The (José Rivera 1987), 102
Pueblos Hispanos, 25
Puerto Rican communities, xxxiii–xxxiv, 59–60
Puerto Rican literature, xxviii–xxix, 52–53. *See also* Nuyorican literature; *specific writers*
Puerto Rican nationalism, 44, 58–59
"Puerto Rican Obituary" (Pedro Pietri 1969), xix, 62–63
Puerto Rican Poets/ Los poetas puertoriqueños (1972), 152

Puerto Rico: and la Generacíon del '40, 51–52; and life writing, 233, 236; literature of, 31; and migration narratives, 47, 49, 62–63, 235, 240; and migration to United States, xxx; and nationalism, 58–59; in 1980s, 107, 109; and Operation Bootstrap, xix, 44–45, 117; and poetry, 150; and Ponce massacre, xviii; and queer literature, 181, 183, 184, 190; and Spanish-language newspapers, 6; and symbolic homelands, 66–67; and transculturation, 166; and U.S. empire, xxviii, 6, 19, 24, 36–37; and U.S.-Spanish War, xviii
Puppet: A Chicano Novella (Margarita Cota-Cárdenas 1985), 108
Push (Sapphire), 197

Queer Latinidad: Identity Practices, Discursive Spaces (Juana María Rodríguez 2003), 179
queer studies, xxvii, 109, 179
"Queer Theory Revisited" (Michael Hames-García), 179
queer U.S. Latina/o literature, 178, 180, 181, 183, 187–188. *See also* LGBTI Latina/o authors; sexuality
Quiñonez, Ernesto, xxi
Quinto Sol Publications, 67, 71n28, 95

race, 10–11, 20, 82, 111, 179, 227
racialization, xxv, xxxii–xxxiii, 20–21
Rag and Bone (Michael Nava 2002), 180
Rag Doll Plagues, The (Alejandro Morales 1992), xx, 216–220, 228
Rainbow's End (Genaro González 1988), 108
Rain God, The (Arturo Islas 1984), xx, 108
Raining Backwards (Roberto Fernández 1988), 108
Rain of Scorpions and Other Writings (Estela Portillo Trambley 1975), 67
Raleigh, Eve. *See* Eimer, Margaret
Rama, Angel, 20
Ramírez, Catherine, 97
Ramírez, Chente, 171
Ramírez, Sara Estela, 147, 150, 153
Ramos, Juanita, 100, 188, 189–190
Ramos Otero, Manuel, 182, 185, 188
Rancho Hollywood (Carlos Morton 1980), 103
Rancière, Jacques, 58
Random House, 67

raúlsalinas, xx, 148, 152
Reading Chican@ Like a Queer (Sandra K. Soto), 179
Reagan, Ronald, 74–75, 87, 197
Rebolledo, Tey Diana, 100, 155
Rechy, John, xix, 108, 181, 182, 188, 189
Recovering the U.S. Hispanic Literary Heritage Project, xxv, xxvi, xxxivn1, 17–18, 70n13, 150, 199
Recuerdo: Short Stories of the Barrio (Mary Helen Ponce 1983), 107
refugees, xxx, 112–113, 241
reggaeton, 148
Republic of Haiti, xvii
Republic of Texas, xvii
"Resolución" (Miguel Teurbe Tolón 1858), 13
Retter Vargas, Yolanda, 188
Return To Centro Histórico: A Mexican Jew Looks for His Roots (Ilan Stavans 2012), 173–174
Return to Sender (Julia Alvarez 2009), 243
Revista Chicano-Riqueña, 95
Revista XhismeArte, 95–96
Revolt of the Cockroach People (Oscar Zeta Acosta 1973), xix, 60
Rice-González, Charles, 181, 190
Riofrio, John, 239
Ríos, Albert Alvaro, 94
Ríos, Alberto, 106, 107, 154
Rites and Witnesses (Rolando Hinojosa 1982), 107
Rituals of Survival: A Woman's Portfolio (Nicholasa Mohr 1985), 106
Rivera, Diego, 30
Rivera, Edward, xx, 109
Rivera, José, xxxii, 102, 103, 129, 138
Rivera, Tomás, xix, 60, 67, 95, 105, 106
Rivera-Servera, Ramón, 181
River Flows North, The (Graciela Limón 2009), 234, 238
Rizal, José, 22–23
Robeson, Paul, 199
Rocafuerte, Vicente, 4
Rodríguez, Andrés, 100
Rodríguez, Jesusa, 186
Rodríguez, Juana María, 179
Rodríguez, Luis J., xxi, 95–96, 106, 171–172
Rodriguez, Richard, xx, 162, 167, 169–170, 172, 188–189
Rodríguez, Richard T., xxix, xxxvn6, 108
Rodriguez-Morales, Maria, 152
Rojas, Bonafide, 152

Román, David, 116, 187, 189
Romano-V., Octavio I., 67
Romero, Leo, 106
Romo-Carmona, Mariana, 96, 180
Roosevelt, Franklin, xviii
Roosevelt, Theodore, 21
Roots: The Saga of an American Family (Alex Haley), 201, 207n7
Rosario, Moisés Agosto, 190
Rúa, Mérida, 196
Rueda Esquibel, Catrióna. *See* Esquibel, Catrióna Rueda
Ruiz, Ramón E., 61
Ruiz de Burton, María Amparo, xvii, 5, 7, 10–12
Rumbaut, Rubén, 235
Rushes (John Rechy 1981), 108

Sadowski-Smith, Claudia, 139
Said, Edward, 7
Saldívar, José David, 17, 100, 142n6
Saldívar, Ramón, 132–135, 140
Saldívar-Hull, Sonia, 120
Salinas, Raúl. *See* raúlsalinas
Salinas, Ric, 92, 103–104
Salles, Walter, 138
Sammy y los Del Tercer Barrio (José Antonio Burciaga 1983), 107
Sánchez, Alex, 180
Sánchez, Edwin, 102
Sánchez, Luis Rafael, 107, 180
Sánchez, Margarita Virginia, 64–65
Sánchez, Marta, 100
Sánchez, Martha, 148, 151
Sánchez, Ricardo, 147, 148, 152, 154
Sánchez, Rosaura, 11–12
Sánchez González, Lisa, 24, 31, 59–60, 67
Sanctuary Movement, 241
Sandino, Agusto César, 30
Sandoval, Chela, 215
"San Onofre, California" (Carolyn Forché 1977), 87
Santiago, Esmeralda, xxi, xxxi, 111, 118, 165, 166, 231, 236
Santiago, Roberto F., 152
Santos, Rosario, 115
Sapogonia (Ana Castillo 1990), 91
Sapphire, 197–198, 205, 206n3
Sarita (María Irene Fornés 1984), 101
Savings (Dolores Prida 1985), 103
Saving the World (Julia Alvarez 2003), 79, 237
Sayre, Amy, 156

Scenes from la cuenca de Los Angeles y otros natural disasters (Susana Chávez-Silverman 2010), 140
Scenes from the Movie GIANT (Tino Villanueva 1993), xxi
Schnabel, Julian, 124n40
Schomburg, Arturo Alfonso, 23–24
School of the Americas (José Rivera 2006), 138
Schulberg, Budd, 62
Schurtermandl, Silvia, 166
Ser islas/Being Islands (Víctor Fragoso), 182
sexism, xxx, 117, 174
sexuality: and Afro-Latino-Caribbean-diasporic identity, 82; and Latin@ poetics, 155; and Latina/o literary studies, xxv; and 1990s, 111; and queer-of-color critique, 179. *See also* queer U.S. Latina/o literature
Sexuality of Latinas, The (1989), 97
Sexual Outlaw, The (John Rechy 1981), 108
"Shades of the Tenth Muse" (Jovita González), 186
Shadow of a Man (Cherríe Moraga), 102
Shaking Off the Dark (Tino Villanueva 1984), 106
Shirley, Don, 99
Short Eyes (Miguel Piñero 1974), xix, 102, 188
short stories, xviii, 31, 47–48, 82, 95, 106–107, 115, 235, 239
Sidibe, Gabourey, 195
Sigüenza, Herbert, 92, 103–104
Silén, Iván, 152
Silence of the Llano, The: Short Stories (Rudolfo Anaya 1982), 107
Silent Dancing (Judith Ortiz Cofer 1990), xx, 165
Silva, Beverly, 100
Simo, Ana Maria, 102
Simply María or The American Dream (Josefina López 1989), 104
Sleeping on Fists (Alberto Ríos 1981), 106
Sleepy Lagoon murder trials, 233
Small Faces (Gary Soto 1986), 106
Smedley, Audrey, 113–114
Smith, Barbara, 96
Smuggler's Blues (Miguel Piñero 1984), 103
Society for the Study of Gloria Anzaldúa, 109
So Hard to Say (Alex Sánchez 2005), 180
Sollors, Werner, 167

Something to Declare (Julia Alvarez 1995), 170, 172–173
Somoza, Anastasio, 73–74
"Song for Wall Street, A" (Salomón de la Selva 1918), 18–19
"Sorcerer and General Bisco, The" (María Cristina Mena), 30
Sor Juana and Other Plays (Estella Portillo-Trambley 1983), 103
Sor Juana Inés de la Cruz, 185–186
Sor Juana's Second Dream (Alicia Gaspar de Alba 1999), 185
Sor Juana: The Nightmare (Carmelita Tropicana 2000), 186
Soto, Gary, xix, 94, 95, 106, 109, 148
Soto, Pedro Juan, xix, xxix, 36, 47–51, 60–61
Soto, Sandra K., 179, 183, 188
Spaces That Time Missed (Olivia Castellano 1986), 105
Spanglish, 91–92, 140, 149, 153, 156, 169, 197
Spanic Attack Artist Collective, 138
Spanish colonialism, 22–23, 118
Spanish language: and assimilation, 169–170; and colonialism, 7–8; and Latina/o literary studies, xxv; and LULAC, 38–39; and newspapers, 42–43; and Puerto Rican authors, xxix; and slang, 140; and U.S. journalism, 22
Spik in Glyph? (Alurista 1981), xx, 104
Spiks (Pedro Juan Soto 1956), xix, xxix, 47–51, 60–61
Squatter and the Don, The (María Amparo Ruiz de Burton 1885), xvii, 10, 15n14, 15–16n15
Stalin, Joseph, 74
Starobinski, Jean, 171
St. Augustine, 171
Stavans, Ilan, 169, 173–174, 187
Steiner, Stan, 67, 152
Sterne, Laurence, 136
Stone, Rosanne Allucquère, 220, 224
Streets and Shadow (Mercedes de Acosta 1922), 187
Suárez, Lucía, xxx, xxxvn8
Suárez, Virgil, xx, 108
Sun Always Shines for the Cool, The; a Midnight Moon at the Greasy Spoon; Eulogy for a Small Time Thief (Miguel Piñero 1984), 103
"¡Surge!" (Sara Estela Ramírez 1911), 153
Svich, Caridad, 101, 138

Swanson, Clare, 181
Swords of Darkness (Jimmy Santiago Baca 1981), 104–105

Tafolla, Carmen, 105, 156, 157
Taking Control (Mary Helen Ponce 1987), 108
Tattooed Soldier, The (Héctor Tobar 1998), xxi, 80–82, 86, 242
Tatum, Charles, 99
Teatro de la Esperanza, 102
Tejada, Roberto José, xxxii, 128–129, 135, 137–138
Tejidos, 152
telenovelas, 140
Telephone Booth Number 190 (Pedro Pietri 1980), 104
Telling to Live: Latina Feminist Testimonios (2001), 121–122
Tenepal, Malintzin, 65
Terms of Survival: Poems (Judith Ortiz Cofer 1987), 105
testimonio, xxxii, 77–78, 81, 86, 104, 109, 121–123, 165, 172. *See also* life writing
Texas Centennial, xxviii, 36–37, 41–42
Texas Rangers, xviii, 38
There Are No Madmen Here (Gina Valdés 1981), 105
Third Woman, 97
Thirty An' Seen a Lot (Evangelina Vigil-Piñón 1982), 105
This Bridge Called My Back (Cherríe Moraga and Gloria E. Anzaldúa 1981), xx, 96, 155, 179, 182, 188
"This Earth" (William Archila 2009), 88
This Is How You Lose Her (Junot Díaz), 82
Thomas, Lorrin, 200
Thomas, Piri, xix, 59–61, 151, 180, 198–200, 233
Three Times a Woman: Chicana Poetry (1989), 98, 105
Tierra: Contemporary Short Fiction of New Mexico (1989), 99
Tiger's Wild (John Rechy 1986), 108
Time's Now (Miguel Algarín 1985), xx, 68, 104
Tobar, Héctor, xxi, xxxi, 80–82, 85–86, 87, 231, 242
To Leveling Swerve (Rodrigo Toscano 2004), 134
Tolón, Miguel Teurbe, 13
Tontons Macoutes, 83
Toro, Vincent, 158

08.30.19

Bebesita,

Aqui te mando tu fondo ☺ jaja porque se que no puedes vivir sin el java. Te extraño mucho bebesita. Gracias por haber venido y por todos los días que compartimos juntas. Estoy muy orgullosa de ti y de todos los cambios para bien que estas haciendo en tu persona. ♡

Pd. Nunca olvides a tus 🦠(celulas) ☺

Te quiero mucho,

Karla ♥

Torres, Edwin, xxxii, 129, 138–139, 152, 180
Torres, Justin, xxii, xxxii, 129, 134
Torres, Manuel, 4
Toscano, Rodrigo, xxxii, 129, 134–135
To Split a Human: Mitos, Machos y la Mujer Chicana (Carmen Tafolla 1985), 105
Trafficking in Broken Hearts (Edwin Sánchez), 102
Traffic Violations (Pedro Pietri 1983), 104
Translating Empire: José Martí, Migrant Latino Subjects, and American Modernities (Laura Lomas), 183
transnational ties, xxvi–xxvii, 235
Treaty of Guadalupe Hidalgo (1848), xvii, 186
Tristan and the Hispanics (José Yglesias 1989), 108
Tropical Rains: A Bilingual Downpour (Sandra Maria Esteves 1984), 104
Tropical Town (Salomón de la Selva 1918), xviii, 18–19, 32
Tropicana, Carmelita, 186
Troyano, Alina, xxi
Trujillo, Carla, 180, 188, 189–190
Trujillo, Rafael: assassination of, xix; brutality of, 82; and Dominican migration literature, 119, 170, 239; and exiles, 76; and "Parsley Massacre," xviii; and U.S. foreign policy, xxix, 74, 79–80
Trujillo, Roberto, 100
Truman, Harry S., 44
Trumpets from the Islands of Their Eviction (Martín Espada 1987), xx, 106
Truth, Sojourner, 199
"Truth about the United States, The" (José Martí 1894), 22
Tubman, Harriet, 199
Turner, Nat, 199
Twain, Mark, 19
Twilights and Chants: Poems (Ray González 1987), 106

Ulibarrí, Sabine, 95, 107, 152
Ultraviolet Sky, The (Alma Villanueva 1988), 108
Umpierre, Luz Maria, xx, 105, 107, 152, 155, 186, 188
Under the Feet of Jesus (Helena María Viramontes 1995), xxi, 234–235
Union Maceo-Martí, 24
United Farm Workers (UFW), 61–62
United Mexican American Students (UMAS), 61–62
United States: and American dream, 26–29, 231–232, 238–240; and Cuba, 84–85; and cultural translation, 20; and diaspora, 204; and El Salvador, 87–88; and empire, 12–13, 18, 22; and English, xxix, 3; and Latin@ poetics, 150, 157; and Latin America, xvii–xx, xxiii, xxvii–xxviii, 73–78; Latina/o population of, 111, 123n1, 128; and *latinidades*, xxx–xxxi, xxxiv, 17; and life writing, 163–164; and *mestizaje*, 167; and Mexico, 58–59; and minority literature, 233; and neoliberal economic policies, 115–117; and Puerto Rico, 44–45, 58–59; and queer literature, xxxii–xxxiii; and queer migration, 181; and race, 23–24, 36, 216; and Spanish, 8; and Spanish-language newspapers, 6
United States of Banana, The (Giannina Braschi 2011), 136–137, 187
Uno, Roberta, 103
Unpeopled Eden (Rigoberto González 2014), 181
Unspeakable Violence (Nicole Guidotti-Hernández), 186
Un trip through the mind jail (raúlsalinas 1980), xx
Ureña, Salomé, 237
Urista Heredia, Alberto Baltazar. *See* Alurista
Urrea, Luís Alberto, 237
Urrieta, Luis, Jr., 196
U.S. Central Americans, and *latinidades*, xxiv, 240
U.S. citizenship, and Puerto Ricans, xviii
U.S. colonial domination, and Puerto Rico, 36–37
U.S. foreign policy, xxix
U.S. Hispanic Autobiography (1988), 100
U.S. interventions, xxiii, xxvii, xxix–xxx
U.S. Latino population, 76
U.S.-Mexican War, xvii, xxvii–xxviii, 5, 98, 178
U.S.-Spanish War, xviii, xxviii, 44, 178

Valdés, Gina, 105
Valdes-Rodriguez, Alisa, xxi
Valdez, Luis, xix, xxx, 64–65, 67, 95, 102, 233
Valens, Ritchie, 102
Valenzuela, Liliana, 156
Valenzuela, Tony, 181

Valle, Carmen, 100
Vallejo, Mariano, 11–12
Valle Senties, Raquel, 154
Valley, The (Rolando Hinojosa 1983), 107
Vargas, Roberto, 149
Vasquez, Richard, 107
Vassilarakis, Roberto, 152
Vázquez, Charlie, 190
Vega, Bernardo, 25, 51–52, 183, 184
Veinte años de literatura cubanoamericana: Antología 1962–1982 (1988), 152
Velázquez, Loreta Janeta, 183, 185
Venegas, Daniel, xviii, 17, 20, 25, 26–29
Venezuela, 76, 115
Versos sencillos (José Martí), 32
Vida (Patricia Engel 2010), 131
Viego, Antonio, 189
Vigil-Piñón, Evangelina, 99–100, 105, 148, 152, 154
Villa, Pancho, 18
Villanueva, Alma, 105, 108
Villanueva, Tino, 99, 106, 148, 158
Villarreal, Edit, 102
Villarreal, José Antonio, xix, xxviii, 36, 42–44, 61, 108, 182, 233
Villaseñor, Victor, 95
"Vindication of Cuba" (José Martí 1889), 20–21
viral *latinidad*, 227–228, 229n5
Viramontes, Helena María, xx, xxi, xxxi, 94–96, 98, 106–107, 231, 234–235, 240–241
Virgins, Guerrillas, and Locas (Jaime Cortez 1999), 190
Voces: An Anthology of Nuevo Mexicano Writers (1987), 99
Voices of Aztlán: Chicano Literature of Today (Dorothy E. Harth), 152
Volando Bajito/Low Flying (Alicia Partnoy), 155
von Hayek, Friedrich, 114
Vourvoulias, Sabrina, 141

Walker, William, xvii
"Washington, A" (José María Heredia 1825), 9–10
Watson, James D., 198–199
We Came All the Way From Cuba So You Could Dress Like This? (Achy Obejas 1994), 235, 238–239
Wedding, The (Mary Helen Ponce 1989), 108
West Side Story (theater 1957; film 1961), 45

We the Animals (Justin Torres 2012), xxii, 134
What of the Night (María Irene Fornés 1989), 101
What's Happening (Jimmy Santiago Baca 1982), 105
What the Body Told (Rafael Campo 1997), 180
When I Was Puerto Rican (Esmeralda Santiago 1994), xxi, 118, 165, 236
When We Were Outlaws: A Memoir of Love & Revolution (Jeanne Córdova 2012), 180–181
Where Sparrows Work Hard (Gary Soto 1981), 106
Whispering to Fool the Wind: Poems (Alberto Ríos 1982), 106
Whitman, Walt, 185
Who Would Have Thought It (María Amparo Ruiz de Burton 1872), xvii, 10–11
Wilde, Oscar, 183
Williams, William Carlos, xviii, 17, 18, 20, 22, 29, 31–32, 148
Winners on the Pass Line (Dagoberto Gilb 1985), 107
"With all and for the Good of All" (José Martí), 23
With His Pistol in His Hand (Américo Paredes), 151
Woman, Woman (Angela de Hoyos 1985), 108
Woman Hollering Creek and Other Stories (Sandra Cisneros 1991), xx, 237
Woman in Battle: A Narrative of the Exploits, Adventures and Travels of Madame Loreta Janeta Velázquez, Otherwise Known as Lieutenant Harry J. Buford, Confederate States Army (1876), 183
Woman of Her Word – Hispanic Women Write (1983), 99–100
Women Are Not Roses (Ana Castillo 1984), 105
Women of Color: Perspectives on Feminism and Identity (1985), 97
Women Singing in the Snow: A Cultural Analysis of Chicana Literature (Diana Rebolledo), 155

X, Malcolm, 57
Xavier, Emanuel, 190

Ybor City, Florida, 183, 199
Year of the White Bear and Two Undiscovered Amerindians Visit the West, The (1992-1994), xx
Yerba Buena: Dibujos Y Poemas (Sandra Maria Esteves 1980), 104
Yes Mrs. Williams (William Carlos Williams), 31–32
Yes Thing, No Thing (Edwin Torres 2010), 138
Yglesias, José, 108
. . . y no se lo tragó la tierra (Tomás Rivera 1971), xix, 60, 67, 106
¡*Yo!* (Julia Alvarez 1997), 79, 170
Y Otras Desgracias and Other Misfortunes (Luz María Umpierre 1985), 107
"You Cramp My Style, Baby" (Lorna Dee Cervantes), 65–66
Young Lords, 62, 68
Young Valiant (Oliver Mayer), 102
Yo-Yo Boing! (Giannina Braschi 1998), xxi, 136, 187

Zamora, Bernice, 148, 152
Zapata, Emiliano, 18
Zapatista uprising, xxi, xxxi
Zenea, Juan Clemente, 13–14
Zeno Gandía, Manuel, xvii, 17, 18, 22, 24–26
Zigzagger (Manuel Muñoz 2003), xxi
Zoot Suit (Luis Valdez 1978), xix, 102, 233
Zoot Suit (Universal Pictures 1982), 102
Zoot Suit riots, 233

Cambridge Companions to …

AUTHORS

Edward Albee edited by Stephen J. Bottoms
Margaret Atwood edited by Coral Ann Howells
W. H. Auden edited by Stan Smith
Jane Austen edited by Edward Copeland and Juliet McMaster (second edition)
James Baldwin edited by Michele Elam
Beckett edited by John Pilling
Bede edited by Scott DeGregorio
Aphra Behn edited by Derek Hughes and Janet Todd
Walter Benjamin edited by David S. Ferris
William Blake edited by Morris Eaves
Boccaccio edited by Guyda Armstrong, Rhiannon Daniels, and Stephen J. Milner
Jorge Luis Borges edited by Edwin Williamson
Brecht edited by Peter Thomson and Glendyr Sacks (second edition)
The Brontës edited by Heather Glen
Bunyan edited by Anne Dunan-Page
Frances Burney edited by Peter Sabor
Byron edited by Drummond Bone
Albert Camus edited by Edward J. Hughes
Willa Cather edited by Marilee Lindemann
Cervantes edited by Anthony J. Cascardi
Chaucer edited by Piero Boitani and Jill Mann (second edition)
Chekhov edited by Vera Gottlieb and Paul Allain
Kate Chopin edited by Janet Beer
Caryl Churchill edited by Elaine Aston and Elin Diamond
Cicero edited by Catherine Steel
Coleridge edited by Lucy Newlyn
Wilkie Collins edited by Jenny Bourne Taylor
Joseph Conrad edited by J. H. Stape
H. D. edited by Nephie J. Christodoulides and Polina Mackay
Dante edited by Rachel Jacoff (second edition)
Daniel Defoe edited by John Richetti
Don DeLillo edited by John N. Duvall
Charles Dickens edited by John O. Jordan

Emily Dickinson edited by Wendy Martin
John Donne edited by Achsah Guibbory
Dostoevskii edited by W. J. Leatherbarrow
Theodore Dreiser edited by Leonard Cassuto and Claire Virginia Eby
John Dryden edited by Steven N. Zwicker
W. E. B. Du Bois edited by Shamoon Zamir
George Eliot edited by George Levine
T. S. Eliot edited by A. David Moody
Ralph Ellison edited by Ross Posnock
Ralph Waldo Emerson edited by Joel Porte and Saundra Morris
William Faulkner edited by Philip M. Weinstein
Henry Fielding edited by Claude Rawson
F. Scott Fitzgerald edited by Ruth Prigozy
Flaubert edited by Timothy Unwin
E. M. Forster edited by David Bradshaw
Benjamin Franklin edited by Carla Mulford
Brian Friel edited by Anthony Roche
Robert Frost edited by Robert Faggen
Gabriel García Márquez edited by Philip Swanson
Elizabeth Gaskell edited by Jill L. Matus
Goethe edited by Lesley Sharpe
Günter Grass edited by Stuart Taberner
Thomas Hardy edited by Dale Kramer
David Hare edited by Richard Boon
Nathaniel Hawthorne edited by Richard Millington
Seamus Heaney edited by Bernard O'Donoghue
Ernest Hemingway edited by Scott Donaldson
Homer edited by Robert Fowler
Horace edited by Stephen Harrison
Ted Hughes edited by Terry Gifford
Ibsen edited by James McFarlane
Henry James edited by Jonathan Freedman
Samuel Johnson edited by Greg Clingham
Ben Jonson edited by Richard Harp and Stanley Stewart
James Joyce edited by Derek Attridge (second edition)

Kafka edited by Julian Preece
Keats edited by Susan J. Wolfson
Rudyard Kipling edited by Howard J. Booth
Lacan edited by Jean-Michel Rabaté
D. H. Lawrence edited by Anne Fernihough
Primo Levi edited by Robert Gordon
Lucretius edited by Stuart Gillespie and Philip Hardie
Machiavelli edited by John M. Najemy
David Mamet edited by Christopher Bigsby
Nelson Mandela edited by Rita Barnard
Thomas Mann edited by Ritchie Robertson
Christopher Marlowe edited by Patrick Cheney
Andrew Marvell edited by Derek Hirst and Steven N. Zwicker
Herman Melville edited by Robert S. Levine
Arthur Miller edited by Christopher Bigsby (second edition)
Milton edited by Dennis Danielson (second edition)
Molière edited by David Bradby and Andrew Calder
Toni Morrison edited by Justine Tally
Nabokov edited by Julian W. Connolly
Eugene O'Neill edited by Michael Manheim
George Orwell edited by John Rodden
Ovid edited by Philip Hardie
Petrarch edited by Albert Russell Ascoli
Harold Pinter edited by Peter Raby (second edition)
Sylvia Plath edited by Jo Gill
Edgar Allan Poe edited by Kevin J. Hayes
Alexander Pope edited by Pat Rogers
Ezra Pound edited by Ira B. Nadel
Proust edited by Richard Bales
Pushkin edited by Andrew Kahn
Rabelais edited by John O'Brien
Rilke edited by Karen Leeder and Robert Vilain
Philip Roth edited by Timothy Parrish
Salman Rushdie edited by Abdulrazak Gurnah
John Ruskin edited by Francis O'Gorman
Seneca edited by Shadi Bartsch and Alessandro Schiesaro
Shakespeare edited by Margareta de Grazia and Stanley Wells (second edition)
Shakespearean Comedy edited by Alexander Leggatt
Shakespeare and Contemporary Dramatists edited by Ton Hoenselaars
Shakespeare and Popular Culture edited by Robert Shaughnessy
Shakespearean Tragedy edited by Claire McEachern (second edition)
Shakespeare on Film edited by Russell Jackson (second edition)
Shakespeare on Stage edited by Stanley Wells and Sarah Stanton
Shakespeare's History Plays edited by Michael Hattaway
Shakespeare's Last Plays edited by Catherine M. S. Alexander
Shakespeare's Poetry edited by Patrick Cheney
George Bernard Shaw edited by Christopher Innes
Shelley edited by Timothy Morton
Mary Shelley edited by Esther Schor
Sam Shepard edited by Matthew C. Roudané
Spenser edited by Andrew Hadfield
Laurence Sterne edited by Thomas Keymer
Wallace Stevens edited by John N. Serio
Tom Stoppard edited by Katherine E. Kelly
Harriet Beecher Stowe edited by Cindy Weinstein
August Strindberg edited by Michael Robinson
Jonathan Swift edited by Christopher Fox
J. M. Synge edited by P. J. Mathews
Tacitus edited by A. J. Woodman
Henry David Thoreau edited by Joel Myerson
Tolstoy edited by Donna Tussing Orwin
Anthony Trollope edited by Carolyn Dever and Lisa Niles
Mark Twain edited by Forrest G. Robinson
John Updike edited by Stacey Olster
Mario Vargas Llosa edited by Efrain Kristal and John King

Virgil edited by Charles Martindale
Voltaire edited by Nicholas Cronk
Edith Wharton edited by Millicent Bell
Walt Whitman edited by Ezra Greenspan
Oscar Wilde edited by Peter Raby
Tennessee Williams edited by Matthew C. Roudané
August Wilson edited by Christopher Bigsby
Mary Wollstonecraft edited by Claudia L. Johnson
Virginia Woolf edited by Susan Sellers (second edition)
Wordsworth edited by Stephen Gill
Wyndham Lewis edited by Tyrus Miller
W. B. Yeats edited by Marjorie Howes and John Kelly
Zola edited by Brian Nelson

TOPICS

The Actress edited by Maggie B. Gale and John Stokes
The African American Novel edited by Maryemma Graham
The African American Slave Narrative edited by Audrey A. Fisch
African American Theatre by Harvey Young
Allegory edited by Rita Copeland and Peter Struck
American Crime Fiction edited by Catherine Ross Nickerson
American Gay and Lesbian Literature edited by Scott Herring
American Modernism edited by Walter Kalaidjian
The American Modernist Novel edited by Joshua Miller
American Poetry Since 1945 edited by Jennifer Ashton
American Poets edited by Mark Richardson
American Realism and Naturalism edited by Donald Pizer
American Science Fiction edited by Gerry Canavan and Eric Carl Link
American Travel Writing edited by Alfred Bendixen and Judith Hamera
American Women Playwrights edited by Brenda Murphy
Ancient Rhetoric edited by Erik Gunderson
Arthurian Legend edited by Elizabeth Archibald and Ad Putter
Asian American Literature edited by Crystal Parikh and Daniel Y. Kim
Australian Literature edited by Elizabeth Webby
Autobiography edited by Maria DiBattista and Emily Wittman
The Body in Literature edited by David Hillman and Ulrika Maude
British Fiction since 1945 edited by David James
British Literature of the French Revolution edited by Pamela Clemit
British Poetry, 1945–2010 edited by Edward Larrissy
British Romanticism edited by Stuart Curran (second edition)
British Romantic Poetry edited by James Chandler and Maureen N. McLane
British Theatre, 1730–1830, edited by Jane Moody and Daniel O'Quinn
Canadian Literature edited by Eva-Marie Kröller
Children's Literature edited by M. O. Grenby and Andrea Immel
The Classic Russian Novel edited by Malcolm V. Jones and Robin Feuer Miller
Contemporary Irish Poetry edited by Matthew Campbell
Creative Writing edited by David Morley and Philip Neilsen
Crime Fiction edited by Martin Priestman
Early Modern Women's Writing edited by Laura Lunger Knoppers
The Eighteenth-Century Novel edited by John Richetti
Eighteenth-Century Poetry edited by John Sitter
Emma edited by Peter Sabor
English Literature, 1500–1600 edited by Arthur F. Kinney
English Literature, 1650–1740 edited by Steven N. Zwicker

English Literature, 1740–1830 edited by Thomas Keymer and Jon Mee
English Literature, 1830–1914 edited by Joanne Shattock
English Novelists edited by Adrian Poole
English Poetry, Donne to Marvell edited by Thomas N. Corns
English Poets edited by Claude Rawson
English Renaissance Drama, second edition edited by A. R. Braunmuller and Michael Hattaway
English Renaissance Tragedy edited by Emma Smith and Garrett A. Sullivan Jr.
English Restoration Theatre edited by Deborah C. Payne Fisk
The Epic edited by Catherine Bates
European Modernism edited by Pericles Lewis
European Novelists edited by Michael Bell
Fairy Tales edited by Maria Tatar
Fantasy Literature edited by Edward James and Farah Mendlesohn
Feminist Literary Theory edited by Ellen Rooney
Fiction in the Romantic Period edited by Richard Maxwell and Katie Trumpener
The Fin de Siècle edited by Gail Marshall
The French Enlightenment edited by Daniel Brewer
French Literature edited by John D. Lyons
The French Novel: from 1800 to the Present edited by Timothy Unwin
Gay and Lesbian Writing edited by Hugh Stevens
German Romanticism edited by Nicholas Saul
Gothic Fiction edited by Jerrold E. Hogle
The Greek and Roman Novel edited by Tim Whitmarsh
Greek and Roman Theatre edited by Marianne McDonald and J. Michael Walton
Greek Comedy edited by Martin Revermann
Greek Lyric edited by Felix Budelmann
Greek Mythology edited by Roger D. Woodard
Greek Tragedy edited by P. E. Easterling
The Harlem Renaissance edited by George Hutchinson
The History of the Book edited by Leslie Howsam
The Irish Novel edited by John Wilson Foster
The Italian Novel edited by Peter Bondanella and Andrea Ciccarelli
The Italian Renaissance edited by Michael Wyatt
Jewish American Literature edited by Hana Wirth-Nesher and Michael P. Kramer
The Latin American Novel edited by Efraín Kristal
The Literature of the First World War edited by Vincent Sherry
The Literature of London edited by Lawrence Manley
The Literature of Los Angeles edited by Kevin R. McNamara
The Literature of New York edited by Cyrus Patell and Bryan Waterman
The Literature of Paris edited by Anna-Louise Milne
The Literature of World War II edited by Marina MacKay
Literature on Screen edited by Deborah Cartmell and Imelda Whelehan
Medieval English Culture edited by Andrew Galloway
Medieval English Literature edited by Larry Scanlon
Medieval English Mysticism edited by Samuel Fanous and Vincent Gillespie
Medieval English Theatre edited by Richard Beadle and Alan J. Fletcher (second edition)
Medieval French Literature edited by Simon Gaunt and Sarah Kay
Medieval Romance edited by Roberta L. Krueger
Medieval Women's Writing edited by Carolyn Dinshaw and David Wallace
Modern American Culture edited by Christopher Bigsby
Modern American Poetry edited by Walter Kalaidjian

Modern British Women Playwrights edited by Elaine Aston and Janelle Reinelt
Modern French Culture edited by Nicholas Hewitt
Modern German Culture edited by Eva Kolinsky and Wilfried van der Will
The Modern German Novel edited by Graham Bartram
The Modern Gothic edited by Jerrold E. Hogle
Modern Irish Culture edited by Joe Cleary and Claire Connolly
Modern Italian Culture edited by Zygmunt G. Baranski and Rebecca J. West
Modern Latin American Culture edited by John King
Modern Russian Culture edited by Nicholas Rzhevsky
Modern Spanish Culture edited by David T. Gies
Modernism edited by Michael Levenson (second edition)
The Modernist Novel edited by Morag Shiach
Modernist Poetry edited by Alex Davis and Lee M. Jenkins
Modernist Women Writers edited by Maren Tova Linett
Narrative edited by David Herman
Native American Literature edited by Joy Porter and Kenneth M. Roemer
Nineteenth-Century American Women's Writing edited by Dale M. Bauer and Philip Gould
Old English Literature edited by Malcolm Godden and Michael Lapidge (second edition)
Paradise Lost edited by Louis Schwartz
Performance Studies edited by Tracy C. Davis
Piers Plowman by Andrew Cole and Andrew Galloway
The Poetry of the First World War edited by Santanu Das
Popular Fiction edited by David Glover and Scott McCracken
Postcolonial Literary Studies edited by Neil Lazarus
The Postcolonial Novel edited by Ato Quayson
Postmodernism edited by Steven Connor
The Pre-Raphaelites edited by Elizabeth Prettejohn
Pride and Prejudice edited by Janet Todd
Renaissance Humanism edited by Jill Kraye
The Roman Historians edited by Andrew Feldherr
Roman Satire edited by Kirk Freudenburg
Science Fiction edited by Edward James and Farah Mendlesohn
Scottish Literature edited by Gerald Carruthers and Liam McIlvanney
Sensation Fiction edited by Andrew Mangham
Slavery in American Literature edited by Ezra Tawil
The Sonnet edited by A. D. Cousins and Peter Howarth
The Spanish Novel: From 1600 to the Present edited by Harriet Turner and Adelaida López de Martínez
Textual Scholarship edited by Neil Fraistat and Julia Flanders
Theatre History by David Wiles and Christine Dymkowski
Travel Writing edited by Peter Hulme and Tim Youngs
Twentieth-Century British and Irish Women's Poetry edited by Jane Dowson
The Twentieth-Century English Novel edited by Robert L. Caserio
Twentieth-Century English Poetry edited by Neil Corcoran
Twentieth-Century Irish Drama edited by Shaun Richards
Twentieth-Century Russian Literature edited by Marina Balina and Evgeny Dobrenko
Utopian Literature edited by Gregory Claeys
Victorian and Edwardian Theatre edited by Kerry Powell
The Victorian Novel edited by Deirdre David (second edition)
Victorian Poetry edited by Joseph Bristow

Victorian Women's Writing edited by Linda H. Peterson
War Writing edited by Kate McLoughlin
The Waste Land edited by Gabrielle McIntire

Women's Writing in Britain, 1660–1789 edited by Catherine Ingrassia
Women's Writing in the Romantic Period edited by Devoney Looser
Writing of the English Revolution edited by N. H. Keeble

Made in the USA
San Bernardino, CA
27 August 2019